MARXISM, FASCISM, AND
TOTALITARIANISM

Marxism, Fascism, and Totalitarianism

CHAPTERS IN THE INTELLECTUAL HISTORY OF RADICALISM

A. James Gregor

STANFORD UNIVERSITY PRESS

Stanford, California 2009

Stanford University Press
Stanford, California
© 2009 by the Board of Trustees of the
Leland Stanford Junior University

Library of Congress Cataloging-in-Publication Data

Gregor, A. James (Anthony James).
    Marxism, fascism, and totalitarianism : chapters in the intellectual
history of radicalism / A. James Gregor.
        p.   cm.
    Includes bibliographical references and index.
    ISBN 978-0-8047-6033-1 (cloth : alk. paper)—
    ISBN 978-0-8047-6034-8 (pbk. : alk. paper)
        1. Totalitarianism—History—20th century.   2. Communism—
Europe—History—20th century.   3. Fascism—Europe—History—
20th century.   I. Title.

JC480.G74   2009

320.53094—dc22   2008022443

Printed in the United States of America
on acid-free, archival-quality paper

Typeset at Stanford University Press in 10/13 Galliard

This work is dedicated to Renzo Morera,
and all those like him,
who paid with courage and dignity
the price of the twentieth century.

Acknowledgments

The author of any book owes an incalculable debt to an inordinate number of persons who have consciously or unconsciously, willingly or unwillingly, assisted in its production. In terms of the assistance I have received over a lifetime, I have been particularly blessed. I have lived long enough, and been given sufficient opportunity, to have spoken with some of the principal protagonists in the story before the reader. Sidney Hook was exceedingly kind to me. He spoke of the ideological disputes that characterized his relationship with some of the major Marxist theoreticians he knew. Giuseppe Prezzolini told me of his experiences with the early syndicalists and the first Fascists. He spoke of his exchanges with the young Benito Mussolini, long before Mussolini was master of Italy. And there have been professors, Russian, Italian, and German, who remembered times, long before the Second World War, when all the issues, joined in the account before the reader, were still current—and moved persons to political action.

To Dr. Renzo Morera, I am grateful for the account of his life, which, to me, conveys something of the dignity and honor with which many paid the price exacted by the political ideologies to which this book is dedicated. The ideologies of the twentieth century made very serious demands on those over whom they exercised influence.

To all those good people, staff and students, who assist all the faculty members of all the universities where I have been fortunate enough to practice my profession—I wish to extend my heartfelt thanks. To the editors of scholarly books—particularly Mr. Norris Pope of Stanford University Press on this occasion—I am more than grateful. It is they who make possible the free flow of ideas in an environment where that flow is essential.

To my wife and sure companion, Professor Maria Hsia Chang, and to all those loving creatures with whom she has surrounded us—my unqualified gratitude. By her example, she has taught me to write with more clarity than otherwise would have been the case.

I wish to publicly acknowledge my gratitude to all these persons. They are responsible for anything that may be good in the work before the reader—I am solely responsible for anything that is not.

A. James Gregor
Berkeley, California

Contents

Preface

The present work constitutes an effort to better understand the origins of the major revolutionary ideologies of the twentieth century. It attempts to reconstruct the evolution of those ideologies from their initial source in the heritage left by Karl Marx and Friedrich Engels—to the rationale for totalitarianism they were to become. Basically, it seeks to track that evolution into Leninism and Italian Fascism.

Some years ago, Zeev Sternhell traced the Fascist ideas of Benito Mussolini to late nineteenth- and early twentieth-century revolutionary ideas in France. At the same time, he made allusion to sources in the specifically Marxist tradition—and spoke of a "second main component" of Fascist ideology as a peculiar "revision" of the Marxism it inherited.*

The present study attempts to trace the influences that shaped that revision—for it will be argued that much, if not all, revolutionary thought in the twentieth century was shaped by just such revisions of traditional Marxism. The tracing is often difficult. There are innumerable asides amidst the attempts by authors, in the revolutionary traditions of Europe at the time, to address and resolve a clutch of critical questions that turned on complex epistemological, normative, and scientific concerns left unresolved by the founders of "historical materialism."

It was left to Marxism's intellectual heirs to address the question of how *materialism*, as ontology and epistemology, was to be understood. There was the notion of "inevitabilities" and the "logic" of history—and the question of just how human choice might function in a deterministic universe.

---

*Zeev Sternhell, with Mario Sznajder and Maia Asheri, *The Birth of Fascist Ideology: From Cultural Rebellion to Political Revolution* (Princeton: Princeton University Press, 1994), p. 12.

And there was the problem of the place of Darwinism, the struggle for existence, and the influence of biology in all of that. With Engels's passing in 1895, all this was bequeathed to the good offices of Marxists who varied in their gifts and perspectives.

Even before the death of Engels, "revisionisms" began to gather on the horizon. Most of the revisionism that was to follow was the result of the efforts made to address all those problems left unsettled by the founders of Marxism. It is to those revisionisms that the present work will direct the reader's attention.

The exposition attempts to fill in some of the intellectual space that separates classical Marxism from its revolutionary variants, and the totalitarian forms to which those variants ultimately committed themselves. It will selectively follow the development of all these variants into political totalitarianism—that peculiar institutionalization that ultimately came to typify their collective goal culture, and profoundly shape the history of the last century.

One might have expected that intellectual historians would make it a priority to explain why totalitarianism was fostered and sustained by both the revolutionary "left" as well as their counterparts on the "right." In fact, remarkably little has been done in that regard.

Martin Malia, for his part, spoke of the "conceptual poverty" associated with Western efforts to come to grips with the reality of "communist" totalitarianism.* I would suggest that much of its failure stems from the opacity that surrounds the ideological discussions that arose out of the very uncertainty of the philosophic and social science claims made by Marx and Engels in the nineteenth century. The present account attempts to outline some of the tortured discussions that collected around those claims. As will be argued, those discussions ultimately shaped the totalitarianism that emerged out of the putative liberality and humanity of classical Marxism.

It is hoped that the present effort will contribute to our understanding of the twentieth century—the century that long will be remembered as perhaps the most destructive in human history. It is something of a cautionary tale, addressed to those who insist on reading revolutionary radicalism as the solitary hope available to the modern world. To the rest of us, it is intended as information, as part of an attempt to settle our accounts with the twentieth century.

---

*Martin Malia, "Foreword," Stephane Courtois (ed.), *The Black Book of Communism: Crimes, Terror, Repression*, translated by Johnathan Murphy and Mark Kramer (Cambridge: Harvard University Press, 1999), p. x.

MARXISM, FASCISM, AND
TOTALITARIANISM

CHAPTER ONE

Introduction

As we move further and further into the twenty-first century, the twentieth takes on more and more an air of unreality. In one sense, its features recede, and in another, some of those same features become caricatures of themselves. Our memories have become uncertain. Mussolini's Fascism becomes a burlesque,[1] and Lenin's Bolshevism the antechamber of gulags and killing fields.[2] One is left with a feeling of disquiet, as though one does not understand any of it.

For a very long time the twentieth century seemed to make sense. The planet was caught up in a Manichean struggle of light against darkness. Marxism, embodying all the values of the Enlightenment, found itself opposed by the irrational evil of reactionary and counterrevolutionary fascism. Fascism, ignominiously struck down in the course of the Second World War, quickly lost whatever cachet it briefly enjoyed among some intellectuals in the West, to be reduced to little more than a public expression of private pathologies.[3] For the nations of the world, antifascism became a compulsory patrimony.

FASCISM AND COMMUNISM

Until the coming of the Second World War, both Mussolini's Fascism and generic fascism had been the subjects of passionate debate. There had been perfectly rational and objective discussion of their respective merits and deficits. Mussolini's Fascism, for example, could be spoken of as possessed of a "complete philosophy" articulated by a number of "young intellectuals" fully competent to argue in defense of their positions. Economists could speak of the "gains and losses" of Fascist economic policy and affirm that "the mass of Italians sympathize with Fascism and, on the whole, support the regime."[4]

After the war, none of that was possible any longer. Antifascism became the negation that unified the capitalist, democratic West and the socialist, nondemocratic East. Fascists were banished from humanity. They became the unprecedented objects of general reprobation. Their very essence was deemed barbarous. Their sole motivation understood to have been war and violence.

Conversely, for years after the Second World War, Joseph Stalin's Soviet Union, triumphant in that conflict, the presumptive embodiment of Marxism, became the hope of a surprisingly large minority of Western intellectuals. Fascism was remembered as the tool of a moribund capitalism—seeking to preserve its profits at the cost of war and pestilence. It was seen as the extreme opposite of Soviet socialism. All the simplisms that had been the content of the Marxist interpretation of fascism in the interwar years were seen by many as having been confirmed by the war. Many on the left were persuaded that monopoly capitalism, in its death agony, had unleashed fascism on the world in its desperate effort to stay the hand of history.

The Second World War was understood to have been a war between imperialists who each sought advantage over the other. The Soviet Union, innocent of all that, became the victim of National Socialist Germany—but had heroically succeeded in emerging victorious. The Red Army was depicted as an antifascist army that had sacrificed itself in defense of humanity. For their part, the Western powers were seen as craven spoilers who sought only profit, and worldwide hegemony, from the defeat of fascism.

Some intellectuals in Europe and North America found such an account convincing. Winston Churchill and Charles de Gaulle, Europe's most consistent antifascists before the advent of the war, were somehow transformed into "cryptofascists." Churchill's postwar "Iron Curtain" speech at Fulton in 1946 was understood to constitute a provocation calculated to support the effort of "industrialists" who hoped to use a contest with the Soviet Union as the pretext for "curbing the claims of the working classes with the help of the authorities and thus complete the [postwar] process of reorganizing production on monopolistic lines at the expense of the community." General de Gaulle, in turn, long known to be an anticommunist, could only be an enemy of the poor and underprivileged, and, as a consequence, one expected to extend aid and comfort to fascists and "reactionaries" of all sorts.[5]

So convinced of all this were some European and American intellectuals that they could only speak of fascism as an excrescence of capitalism. Some Europeans solemnly maintained that "those who have nothing to say about capitalism should also be silent about fascism."[6] The relationship between the two was conceived as one of entailment.

Marxists, for more than half-a-hundred years, had argued that there could only be "two paths . . . open before present society. . . . [The] path of fascism, the path to which the bourgeoisie in all modern countries . . . is increasingly turning . . . or [the] path of communism."[7] Marxists and leftist liberals in the West had been convinced by the war that Soviet theoreticians had always been correct. Capitalism was the seedbed of fascism, and the only recourse humanity had was to protect, sustain, foster, and enhance Soviet socialism and its variants. Only with Nikita Khrushchev's public denunciation of Stalin's crimes at the 20th Party Congress of the Communist Party, did the support of Western leftists for the Soviet Union show any signs of flagging.

Immediately after Stalin's death in March 1953, oblique criticisms of his regime, by the leaders of the Communist Party of the Soviet Union, signaled the forthcoming denunciation—and in February 1956, Khrushchev delivered his catalog of charges against the departed leader in a "secret speech" to the leadership of the Party. In that speech, Stalin's dictatorship was characterized as tyrannical, arbitrary, and homicidal, having created a system in which many, many innocents perished, and in which prodigious quantities of the nation's resources had been wasted. Largely unexpected both within and outside the Soviet Union, the disclosures of the 20th Party Congress created political tensions within the Party and among Soviet sympathizers throughout the West.

Stalin's successors were burdened with the unanticipated necessity of renouncing the tyrannical and homicidal rule associated with his name, while seeking to perpetuate the regime he had created. They were obliged, by their leadership responsibilities, to continue to speak of "socialism in one country," while at the same time, denouncing its architect. They spoke of a "return to Leninism" while abandoning some of Lenin's most important policies. They spoke of the commitment to classical Marxism, while at the same time beginning the process that would conclude with the creation of a socialist "state of the whole people"—an arrant affront to classical Marxism's emphatic insistence that socialism would see the inevitable "withering away of the state."[8]

Nikita Khrushchev fashioned himself master of a system that revealed itself as increasingly nationalistic in inspiration, militaristic in deportment, industrializing in intent, and statist by choice. It was a system that sought uniform control of all the factors of production, enlisted in the service of an economic plan calculated to make the nation a major international power, restoring "lost territories" to the motherland, and securing its borders against external "imperialists." It was an elitist system, with minority rule legitimized by a claim of special knowledge of the laws governing the dialectical evolution of society.[9]

In the years that followed, more and more Soviet intellectuals reflected more and more critically on the properties of their political and economic system. They seemed to recognize, at least in part, that the special claim to wisdom and moral virtue by the ruling elite had occasioned the creation of a "cult of personality" around their leader, Joseph Vissarionovich Stalin, from which they had all suffered. They appreciated the fact that Stalin had proceeded to implement views that "in fact had nothing in common with Marxism-Leninism"—but which he invoked in order "to substantiate theoretically the lawlessness and the mass reprisals against those who did not suit him."[10] Possessed of "unlimited power" in an "administrative system"—typified by "centralized decision-making and the punctual, rigorous and utterly dedicated execution of the directives coming from the top and, particularly, from Stalin"—Stalinism devolved into a morally defective system in abject dependence on the whims of a single man, whose sense of infallibility and omnipotence, ultimately and irresistibly, led to his utter "irrationality."[11]

Before the close of the system, Soviet theoreticians had begun to draw conclusions from the role played by Stalin in their nation's revolutionary history. They suggested that "Stalin quickly grew accustomed to violence as an indispensable component of unlimited power"—to ultimately conceive it a "universal tool"—a conception that opened the portals to a "tragic triumph of the forces of evil."[12] Soviet analysts concluded that all of that, apparently, "was payment for building socialism in a backward country—by the need to build in a short space of time a heavy (above all, defence) industry, and thousands of enterprises in these industries," in circumstances in which the motherland was "surrounded by enemies."[13]

By the time of its passing, the apologists for the Soviet system, under the uncertain leadership of Mikhail Gorbachev, had taken the measure of the system they staffed. They sought to abandon all its ideological pretenses as well as its institutional forms, to replace them with the values and fashions of the liberalism Marxism-Leninism had long deplored. In the years between Stalin's death and the appearance of Gorbachev, all the properties associated with Lenin's Bolshevism, and Stalin's "socialism in one country," were made subject to corrosive review by Soviet Marxist-Leninists themselves — and were found wanting.

The impact of all that on Western academics varied from person to person.[14] Some saw their earlier commitment to the Soviet Union the product of an infatuation with an unattainable dream — and proceeded to abandon socialism as the only alternative to fascism. Others dismissed the entire Soviet sequence as the consequence of one man's perversity. Others simply shifted their allegiance to other, more appealing, socialisms — in China, Cuba, or Ethiopia. The schematization of history, with exploitative capitalism at one pole and socialist liberation at the other, was simply too familiar and attractive to forsake. What would change would be the socialist country that would be the object of their allegiance. Marxist socialism as the paradigm of virtue appears fitfully in the writing of intellectuals to the present day.[15] The possibility never appears to have occurred to them that the socialism they had embraced, in the form it had assumed in the twentieth century, was hardly the incarnation of the Marxism of which they approved.

SOVIET COMMUNISM, NATIONALISM, AND FASCISM

Before Khrushchev's "secret speech" at the 20th Party Congress in 1956, there had been scant tolerance for any resistance to the political systems imposed on Eastern Europe by the Soviets at the conclusion of the Second World War. At the end of the Second World War, among the first responses of many Western intellectuals, was the depiction of the entry of the Red Army into the heartland of Europe as the coming of an avenging host of decency and liberation. Soon, however, the restiveness of those "liberated," and the heavy-handed suppression that followed, produced disquiet among intellectuals in the industrial democracies.

The system imposed on a fragment of what had been Germany, for example, was a purgatory of expiation for the atrocities committed by Adolf Hitler's National Socialism. East Germany, under Soviet occupation, and the regime imposed upon it by Moscow, was expected to provide prodigious amounts of industrial goods and material resources to the Soviet Union as compensation for the destruction of assets and loss of life that resulted from the Nazi invasion of the homeland. Even after the East Germans emerged from the desolation of the war, the "German Democratic Republic," cobbled together by the Soviets, soon revealed itself to be an ineffectual, incompetent, and unpopular police system, which, in the final analysis, was justified only by its "antifascist" credentials.[16] In fact, through the long years between the Second World War and the collapse of the Soviet Union, Moscow employed its certification as antifascist to legitimate its rule over much of Eastern Europe.

During that same period, international communism, with Moscow at its core—having achieved its apotheosis in its defeat of fascism in the Second World War—faced the first critical challenge to its dominance and control in the defection of Tito's Yugoslavia. It was immediately clear that Tito's defection from the highly centralized organization constructed around the Soviet center was not the consequence of ideological disagreement. Originally, there were no doctrinal problems between Tito and Stalin. Their shared ideology notwithstanding, Tito simply refused to surrender control over any of his nation's sovereignty to Moscow. The Yugoslav defection from "proletarian internationalism" brought to public attention what long had been a private apprehension among Marxist thinkers. "Titoism" was to be symptomatic of a critical problem at the heart of "international socialism."

Since its very founding, Bolshevism had struggled not only against "bourgeois nationalist," but "national communist," factions as well. Even before the Bolshevik revolution, Lenin had been bedeviled by the nationalisms of Polish, Baltic, and Jewish revolutionaries. Dismissed as apostasies by Lenin and his followers, after the October revolution, the leaders of those factions were incarcerated, exiled, or murdered.

There could be none of that in dealing with Tito. Tito Broz was a heretic of a different sort. He could not be dealt with as others had been. Tito was the leader of an independent nation, and his national communism heralded the prospect of a proliferation of just such state systems.

While, in the past, there had been any number of Marxist heretics who had advocated various forms of national communism, it was only with Tito that heresy spread to a ruling party and to an extant state. Tito's "nationalist deviation" compromised the proletarian international. The vision of an international proletarian revolution that would result in a worldwide socialism lost whatever credibility it had hitherto enjoyed. At the time, observers could not know that a new chapter in the history of communism had begun with the long anti-Tito Cominform resolution of June 1948.

What Tito had done was to reaffirm the coupling of the ideas of nationhood and revolution. In declaring his independence from institutional Stalinism, Tito demonstrated that the sentiment of nationality might serve as a fulcrum for revolutionary mobilization—all the counterarguments of Leninism notwithstanding. The schismatic of Belgrade had raised questions for international communism that could not be laid to rest by political suppression, incarceration, exile, or terror. National communism would demonstrate more resonance than any, at the time, anticipated.

About a decade later, the disaffection of Mao Zedong became public knowledge—and confirmed to even the most skeptical, that international communism had fallen on evil times. National communism revealed itself an endemic factional threat to revolutionary Marxism—with the defection of Mao to be followed by the national Marxists of tiny Albania, Fidel Castro's Cuba, and the dedicated nationalism of Ho Chi Minh. Even the hermetic regime of Kim Il Sung and his heir would ultimately take on nationalist coloration. Titoism no longer was a personal idiosyncrasy; it was to be an irremediable and ongoing affliction of international Marxism-Leninism.

The Soviet leadership that long had been self-congratulatory in claiming to have solved the "nationalities problem" within its own boundaries, could not control political nationalism in the world outside. It was to be a recurrent concern for the quondam leaders of what had been a conjectured international proletariat.

Tito, originally a militant Stalinist, was prepared to oppose Stalin in the service of political autonomy from Moscow—an autonomy that could accommodate significant nationalist sentiments. While Tito could allow direct expression of such values, a similar option was not available to other nations of the "Soviet bloc." Nonetheless, it can be argued that after 1948, it was just those sentiments that made communism at all viable in the Soviet satellite nations.

What seemed reasonably clear was the fact that most of the communist governments, sponsored by Moscow in Eastern Europe, remained at all effective only because their communism was sustained by national sentiment. Domestic communists had coupled nationalism with the postwar aversion to Germans, who, as Nazis, had destroyed, pillaged, and butchered their way across vast territories in their conquest of Europe. Those circumstances provided Moscow its most effective raison d'être: its "antifascism." The Soviet treatment of the states of Eastern Europe was vindicated by an argument that warned of a possible rise of a revanchist, "neonazi" Germany, which would threaten regional security in the future. Rather than the putative merits of communism to hold its satellites together, Moscow fell back on its antifascist credentials.[17] It was not Marxism-Leninism that tied the Eastern European communities to Moscow; it was Moscow's "antifascism."

For all that, in the years that were to follow, national sentiment, quite independent of the overlay of communist antifascism, would successively animate national political life throughout the satellite nations of Eastern Europe, in Poland, Hungary, Romania, and Czechoslovakia. Gradually, and in varying measure, the national communisms of each of those nations found expression in its own developmental "socialism in one country," several with their own respective "charismatic leader," and corresponding unitary party—until national independence from Moscow became the dominant imperative. The truth is that the issue of the connection of nationalism and revolution had never been resolved by Marxist revolutionaries in the twentieth century.

"FASCISM," AND "NEOFASCISM," AS CONCEPTS

Until the collapse of the entire system, "antifascism" had served as the linchpin of the international policies of the Soviet Union. For about two decades after the end of the Second World War, Moscow reiterated its "interpretation of fascism," first fully articulated in the mid-1930s, identifying fascism the "terrorist tool" of "finance capitalism."[18] The singular difference that distinguished its interpretation after the Second World War was Moscow's ready identification of any political system, any political leader, or any political movement, that opposed itself to Soviet Marxism-Leninism, not only as "capitalist," but as "neofascist" as well. Thus, almost immediately after the end of the war, Winston Churchill, Harry Truman, and Charles de Gaulle, who warned the industrial democracies against Soviet machinations, became "neo-," or "protofascists," according to Moscow. To satisfy Moscow's entry criteria into the class of "neofascisms" required only that one's policies be conceived "capitalist," or "anticommunist." Thus, according to Moscow, the "McCarthy era" in the United States, with its "hysterical anticommunism," signaled the "rise of fascism" in the Western Hemisphere.

By the end of the 1960s, whatever the revisions in the Soviet "standard version" of "fascism," Moscow continued to employ the term to identify its "class enemies." The treatment of "fascism" was stereotypic, abstract, and

largely ahistorical. At best, Soviet spokesmen identified fascism with a catalog of horrors. The account of fascism's rise and appeal was delivered in
an unconvincing and insubstantial rendering. According to the prevailing
opinion in Moscow in the 1920s and 1930s, the propertied elites of Germany had invoked, mobilized, organized, directed, and ensconced in power,
Adolf Hitler and his henchmen.[19] Throughout the years before the Soviet
Union disappeared into history, Moscow insisted that the selfsame propertied elites in the United States, and the Western industrialized powers, in
their eternal search for "corporate profits," were preparing, once again, to
visit the same horrors on the world.

At the same time, driven by its abstract and stereotypic interpretation of
world history, Moscow discovered a totally unanticipated "fascism" on its
long borders to the East. By the mid-1960s, Soviet theoreticians began to
characterize Maoism as an "anti-Marxist, petty bourgeois nationalism."[20]
Given the generous criteria for admission into the class of "fascisms," the
People's Republic of China, in Moscow's scheme of reality, became a fascist
power, ultimately to make common cause with international finance capitalism.

The late 1960s actually saw the two "socialist" powers in armed conflict on the Sino-Soviet border. In the course of all that, Beijing tendered
its assessment of what had been transpiring in the Soviet Union. Maoists
began to identify "capitalist-roaders" among the post-Stalinist leadership
in Moscow. There was easy talk about the "restoration of capitalism" in
the Soviet Union.[21] To Beijing, with that putative restoration, the Soviet
Union quickly made the transition to "social imperialism," to finally morph
into "social-fascism."[22]

Genuinely puzzled by the appearance of "fascism" in "socialist states,"
most commentators in the West refrained from treating such identifications
as instructive. Such conceptual notions created theoretical stress in their
antifascist repertory. They simply identified the exchanges as a form of political abuse that accompanied the political, military, and economic tensions
between the two "socialisms."

Most anglophone commentators chose to extend credit to generic communism, surrounding it with the deference due the Marxist ideas it supposedly incarnated. They seemed to find impossible the notion that either
the Soviet Union, the heir of Lenin, or China, the product of a "Marxist
Long March," could qualify as "fascist." Whatever they were, or had become, Western intellectuals had difficulty imagining that fascism could find
place among the heirs of classical Marxism and Marxism-Leninism.

The fact that both revolutionary socialist systems employed the concept "fascism" to describe the other was dismissed as a product of international tension. The term could not have meant anything in such an exchange.

Thereafter, Western scholarship has sought, largely in vain, for some definition of "fascism" that minimally would satisfy research requirements. To date none has been forthcoming—or at least none that satisfies all participants in search for fascism or neofascism.[23] In the interim, hundreds of books, and thousands of articles, have been published dealing with both topics. None have been notably successful.

"Fascism" and "neofascism," at one time or another, have been identified with conservatism, a defense of capitalism, anticommunism, right-wing extremism, genocidal intent, racism of one or another sort, thuggery of whatever sort, chauvinism, militarism, military rule, authoritarianism, xenophobia, homophobia, tax protests, terror bombings, religious fundamentalism, simple irrationalism, sexism, violence at soccer matches, religious bigotry, vandalism in graveyards, and hate speech.[24] What they have not been identified with is communism—no matter how murderous and bestial some Marxist dictatorships have been.[25]

Part of the responsibility for this derives directly from the fact that during the Second World War, the Allied powers had chosen to identify the conflict with the Axis powers as a "war against fascism"—with Hitler's National Socialism conjoined with Mussolini's Fascism, to become a generic "fascism," sometimes carrying a "fascist" imperial Japan in its train. By the end of the war, "fascism" was identified with every bestiality from unprovoked attack, to the mass murder of innocents, that could be attributed to the forces of National Socialism or imperial Japan. The noncommunist Allied powers, for a variety of reasons, were as prepared as Moscow to identify any and all of their opponents in the war as "fascists." The consequence was the artless identification of a generic "fascism" with every enormity committed by any of the Axis powers, anywhere in the world, in the course of the Second World War. By that time, the term had dilated to such an extent that it hardly commanded any cognitive reference; it was little more than a term of abuse. All that notwithstanding, Soviet forces, and communist partisans, however egregious their conduct, were never associated with fascism.

As has been suggested, it was in that parlous condition that the term entered the lexicon of then current Western academic inquiry. It was used then, and still used now, to refer indifferently to Hitler's National Socialism and Mussolini's Fascism (as well as to an expanding number of other sociopolitical systems as time progressed). Together with a general leftist-liberal disposition to forever see merit in Marxism, all of that reinforced the interpretation of contemporary politics as divided along the fault lines of "capitalism-fascism" and "socialism."

Leftist European intellectuals then, and largely continue to this day, to labor the thesis that fascism was the lamentable and inevitable by-product of capitalism. In places like the German Federal Republic and Great Britain, professors, academicians, and journalists regularly made a case for the "bourgeois" and "capitalist" essence of fascism. Fascism was, and continues to be, portrayed "as a form of counterrevolution acting in the interests of capital." The only "lasting alternative" to fascism was, and is, seen in the creation of "a root-and-branch socialism" that will render capitalism and the existence of the bourgeoisie no longer possible.[26] Given such convictions among those who shape opinion, the long revolutionary, anticapitalist, and antibourgeois tradition of Italian Fascism disappears into a stylized, amnesiac, historically inaccurate reconstruction.

Not all the history of the interwar years slipped away. Some scholars conjured up a half-remembered concept that early in the interwar years had been used, in its time, to subsume both fascism and communism. During those years, Fascist intellectuals themselves acknowledged the institutional and structural similarities their "corporative state" shared with the "dictatorship of the proletariat." Those similarities were collected under the rubric: "totalitarianism."

Fascist theoreticians recognized the logic that sustained all single-party systems—communist and fascist alike. In the identification of the individual with the single party state, and the identification of the single party state with a leader, "whose will is the will of the governed,"[27] they recognized a shared "totalitarianism."

The rationale of totalitarianism was articulated before the Great War of 1914–1918 by Giovanni Gentile—the author of the variant of Hegelian idealism that ultimately came to animate Mussolini's Fascism. Before the First World War, Gentile had proposed a conception of political rule that conceived individuals organically united in a society that found its identity in an "ethical state." Gentile conceived society and the state intrinsic, rather than extrinsic, to the individual. Like Hegel, and Aristotle before him, Gentile conceived the individual outside society and the state only an "abstraction."[28]

From that fundamental identity of the individual, society, and the state, all the subsequent identities followed. There followed a conceived unity of political opinion, culture, and aspirations—and the corresponding institutional structures that endowed those identities physical substance.

Fascist ideologues not only saw in that social philosophy the rationale of their system—but they recognized its appearance in the political rule of V. I. Lenin in Bolshevik Russia. "Totalitarianism" was understood to cover antidemocratic and antiparliamentarian systems of both the political left and right.

In December 1921, Mussolini had himself acknowledged the affinities shared by his Fascism and Lenin's Bolshevism. He spoke of their common recognition of the necessity of creating "a centralizing and unitary state, that imposes on all an iron discipline."[29]

In the course of time, Fascist intellectuals identified a similar rationale in the ideology of Adolf Hitler's National Socialism, and in the political rationale of Chiang Kaishek's Kuomintang. In effect, Fascists saw totalitarianism as a novel form of governance, as a singular product of revolution in the twentieth century. In origin, it was neither of the left or right.

TOTALITARIANISM

Fascist ideologues spoke affirmatively of totalitarianism. They spoke of the primacy of politics over economics, and leadership over consultation. They spoke of obedience and belief, and a readiness to struggle against the reactionary forces of wealth and privilege. They spoke of creating a "new humanity" for a "new society" under the auspices of an "ethical state." Totalitarianism was understood to be a unique political creation of the modern age.

For their part, Fascism's opponents, as early as 1923, identified totalitarianism as an oppressive system of "absolute political dominion" over citizens.[30] Thereafter, the term appeared sporadically outside Fascist environs—almost always accompanied by negative connotation. In the fall of 1929, for example, the term appeared in the London *Times*, and was applied to both Fascist Italy and Stalin's Russia. In 1934, George Sabine spoke of a "new type" of state that found expression not only in "fascist totalitarianism," but in the "very similar" conception of the state that had manifested itself in Stalin's Russia.[31]

In the mid-1930s, the term "totalitarianism" was used, with some frequency, to identify not only the political systems of Mussolini and Hitler, i.e., fascist states, but that of Stalin's Russia as well.[32] Marxist-Leninists, predictably, took exception to the usage. They had first used the term in 1928, and thereafter applied it exclusively to what they considered fascist state systems. They had decided that totalitarianism was a by-product of the final crisis of industrial capitalism.[33]

With the coming of the Second World War, "totalitarianism" was used almost exclusively to refer to the Axis powers. The Soviet Union, by that time an ally in the "war against fascism," was generally exempt, with the often unspoken suggestion that Stalin's Russia was some sort of incipient democracy. Those sympathetic to Stalin, Marxists of one or another degree of commitment, given their identification of fascism and monopoly capitalism, insisted that "totalitarianism" could only refer to fascist systems—with fascism representing the pathological reaction of capitalism in decline.[34]

The identification of Stalin's Russia as a totalitarianism was largely left to democratic, or anti-Soviet, Marxists—Mensheviks, Trotskyists, and social democrats. Only with the end of the Second World War did the term become increasingly inclusive, to refer to socialist, as well as fascist, systems. Such usage had survived throughout the war years in publications such as Arthur Koestler's *Darkness at Noon*, and in more academic works such as Franz Neumann's *Behemoth* and Sigmund Neumann's *Permanent Revolution*. George Orwell reported that the idea for his premonitory, antitotalitarian novel, *Nineteen Eighty-four*, had come to him in 1943. For Orwell, a victorious Soviet Union held out the prospect of something other than social democracy.

With the end of the Second World War, the referents of the term once again included Stalin's Soviet Union. The criterial traits that governed admission into the category included the features that had been common to totalitarianism since the first years of the 1930s. They included a "charismatic leadership," inspired by a formal ideology of pretended infallibility, leading an elite vanguard housed in a single, dominant party, which administered a disciplined system of potential controls over all aspects of civil life, ranging from the economy, the flow of information, to culture.[35]

The war having been won, the leaders of the industrial democracies no longer had to concern themselves with the sensibilities of their counterparts in Moscow. There were enough critics of the political system in the Soviet Union to provide the energy to once again address the issue of the relationship between political democracy and totalitarianism. Deteriorating relations between Washington and Moscow precipitated the development—and signaled the advent of the "cold war."[36]

A wave of publications, both popular and academic, made an issue of the "threat of totalitarianism." In 1950, the United States Congress passed the McCarran Internal Security Act, which proscribed the entry of "totalitarians" into the United States—a proscription that explicitly included "communists"—transcending the customary distinction between the political left and right.

For a time, the expression "Red fascism" enjoyed a certain vogue.[37] Anti-Soviet leftists had persisted in their employment of "totalitarianism" to include Stalinism throughout the war—and immediately fell into line behind Washington. Soviet Marxists, in opposition, reaffirmed their standard theoretical argument. In 1946, a Soviet official contended that although the war against the fascism of Hitler and Mussolini had been successfully concluded, the fascist threat remained. "Fascism," he contended, "is a manifestation of capitalist society in its imperialistic phase," and could be expected to resurface as capitalists feel the necessity to "oppose Soviet democracy."[38]

Throughout the course of the cold war, "totalitarianism" became a contested political concept. Senator Joseph McCarthy created a political firestorm with his crusade against communists, and "fellow-travelers." Liberal journalists objected that McCarthyism had taken on totalitarian features—an objection that suggested that liberal democratic systems themselves might well share traits with totalitarianism. Totalitarianism, it was contended, was not uniquely limited to fascism or communism. Its properties might be found anywhere. It is a contention that continues to resonate in Western academic and journalistic communities to this day.

As early as the McCarthy committee meetings, liberals and leftists developed a strategy in dealing with totalitarianism. "Totalitarianism" was to be a term to be employed against any "reactionary" or "quasifascist" opponents of "democracy." Fascism and capitalism might be its proper referents—but could hardly apply to Marxist or Marxist-Leninist systems since Marxism was understood to be in the democratic traditions of the French revolution.[39]

As the concept entered fulsomely into academic discourse, it became increasingly complex and uncertain. Hannah Arendt delivered her *Origins of Totalitarianism* in 1951 to general acclaim, but her account created problems.[40] She had argued that the term "totalitarianism" covered the Soviet system as well as that of Adolf Hitler—but her treatment of the Soviet Union appeared somewhat contrived, as though it were something of an afterthought. She had managed to trace the totalitarianism of National Socialist Germany to conditions created by the "bourgeoisie" of the nineteenth century—to unbridled economic competition, the dissolution of class and caste identities, resultant alienation, and the creation of the political "mob." The bourgeois economic system had left individuals bereft of particularity, and reduced them to search for their identities in such nebulous concepts as race. It was that which fueled the *völkisch* thought of nineteenth-century Germany that, in turn, provided much of the substance of National Socialist ideology.

On the other hand, Arendt's treatment of Soviet totalitarianism was deemed, even by her admirers, as being far less penetrating and substantive.[41] She did assign some responsibility to Marx for having reduced law and governance to simple "reflexes" of economic factors, and she alluded to the collectivistic and deterministic aspects of his social philosophy as factors. How that lent itself to the rationale that underwrote totalitarianism was not clear. One comes away from the text with a sense that, somehow or other, "capitalism" and the "bourgeoisie," and not Marx, are really responsible for totalitarianism. As a consequence, the ultimate sources of Soviet totalitarianism remained more than a little obscure.

Arendt's volume was one of a collection of notable volumes that appeared about the same time. Karl Popper's *The Open Society and Its Enemies*, and Jacob Talmon's *The Origins of Totalitarian Democracy* and his *Political Messianism* contributed to the ongoing discussion. By the 1970s, interest in the origins of totalitarianism, in some measure, had begun to flag, and more and more academics found reason to object to the concept's employment.

"Destalinization" had presumably taken hold in the Soviet Union, and there were many who sought to reduce international tensions by no longer invoking "inflammatory" political characterizations. Besides, it was argued, the term "totalitarianism" was hardly sufficiently nuanced to allow its use in social science and historical exposition. As a case in point, it was argued, Lenin's ideas were very complex, and so were the ideas of other Bolsheviks. Their individual and collective behaviors were hardly the consequence of holding fast to some collection of uniform political convictions. They were rather the results of a complex of factors far too numerous to be captured by so broad gauged a term as "a formal totalitarian ideology."[42]

It was further argued that Mussolini's regime, whatever the Duce's boasts, was never really totalitarian. Fascism never succeeded in absorbing the Italian monarchy, the Roman Catholic Church, or the officer corps of the armed forces.[43] Worse still, Mussolini hardly massacred anyone. Guilty of employing toxic gas in the Ethiopian war, and brutality in suppressing uprisings in Libya, Mussolini killed remarkably few of his own citizens during his reign of a quarter century.[44] Hannah Arendt noted that failure, and decided Italian Fascism did not qualify for entry into the class of totalitarianisms.

Others emphasized that the term "totalitarian" suggests a depiction of a systematic integration of all the component parts of a society under the control of the omnicompetent state. In fact, critics contended, so-called totalitarian systems were anything but omnicompetent. Hitler's regime was disorganized, and many lived throughout his tenure with little change in their day-to-day lives—until the devastation of the Second World War. In the Soviet Union, party rule varied from place to place, and in Mao's China there was much disorder—and at times, pandemic incompetence. Somehow or other, for critics of the concept, all of that seemed to mean that "totalitarianism" as a social science concept was of little cognitive use. Many recommended that it be abandoned. Its use generated hostility between the superpowers, and provided little insight as compensation.

Other than that, many intellectuals felt that any association between "socialism," in whatever form it took, and fascism of any sort, was to be rejected. The suggestion that there might be some sort of association between the two could only serve the purposes of capitalism in its struggle against socialist liberation.[45] There was fulsome support for the use of the designation "antifascism," rather than "antitotalitarian," to identify the true enemy of modern democracy.[46] Fascism, not socialism, was the foe.

And yet, there were those who continued to argue that the term "totalitarian" had as its referents political regimes of both the left and the right—and that those regimes were of a new type, unique to the twentieth century.[47] Totalitarian regimes featured distinctive political rule, in terms of the singular leader himself, his preclusive ideology and the dominant party it animated. It was not just a police state—or simply a personal dictatorship. It was a political system that arrogated to itself the power to fashion, and emit legislation without the semblance of those "checks and balances" that typify pluralistic arrangements. In such systems, the distinction between legislative and executive branches is deemed anachronistic—and the suggestion that judicial review should be independent of the other branches of government is considered dysfunctional. Such systems, it was held, could be politically either of the left or the right, socialist or fascist as the case might be.

Law in such systems is conceived an adjunct of ideology—an expression of "the will of all." It is generally formulated and administered through the bureaucracies of the state—with the courts playing an uncertain, ill-defined role. The machinery of the state is designed to serve the ideological purposes of the party as those purposes are understood by the leadership. Individuals, under surveillance by police and party, are enrolled in age cohorts, political, paramilitary, and functional associations, and expected selflessly to serve the system.

It seems evident that such a syndrome of properties serves heuristic, didactic, and mnemonic purposes.[48] It suggests possible research topics; it serves to organize complex materials for pedagogical ends; and it assists in ready storage and recall of fugitive information. What "totalitarianism" is not is a "theory." It can neither explain, in any comprehensible scientific sense, nor predict. At best, it advances a very general description of a syndrome of traits that seem to hang together. It is not clear that all members of the class share *all* its defining traits—nor is it clear how many of those defining traits, or in what measure, are required for entry into the class.

In the past, the concept has assisted social scientists to explore the actual functioning of those systems tentatively identified as totalitarian. Some seem to display more of the traits than others, and some in more emphatic measure.

Some of the systems so identified pass through stages. Stalinism was something quite different before the death of Stalin than after. Maoism was transformed by the death of its "Never Setting Red Sun." Conversely, Kim Jong Il's Democratic People's Republic of Korea has remained stolidly the same after the death of Kim Il Sung. Castro's regime in Cuba displays some of the major features of totalitarianism, and yet is somehow different. Stalinists, Maoists, and Marxists of sundry sorts have teased out diaphanous totalitarian features even in pluralistic systems.

The fulsome traits associated with the term "totalitarianism" refer to a distinctive form of governance that first became possible in the age of mobilizable masses, of nationalism, of rapid industrialization, and modern technology. For our immediate purposes, it is interesting that some specialists insist that only right-wing political movements in capitalist environs can ever be totalitarian—while others maintain that only "a socialist or communist system can achieve full totalitarianism, since total control requires total institutional revolution that can only be effected by state socialism."[49] In Eastern Europe, as Soviet controls weakened in the 1980s, more and more socialist scholars acknowledged the features shared by fascist and Marxist-Leninist systems.[50] By the mid-1980s, writers and academics in the Soviet Union were prepared to recognize the totalitarianism of their system, particularly that of the Stalinist period.[51] Thereafter, anglophone scholars have either unself-consciously used the characterization to identify entire stages in the history of the Soviet Union, or as part of their analysis.[52]

What seems to survive out of all of this is an acknowledgment that fascism, however understood, and Marxism-Leninism, in whatever variant, share some identifiable features. Only the most doctrinaire of Marxists still insist that only fascism was totalitarian in practice or intent. Most comparativists, with however little enthusiasm, are prepared to grant important, if abstract similarities. By the last decade of the twentieth century the debate on the issue of "totalitarianism," its scope, interpretation, and applicability, had run its course. Fascism, in some of its forms, was somehow related to Marxism, in some of its forms. There was little agreement on how similar these two classes of political systems might be, but many attest to the similarities.

From the interwar years, when fascism and communism were classed together, through the war years when only fascism was identified as totalitarian, until the final years of the twentieth century when, once again, similarities were attested between fascism and communism in however attenuated a form, a search for ideological and historical origins has recommended itself. Enough political systems remain that continue to share totalitarian traits to make the enterprise worthy of the time and energy required.

All that notwithstanding, there have been those, at the close of the last century, who have held that concern for a generic totalitarianism has little, if any, place in the social science of our time. Communism had collapsed both in the Soviet Union as well as in its Eastern European satellites. In the People's Republic of China, Maoist communism transformed itself into something significantly different almost immediately after the death of its "Chairman."

The consequence was an almost immediate refocus of political attention. Among many, fascism reappeared as the exclusive concern. Soon there was the suggestion that fascism, alone, was the "pathological" cause of the mass murders that darkened the history of the twentieth century. Fascism was understood to have been so destructive a political alternative that it, and it alone, occupies a unique place in the ideological and institutional history of our time. Marxism, in all its variants, recedes into history. It is "fascism," not "totalitarianism," that is invoked to "understand" a unique barbarity and inhumanity that apparently exceeded anything that transpired under communist auspices.

A spate of monographs appeared that argued that only fascism could be responsible for the horrors of the twentieth century. The argument was made that Marxism and fascism were, and could only be, diametric opposites. Marxism was a product of the Enlightenment, and was a rational, progressive ideology—while fascism was irrational, reactionary, and intrinsically evil, committed exclusively to "violence and war" for their own sake. Marxism, on the other hand, was "as much an ethical doctrine as an economic one."[53] Their respective morality and ethics distinguished the two systems.

In general, the argument employs Hitler's National Socialism, infamous in its genocidal malevolence, as paradigmatic of the class of "fascisms." That given, many have sought to dilate the term "fascism" to include a variety of political systems—all understood to share in the special evil that was Nazism. That having been established, Marxism and its variants have been accorded a distinctive moral superiority.

It is an intellectual strategy that has left more than one scholar unconvinced. As late as 1994, Walter Laqueur could still speak of the properties shared by Stalin's Soviet Union and Hitler's National Socialist Germany—and others were to catalog the long list of unimaginable moral outrages that stained the history of both.[54]

SOME ISSUES IN THE INTELLECTUAL HISTORY OF REVOLUTION

For all the efforts made to distinguish Marxism from fascism in any of its real or fancied forms, there is a lingering suspicion that the two ideological systems are somehow related. The similarities were noted even before Italian Fascism had reached political maturity.

Many Marxists were there at the birth of Fascism. However strenuously resisted by some, the relationship was recognized in totalitarianism. During the tenure of the regime, it was acknowledged by some of Fascism's major theoreticians. And after the passing of Leninist communism, its relationship to fascism, in general, was acknowledged by many of its erstwhile practitioners.[55]

The difficulty that many have had with all that is the consequence of political science folk wisdom that has made fascism the unqualified opposite of any form of Marxism. So fixed has that notion become in the study of comparative politics that the suggestion of any affinities between the two is generally dismissed. And yet, some contemporary comparativists recognize that there was an unmistakable "essential ideological kindredness" shared by fascism and Leninism. It was equally clear that at "certain pivotal ideational junctures, *les extremes se touchent.*"[56]

It is important to try to understand how that could be possible. In answering that, one has a foothold on how one might explain the concept "totalitarianism"—that has fascism and the variants of Marxism as its referents. Attempting to begin to explain the relationship is part of the story of revolutionary thought at the turn of the twentieth century. It is a story that merits telling. It is part of a long and complicated narrative in the intellectual history of ideology. It is an account that hopefully lends some substance to the relationship between Marxism in its various modern guises—and the Fascism of Mussolini. It is a chronicle that perhaps also serves to distinguish that Fascism from other candidate fascisms.

Italian Fascism was not Hitler's National Socialism, and it was not Lenin's Bolshevism—but all three shared some sort of affinity, however minimal. For the purpose of the present exposition, the relationship between Mussolini's Fascism and Lenin's Bolshevism is of central concern. It speaks to the ideological relationship shared by Italian Fascism and one or another variant of Marxism, and helps us understand why relevant similarities regularly resurface in any study dealing with modern revolutionary political systems. It is a story that covers almost half a century of European radical thought—and involves some of the major intellectuals of the first quarter of the twentieth century.

While it is only a thread in the complex tapestry of revolution in our time, it is an important and interesting concern. It deals with revolutionary morality and the ethical system that sustains it. It addresses the issue of how the revolutionary theorists at the beginning of our time attempted to understand human choice and political decisions. It deals with revolution and its motives, and violence and its uses.

In the course of time, all these concerns were addressed by self-selected Marxist revolutionaries at the end of the nineteenth century, some of whom were to become the leaders of revolutionary movements in the twentieth. History was to subsequently identify some as "Marxists" and others as "fascists." Those with whom we shall concern ourselves were all Marxists of one or another persuasion. The most interesting, for our purposes, were to ultimately be identified as "Mussoliniani," intellectual leaders of Italian Fascism.

It will be surprising to some—though certainly not everyone—that among the first issues engaged by the revolutionary thinkers at the turn of the twentieth century were those having to do with choice and determinism, with morality and ethics, with nationalism, with leadership, with the mobilization of masses, and how revolution was to be understood in the broad expanse of history. They are questions that continue to shape the revolutionary thought of our time.

CHAPTER TWO

The Roots of Revolutionary Ideology

The discussion that follows does not constitute an attempt to *explain* revolution in our time. It is an effort to outline something of the reasons, empirical and normative, advanced by its advocates to *justify* violent social change.

Human beings characteristically pretend to provide moral justification for their most abominable acts. In that fundamental sense, revolutionaries are eminently human. The twentieth century was a century of almost unremitting revolution, mass murder, and destruction. Throughout that time, history witnessed the most heinous acts against humanity—and in not a single case did the major protagonists fail to advance a moral and/or empirical rationale, however unpersuasive, to legitimate their behaviors. The effort, here, attempts to make the case that much of the justificatory rationale for revolution in the twentieth century found its origins in the nineteenth-century intellectual labors of Karl Marx and Friedrich Engels. Marx died in 1883, to be followed twelve years later by Engels. Thereafter, Marxists were left to their own devices in attempting to provide a moral rationale for the violence, mayhem, and death that attended the revolution to which they devoted their efforts. It will be argued that out of that attempt emerged much of the moral reasoning used to justify totalitarianism and the massive destruction of life and property that darkens almost the entire past century.

In retrospect, out of the enormous body of reasoning devoted to Marxism as a revolutionary belief system, one can tease some of those elements with which we are today all-too-familiar. There is, in the texts left to us by Marx and Engels, an argument for the rejection of any "absolute" morality. Morality, we are told by the founders of classical Marxism, is that code of conduct that results in "the overthrow of the present, [and] represents the future."[1] Why overthrowing the present should recommend itself as moral is part of the story of the role played by normative reasoning in the twentieth century. Out of that reasoning, in large part, was to emerge the totalitarian rationale of Leninism, Stalinism, Maoism, National Socialism, and Italian Fascism in all their variants.

At the end of the nineteenth century, a surprising number of aggressive intellectuals arose throughout continental Europe who were to serve as leaders of those revolutionary forces that were ultimately to visit unimaginable destruction almost everywhere. Those leaders were to be found in imperial Germany and Austria-Hungary, czarist Russia, monarchial Italy, and republican France. They collected around themselves restless forces they were to animate with revolutionary ideas. It will be argued that almost all those leaders and those forces were directly or indirectly, legitimate or illegitimate, heirs of the revolutionary thought of Karl Marx and Friedrich Engels.

MARXISM AND "PHANTOMS FORMED IN THE BRAIN"

Morals and ethics lie at the core of revolutionary commitment. As such, moral and immoral behavior, sustained or abjured by appropriate ethical assessment,[2] becomes critical to any revolutionary enterprise. That enterprise is inextricably associated with the advocacy of, or resistance to, violence. At some stage in the process it becomes necessary to systematically address ethical and moral questions. At the very least, the proponents of revolution must justify to themselves or others their endorsement of real or potential violence.

As early as his first efforts at revolutionary analysis, Karl Marx extended what could only be characterized as a slack interpretation of morals and ethics—as well as a singular account of human conceptual life in general. In *The Communist Manifesto* of 1848, he simply dismissed the notion that there were "eternal truths, such as Freedom, Justice, etc.," or that any such ideas should independently influence the course of human conduct. He argued, instead, that such ideas, other than eternal, were relative, a function of the time, place, and circumstances in which they find expression—and whatever influence they exercise, as we shall see, was to be understood to be the derivative result of objective factors that, taken together, he identified as time-specific "modes of production."

In the *Manifesto*, Marx simply affirmed that "man's ideas, views, and conceptions, in one word, man's consciousness, changes with every change in the conditions of his material existence, in his social relations and his social life." Notions such as "freedom" and "justice" are artifacts of a peculiar set of objective and time-sensitive conditions. Marx concluded with the pronouncement that "what else does the history of ideas prove, than that intellectual production changes its character in proportion as material production is changed?"[3] Moral judgments, apparently, as well as the rationale given in their support, can only be relative, transitory, intrinsically related to the peculiar conditions attendant on the prevailing mode of material production at any given time.

Thus, about a year before the publication of the *Manifesto*, Marx had affirmed that "a change in men's productive forces necessarily brings about a change in their relations of production. . . . The same men who establish their social relations in conformity with their material productivity, produce also principles, ideas and categories, in conformity with their social relations." Thus, "productive forces" employed in the provision of goods gave rise to corresponding "social relations," which together make up the mode of production.[4] Morality, both in behavior and in principle, was understood to be contingent and derivative of a prevailing mode of production.

A few years earlier, in 1844, the young Marx characterized such a conception of a derivative human consciousness as a "fully developed naturalism" or "humanism," that necessarily implied that "religion, family, state, law, morality, science, art, etc., are only *particular* modes of production, and *fall under its general law*."[5] How that was to be understood was less than transparent.

What Marx's cryptic formulation seems to mean is that the generation of moral concepts was the predictable consequence of a given "mode of production"—that, somehow or other, the provision of moral precepts "fell under the 'general law' of production."[6] Precisely how that might have been accomplished remains obscure to this day.

At the end of 1845, in an obvious effort at clarification, Marx spoke of the "mode of production," which produced the "means of subsistence" for human communities, as somehow giving rise to an inclusive "definite mode of life" that was conceived responsible for the shaping of human behavior. We are told that "what human beings are," what the "nature of individuals" might be, "coincides with" and "depends on, the material conditions determining" the production of their subsistence—both "with what they produce and how they produce."[7]

The central thesis of what Marx called, at that time, the "materialist method" was that "individuals who are productively active in a definite way enter into . . . definite social and political relations"—which are, apparently, "independent" of their individual and collective wills. The manner in which material subsistence is made available, and the corresponding social and political relations that result, together "produce" the "ideological reflexes and echoes of this life process. Morality, religion, metaphysics, and all the rest of ideology as well as the forms of consciousness corresponding to [the mode of production], thus no longer retain the semblance of independence. They have no history, no development; but men, developing their material production and their material intercourse, alter, along with this their actual world, also their thinking and the products of their thinking. It is not consciousness that determines life, but life that determines consciousness."[8]

To speak of "politics, laws, morality, religion, [and] metaphysics . . ." as "phantoms formed in the human brain" that are "necessarily sublimates" of the "mode of material production," constitutes one of those attempts at formulating complex social science claims that are necessarily preliminary to serious empirical inquiry. Omnibus claims such as those tendered by the youthful Marx are familiar to social science practitioners. They are characteristically formulated in terms of analogy and metaphor. "Phantoms" are somehow "formed" in the brain through a process vaguely characterized as "sublimation." All of which simply defies convincing confirmation unless the central concepts are unpacked in terms of some kind of operational definition, and the relationships between concepts are specified in measurable terms.[9] Unless such a procedure is undertaken, precursory claims, like those found in the youthful writings of Marx, never constitute anything more than research suggestions. Establishing their empirical truth requires relevant observational evidence, and that would require far greater conceptual specificity than anything to be found in the early Marx accounts. The claims advanced are preliminary to serious inquiry and serve, at best, heuristic purpose.

To be told that "the form of intercourse determined by the existing productive forces . . . is civil society," and that "civil society in its various stages, [is] the basis of all history . . . explaining how all the different theoretical products and forms of consciousness, religion, philosophy, morality, etc., etc., arise from it,"[10] is not to be told anything that might be empirically confirmed in the "real" world. The claim is too vague and the relationship between what is understood to be "civil society"[11] and the "different theoretical products" far too uncertain to allow confirmation.

Such claims are complicated still further by introducing the conviction that "the class which has the means of material production at its disposal . . . also controls the means of mental production," is not helpful. To be told that "the individuals composing the ruling class . . . rule also as thinkers, as producers of ideas, and regulate the production and distribution of the ideas of their age . . ." clarifies very little—and once again, defies empirical substantiation. It pretends that the truth of such a further affirmation is unmistakably evident, when in fact it merely further confounds the original, convoluted claim that the "mode of production" somehow *explains* the "rise" of "all the different theoretical products and forms of consciousness, religion, philosophy, [and] morality . . ."[12]

A still further complication is added when we are told that in the production of such "different theoretical products," as in all cases of collective productive activities, there was a "division of labor" among the component subsets of the "ruling class." On the one hand, there are the "thinkers . . . [who] make the formation of the illusions of the class about itself their chief source of livelihood." On the other, there are those active owners of the means of production who, having "less time to make up illusions and ideas about themselves," may develop a "certain opposition and hostility" directed toward those charged with fashioning the system's ideological fictions.

Those thinkers who specialize in the intellectual defense of the very class privileges they all enjoy may be seen by the members of the class responsible for *real* production as providing "illusions" that are inadequate, unimpressive, or counterproductive. Any "opposition or hostility" that might arise between such subsets of the ruling class, however, Marx went on to add, would "automatically vanish . . . whenever a practical collision occurs in which the class itself is endangered." At that juncture, the ideas of the more active members, the actual owners of the means of production, become dominant. They supercede those of the apologists for the class.[13]

Given all the patent intricacies involved in such notions, it is hard to imagine how any one of them might be convincingly established as true by available evidence. At best, such an account delivers a plausible story of a very tangled set of social and intellectual exchanges understood to apply to all of human history. More interesting for the purpose of exposition, Marx advanced an account of the advent of revolutionary ideas that has immediate relevance to any understanding of systemic change in the modern world. According to Marx, *revolutionary ideas*, as distinct from those standard legal, philosophical, and moral ideas that are "class illusions," manifest themselves in any given environment only when "productive forces and means of intercourse are brought into being which, under the existing relations, only cause mischief, and are no longer productive but destructive forces." What that seems to mean is that in the course of time "productive forces," somehow or other, enter into "conflict" with "social intercourse."[14] That, in turn, creates conditions that give rise to those who would serve as *agents of revolutionary change* together with the very *revolutionary ideas* that animate their undertaking. Tensions between the productive forces (whatever they are understood to include) and productive relations, give rise to a class of persons prepared to overthrow the old system for one that is new.

For Marx, the explication of such general notions involves an account that demonstrates how modern industry has produced "a class . . . which was to bear all the burdens of society without enjoying its advantages."[15] It was just such a class that Marx understood would serve as a conscious instrument of the kind of change he had in mind. Such an oppressed class would be fundamentally revolutionary—but more than that, because Marx conceived history's developmental energy arising from the "conflict" between productive forces and prevailing social relations, he argued that beyond the unproblematic recognition that such a class might serve as revolutionary agent, its existence was understood to reflect a still more fundamental reality festering in society's "economic base." In some determinate sense, human beings did not simply become revolutionary. The very existence of such an oppressed class in modern industrial society is the "inevitable" (*unvermeidlich*) consequence of what Marx understood to be dysfunctions, independent of the will of all participants, which lay at the very productive base of social life. According to Marx, human beings became revolutionary because the "objective facts" of history compelled them.

It is clear that for Marx revolution could hardly be simply the consequence of felt grievance, or an individual or collective decision to act. Marx was prepared to argue that revolution was a function of causes having little to do with willed choice. He argued that the very existence of a revolutionary class was evidence of impersonal tensions between entirely objective existing and emerging productive forces as well as the constraints imposed on those forces by prevailing social relations. It is precisely those tensions that engender a class of persons compelled to assume revolutionary responsibilities. A revolutionary class arises because of tensions at the economic base of society, and only derivatively because of felt grievance on the part of its members. Once the conscious agents of change become available, the entire system enters into transformative crisis. Marx devoted the remainder of his intellectual life to the attempt to explain precisely how such a process initiated and sustained itself.

What was abundantly clear was Marx's conviction that an *inevitable* and entirely objective process "reflected" itself in the consciousness of proletarian agents of change. The process gave rise to a functional revolutionary ideology through, and with which, the crisis would be resolved. The requisite ideology would inevitably infill the consciousness of a revolutionary class that then would proceed to give body and expression to the "necessity of a fundamental revolution."[16]

There is a quaint automaticity in all of this. Specific moral ideas apparently appear precisely when they are required. They are destined to overwhelm those "reactionary illusions" that support the class profiting from the existing dysfunctional relations of production. Functional revolutionary ideas are a product of a consciousness conjured up by the tensions produced by emerging productive forces that can no longer be accommodated by the existing mode of production.

For Marx, the material productive forces and corresponding relations of production together constituted "the real *ground* of history"—and explain "the formation of ideas from material practice."[17] Ideas, moral, philosophical, or legal, are *epiphenomenal*; they are reflections of collective, essentially material, productive processes, and the social relations to which those processes, taken together, give rise.[18] When emerging productive forces can no longer be housed within existing social relations, new ideas, religious, moral, philosophical, or legal, appear—in the form of advocacy of revolutionary change. Revolutionary ideas, in whatever form they appear, emerge in order that those social practices that have begun to act as "constraints" on the expanding forces of production might be "overcome."[19] The apposite moral, ethical, religious, and philosophical ideas that come to animate the revolutionary class arise simply because those ideas correspond to the productive needs of given historic circumstances.

As the forces of production "outgrow" the corresponding relations of production to which they originally "gave rise," a class emerges representing new productive forces that cannot flourish within the prevailing social and political constraints of a given arrangement. That class is somehow "ineluctably" and "inevitably" inspired to revolutionary enterprise. Correlative to this, revolutionary ideas make their appearance to supply a normative rationale for just such radical social change.

Thus, while generic communist ideas may have made their appearance at various times in history, all the moral and philosophical principles implied by such ideas could only become historically significant when certain material, i.e., productive, conditions make their appearance. When new forces of production can no longer be accommodated in a given society's economic base, a revolutionary class, animated by corresponding revolutionary convictions, necessarily rises to clear passage.

Such was the discussion Marx provided as an account of how revolutionary ideas arise, prevail, and prosper. He makes them a function of material preconditions identified as necessary for the appearance of a truly revolutionary class, its moral epiphany, and its ultimate success in establishing a communist society. Only when material conditions have fully matured might one predict the rise of a genuinely revolutionary class, its specific philosophical and moral inspiration, as well as the real possibility of its success. Those conditions, themselves, render both the appearance of the revolutionary proletariat, as well as its mastery, historically "necessary." Independent of those preconditions, generic communism could only remain a distracting velleity. We are told that if "material elements of a complete revolution are not present . . . it is absolutely immaterial whether the *idea* of this revolution has been expressed a hundred times already." Without their necessary material premises, such ideas would remain little more than "idealistic humbug."[20]

At times, somehow or other, such humbug persists in society for an unconscionable length of time. There are many political, religious, moral, and philosophical ideas, that anachronistically survive into our own time, that could only be the products of earlier productive modes. Marx had very little to say that might explain their persistence. He did remark, however, that their continued existence would be, at best, temporary. "Reality," after some unspecified interval, would dissolve all "theoretical bubble-blowing," all "ready-made nonsense," simply because such irrelevancies fail to satisfy any of the requirements of the actual processes of "earthly" production. At some indeterminate time, everyone would understand that "such nonsense" was to be explained, not on its merits, but as nothing other than an ideational by-product of "life conditions."

Those were the convictions that shaped Marx's view that it would soon be the case that the "mass" of contemporary revolutionaries, the proletariat, would no longer entertain archaic notions about religion and the whole attendant "learned" nonsense about a transcendent morality emanating from the "realm of God."[21] Marx informed the revolutionaries of his time that the morality of the proletariat would represent the "interests" of the emerging productive forces—the productive forces of the future—and as such would represent the only defensible morality for rational actors.

What emerges from Marx's account is a very singular conception of revolutionary thought—and the motives that inspire human beings to assume the moral responsibilities that attend violence and mayhem. In *The Communist Manifesto*, the conception finds expression in a set of mutually supportive convictions turning on the premise that the course of history is, in the last analysis, *inevitable*—and that the modern agents of production, the bourgeoisie, are somehow compelled to produce the proletariat, destined to be their "grave-diggers"—to inaugurate a new epoch of universal liberty and abundance.[22]

Over the years, Marx's formulations concerning the general outlines of the materialist conception of history—and the implications of such a conception in terms of morality and ethics—did not substantially change irrespective of the introduction of some more complicated surface features that found articulation in synoptic propositions and epigrammatic turns of speech.[23] Thus, in his youth he informed his readership, as an illustrative instance, that "the hand mill gives you society with the feudal lord; the steam mill, society with the industrial capitalist." Then he proceeded to insist that "in acquiring new productive forces men change their mode of production, in changing the way of earning their living, they change all their social relations. . . . The same men who establish their social relations in conformity with their material productivity, produce also principles, ideas and categories, in conformity with their social relations."[24] These central notions, however complex and difficult to confirm, remained constant with Marx throughout his maturity—and in the major work produced in that full maturity, he wrote, "Technology discloses man's mode of dealing with Nature, the process of production by which he sustains his life, and thereby also lays bare the mode of formation of his social relations, and of the mental conceptions that flow from them."[25]

In much the same fashion as he had expressed such notions two decades before, Marx maintained that it was technology that was ultimately responsible for mental conceptions[26]—expressing synoptically the claims he had advanced between the fall of 1845 and the summer of 1846.[27] If the "hand mill" must necessarily "give rise" to feudal society, together with all its associated ideas, the evident implication, given everything Marx had written over the years, was that technology must somehow be responsible not only for corresponding social relations, but for the provision of the appropriate moral and legal principles, as well as the customary usages, that sustain public security and social stability in any given society, feudal or otherwise.

Whatever might be said concerning such speculations, it seems clear that something more was required to provide a persuasive account of an eminently complex process. Stitching together the generalizations that make up the core of the materialist conception of history demanded some elaboration if a persuasive account of ethical reasoning and adaptive moral behavior was to be forthcoming. Over the years, other Marxists attempted to supply just that elaboration. What they delivered, however unpersuasive, was calculated to supply what would pass as a general theory of ethics and a behavioral account of moral conduct.

MARXIST ETHICS AND DARWINISM

By the early 1850s, soon after the appearance of *The Communist Manifesto*, revolutionary effervescence had dissipated in Europe. All the revolutionary activity of the preceding few years had abated, and "reaction" once again reasserted itself. Both Marx and Engels recognized as much, although they continued to anticipate yet other revolutionary episodes in the immediate future.[28] To prepare for just such eventualities, Engels urged that Marx write a "thick book" that would provide the scientific grounds to support their revolutionary expectations.[29] In response, Marx undertook just such a responsibility, and over the years dutifully pursued his "Critical Analysis of Capitalist Production"—to produce, in 1867, what is now identified as the first volume of his *magnum opus*, *Das Kapital*.

About that time, in 1863, Ferdinand Lassalle, an intellectually independent socialist, founded the German Workers' Union in Leipzig.[30] In 1869, the Social Democratic Workers' Party was founded in Germany by some of Marx's disciples—and soon Lassalleans and Marxists attempted a collaborative union. Neither Marx nor Engels endorsed Lassalle's ideological or political efforts, but they were not in a position to significantly influence the collaboration between him and their followers. Barred as he was from Germany as a consequence of his earlier exile and renunciation of citizenship, Marx could only level objections from afar.

Both Marx and Engels found ready reasons to object to the ideological convictions and political behaviors of Lassalle. In the judgment of the founders of Marxism, neither Lassalle's beliefs nor his leadership of the German workers' movement adequately reflected the realities of the then prevailing economic base.

Marx's critical mistrust of Lassalle was not particularly unique. For some reason, most of Marx's compatriots in the socialist movement never won his full intellectual approval. In Marx's judgment, almost all the socialist thinkers of his time failed to capture prevailing reality either in their assessments or in their policy recommendations. According to Marx, all of his revolutionary contemporaries succeeded in being wrong—each in his own fashion. There were "feudal socialists" and "clerical socialists," and there were "petty bourgeois socialists," and all sorts of "true socialists"—all wrong in all the ways they could be wrong. They were either confused, suborned, or intellectually impaired. Proudonists and Lassalleans, Fourierists and Owenites, were all to be found in their ranks—all emphatically and irreparably wrong.

It was in that contentious environment that the German Social Democratic movement made its appearance under the acknowledged influence of Karl Marx. More and more intellectuals gathered around its standards, and a formidable body of specifically Marxist argumentation made its appearance. Not always faithful to the original Marxist texts, it bore witness to both the richness of the original material as well as its intrinsic vagueness and ambiguity.

About the same time that the new Social Democratic movement took on institutional shape, Josef Dietzgen,[31] a follower of Marx and Engels, undertook to provide German workers with an easily accessible account of the new party's convictions. In 1869, at the time of the founding of the German Social Democratic party, Dietzgen published his *The Positive Outcome of Philosophy*, a loosely structured discussion of a catalog of philosophical problems. Within that context, Dietzgen outlined his first notions of what a Marxist ethics might be.

At the time of the publication of the work that led to his identification as the "philosopher of the proletariat,"[32] Dietzgen sought to explain all the complexities of Marxist ethical judgment and moral behavior by referring to "the wants of the senses," which he conceived to be "the material out of which reason fashions moral truths."[33] He imagined that such a conception captured the central convictions of what he called "the materialistic conception of morality."[34] At that time, his conception of the nature of ethical reasoning as well as the formulation of moral prescription was hardly more complicated than that.

Whatever the subsequent changes in his analysis, Dietzgen was forever to argue that Marxist ethics was an *inductive science*. Like most of the positivists of the period, he held that "the understanding of the method of science . . . is destined to solve all the problems of religion and philosophy."[35] What that seems to have meant to him at the time was, should one wish to study morality, one would have to proceed to descriptively catalog human needs—for "that which is good corresponds to our needs, that is bad which is contrary to them . . . [for] morality, or the determination of that which is right, has a practical purpose." He simply affirmed that "man with his many wants is the standard of moral truth"—and further, it was just those "human wants [that] give to reason a standard for judging what is good, right, bad, reasonable, etc."[36]

Those preliminary formulations were to be bound together in one universal prescription: "The one and sole absolute end" of moral deliberation was, in Dietzgen's judgment, "human welfare"[37]—and "human welfare" was understood to constitute "an end which sanctifies all rules and actions, all means, so long as they are subservient to it." Granted that, Dietzgen was sufficiently astute to recognize that "human welfare" was an omnibus term that was intrinsically difficult to define. He duly acknowledged that "human welfare," as such, was nowhere to be empirically observed in its simplicity. The proper referent for "human welfare," he seemed to argue, was a generalization drawn from a series of observations of historic instances of individual and collective well-being. Dietzgen was prepared to argue that the satisfaction of human welfare, the "sole and absolute end" of all ethical reasoning, could only be understood, inductively, by inspecting some indeterminate set of "empirical . . . concrete cases."[38]

It is hard to make a great deal out of all this. It is not at all evident what general and transhistorical "human welfare" might be, and consequently, what particular behaviors, at any given time, might duly serve its ends. And yet, understanding what might be implied in terms of behaviors that support that welfare is critical to Dietzgen's presentation of the "materialistic conception of morality"—for he was convinced that "a morality worthy of that name . . . can be exercised only through the understanding of its worth, of its value to our welfare." He went on to insist that "morality is eternally sacred, in so far as it refers to considerations which a man owes to himself and to his fellowmen in the interest of their common welfare."[39]

Fully comprehending what a generic, universal, and absolute human welfare requires becomes essential to a full appreciation of Dietzgen's effort to provide an account of "materialistic morality." He tells us, for example, that "means which are generally unholy may become . . . sanctioned by their relation to some . . . welfare." Thus, he was prepared to maintain that "when . . . man seeks his salvation in war, then murder and incendiarism are holy means." The end, he consistently argued, justifies the means.[40]

In the same vein and in the same place, he went on to tell his readers that the only reason we find "sly tricks and intrigues, poison and murder . . . unholy" is because those behaviors do not seem to serve human welfare.[41] It would seem that if it could be shown that they might so serve, they would presumably thereby be held "holy."

Other than the very unconvincing quality of the discussion, Dietzgen provided a number of puzzling addenda to his account. At one point he proceeded to announce that it would be "a disastrous deception . . . if any age or class . . . proclaims its own peculiar purposes and means to be for the absolute welfare of humanity."[42]

The "philosopher of the proletariat," in effect, in the course of attempting to provide a compelling account of the "science of ethics," counseled the revolutionary working class that it could not, and should not, declare its purposes, and the means it chose for achieving those purposes, as "absolutely moral." At best, morality was relative to time and circumstances. They would dictate proper conduct. There could never be a "timeless" right or wrong.

It seems evident that Dietzgen could not leave his account of the moral philosophy of German Social Democracy in such a state. It was evident that his first effort to provide a coherent, Marxist account of "proletarian morality" was not in the least persuasive. More than that, other than Dietzgen's ready references to the proletariat, it is not difficult to appreciate that there was really very little in his account that was directly attributable to the conjectures found in the early work of Karl Marx and Friedrich Engels.

It is easy to appreciate why, by the middle of the 1870s, Dietzgen chose to undertake a more coherent and convincing treatment of Marxist normative theory. In making the attempt, he made every effort to remain true to the fundamental premises of his Masters. What was singular about the new attempt was the introduction of distinctively *Darwinian* elements into his exposition. Between Dietzgen's two attempts at proposing a Marxist ethical theory, the impact of Darwinism on his thought made itself evident.

The first steps in Dietzgen's attempt at assimilating Darwinist notions into the "materialist conception of history" were facilitated by insisting, once again, on the *scientific* character of the entire endeavor. Dietzgen consistently argued that the most unique feature of Marxist ethics was precisely its scientific character.[43] According to him, Marxist normative notions, like all of Marxist theory, were unalterably and irreducibly scientific. He reiterated his conviction that the moral and ethical convictions of Marxism were somehow the *inductive* consequences of direct or indirect, individual, and collective, sensory observation. For him, "moral truths" were somehow indistinguishable from those truths that were empirical. In some significant sense, morality was, for Dietzgen, something like a "natural science"[44]—and as Darwinism was one of the major accomplishments of natural science in the nineteenth century—it simply had to be accommodated.

By the time Dietzgen put pen to paper in the 1870s, Darwinism had already exercised influence on the European continent for more than a decade—and Marx himself had identified Darwinism as an intellectual activity sharing "affinities" with his own "historical materialism."[45] In those circumstances, what Dietzgen did was to take some of the central propositions of Darwinism—"the struggle for survival," "survival of the fittest," and the conception of "progressive evolution"—and tailor them to fit what he took to be the Marxist inductive "science" of moral judgment.

As a sometimes Darwinist, Dietzgen began his revised account of the science of Marxian ethics with the conviction that human welfare, the basis of materialist ethics, was shaped by the natural imperative to survive.[46] In *The Communist Manifesto*, Marx had, in fact, alluded to the reality that in contemporary "bourgeois society," because of the exploitative nature of the economic system, the proletarians were threatened with extinction—a circumstance that did, in fact, engage their instinctive will to survive.[47]

Dietzgen took that notion and combined it with the generalization that life on the planet exemplified, over geologic time, progressive development—from the simpler to more complex forms. Among sentient, mobile creatures, evolutionary development was accomplished through a struggle for existence, a competition in which the "fittest" survived, allowing them not only the occasion to reproduce and perpetuate the species, but to serve as vehicles of progressive change as well. Animal life, Dietzgen argued, was characterized by an irrepressible will to survive, and that survival impulse directly contributed to just such an outcome.

Through a series of quasideductive steps, Dietzgen argued that since all life seeks its own survival, the will to survive might well be understood as an imperative that contributed, through the struggle for existence, to the progressive evolution of the species. The will to survive created competition and competition would select, for survival, and reproduction, the fittest among competitors. Dietzgen concluded that, within such circumstances, it was evident that individual survival, per se, was of only instrumental, rather than intrinsic, significance. Survivors carried within themselves the biological potential of both survival and reproduction of their species. More than that, in surviving they would further the "fitness" of the species and contribute to the progressive evolution of life. The competitive impulse to survive allowed only the fittest to prevail and reproduce—to the progressive advantage of the species. Thus, individuals might be consumed in the process, but they would, in the last analysis, serve the "absolute welfare of humanity." Dietzgen had closed the circle of "materialist ethics." He could point to the Darwinian realities that gave substance to his notion of the "welfare of humanity."

It was the confirmed reality of human evolution that provided Dietzgen the "scientific" evidence for that which he had insisted was the "sole and absolute end" of moral calculation—the ultimate normative imperative of Marxist ethics. For him, evolution provided the scientific demonstration of what "human welfare" was to be taken to mean. More than that, the entire process of human evolution established that individual life must necessarily be subordinate to the survival and developmental needs of collective "human welfare." Life, in general, seeks its own defense and selective perpetuity—in the course of which individual lives may well be sacrificed for the collective good—all in the service of ultimate human welfare.

It was within that understanding that Dietzgen sought to provide an account for ethics and moral conduct that was collectivistic in orientation. Moral behavior, he argued, is simply one way by virtue of which the group ensures its own survival and evolutionary betterment in the Darwinian struggle for existence. The compliant behavior of its members, the readiness to sacrifice for the community, for example, reinforces group enterprise and survival potential in the struggle. Moral behavior, Dietzgen argued, is revealed as a necessary condition of group life and collective biological development.

Based on just such a set of conjectures, Dietzgen was prepared to argue that, given the biological circumstances surrounding group life, one would expect "nature" to "implant neighborly love in the heart of each of us"[48]—simply because fellow feeling provides the basis for self-discipline, collaboration, and a readiness to sacrifice for the community. In any challenging environment such fellow feeling, while prejudicial to individual survival, would enhance group survival and provide a greater probability of competitive success.

Dietzgen maintained that Darwin had demonstrated that social life was simply one form within the multiplicity of forms that make up the totality of organic and inorganic reality. The social life of humans represented but one form through which the general organic, evolutionary laws that typify cosmic change find expression. While all matter evolves, only human beings attain conscious awareness of the process. It is that consciousness that inspires the effort to produce a persuasive ethical rationale for what, in terms of human evolution, was functional behavior. In fact, and in the last analysis, it is evolution itself that Dietzgen understood to be the initial wellspring of both individual and collective behavior as well as their sustaining impetus. For Dietzgen, it was evolution that inspired the heart and supplied the rationale for moral behavior and ethical judgment.[49]

Although there was some suggestion of all that in the works of "scientific communism,"[50] it was left to Dietzgen to make the explicit case for a Darwinian overlay for what he considered to be Marxist ethics. Many of Dietzgen's injunctions were clearly Marxist in expression, but rested on grounds that were distinctly non-Marxist and essentially Darwinian.

As a consequence of all that, it was evident to Dietzgen that in the natural world of animal evolution—no less for humans than the beasts of the field—individual life must necessarily subordinate itself to the demands intrinsic to life lived in common. Individual interests and individual well-being, in and of themselves, contributed little, if anything, essential to group survival and biological evolution—the foundation of human progress and the substance of ultimate "human welfare." For Dietzgen, it was only "unlimited progress" that was "absolutely moral"—and that "scientifically established" dictum provided the "objective" grounds for Marxist ethics and an impeccable guide for individual and collective human conduct.[51]

The implications of such an interpretation became almost immediately evident. According to Dietzgen, science had established that human life was governed by the cosmic principles of progressive evolution. Those were the ethical principles, derived from inductive science, which provided the ultimate moral substance to human life. Within the compass of human life lived in society Dietzgen went on to argue that, in principle, "absolute morality demands nothing less than radical progress or 'revolution in permanence.'"[52] Nothing was to obstruct the continual evolutionary progress of humankind. To attempt to impede such progress was not only reactionary; it was, in his judgment, evil. Within that context, Dietzgen introduced all the constituents of historical materialism that had become standard by that time. Thus, while *biological* "progress" was the governing principle—the ultimate and "absolute" source of morality—the trajectory of human *social* evolution, from the most primitive times to the present day, followed stages determined by the progressive unfolding of material production.[53]

Thus, from the ultimate and absolute moral principle of biological development, one could proceed to deal with the successive stages of societal evolution—which followed essentially the same developmental processes. Progressive social evolution took place through the competition of groups that characterized the history of communal life. Evolving social life required productive systems that serviced life lived in collectivities. Meeting those needs thus become moral responsibilities—and find expression in collective consciousness. Ethical dictates, moral imperatives, customary deportment, deferential conduct, and all the familiar patterns of proper behavior are directly or indirectly the "reflection" of particular social and productive needs—at particular historic junctures—within the unfolding mode of production—all as social reflections on the realities of Darwinian evolution.

Given such an evolutionary perspective, one can argue that primitive modes of production promote corresponding primitive modes of conduct—that are at a survival disadvantage when confronted by more advanced modes. The barbarism of primal peoples, the savagery and superstition, the oppression and the exploitation, is a reflection of the primitive mode of material production—destined to fail in the competitive struggle for existence. Only the full maturation of the economic base of society would produce the more advanced, and eminently survivable, "really human moral order"[54] anticipated by the revolutionaries of late nineteenth-century Germany.

Before the advent of such a morality, however, all the terms characteristic of moral discourse—"freedom" and "justice" as cases in point—necessarily alter in their respective meaning when applied to the various stages of productive evolution. Moral terms, and their binding implications, take on varying significance at each stage in human social evolution. Whatever the religious fantasy, expressions like "brotherly love" have no "absolute" or eternal meaning. The "brotherly love" of hunters and gatherers is, and can only be, fundamentally different from the "brotherly love" of the modern proletariat, the product of the modern mode of production.[55] Which conception survives and prevails would be a function, not of intrinsic merit, but of the survivability and prevalence of the more highly evolved mode of production of which it is a product.

Dietzgen understood ethics to be an inductive science, with its "commandments" and enjoinments a function of coming to understand the "real processes governing the world [*der reale Weltprozess*] with its material, living, human history." Dietzgen argued that it was from an understanding of the biological and evolutionary history of human society that Marxists "have produced an awareness of an ideal, abstract notion of morality." We come to understand morality, its genesis and its function, once we understand its source. Morality is the product of understanding cosmic evolution and the role played by human beings in the biological and societal process. It is only within such a context that human moral activity is justified and understood.

Such notions are clearly the product of a conviction that at the bottom of all ethical reasoning and all moral conduct are well confirmed *empirical* generalizations. Morality is simply a part, however distinctive, of that standard science that governs our knowledge of the world, the biological and social history of humankind, and their respective sustaining lawlike processes.

This was the normative theory that seemed to enjoy the tacit support of Marx and Engels[56]—and that, in part, inspired the German Social Democratic movement during the last quarter of the nineteenth century. Parts were to survive into the twentieth century and, as will be argued, influenced the ethical reasoning of those revolutionaries who would shape their time.

KARL KAUTSKY AND A DARWINIAN MARXISM

To some Marxist thinkers it became obvious, almost immediately, what such a construction of Marxist ethics and morals might imply.

Karl Kautsky, one of Marx's most important intellectual heirs—clearly familiar with the work of Dietzgen—recognized that the role played by Darwinism in the materialist conception of history would have to be very carefully considered.

Engels had accorded Darwinism a critical place in the philosophical articulation of Marx's views. He held that "dialectical materialism," the more "philosophical" component of Marxism, was predicated on three major developments in natural science, among which Darwin's theory of organic evolution occupied a central position. In his *Anti-Dühring*, Engels made a spirited defense of Darwin and Darwinism.[57]

Nonetheless, it soon became evident to Kautsky that Marxist theory had ventured into troubled waters. After the death of the founders of scientific socialism, the question of how Darwinism might be assimilated into a specifically Marxist ethical system remained. It was clear that anything other than the most careful accommodation might bring objectionable implications in its train. Like Dietzgen, Kautsky was prepared to acknowledge that human beings evolved as a consequence of a "struggle for existence"—but he hesitated to conceive such evolutionary "progress" an "imperative" governing either the human struggle with the external environment or conflict against other communities. He chose not to impute a cosmic purpose to nature. Rather, he spoke of human beings, moved by the instincts of survival and procreation, developing their respective skills in their effort to survive and reproduce in the midst of challenge.

Animated by social instincts and associative impulse, human beings organized themselves in communities in which the division of labor imparted an "organic" quality to their association. Instinct and impulse found expression as ingroup sentiment, a disposition to submit to the will of the community, to display courage and commitment in the pursuit of collective purpose. Given the biological basis of social impulse, a sense of pride and fulfillment normally accompanies such seemingly voluntary behaviors. Kautsky spoke of such "sublime virtues" as essentially nothing other than biologically based "social drives [*sozialen Triebe*]," capable, at times, of overwhelming the individual's very instinct of survival.

Darwin had shown that among group animals it was not uncommon for individuals to sacrifice themselves for the offspring of their community—or to be equally sacrificial in the service of those with whom they shared life and circumstance. In effect, Kautsky told his readers, Darwin had shown that the most exalted moral virtues found their immediate origin in animal impulse. Where philosophers and social thinkers had for millennia spoken of the moral virtues of humankind as "spiritual" in nature, Darwinism had demonstrated their all-too-biomaterialistic origin. Recognizing perhaps where such an account of ethical judgment and moral behavior might lead, Kautsky went on to point out that human beings cannot be expected to simply follow instinctual impulse. Human beings are subject to conflicting impulses and one must explain why one or another impulse prevails at any given time or under any given circumstance.

In effect, Kautsky argued that a simple Darwinism will not do to fully explain human morality, nor the reasoning that sustains it. Human beings, gifted with speech, clearly appeal to ideals and principles to govern their behavior—and, in many instances, individual behavior seems inexplicable unless one takes into account the life circumstances within which moral choices are made. The question of how human beings decide on appropriate behavior, or respond to impulse in morally conflicted situations, remains after Darwinian insights are fully considered. Kautsky turned to the thought of Marx and Engels for a supplementary and persuasive answer.[58]

MARXISM, MORALS, AND SCIENCE

In formulating his account, Kautsky addressed himself to the rise of social science in the modern period. He spoke of the rise of statistical science and the discovery that collective human behavior—the rise or diminution in crime, the increase in matrimonies, and the increase or decline in the rate of childbirth—could be systematically correlated with similarly calculated determinant economic factors. No one, he argued, would deny that sexual instincts are biological in origin, but it was equally evident that their variant expression at any given time and in any given circumstance was largely the product of then prevalent material conditions. Similarly, one could speak of the social instincts of human beings—instincts to be explained by Darwinian realities—but how such instincts manifested themselves at any given time or juncture was, in Kautsky's judgment, a reflection of determinate economic circumstances. Those circumstances required careful analysis.

Principal among those economic determinants, Kautsky argued, was the state of the class struggle at any given time. That the social thinkers of the past were unaware of that was the simple consequence of the fact that all the dominant economic classes of the past were either incompetent, or had set themselves against any efforts at cognitive understanding. All past dominant classes, prior to the modern period, opposed, in principle, all and any change. They viewed any change as a threat to their dominance. Only in the modern epoch, with the rapid maturation of the forces of production, did the opportunity arise for the emergence of a truly *social* science.

As commodity production became increasingly a merchandizing, profit-making activity, statistics, as a discipline, was required in order to assess cost and profit ratios, insurance risks for commercial entrepreneurs, to determine rates of return on investment assets, and fix tax obligations. Out of just such preoccupations there arose a gradual recognition of the need to comprehend social regularities—"social laws."

Thus, with the appearance of the modern bourgeoisie—with its demand for standardized information on economic matters—there was a correlative growth in investment in social science. It further became evident that science prospered best in an environment of intellectual freedom. Intellectual freedom in the pursuit of science recommended itself, because knowledge of social laws enhanced, in a variety of fashions, the opportunities for profit.

Because of the peculiar life circumstances of the bourgeois mode of production, inquiry into natural, and subsequently, social, laws became the subject of systematic study. At first uncertain, the systematic study of society was finally accepted by the dominant bourgeoisie. Social science urged itself on emerging capitalist society, together with the intellectual freedom that seemed to be its natural climate.

As a consequence, intellectual freedom and the pursuit of science emerged as "bourgeois" values. Together with a gradual recognition of the economic laws governing the production of social necessities, social laws made their appearance—and with Marx and Engels, according to their followers, the *necessary* laws of social development were finally appreciated. In the view of Marxists at the end of the nineteenth century, the articulation of a true social science became possible. The group life of human beings, in the context of general evolution, became comprehensible.

It was in that context that Kautsky spoke of a special branch of social science, that science that dealt with the mentality of human beings living in community. He alluded to empirical studies that dealt not only with the behavior of group animals, but with the differential conduct of human beings when in intimate association with their peers.

Like Engels, Kautsky expanded on the specifically evolutionary circumstances that made human beings unique among group animals. He referred to the fact that human beings, in the course of development, came to distinguish themselves from other animals by becoming essentially *tool-making* creatures[59]—and with the making of tools to commence a path of development distinctly their own.[60] Evolution had created the potential among humans that would provide them a distinctive future.

Kautsky went on to maintain that the process once begun pursues an ineluctable course. Such an interpretation was the product, at least in part, of the stylized speech that had become common to Marxist theoreticians. The "productive forces" and the "instruments of production" were regularly spoken of as active, as "developing," for example, rather than being developed.

Revolution was referred to as "the rebellion of the productive forces," or "the mode of production being in rebellion against the mode of exchange."[61] We are further told that social relations are, in turn, "dictated by the instrument of labor itself," as though the instruments are, once again, both active and determinant.[62] Ideas, conceptions, principles and laws are then spoken of as being "reflections" of just such a complex, inevitable process. There is, Kautsky maintained, "an inevitable effect that results from the invention of new tools, which in turn provides the impulse for more inventions and subsequent, reactive variation in the mode of life—in an unending chain of development."[63]

Within the span of law-governed general evolutionary and social development, in the necessary association required by survival itself, human beings, as distinct from lower primates, fashion articulate speech, out of which thought emerges, reinforcing shared commonality. With thought and common purpose, human beings expand their range of activities. They begin to produce in greater abundance and begin to compete for land and advantage. They enter into conflict with other communities—with war one of the predictable consequences.

As conflict becomes more insistent, given the progressive sophistication of the very instruments of conflict, the group becomes more and more cohesive and individuals more and more identify with the community in mortal conflict with opponents. In the course of those developments, the "sublime virtues," self-sacrifice, discipline, commitment, the sense of duty, all become more emphatic. Individuals conceive their very survival entirely dependent upon the survival of their community. In the course of these developments, the immediate cause of war alters. War is no longer the consequence of immediate survival needs—the seizure of foodstuffs and mates—but becomes a search for security of property.[64]

The evolution of war follows developments at the productive base of society. Soon wars are conducted not to protect communal or tribal property, but the property of dominant classes. Wars in the defense of property are fought by the dominant class itself, with the unpropertied classes not directly involved except as victims and occasional mercenaries. With the development of the instruments of production and the rise of the bourgeoisie, the character of group association changes dramatically.

In responding to the demands of the new techniques of production, the political conceptions of the bourgeoisie come to dominate society. Not only did the rising bourgeoisie demand increasing freedom from feudal constraints, they began to introduce "myths" calculated to serve their economic interests. The myth of "freedom," for example, arose and was accompanied by the introduction of a "popular" demand for secure and unobstructed commodity and resource markets for the bourgeoisie—in order to "freely" generate wealth "for everyone." Together with the other operative myths, there was the emergence and increasing prevalence of the myth of nationality. With the prevalence of that myth, there arose an increasing demand for popular participation in the defense of the "nation." Gradually those demands, the consequence of the absolute control of the intellectual environment by the dominant bourgeoisie, drew the entire mass of the propertiless population into political activity.

As a consequence of the rise of the bourgeoisie, with its appeal to generic freedom, and national identity, the "people" were drawn into conflict with the feudal nobility and its absolute monarch. The revolution that characterizes the modern epoch thus began with the increasing involvement of the masses in the business of society—a society unified around the nation as a politically defined geographic space—a "national" space that afforded the bourgeoisie a ready and accessible market.

As the bourgeoisie expanded its interests through increased production and commerce, an essential part of that business became the conduct of war—an activity that increasingly involved the nation's masses. The virtues of "solidarity, the spirit of sacrifice, and ingroup sentiment"—duty, commitment, and patriotism—become broadcast among all the members of the community,[65] in order to service the economic interests of the emergent bourgeoisie.

Only social evolution might change those circumstances. Peace and "true" brotherhood would only be possible with changes in the mode of production. Only when the productive system is capable of fully satisfying all human needs would the "premature" virtues that make up the panoply of Christian moral enjoinments, the "loving" of everyone, including one's enemies, attain any prospect of implementation. Only with the full maturation of the productive forces of society could a new class arise whose material interests would be those of all humanity. Only then could the "premature" virtues with which human beings long have been familiar become a reality. True humanity, without distinctions of class, nationality, or race, would only appear with the advent of the modern, urban proletariat—the objective indicator that the industrial system had reached productive maturity. Classical Marxists had demonstrated that each "economic development creates its own particular . . . moral canon."[66] The full maturation of the modern industrial system would generate that singularly human morality of which Engels has spoken.

In Kautsky's account of a "materialist ethics," which by that time included Darwinian insights, human societies are understood to be "organic" communities, composed of interrelated components that together further the "purposes" of some sort of progressive economic "dialectic." In the course of social history, conditions arise in which social relations—initially a reflection of the needs determined by the extant mode of production—begin to impede further development. Social revolution inevitably surfaces out of the crisis.

There has been a succession of such revolutions since the prehistory of humankind. The distinctiveness of the social revolution of our time is determined by the full and unique maturation of the productive base—a development destined to provide the material basis for both the universal ethical rationale for human fulfillment as well as the moral proscriptions and prescriptions appropriate to that realization.[67]

Out of the intense discussions turning on the nature of ethics and morality at the turn of the twentieth century, Kautsky thus sought to provide a Darwinist basis for a defensible account of Marxist normative theory. He maintained that his narrative captured the essence of the formulations found not only in the writings of Darwin and the founders of Marxism, but in those of Josef Dietzgen as well.[68] However successful or unsuccessful Kautsky's efforts may be judged to have been in terms of intrinsic plausibility, the entire discussion turned on several critical concepts that continued to provide the substance of competing revolutionary ideologies throughout the twentieth century.

One of the most important concepts with which Kautsky sought to deal was what the role of individual and collective will might be in the making of human history. It was an issue that lay at the very heart of revolutionary morality. It was an issue that dealt with the human decision to undertake, and the willingness to serve, the revolution. It was an issue that found only schematic expression in the conceptual framework Marx offered as early as the summer of 1846, two years before the appearance of *The Communist Manifesto*.

In the text of the *German Ideology*, we are told that the behavior of individuals, as well as that of communities of individuals, is neither the product of willful caprice nor philosophical reflection, but of the material circumstances surrounding the mode of life at any given time. It is the "mode of production," once again, that "determines" for individuals "a definite mode of life." That life, which manifests itself in conscious acts and the normative rationale informing those acts, "coincides with . . . production. . . . What individuals are depends on the material conditions of their production."[69] What they do is determined by a prevailing "mode of life."

More specifically, the Marxists at the end of the nineteenth century were prepared to maintain that the will that animates individual and group activity is both "conditioned and determined by the material forces of production." As a consequence of just such a notion, Marxists argued that individuals did not choose to behave in any specific fashion—they responded to prevailing custom and usage—and both were products of a dominant class ideology.

MARX AND ENGELS AND THE CLOSE OF THE SYSTEM

None of this was argued with much coherence. It was not immediately evident how ideology was the exclusive product of a given class or how such ideological convictions shaped the overt responses of members of other classes. The entire account was affirmed with impressive conviction by Marx and Engels and initially repeated, with very little elaboration, by their followers throughout the final decades of the nineteenth century.

Marxists argued, throughout the final years of the century, that they could demonstrate the putative relationship between any prevailing mode of life, the "reflection" of that mode in class "ideology," and corresponding human moral behavior. In one case the argument used to provide evidence of such contentions proceeded in something like the following fashion: Because the German bourgeoisie of Marx's time—given the backward state of available productive forces—remained "impotent," their theoretical, normative, and legal conceptions were correspondingly retrograde. Nothing else was to be expected. The "*inevitable* consequence" of such retrograde economic conditions was a peculiar form of monarchical absolutism and attendant political nationalism. It was simply asserted that both the forms and the "theoretical ideas" that gave feature to those institutions had "as their basis . . . a *will* that was conditioned and determined by the material relations of production."[70]

Marxists simply asserted that the beliefs that provided the rationale for the institutional stability of such a society were "reflections" of the peculiarities of the "economic base." Stability was seen to be a function of the "class beliefs" that reflected the functional requirements of the economic system. Individuals, inculcated with prevailing beliefs, behave *morally*, that is, they conform to the prevailing class ideology. There was no independent source of morality. Morality was a function of time, circumstance, economic imperative, and class interests.

Only when emerging productive forces can no longer develop within the existing social relations does another morality make its appearance. The social system enters into crisis. A new revolutionary class makes its appearance and becomes the agent of fundamental social change. The human beings who become conscious participants in the process reflect the necessity of change in the form of an apposite revolutionary ideology. In the final analysis, all moral aspirations and ethical enjoinments that become part of that revolutionary ideology are the necessary by-product of the productive conditions at the economic base of society.[71]

On the basis of such an analysis, an elaborate normative system like that of Immanuel Kant—that precludes the use of human beings as means rather than ends—could only be seen, at best, as little more than a body of "abstract ideas" and "pious humbug," penned as a rather primitive response to challenges confronting an equally primitive bourgeoisie. All of Kant's "self-determination of the will," together with his "categorical imperatives," were dismissed as rather pathetic distortions of the material interests of the emerging German commercial and industrial bourgeoisie.[72]

At the end of the nineteenth century, human will, both in its overt as well as its theoretical expressions, was conceived by classical Marxism to be a determinate product of material life circumstances—which meant essentially, that the will to behave, together with its corresponding rationale, were but the "reflexes" of "a certain mode of production, or industrial stage . . . combined with a certain mode of cooperation . . ."[73]

In effect, human will,[74] and the behavior to which it gives expression, were conceived by Marx and Engels, and their followers, to be a function of "social organization evolving directly out of production and intercourse, which in all ages forms the basis of the state and of the rest of the idealistic superstructure." It was, in their judgment, the recognition of the inevitability of that relationship that "shattered the [independent] basis of all morality."[75]

Both Marx and Engels understood morality, and its associated "voluntary" behavior, to be the predictable result of conditions governing material production and the social relations to which that production gave rise. In any given historical period, those who dominate the means of production "assert their common interests" through the apparatus of political control—rationalized by fostering the illusion that human behavior is the product of individual and collective "free will." In fact, the political ideology of any given time is the exclusive product of the "social organization evolving directly out of production and intercourse."[76]

As has been suggested, all of that is unpacked into a notion that understood philosophy, national sentiment, morality, religion and law, together with all the willed products of consciousness, the predictable consequence of the prevailing mode of production. Marx himself spoke of human behavior as being the necessary consequence of "forms of intercourse"—that arise out of lawlike processes independent of individual or collective choice. Since that time, Marxist theoreticians have regularly spoken of the "productive forces" *determining* the "forms of social intercourse"[77]—which all together produce the "phantoms in the brain": religion, philosophy, collective sentiment, morality, and law.

Given that collection of convictions, the "superstructural" ideas of any particular historic period are understood to be the determinate by-products of that period's economic base, with the prevailing ideas being those of the dominant possessors of the means of material production. Controlling the means of survival, they impose on the dispossessed their will as law, as philosophy, and morality.

As has been indicated, at some stage in the historic process, the productive forces of society enter into "contradiction" with the prevailing forms of social relations. In some sense or another, the social relations—the manner in which production is distributed and employed—becomes a "fetter" on production. Production is somehow obstructed by the manner of distribution—and "a class is called forth" that is burdened with all the disadvantages of the productive system and none of its advantages. That generates the explicit "consciousness of the necessity of a fundamental revolution."[78]

The will to revolution, the sense of the moral necessity to act, is a function of the relationship between the material productive forces and the "contradiction" that obtains between them and the social relations those very forces produce.[79] The call to revolution, the very *idea* of revolution, would be "absolutely immaterial for practical development," unless the existing relations of production already stood in conflict with the forces of production. Thus Marx could confidently insist that "all collisions in history have their origin, according to our view, in the contradiction between the productive forces and the form of intercourse."[80]

By the summer of 1846, Marx had provided the schematic outline of what was to be forever identified as the "materialist conception of history." Clearly evident in these early writings is the *determinism* that governed the entire speculative system.

Written in the years of their early collaboration, *The German Ideology* was the first coherent effort by Marx and Engels to "prove" with "scientific precision" that a communist revolution was the inescapable, "ineluctable," "inevitable," consequence of the forces then in act in industrial society. *The Communist Manifesto*, which followed in 1848, was little more than a summary statement of that same speculative effort.

What became clear almost immediately to anyone seriously interested in the science of society, was the realization that nothing in these early writings provided anything like empirical confirmation of any of the clutch of cosmic claims that made up their substance. Both Marx and Engels understood as much—and Marx spent the remainder of his life attempting to produce the missing substantive grounds that might support his early conjectures. The result, as has been indicated, was the first volume of *Das Kapital*, which survives today among the unfinished volumes as they were left to us by Engels.[81]

By the turn of the twentieth century, the work of Marx and Engels, amended and interpreted by their immediate followers, provided the substance of the revolutionary aspirations of the time. Out of the body of that work, a number of critical concepts can be isolated that were to invoke reactive response among the most gifted thinkers of the epoch. There were efforts to understand the nature of willed choice—and the role played by sentiment and morality in the history of humankind. Darwinism, as science and speculation, exercised unmistakable influence on Marxist revolutionary thought.

Out of all this, revolutionary variants of classical Marxism arose. Several made their appearance at almost the same time. After the death of Friedrich Engels in 1895, no longer was there an authoritative control over developments of what might pass as ideological orthodoxy. Almost immediately after Engels's death, Eduard Bernstein's first efforts at theoretical revision made their appearance. There no longer was an "official" guide for what was to be considered Marxist "orthodoxy."[82] The result was a rapid unraveling of the dense ideological system as it had been left by its founders. As will be argued, by the end of the nineteenth century, the first elements of German National Socialism, Italian Fascism, and Russian Leninism grew out of the funded system to cast their shadows across the new century.

CHAPTER THREE

The Heterodox Marxism of Ludwig Woltmann

With the death of Friedrich Engels in 1895, Marxism found itself bereft of an authority who commanded the respect of all those in its ranks. There no longer was a single arbiter to resolve theoretical disagreements among those expected to provide the intellectual and moral leadership of the revolution—and there was no longer anyone who could establish orthodoxy, or "creatively develop" doctrine to better accord with emerging facts, new scientific developments, or altered political circumstances. Without Engels to guide them, revolutionary intellectuals could hardly pretend to be able to identify, with finality, what was a "true" rendering of an intrinsically porous doctrine. With the passing of Engels, any and every change whatever in the inherited doctrine ran the risk of being seen as "revisionism"—as an abandonment or corruption of Marxism. As it happened, perhaps most of the abandonment and corruption of Marxism can be traced to those thinkers who pretended to be its most faithful spokespersons.

After the death of Engels, the most prominent of the first intellectuals who were to candidly venture on conscious revisionism was Eduard Bernstein. No more than two or three years after the death of Engels, Bernstein advanced a number of major emendations.[1] He argued that as a scientific enterprise, it was incumbent upon Marxism to continually test the accuracy and reliability of its factual claims. Furthermore, the canons of empirical science required that Marxism be prepared to confirm or disconfirm its predictions against the evolving reality of the modern world. If inherited Marxist theory maintained that then contemporary capitalism must inevitably collapse in a final catastrophic dysfunction, it was essential for Marxist theoreticians to assess existing data to determine the real possibility of such an outcome. If inherited Marxism predicted the inevitable reduction of classes in modern society to but two—the bourgeoisie and the proletariat—Bernstein urged an inspection of available descriptive and predictive demographic statistics to determine if such a trend could be, in fact, discerned. If Marxism insisted that, over time, capitalist development would produce increasing "emiseration" among the working classes, Bernstein argued that it behooved Marxism's intellectuals to inspect the growing body of economic data to provide confirmation.

In almost all the cases to which Bernstein alluded, he claimed that existing data, and measurable projections, tended to disconfirm the empirical claims and substantive predictions of the founders of revolutionary Marxism. While still a convinced, if qualified, Marxist,[2] Bernstein argued that a systematic distinction should be made between the *theory* entertained by Marxists and its *application* in prevailing circumstances. He seemed to want to make a distinction between the "postulates" of the theory and application of its "theorums" in actual practice. He sought to draw a meaningful and consistent distinction between "pure and applied Marxism."[3]

It remains uncertain what Bernstein expected to accomplish in attempting such a distinction. In science, irrespective of the introduction of any number of *ad hoc* causes of error, regular disconfirmation of empirical claims necessarily leads to change in theory itself. One could not consistently hold that a theory was true if its descriptive or predictive claims were regularly disconfirmed. Whatever the case, what is important for the present account is the fact that Bernstein continued to urge fundamental changes in the body of inherited Marxist thought—and yet considered himself, and was generally considered by others, to be a Marxist.

It seems that the more such discussion commanded attention among party intellectuals, the greater the frequency and magnitude of changes proposed. By the turn of the century, as a consequence, a variety of Marxisms had made their appearance—each arguing that it was true to the ideas of the founders.[4] Marxism had begun to take on some of the properties of religious conviction.

Like religious beliefs, in general, the Marxism of Marx and Engels was subject to regular reinterpretation by adepts, with each precipitating outcries of heresy and unorthodoxy. The faithful of whatever "orthodoxy" were convinced that a "true" faith might be discerned amid the growing confusion. Whatever their interpretation, the faithful tended to believe it to be the one true expression of inherited doctrine. Each community of believers conceived their own construction to be impeccably true—and that of others grievously, and perhaps maliciously, flawed.

As was the case in religious disagreements, such disagreements led to abuse, mutual disdain, and in far too many cases, violence. Those Marxists, of whatever persuasion, who succeeded to power in whatever circumstances, did not hesitate to use vituperation, excommunication, and ultimately, deadly force against other Marxists who embraced an alternative interpretation of the sacred texts.

Thus while Bernstein represents a clear instance of a Marxist who was prepared to critically review all the propositional commitments of classical Marxism and admitted his heterodoxy, there were others equally revisionistic, who insisted on their pious orthodoxy. There was yet a third group: those who undertook critical review of Marxism, but conceived such a venture as neither orthodox nor revisionist. They simply undertook their work as an intellectual obligation. Ludwig Woltmann was of their number.

MARXISM AND LUDWIG WOLTMANN

At almost the same time as the appearance of Bernstein's *Der Voraussetzungen des Sozialismus und die Aufgaben der Sozialdemokratie*, one of the more important Marxist intellectuals of the period—Ludwig Woltmann— authored a major explication of Marxism as a theory of socioeconomic change and development: *Der historische Materialismus*.[5] It was the third of the major works written by the young Woltmann (who was born in 1871) specifically dedicated to the interpretation and the advocacy of an essentially Marxian socialism.[6]

For our purposes, the most important feature of Woltmann's work is that one can find in it insightful treatment of some of the critical issues that were to give ideological shape to the most important revolutionary doctrines of the twentieth century. Only with the passage of time has it become obvious that the issues to which Woltmann directed his attention might prove instructive in coming to understand the revolutions that have overwhelmed humanity over the past one hundred years.

Among those issues that were to prove so important, the question of the role of morality, and its rationale in Marxist theory, was one that occupied critical place. Woltmann was to consistently argue that the account found in the writings of the founders of Marxism, that pretended to explain the origins of morality and ethics, was less than adequate. Its inadequacy more often then not led Marxist intellectuals to lapse into a caricature of the actual claims. Moral and ethical ideas were simply spoken of as "reflections" of "substructural" economic conditions. Moral principles, and their ethical rationale—according to "orthodoxy"—apparently had no independence of the "material life conditions" of which they were a determinate product.

Given such a conception of the relationship of thought to the "mode of production," the moral principles governing Immanuel Kant's ethical philosophy, as has been suggested, were understood to be passive reflections of the peculiar circumstances surrounding the emergent bourgeoisie in eighteenth-century Germany. Similarly, the moral enjoinments of the French Revolution were by-products of the economic circumstances surrounding the rise of a "triumphant" bourgeoisie; those of the early Christians, a simple reactive response to the extant economic and class conditions of the initial centuries of the first millennium.[7]

Woltmann attributed the fact that such a caricature of how ethical thought is generated and progresses was possible only because there really was no coherent or consistent moral "theory" to be found in classical Marxism. While Woltmann, like Dietzgen, argued that Marxism, as a doctrine, was much more sophisticated and complicated than most of its adherents appreciated, he granted that there were issues that neither Marx nor Engels had adequately addressed. More important still, in Woltmann's judgment, was the reality that Marx and Engels had significantly modified their views over half a century—and the changes made were sometimes dramatic.[8] If one sought to provide a full account of the moral and ethical thought of the founders, that rendering would have to incorporate all changes that had been made over time. Finally, Woltmann argued that both Marx and Engels often spoke schematically of very complex historical processes—content to allow enormously complex sequences to find expression in metaphor and to remain concealed beneath epigrams. All of that left a literary legacy that often was more confusing than enlightening.

Taking all that into account, Woltmann argued that with respect to the founders' theory of the nature, origin, and evolution of moral judgment and ethical principles, Marxism was incomplete. Not only were there significant gaps in its account of the historical, social, economic, and psychological processes involved—but it left fundamental philosophical issues unexplored. All of that prompted others to sometimes attempt rescue.

Woltmann specifically held that neither Marx nor Engels entertained a sufficiently nuanced conception of the *psychological* dynamics implied in their conception of the relationship between the ideational products of human beings and socioeconomic change and development. He held, for example, that the founders of Marxism made far too easy transit from physical, material, and class-specific needs to the psychological expressions in which those needs were presumably "reflected."[9] As a consequence there were those, like Dietzgen, who attempted to supply plausibility of various sorts in the effort to provide more convincing reconstruction.

More than that, Woltmann held that to suggest that one might account for the philosophical thought of Aristotle or that of Kant by conceiving it simply a "superstructural reflection" of the economics of a slave holding or an emerging bourgeois society was entirely too simplistic.[10] The thought of either was far too complex and intricate to even pretend that any such reduction was credible.

Once these issues were joined, a number of further concerns urged themselves on Marxist intellectuals at the turn of the twentieth century. While Woltmann was prepared to argue that human thought was conditioned by material considerations, he was not prepared to allow that the thought that resulted was their simple psychological "reflex."[11] He was prepared to accept the notion that thought, in general, could be understood as a functional response to immediate external physical and social stimuli.[12] Granted that, however, what he did insist upon was that once conscious thought manifested itself, it was governed by principles or regularities that were, in significant measure, independent of material circumstances.

With that understood, Woltmann proceeded to attempt to put together arguments that might better support the ideas of Marx and Engels. Like them, he argued that "material life conditions" provided the foundation of life in general. Like them, he argued further that human evolution itself was the product of material processes governed by natural laws. Marxists, he continued, recognized that organic evolution was governed by the "struggle for existence," and the corresponding "natural selection" implied by "the survival of the fittest." These were among the "natural laws" identified by Woltmann as governing *organic* evolution.

It was at that point that Woltmann insisted that whatever the laws governing evolution, such laws could not be projected over *social* evolution without recognizing the possibility of grievous error.[13] He dismissed the attempt on the part of "bourgeois Darwinists" to see the direct operation of Darwinian laws in human behavior. When Social Darwinists attempted to apply the laws of organic evolution to society, by conceiving *laissez faire* business practices, for example, the economic equivalent of the "struggle for existence" that typified the animal world, Woltmann argued that they made the same mistake made by those who seek to impose social "laws" on the "laws" of thought. It was at that point that Woltmann introduced a major modification in the Marxist system as it had been inherited.

Woltmann maintained that once some collection of higher primates were no longer content with the spontaneous groupings in which they found themselves in nature—and created the first human societies, there was a qualitative change in the processes governing their association. *Social* evolution in organized human communities, he insisted, does not follow the same identifiable regularities as general *biological* evolution. Animal societies may follow the laws of biological evolution, but social evolution among human beings was, in his judgment, qualitatively different. Social evolution among humans proceeds with considerable independence of the laws of biological development—following regularities peculiar to itself.

While Darwinism discovered the natural laws governing organic evolution, Marxism, Woltmann contended, identifies the specifically *social* laws that shape human society. Those laws are the laws governing the relationship of the material productive forces and the social relationships to which they give rise. Woltmann's argument was that while the founders of Marxism had carefully distinguished the regularities governing social evolution from those governing organic evolution, they had not succeeded in making the same distinction between the laws of social life and those of human thought. Rather, they pretended to have discovered how society's economic foundation produced and governed the "phantoms formed in the brain"—the processes peculiar to human thought.

Woltmann argued that in advancing such an account, the founders of Marxism had failed to make a critical distinction. While it was evident that thought arose out of natural evolutionary processes, and that thought was conditioned by social circumstances, human reflection, nonetheless, operated with considerable autonomy, responding to domain specific extrinsic and intrinsic stimuli as well as distinctive criteria governing truth ascription. Woltmann was to argue that in the same measure that differences distinguish the regularities governing biological, from those of social, evolution, differences of the same order of magnitude characterized the distinctions between the regularities governing the "higher domain" of human culture—morality, ethics, epistemology, science, and thought, in general—and those of organic or social development.[14]

Woltmann contended that complex human thought could not reasonably be understood to be a simple "reflection" of anything—neither as reflections of anything going on in the processes of biological, nor anything transpiring within the domain of social, evolution. That was true for at least one reason: all Marxists recognized that throughout human history, there have been those who articulate "premature" moral concepts. That is to say, the Stoics of antiquity, the first Jews and Christians, and some thinkers of the earliest societies, advanced notions of fundamental human equality, unqualified brotherhood, universal compassion, and world peace, long before there existed any "mature economic base" to which any of that might "correspond."[15]

As a case in point, in speaking of the Peasant War in Germany in the sixteenth century, Engels spoke of Thomas Münzer, leader of the most oppressed of the peasants, as entertaining a clutch of "fantastic" notions of revolutionary change that had "little root in then existing economic conditions." Münzer advocated a society of equals, innocent of class differences and private ownership—a fellowship of "Christian equality and evangelical community of property." Engels went on to speak, with a discernable measure of contempt, of "the chiliastic dream visions" of those early Christians who had inspired Münzer—with their advocacy of common property, equality, and universal love. Engels was to argue that the ideas that inspired both the early Christians and Münzer had no prospect of success because the "level of production . . . [was] not ripe" for them.[16]

The question arises: if prevailing economic conditions were primitive, how is it possible that the ideas of the early Christians did not "reflect" them—but rather those social and economic conditions that would not mature for two thousand years? Clearly Münzer's "chiliastic dream visions" were not a simple reflection of the existent economic base. They were moral convictions that were somehow "premature." The notion that a "reflection" might be premature can only leave one puzzled. Somehow, the moral ideas of the early Christians, and the peasant revolutionaries of the sixteenth century that seized upon them, anticipated the future appearance of the full maturation of the productive forces of society—when such ideas would no longer be "fantasies," but would actually "correspond" to their "real" foundation in the economic base.

Woltmann was to contend that the most persuasive answer to that kind of puzzle lay in the recognition that once human beings developed the faculties that allowed recall, reflection, calculation, association, and inference, they proceeded to anticipate futures, undertake analyses, and render judgments, all against a catalog of preferences and felt objections—which made ethics and moral argument not only possible, but inescapable. More than that, the process of moral assessments and its rules were significantly independent of any given economic base.

What followed was Woltmann's argument that while some more "orthodox" Marxists were correct in pointing out that certain doctrinal objectives have little prospect of success in given economic circumstances, that reality does little to account for the moral behavior and ethical reasoning of participants in what might well be a futile struggle. Individuals, singly or collectively, often undertake quixotic enterprise because their ethical principles demand it of them. Wars have been fought for moral purpose; and it can be argued that, on important occasions, human thought and human conviction, alone, have changed history quite independently of the prevailing economic base. Moreover, however unlikely of realization any set of social, economic, or moral prescriptions might be, their relative independence from the economic base of society is not thereby compromised.

Woltmann's argument was that the thought of human beings enjoyed a relative independence of biological and economic conditions—just as the regularities of social life display a relative independence of the laws of biological evolution. Woltmann admitted, with Josef Dietzgen, that biological and economic needs provided the raw incentives of human behavior, as well as establishing the parameters in which success is sought, but he went on to argue that the behavior of even the most primitive of humans distinguished itself from that of the most advanced lesser primates by its independence from just such material constraints. What makes behavior human is the fact that whatever may prompt it, it is characteristically filtered through fairly elaborate empirical and ethical considerations. Those considerations are exclusively human and proceed in an atmosphere governed by regularities that are intrinsically different from those of organic or social evolution.

As a consequence of his argument, Woltmann went on to advocate that revolutionary Marxism, before proceeding any further, undertake serious philosophical, epistemological, and ethical reflection—as intended, but never accomplished, by Marx himself. Marxism, in Woltmann's judgment, required a careful reworking of its epistemological and ethical analyses. It was in that context that Woltmann advocated a "return to Kant."[17]

BACK TO KANT

Woltmann made it clear that a critical confusion lay at the very core of Marxism as a revolutionary ideology. In the course of his account, Woltmann pointed to an issue that was to remain contested throughout the twentieth century. While Dietzgen and Karl Kautsky argued that moral injunctions ultimately rested on an empirical basis,[18] Woltmann asserted that moral imperatives required something more than empirical facts as warrant.

Woltmann reminded Marxist intellectuals that while it was clear to Marx that individuals and groups differed on the basis of any number of physical and psychological properties, empirical reality did not in any way influence his unqualified *moral* commitment to equality and freedom for all—whatever the difference.[19] That clearly implied that the moral commitment to full equality for all human beings did not require empirical legitimation. Woltmann argued that moral judgments were to be systematically distinguished, in kind, from empirical truths.[20] One's moral judgments are not *determined* by facts. Facts can be, and almost invariably are, components of moral calculation, but the warrant for the moral judgment itself—that which makes the calculation moral—must be distinguished from any collection of facts.

Woltmann held that *normative* truths, in general, were distinctive and to be distinguished from those that were logical or empirical. Normative truths had different truth conditions determining their truth status. He understood normative truths to be neither simply logical nor empirical. They are, in the last analysis, uniquely and inextricably predicated on *felt* experience. He held that normative experience invariably involves one's *feelings* about art, religion, or ethics, and that feelings constitute an inextricable and fundamental constituent of normative evaluation. However much moral deliberation—as part of human normative concerns—involves simple logic or empirical facts, it is moral sentiment that ultimately informs its public rationale, and distinguishes it from the assessment of facts and logic alone or in combination.[21]

More than that, Woltmann was to argue that human knowledge, in a real and profound sense, ultimately rests on feelings—for in the last analysis knowing anything ultimately rests on a sense of adequacy. The search for truth itself, in the last analysis, is satisfied by a sense of conviction.

Clearly there are pragmatic reasons for seeking the truth. Truth is necessary to negotiate the difficulties of life. It is equally clear, however, that human beings can reject truths of any kind in order to defend some other deeply felt conviction—moral, religious, or political. There have always been consistent skeptics, philosophical or otherwise, throughout human intellectual history. What distinguishes them from ordinary persons, who accept as true those propositions that meet the truth conditions of logic and experience, is their indisposition to accept as true anything that offends collateral beliefs more deeply felt.

It is clear from everything he wrote that Woltmann conceived morality to be a critical part of human life. The product of organic and social evolution, human beings, nonetheless, governed their lives, consciously or unconsciously, mechanically or deliberatively, by ideas, desires, needs, volition and, ultimately, significantly autonomous, moral sentiment. Woltmann insisted that without some such appreciation on our part, human experience becomes not only incomprehensible, but meaningless as well.

For Woltmann, none of that reduces the "objectivity" of empirical, logical, or ethical deliberation. Propositions are identified as "true" when they meet public criteria. Logical and empirical truths are true because they meet the specific, intersubjective criteria for logical and empirical truth. What distinguishes candidate moral truths from any others is that feelings constitute part of the admissions criteria.[22] That does not render them "subjective." Moral sentiments can be expressed and relative behavior observed. Their truth is no more intrinsically subjective than any truth entertained by anyone.

Woltmann was to argue that there is a common moral sentiment that reveals itself in the study of the history of humankind—just as there is common color vision that takes precedence over idiosyncratic color blindness.[23] As a consequence, he maintained that ethics could be the proper object of "scientific" study—in the broadest Germanic sense of *Wissenschaft*—that is to say, a subject amenable to systematic and "objective" scrutiny.

Woltmann distinguished his position from that of Josef Dietzgen and the early Karl Kautsky in that he rejected their contention that empirical facts *alone* might provide the warrant for moral truth claims. *All* truth claims, in an ultimate sense, require more than empirical facts as warrant. That fact simply becomes more specific, emphatic, and evident in the case of ethical and moral claims.

Woltmann argued that both David Hume and Immanuel Kant had made just such a case for the nature of truth and morals.[24] In fact, Woltmann was to serve as a spokesman for those who held that an effective Marxism required a return to some variant of Kantian "idealism."[25]

At almost the same time that Woltmann ventured upon his assessment, Eduard Bernstein himself invoked Kantianism as a corrective to a kind of Marxist dogmatism that had grown up around the thought of its founders. It was evident that the efforts at reinterpretation of the philosophical and epistemological foundations of Marxism were creating tensions among believers. By 1908, Franz Mehring complained that the effort to introduce Kantianism into revolutionary Marxism had produced an intellectual scandal among Social Democrats.[26] Whatever the case, the issues raised by Woltmann tormented revolutionary Marxism throughout the twentieth century. For the present, it is enough to understand why Woltmann thought a return to Kant was essential to Marxism as a creed intended to mobilize the moral sentiments of revolutionaries.

The argument concerning the epistemological rationale behind moral judgment and ethical assessment was only one, if an important, part of Woltmann's general argument concerning the relative independence of philosophical thought from its material base. While he was fully prepared to acknowledge the fact that material life conditions clearly influenced human reflection, Woltmann maintained that reflection, once initiated, had a "logic" of its own. Philosophical thought often proceeded with its own intrinsic dialectic—each problem precipitating a set of responses which in turn provoked still further issues. The result was a pattern of thought and associated reflections having very little to do directly with the economic base and class structure of any given society. Woltmann insisted that the history of thought taught nothing less.

Once one is prepared to recognize that human thought is governed in large part, if not exclusively, by its own criteria of truth and falsehood, of plausibility and implausibility, of approval and disapproval, of logic and illogic, then any proffered theory, scientific or ethical, must both acknowledge and be prepared to meet them. The necessary consequence of such an analysis is a preoccupation with *epistemology* and *ethics*—the systematic study of truth assignment—and its deontological application.[27]

Woltmann maintained that Marx had fully intended to write a treatment of just such a comprehensive "theory of knowledge," but did not have the opportunity in a life overwhelmed by other responsibilities. As a consequence, Woltmann lamented, one is left with only *intimations* of what might well have been a relatively sophisticated system.[28] Woltmann's own work was an attempt to supply the missing constituents.

Several things emerge from the effort. First of all, Woltmann was prepared to contend that human thought itself with its relative independence can, and frequently does, act as a determinant in human history. Human thinkers, individually and collectively, through the use of empirical, logical, and normative truths, managed to sway the commitment and behavior of others to historic purpose. Woltmann was to argue that together with all the other factors with which Marxists were familiar, human convictions, and the doctrines that influence those convictions, independently shape events.

More than that, Woltmann was prepared to argue that given the efficacy of thought, its spokespersons bore a special responsibility. Time and circumstance often created conditions that allowed particular individuals or groups of individuals to influence events in a fashion not possible at

other junctures. Clearly, many factors were operative in any such environment—but the peculiar intellectual and political gifts of particular individuals were critical among them.[29] Woltmann was prepared to argue that, in
some sense, and under singular circumstances, "great men" do make history.

In at least one notable place, Engels seemed to support something like
Woltmann's analysis by intimating that Marx, with his ideas, played a singular role in the making of modern revolution. He affirmed that without
Marx revolutionary theory "would not be by far what it is today."[30] That,
combined with the conviction that revolutionary theory plays a role in the
success of revolution, would mean that individuals and their ideological
convictions may very well help to direct the course of human history.

None of that is at all certain. Elsewhere, Engels seems to deny Marx, or
his revolutionary thought, any special role in influencing historical events.
Engels tells us that "while Marx discovered the materialist conception of
history . . . the discovery of the same conception [by others] proves that
the time was ripe for it and that it simply *had* to be discovered."[31] It would
seem that Engels was prepared to argue that if Marx had never existed,
something like Marxist theory would have manifested itself to serve the
same historic purpose. With the absence of Karl Marx, nothing in history
would have changed.

Dealing with counterfactuals is, of course, very difficult. It does seem,
however, that Engels wished to affirm that revolutions in history proceed
through their own intrinsic dynamic—in terms of which neither individuals nor their special gifts play a role. As a youthful theoretician, Engels insisted that "revolutions are not made intentionally and arbitrarily, but that
everywhere and always they have been the necessary consequence of conditions which were wholly independent of the will and direction of individual
parties and entire classes."[32]

That seems to have been the position most consistently held by Engels
throughout his life. More than forty years after having written that revolutions occur independent of the will and direction of human agents and
agencies, he wrote that history is to be "viewed as the product of a power
which works as a whole, *unconsciously* and without volition. . . . History
proceeds in the manner of a natural process and is essentially subject to the
same laws of motion."[33]

None of this is unambiguous. Certainly Engels insisted that human beings make their own history. Invariably, when "orthodox" Marxists make
that submission, it is quickly qualified by the affirmation that the making is
undertaken under "very definite" conditions—among which "the economic

ones are ultimately decisive."[34] What all that means is exceedingly obscure. Is it intended to mean that human beings are the agents of history, but must perform in obedience to its "laws of motion"? Is it understood to mean that individual and collective human participation, motivated by individual and collective volition, is somehow the *necessary* product of "material life conditions" and could not have been otherwise?

Marx himself maintained that "the ideal," that which inspires human participation in the world, "is nothing else than the material world reflected by the human mind, and translated into forms of thought"[35] — suggesting the kind of automaticity that would seem to deny human reflection any independent role in history. Humans may be the makers of their own history, but the founders of Marxism seemed to imagine that the making followed regularities that human beings could neither influence nor control.

Woltmann's position was that human volition, the product of human thought and moral judgment, was not *determined*, although it might be *conditioned*, by economic factors. He argued that it could not be shown with any degree of empirical plausibility that human thought submissively followed socioeconomic "laws of motion." He insisted that every piece of evidence available indicated that human thought and human will were governed by processes peculiar to themselves. Human thought was governed by epistemological criteria of its own—and the truth that emerged informed the will—and while human beings possessed of truth certainly did not always prevail in history, they did, on occasion, and under certain circumstances, significantly influence its passage.

The issue was to prove important for Marxists and revolutionaries throughout the twentieth century. Almost every Marxist theoretician throughout the century attempted to persuasively explain how economic conditions energized the revolutionary will of individuals and multitudes. If accepted, it would have to be an explanation that accounted for the felt sense of freedom that attends human choice and commitment, and still demonstrate that history, nonetheless, is relentlessly deterministic in character. No single Marxist has yet succeeded in doing all that to everyone's satisfaction.[36]

By the turn of the twentieth century, it was evident that Marxism was undergoing fundamental revision. Not a few Marxists were reshaping revolutionary doctrine and policy by reinterpreting some of the basic tenets of doctrinal Marxism. Woltmann was clearly numbered among them—and while the analyses of the nature of science and truth, human thought, will, and morality were issues employed in the reshaping, it was Darwinism that was to have the most radical impact.

WOLTMANN, DARWINISM, AND MARXISM

In retrospect, Woltmann's efforts to assimilate Darwinian reflections on the nature and consequences of human evolution into the loose structure of Marxist theory was to influence revolutionary thought in the twentieth century in a totally unexpected manner. Woltmann's accidental death in 1907 did not stop the spread of his ideas to others, and by the mid-1930s their influence was apparent in the revolutionary literature of the time.

In 1899, Woltmann published a major study on the relationship of Darwinism to Marxism.[37] In that study, and in subsequent works, Woltmann demonstrated an impressive familiarity with the abundant literature devoted to Darwinism. He made evident his knowledge of the then available literature devoted to plant and animal biology. He understood the mechanics and circumstances of evolution as it was understood by the specialists of the time. As a medical doctor, he seemed to fully comprehend the particulars of the professional literature devoted to both plant and human genetics.

The reason Woltmann gave for embarking on a special study of organic evolution turned on his study of theoretical Marxism over the fifty or sixty years of its articulation at the hands of its founders. Like Josef Dietzgen, Woltmann conceived Marxism as essentially *scientific* in essence—and Darwinism was the major scientific achievement of the last half of the nineteenth century. Woltmann sought to reaffirm Marxism's scientific properties by showing that it was not only compatible with Darwinism but that Darwinism and Marxism were mutually reinforcing.[38]

Woltmann proceeded to provide evidence that Marx had early signaled his interest in Darwinism. In *Capital*, for example, Marx argued that just as Darwin had shown how "the history of Nature's Technology, i.e., in the formation of the organs of plants and animals" provided the key to an understanding of the processes governing the organic evolution of sentient life, he himself had demonstrated that the "productive organs of man," *tools*, supplied the "material basis of all" social evolution.[39] Somehow or other Marx understood that Darwinism, like his own system, afforded a "key" to the law-governed processes of evolution as evolution applied to both organic and social development.[40]

In some imprecise sense, Marx pretended to see symmetry between Darwin's notions of the biological descent of man and his own theory of social evolution.[41] Marx apparently imagined that he increased the credibility of his system by somehow associating it, however indirectly, with Darwin's theory of the descent of man.

Whatever his ulterior purpose, it seems clear that Marx imagined that Darwinism somehow contributed to the credibility of his own conception of human social evolution. From the perspective of the twenty-first century, other than the fact that both systems trafficked on "struggle" and were developmental in character, the one really had very little to do with the other. At the end of the nineteenth century, however, given the fact that many socialists imagined that Darwinism was an affirmation of Marxism,[42] the differences could only be apparent to those profoundly familiar with both.

Darwin understood evolution in biological terms—while Marx and his followers sought to account for social change over time by appealing to culturally transmitted technological change.[43] In retrospect, it seems apparent that the processes involved require entirely different mechanisms for their accomplishment. Darwin spoke of the inheritance of morphological properties that survive competitive selection in a "struggle for existence." Marx addressed what he understood to be tensions that arose over time between material productive forces and the social relations within which they were accommodated—tensions that manifested themselves in "class struggle." Other than the superficial similarities in nomenclature, the systems really had very little to do with each other.[44]

It was Engels who chose to assume the responsibility of attempting a serious theoretical accommodation between the two bodies of thought.[45] The effort was to prove uncertain at best.

There is no question that Engels, in general, was very supportive of Darwinism. With the exclusion of any Malthusian elements to be found in the doctrine, Engels provided its spirited defense in his *Anti-Dühring*. In one curious passage, Engels even spoke of industrial competition, both national and international, as analogous to "the Darwinian struggle of the individual for existence."[46] However odd the notion, there is no reason to imagine that Marx objected either to Engels's general position or his Darwinian characterization of economic competition and the class struggle.[47]

That granted, within their lifetimes the founders of Marxism never really settled their accounts with Darwinism. Only in an essay, "The Part Played by Labour in the Transition from Ape to Man," written in 1876—published in 1896 after his death—did Engels attempt to establish some sort of theoretical connection between Darwin's conceptions of human evolution and those of historical materialism.[48] The effort was not a notable success.

In his essay, Engels proceeded to argue that in the course of human evolution human beings developed the capacity to fashion *tools*. More sophisticated in almost every way compared to those put together by lesser creatures, human tools came to serve not only in the fabrication of products that sustained and fostered life, but over thousands of years of use they somehow managed to "create" man himself. The claim was exceedingly curious. Somehow Engels thought he might close the distance between Darwinian evolution and the full maturation of humankind by using man's tool-making abilities to bridge the gap.

Having made the claim, Engels proceeded to attempt to render it credible. He went on to say that human labor, employing tools, made human beings what they are. "Only by labour," Engels maintained, "by adaptation to ever new operations, by inheritance of the thus acquired special development," did human beings achieve that high station they enjoyed.

More than that, Engels continued, labor involving tools brought "members of society closer together by multiplying cases of mutual support." That in turn made communication an increasing necessity—and Engels informs us, "the urge created its organ; the underdeveloped larynx of the ape was slowly but surely transformed" until primitive humanity began to speak.[49] The invention of tools had created the necessity to communicate intelligently. Humans could then effectively collaborate. Armed with tools and speech, human beings created social arrangements that underwrote initiative and spatial expansion—the beginnings of increased productivity and commerce over increasingly greater distances. The true social history of humanity had begun. Engels believed he had thereby made the theoretical transition from humanity's organic, to its social, evolution—an apparently unbroken transition from Darwinism to historical materialism.

Like Dietzgen, Engels sought to render Darwinian evolution propaedeutic to the social theories of historical materialism. If that could be done, he would have established not only the compatibility of the two bodies of thought, but their interactive support.

In fact, whatever the measure of success, it was achieved only at considerable intellectual cost. Like Dietzgen, Engels was prepared to accept that human beings had evolved in precisely the fashion described by Darwin in his major work. Environmental challenge and competition had ultimately produced a bipedal higher primate. At that point, Engels sought to tie that to the elements of Marx's historical materialism. He attempted to establish that it was "labor" that was somehow responsible for making of that primate produced by the "struggle for existence," "natural selection," and "survival of the fittest," an intelligent, articulate human being whose life came to exemplify the dynamics of historical materialism.

In order to accomplish that, Engels argued that of all the creatures produced in the course of evolution, it was only humankind who, through the use of tools, achieved true humanity. Somehow human evolution, as distinct from all other forms of organic evolution, no longer proceeded through morphological variability, competition, and selection. Humans, after the advent of tools, advanced to full humanity only as a consequence of the use of the instruments of material production.

Marxism, from the time of its first formulation, argued that technology—tools—lay at the very foundation of social and historic change. If Engels could successfully link human evolution to the use of tools, a transition could be effected from Darwinian to Marxian evolution. The problem was that it was not at all clear that any of that could be accomplished with any degree of plausibility.

As it turned out, in the effort to make his account in the least tenable, Engels was compelled to press into service scientific conjectures that were already subject to reservation by the time he wrote "The Role of Labour . . ." To show that tools produced the changes that made higher primates truly human, Engels appealed to the notion of the inheritance of acquired characteristics first suggested by Jean Baptiste Lamarck early in the nineteenth century.

If it could be shown that the use of tools produced competencies that could be inherited, Engels's case would be credible. If some highly advanced primates used tools, and their use required various forms of dexterity, as well as a disposition to social cooperation through speech, that were then directly transmitted to their biological heirs, Engels would have begun to make his case.

Unhappily the notion that acquired characteristics could be directly inherited had already become suspect to the scientific community by the time Engels wrote his essay. By that time, there was the evidence that was to be confirmed in the results of the genetic research of Gregor Mendel and August Weismann.[50] In substance, the best science of the time had begun to question that acquired characteristics could be inherited in the fashion required by Engels's speculations. Neither tools nor labor, per se, could explain the evolution of humanity upward from the ranks of lesser creatures. Engels's attempt to provide a theoretical coupling between Darwinism and Marxism, in essence, was entirely unpersuasive.

After the death of Engels, as a consequence of that failure, the intellectual crisis that gradually collected around Marxism, as a system of beliefs, intensified. There was a palpable unraveling of some major aspects of the entire system. That was nowhere more apparent than in the later work of Ludwig Woltmann.

THE RACISM OF LUDWIG WOLTMANN

All the elements of a variant worldview—other than that of Karl Marx and Friedrich Engels—were already to be found in the first works published by Woltmann immediately after the turn of the twentieth century. While not frequently acknowledged, Woltmann was to emerge as one of the major theoreticians of an alternative revolution, one whose rationale would bring "biology and anthropology to bear on the historical sciences, sociology and politics."[51]

In articulating the worldview that grew out of his criticism of Marxism, the "general laws of heredity" were among the critical issues addressed by Woltmann.[52] That was the issue on which Engels's efforts to unite Darwinism and Marxism had foundered. For Woltmann, Engels had betrayed the secret of Marxism's failure. The truth, according to Woltmann, was that Engels misunderstood the relationship between Darwinism and Marxism. Woltmann argued that Engels's entire effort to assimilate Darwinism into the body of classical Marxism only led to scientific embarrassment. First, Engels attempted to portray Darwinism and Marxism as two aspects of the same theory of man and history.[53] Then he attempted to smuggle the notion of human *reproduction* into the Marxian concept of *production* as the motor of history.

Woltmann pointed out that in discussing the origins of the family and private property, in an account written after Marx's death, Engels pretended that while the materialist conception of history turned on *production* as the "determining factor in history," one must understand production to include the "*reproduction* of immediate life."[54] According to the later Engels, Marxism was apparently supposed to accommodate biological reproduction as part of that production that served as the "determining factor" in history.

Woltmann argued that if that were the case, then all the relevant laws of biology had a place in what had been, essentially, an economic interpretation of history. That is why Engels had made *heredity* an issue in his exposition. Woltmann went on to contend that if one took biology, Darwinism, and the laws of Mendelian heredity seriously, Marxism, as it had come to be understood, would have to be significantly amended. Woltmann's criticisms of Marxism were to turn on, but not be restricted to, Marxism's failure to answer questions raised by Engels's efforts to incorporate Darwinism, human reproduction, and the laws of heredity into the theoretical foundation of historical materialism.

Woltmann had addressed these issues in his first public discussions of

Marxism. In those publications, Woltmann rehearsed the logic of classical Marxism. He characterized Marxism as a system predicated on the primary importance of "the forces of production." However the forces of production were understood, they were conceived "dependent on the evolution of technology and tools." The forces of production, in turn, gave rise to apposite "social relations." The forces of production, together with the prevailing social relations, provided the reality "reflected" in the mind of participants.[55]

That account granted, the fundamental question raised by Woltmann, early in his discussion of the social theories of Marxism, turned on what was understood to govern technological change and the invention of tools. His understanding of Darwinism suggested to him that human intelligence and inventiveness might function in the process in fundamental fashion. Technology does not invent itself—it must be invented. That requires creativity and intelligence. He went on to suggest that both Marx and Engels, themselves, wrestled with just that consideration.[56]

In one place, for example, Marx identified "race" as one of the natural "physical conditions" that influences the productivity of labor. That productivity, in itself, was critical to social development.[57] Somehow or other, it would seem, racial traits influenced the very fundamentals of human social life. Engels, in his fullest maturity, in the year before his death, did speak of "economic conditions" as the factor that ultimately shapes historical development, to quickly add, "but race is itself an economic factor."[58] Woltmann pointed out that it was uncertain how such notions were to be understood if they did not allude to heritable racial properties.

Woltmann employed such references to argue that both Marx and Engels were prepared to include biological *race*—alongside, and perhaps as part of, the material productive forces—as a determinant in social development. Woltmann maintained that his interpretation was further supported by Marx's comments concerning some of the properties displayed by workingmen's castes and guilds as they have arisen, and been sustained, in history. In various cultures, the members of castes and guilds display proficiencies of performance that distinguish them from other members of society. In making reference to those proficiencies, Marx spoke of "the natural laws" that "regulate" them. Differential performance is the result of natural laws. They are the same natural laws that "regulate the differentiation of plants and animals into species and varieties." Marx clearly seemed to identify those laws, that made caste and guild members what they were, as the same "natural laws" responsible for *hereditary* biological variation and speciation.[59]

Woltmann granted that neither Marx nor Engels had a sure grasp of the implications of what they had written. Engels's Lamarckianism clearly obscured the theoretical implications. If both Marx and Engels identified *race* as an economic variable—and economic variables were determinant in understanding human history—it would seem that race would play at least an important, if not a critical, part in the social evolution of humankind.

Only if racial differences were understood to be the direct and heritable product of surrounding *economic* circumstances might the integrity of Marxist historical determinism be secured. Only if the heritable psychophysical differences that distinguished races were understood to be consequences of environmental influences would the primacy of "material life conditions" be restored. Just such considerations would help to explain Engels's readiness to invoke the suspect biological speculations of Lamarck to paper over what was for Woltmann a critical issue of scientific integrity.

Woltmann suggested that both Marx and Engels recognized, consciously or subconsciously, that some form of Lamarckianism was necessary for the defense of their system. The notion that acquired characteristics would be inherited was necessary to protect the coherence of their worldview. Without such a notion, acknowledging that the properties that differentiated species, varieties and races were genetic, and not environmental, in origin, would create theoretical problems for historical materialism. If race was an economic factor, as both Marx and Engels suggested, and economic factors were historical determinants, as their theory insisted, then biology would become part of the "material life conditions" that determined the course of human history.[60]

Woltmann argued that if invention—technology in general, and tools in particular—involved talents that were biogenetic in origin, some fundamental Marxist theses would have to be significantly modified. If technological innovation moved history,[61] and genetically determined talents supply innovation, Marxists would have to try to understand how differential talents arise—in individuals as well as groups of individuals.[62] To explain the course of history, one would have to explain the course of technological innovation. To explain the course of innovation, one would have to explain the rise and prevalence of individual and collective innovative talent.

From that point, Woltmann devoted his time to an account of historical development predicated on the conviction that development turned on a biological foundation of differential individual and collective talent. Thereafter, he was to speak of his "study of political development . . . as predicated on understanding natural science, that is to say, the biological and anthropological . . . inborn, heritable and acquired traits . . . that are the physiological bases of all political dispositions, behaviors, and conceptions." Thereafter, he proceeded to argue that all mankind's history was to be understood as a function of the "natural laws of selective variation and inheritance, adaptation and selection, inbreeding and genetic mixture, progressive evolution and degeneration of human races themselves."[63]

Woltmann argued, as had Dietzgen, that Darwinism did, indeed, provide a scientific foundation for Marxism. The difference was that Woltmann drew entirely different inferences from that consideration. The conclusion Woltmann drew from the fact that Darwinism was part of the scientific foundation of Marxism was that Darwinian "natural laws," minimally, conditioned those social laws Marx and Engels had made the basis of historical materialism. Woltmann conceived technological invention and development, the foundation of historical materialism, to be the result of human creativity and talent, differentially distributed among extant human races.[64] Woltmann believed he had enough evidence to support his thesis: not only did he turn to the social sciences of his period, he conducted his own research. He was thus prepared to resolve the economic determinism of classical Marxism into a broadly conceived form of bioeconomic determinism. Woltmann had finally succeeded, to his own satisfaction, in assimilating Darwinism into his Marxism. The price paid was to entirely transform Marxism as a theory of historical development.

Given the new set of convictions that lay at the foundation of what had been his "orthodox" Marxism, Woltmann then turned to the evidence of history to try to decide if different human races, distinguished by observable physical properties, displayed unmistakable differences in heritable intellectual and creative gifts. That would influence the course of social development—with those races more abundantly gifted with creative talents necessarily having a different history than any lesser endowed race. Once again, Woltmann was to find in the abundance of the Marxist legacy enough material on which to hang his interpretation.

There was more than a suggestion of differential creative potential among peoples in the writings of Marx and Engels. In a letter to Engels, dated the second of December 1847, for example, Marx wrote that "the Spaniards are indeed degenerate. But a degenerate Spaniard, a Mexican, that is the ideal. All vices of the Spaniards—boastfulness, grandiloquence, and quixoticism—are found in the Mexicans raised to the third power." Nor did that seem to be the result of a fit of pique, for Engels expressed some very similar judgments in a communique on the U.S.-Mexican war he provided for publication.

In his account, Engels opined that the American expansion into the West and Southwest of North America served "the interests of civilization," since "the lazy Mexicans . . . did not know what to do with it." The "energetic Yankees," on the other hand, opened the entire region to trade and industry. Engels was convinced that more highly developed industrial nations were destined to bind "tiny, crippled, powerless little nations together in a great Empire, and thereby [enable] them to take part in an historical development which, if left to themselves, would [remain] entirely foreign to them!"[65]

Both Marx and Engels seemed convinced that there were "peoples" who "have never had a history of their own" and who were destined to be "forced into the first stages of civilization through a foreign yoke, have no vitality, [and] will never be able to attain any sort of independence."[66] Marx spoke of the Chinese as being afflicted with "hereditary stupidity," while Engels deemed the Slavs of Eastern and Southeastern Europe to be nothing more than "ethnic trash."[67]

Both founders of Marxism conceived of a class of peoples as "history-less," as somehow deficient in energy, who entered history only through the agency of "more vital" agents—to be "absorbed" into "more energetic stock."[68] Engels regularly spoke of Slavs as "dying," "retrograde" peoples, as "phthisical bodies," to enter history only through the "mighty Germans," to remain forever as "ethnographic monuments" within the German Empire.[69] He seemed to imagine that only the Germans were capable of saving civilization, for he argued that when it is a "question of saving European civilization, what [matters] the fate of a few nationalities?"[70]

All of this fed into the formulations that more and more dominated Woltmann's thought. By the end of the nineteenth century, Woltmann was prepared to argue, indeed, that there was a human race destined to "save civilization." It was a race he identified as the sole creator of civilization.

Convinced that Marx had argued that *race* was a critical factor in technological development, Woltmann proceeded to draw out what he held to be some significant historic and moral implications. Among the human races, Woltmann argued, some were endowed with greater creative potential than others. Marx and Engels seemed to have suggested as much. Putting all of that together, Woltmann proceeded to identify that race most responsible for economic and cultural evolution. He settled on Nordics—tall, long-headed, narrow-faced, depigmented Europeans—as humankind's most creative racial community.[71] In the years that immediately followed, in a systematic effort to provide the scientific evidence in support of his claims, Woltmann undertook a number of empirical studies that involved attempting a statistical assessment of the measure of Germanic, or Nordic, genetic potential that might be found among the minorities of France and Renaissance Italy—and correlate that with their respective creativity.[72]

On the basis of that sort of research, together with his familiarity with available literature,[73] Woltmann felt himself prepared to tender sweeping generalizations concerning biological race and culture creation within the context of what he by then called "the anthropological theory of history"— the essence of which was that an "Aryan race," Nordic in features and talent, has been responsible for virtually all the world's cultures, ranging from those of India, Persia, Hellas, the Italic peninsula, Gaul, as well as those of Northern, Eastern, and Southeastern Europe. That creative race also "strongly influenced" the great civilizations of the Far East as well.[74]

By the time Woltmann published his *Politische Anthropologie*, his heterodox Marxism had been transformed. Darwinism dominated not only his conception of human evolution, but social evolution as well. The social dynamics we continue to identify with historical materialism remained largely inviolable, but the motive force behind technological invention Woltmann identified with heritable properties—creativity and intelligence—traits he increasingly identified with select individuals and select racial communities.

By the first years of the twentieth century what emerged was a political ideology that had originally found its inspiration in classical Marxism—but which, as a consequence of systematic and sustained criticism, had been so altered that it could only be identified as a Marxist heresy. Whatever that is taken to mean, it obscures the reality that Woltmann's racism was the natural child of classical Marxism.

Woltmann was not the only Marxist who traveled that path. In 1862, decades before Woltmann's "heresy," Moses Hess, the "communist rabbi"—the person who purportedly made a communist of Karl Marx—made very clear his racist and nationalist predilections with the publication of his *Rome and Jerusalem*.[75] After having worked with Marx and Engels on some of their most important early publications, with the appearance of *Rome and Jerusalem*, Hess was to leave them behind.

In his book, Hess made the case for Jewish psychobiological superiority, to advocate the creation of a Jewish homeland in the effort to assure Jewish survival—in order that they might continue to provide benefits for all of humanity. The Marxism of his young manhood had been transmogrified in much the same manner as had the Marxism of the young Ludwig Woltmann.

Woltmann's philosophical curiosity was to propel him still further. He took his studies of Darwinism, and his allusions to the role of race in the economic history of human kind, and tied them to the moral principle that Josef Dietzgen had made the lodestar of Marxist ethics. In his final works, the highest good that shaped Woltmann's individual and collective ethics was, as it was for Dietzgen, the "general welfare of humankind."

What distinguished Woltmann's conception of the general welfare of humankind from that of Dietzgen turned on Woltmann's conviction that the biological survival and collective integrity of Nordics constituted the agency responsible for what that general welfare might be taken to be. Woltmann could affirm, with profound conviction, that if the secular progress of which all Marxists spoke was a function of the intellectual and creative talents of a racial minority of human beings, then the security, sustenance, and fostering of that race became a moral imperative of the highest order.[76] Its survival and expansion was the necessary condition for the production of all the welfare benefits, material and spiritual, of which Marx had spoken—and to which Dietzgen had alluded.

Like Marx, Woltmann deplored capitalism. He spoke of its dysgenic effects. He spoke of its profligate use of human beings in its search for profit. He spoke of the physical and mental costs to workers marshaled by industrial capitalism into the ranks of factory hands. He spoke of the physical decline in the production of offspring and of the increasing number of the unfit that had begun to appear in the cities. He spoke of the need to mobilize social sentiment behind mass eugenics programs, through moral suasion if possible, or by law if necessary.

Finally, Woltmann identified the Jews as an "alien" community. They contributed to those forces unwilling to defend the future of humankind by protecting the Nordic culture race.[77] He spoke of their behavior as hereditary singularities—the unfortunate consequence of their millennial struggle to survive in pathogenic circumstances.

Before his accidental death in 1907, Woltmann pursued his modifications of classical Marxism—putting together elements to be found there, augmented by the early moral preachments of Josef Dietzgen—to fabricate an ideology that was to inspire millions in the years that were to follow, thereby contributing to making the twentieth century what it was to be. His racism entered into a stream of convictions calculated to identify Germans, in general, as a special people. A decade later, by the end of the First World War, Germans, as a community, felt themselves unjustly humiliated at the hands of their wartime opponents. The peace treaty that ended the conflict identified them as collectively responsible for the catastrophic conflict that cost Europe millions in treasure and lives.

Germany was burdened with disabling reparations payments and, for an unconscionable length of time after the end of hostilities, remained under blockade. The rancor and bitterness that resulted, prepared the soil for the reactive nationalism that was to follow. It was to be a nationalism having more to do with race than nation[78]—and Woltmann was to be found in the pantheon of thinkers revered by its leaders.[79]

A population so devastated by events proved itself eminently susceptible to the blandishments of theories that promised to identify their community as special—as the ultimate and exclusive source of world culture. All those factors contributed to the proliferation of racist literature that followed the end of the First World War—and it was Woltmann's name that was to surface in many of its volumes.

In our own time, Woltmann's intimate association with Marxism is rarely, if ever, cited—and one of the principal sources of the revolutionary racism of the twentieth century thereby obscured. It was the decay of classical Marxism that contributed racism to the mix of revolutionary ideas that were to torment our time. Neither Moses Hess nor Ludwig Woltmann can be dismissed as anomalies. As the subsequent history of revolutionary Marxism was to reveal, racist and reactive nationalist variants of Marxism were to inspire revolutions throughout the doleful history of our most recent past.

THE LEGACY

However important in the intellectual history of revolution, it would be a mistake to reduce Woltmann's assessment of classical Marxism to his racism. There were themes in Woltmann's work that were to resurface in the thought of the major ideologues of revolution after his passing. Among those themes were fundamental philosophical questions that turned on epistemology and morality and how they were to be resolved—and what role morality and ethics played in human behavior. Any attempt to provide a studied response to any of those topics very quickly introduced epistemological questions as well as those that turned on the "free will" of individuals in conflicted situations. Any attempt to answer the latter question took on psychological as well as philosophical dimension. Revolutionaries were required to answer questions of human motivation as well as how one might justify commitment. Almost immediately one faced the collateral problem of the role of individuals in shaping the behavior of others. Throughout the history of revolution in the twentieth century, the question of the role of the individual in history resurfaces again and again—and the answers vary in any number of ways.

Woltmann was more than a racist. He was a sophisticated Marxist who offered calculated response to all those issues. He teased many of the answers out of the abundant literature of Marxism itself. In effect, Woltmann, perhaps more than any other thinker at the beginning of the twentieth century, identified the topics that transformed the Marxism of Karl Marx and Friedrich Engels into ideological variants that were to inform the revolutionary movements destined to overwhelm the world.

It is a relatively simple matter to trace Woltmann's ideas from Marxism to racism—and from there into the ideology of Adolf Hitler's National Socialism.[80] Far less easy is relating Woltmann's thought to those forms of Marxism that pretended to be true to the thought of the masters. V. I. Lenin never admitted he had taken liberties with the Marxism he inherited. The "Marxism-Leninism" that resulted was to emerge as Stalinism in the late 1920s and the 1930s, to further devolve after the death of the "Leader" into the post-Stalinist and post-Soviet curiosities now identified with the Communist Party of the Russian Federation.

At the same time that Lenin was putting together his "creative developments" of revolutionary Marxism, another Marxist, a leader of a revolutionary socialist party in Italy, was undertaking similarly creative developments. The result was yet another Marxist heresy: Fascism.

Over the years, the direct connection that related all these revolutionary movements with the revisions of Marxism to be first found in the work of Josef Dietzgen and Ludwig Woltmann have become increasingly diaphanous. Nonetheless, the themes Dietzgen and Woltmann addressed run like red threads through all the belief systems that pretend to somehow represent the Marxism of Marx and Engels. Almost every one of the issues with which both Dietzgen and Woltmann dealt proved to be critical to the intellectual integrity and the justificatory rationale of the major revolutionaries of the twentieth century.

The intellectual legacy left to our time by the founders of Marxism requires almost fifty Germanic volumes for its containment. The ideas embodied in that corpus were developed, modified, elaborated upon, and synoptically expressed in so many ways and in so many permutations by Marx and Engels themselves, it is not surprising that acolytes have found almost everything there—from the rationale for Chinese Maoism, Castro's "Fidelismo," and all the curious notions that make up the intellectual substance of the Marxisms found in such quaint places as Cambodia, the Philippine islands, Ethiopia, and the highlands of Peru. The very richness of Marxism assured that there would be many Marxisms, almost Marxisms, and not-so-much Marxisms, that would inspire revolutionaries to destroy half a world with their enthusiasm.

Almost every serious revolutionary in the twentieth century has had to settle his accounts with the Marxism of the nineteenth century. Hitler's National Socialism, for one, adopted and adapted some of the central Leninist convictions, and their institutional expressions concerning the control of subject populations. Some of that, it will be argued, can be plausibly traced to convictions central to classical Marxism—to become thematic in the analysis of both Dietzgen and Woltmann. Quite independent of the specifically racist themes that can be traced to Woltmann's work, there are those general themes explored by both Dietzgen and Woltmann that resurface in the institutional features of Leninism, Stalinism, and National Socialism, together with the rationale advanced in their support.

Of Mussolini's Fascism, a great deal more requires the saying. Fascism, whatever its affinities with National Socialism, was informed by a fundamentally different belief system. It will be argued that it was Fascism, more than any other revolutionary movement, that embodied whatever elements of classical Marxism were to survive into the twentieth century—and some of the themes that grew out of Woltmann's work provide insight both into the fabric of Fascist thought as well as its ideological origins in Marxism.

Before any of that can be attempted, it is necessary to review Leninism as the first "creative development" of classical Marxism in the effort to trace its relationship to those themes we have identified in the work of Dietzgen and Woltmann. Directly and indirectly, Lenin was compelled to address some of the theoretical problems that made up much of their analysis of classical Marxism. It will be argued that Lenin's resolution of those problems created a system that shared unmistakable ideological and institutional similarities, at one or another level, with National Socialism and Fascism. Woltmann's arguments provide us a convenient point of departure.

Lenin was among the first ruling Marxists who attempted to address almost all those themes. He was familiar with the work of Dietzgen and Woltmann—just as he was familiar with the work of Giovanni Gentile—who was to serve as the official philosopher of Mussolini's Fascism. Lenin remarked on the importance of both Woltmann and Gentile in the serious study of Marxism. He spoke of Woltmann's book, *Der historische Materialismus*, as among the most "outstanding" works devoted to Marxism—and of Gentile's work on the philosophy of the young Marx as "noteworthy" and "important."[81] At the very commencement of the twentieth century, Lenin spontaneously identified authors who were to shape Marxism into ideologies that were to influence history in ways no one, least of all Lenin, could have possibly anticipated. But before their ideas were to fully work their influence, Georges Sorel's interpretation of Marxism was to intervene.

CHAPTER FOUR

The Heterodox Marxism of Georges Sorel

On the cusp of the twentieth century, as discussion swirled around the doctrinal meaning and applied politics of their belief system, Marxists in each of the Western European nations developed interpretations and practical orientations that were seen by others as increasingly heterodox. In Germany, following the efforts of Joseph Dietzgen, and the Lassallean interlude, the German Social Democrats sought to settle on a Marxism whose orthodoxy was assured by the direct, if episodic, intervention of Friedrich Engels.

With the death of Engels in 1895, however, there was no longer the restraint supplied by a keeper at the gate. As indicated, Eduard Bernstein announced his critique of the classical doctrine almost immediately after the disappearance of Engels. More an effort to make doctrine conform to practice, Bernstein recommended a careful review of Marxism's central empirical claims. In substance, Bernstein asked Marxists to consider what tactical policies recommended themselves to revolutionary leaders if some of Marxism's most entrenched predictions proved to be incorrect.

Bernstein's entire enterprise was predicated on the implication that policy, in significant measure, was a function of the truth of Marxism's empirical claims. If the capitalist system really could not be expected to spontaneously collapse at some point, revolutionary leaders were compelled to devise a strategy to deal with a protracted political struggle for workers' rights. Every empirical claim made by either Marx or Engels was subject to review—and any claim found to be wanting would require a deliberate change in revolutionary policy. Revolutionaries would have to accustom themselves to a reality in which neither doctrinal nor policy stability could be expected. Marxism would be subject to constant revision under the pressure of new evidence, with policy expected to change with each modification in doctrine.

Bernstein's revisionism revealed something about Marxism that almost everyone seriously interested in the doctrine was ultimately forced to accept. Classical Marxism, at its very birth, was an enormously complex and precariously balanced ideological construction—composed in part of speculative factual claims, in part of an uncertain logic, and in part of unargued moral convictions. As a consequence, throughout its history over the next four or five decades, almost all its critical concepts were to remain contested. Typical of the problem was Marxism's use of the term "class." Like most of its central concepts, it was nowhere rigorously defined.[1] The predictable result was that over the years, the interpretation and reinterpretation of such concepts by both followers and detractors produced variants of Marxism that were to shape political activity throughout the twentieth century.

Drawing out the implications of some of the concepts of classical Marxism, Ludwig Woltmann fashioned the "political anthropology" that was to inspire some of the leaders of National Socialism. He was only one of the many authors at the dawn of the emerging century who were to father variants of Marxism—each of which helped make of our time what it was to become. That is the reality against which one can measure the consequences that follow from the original vagueness and ambiguity of the Marxism left as a legacy by its founders.[2]

Woltmann's explication and ultimate reformulation nowhere departed unequivocally from the Marxism he knew. His interpretation turned on his construal of terms like "race" that are found in the body of Marx's work—and concepts of heritability found in the work of Engels. Decades later, even after it had become evident where Woltmann's heresies had led him, Karl Kautsky could still agree that Woltmann was correct in affirming that "historical materialism implies a biological materialism" and that he was right to incorporate into its "theoretical structure the teachings of Darwinian evolution."[3]

These were the circumstances in which the proliferation of heresies began. Woltmann's heterodoxy was only one of the first—if perhaps the most arresting. In the course of time, as Marxism became the belief system of a political party, rather than a preoccupation of solitary authors, the demand increased for a single, coherent "theory" around which followers might collect. If hundreds of thousands of German workers were to be enlisted in a "Marxist party," institutional demands, if nothing else, recommended doctrinal coherence and consistency. With the passage of time, in Wilhelminian Germany, Karl Kautsky emerged as the standard bearer of the required orthodoxy.

By the first decade of the twentieth century, whatever their political tactics, German Marxists began to acquire a reputation for being dogmatic and inflexible in doctrinal matters. More often than not, party members identified Kautsky's peculiar orthodoxy with the "thought of Marx." In the minds of the members of the German Social Democratic Party, the thought of Joseph Dietzgen, Ludwig Woltmann, and Eduard Bernstein receded further and further into heterodoxy.

Roberto Michels tendered a contemporary judgment when he spoke of German Social Democratic intellectuals as seeing themselves the "most authentic heirs of Marx's profundities," and, as a consequence, given to a kind of "dogmatic intolerance" of any interpretations that did not fully correspond to that of the leadership of the party.[4] Any Marxism that did not conform to that of the party intellectuals was to remain forever "heterodox" and "heretical," if not in fact an "apostasy." Outside of Germany, things were different.

In both France and Italy, while there were authors who sought to articulate an interpretation of classical Marxism true to the fundamental intentions of its founders, there was no one who exercised the same dominant intellectual influence as did Kautsky in Germany. As a consequence, by the first decade of the new century, a number of variants of Marxism had made their appearance among both French and Italian intellectuals. In both countries, interpretations of classical Marxism appeared, each of which, almost without exception, was a major departure from that endorsed by Kautsky and the German Social Democratic Party.[5]

Developments of Marxist doctrine in both countries followed careers of their own. In France, as early as the first years of the 1870s, a group of radicals in Paris, each with independent interpretation, sought to influence the development of the domestic labor movement. By the end of the decade, the movement had attracted the attention and support of Jules Guesde, who was to go on to become a major figure in the evolution of French socialism. Articulate and commanding, Guesde became spokesman for French "scientific socialism." The movement did not remain united very long. By the beginning of the next decade, the advocates of labor reform through participation in parliament separated from anarchocommunist elements who conceived all "bourgeois" political institutions, without exception, agencies of oppression. They held capitalists to be intrinsically unresponsive to reform. They conceived the participation of workers' representatives in the national parliament as nothing other than the occasion for stultifying compromise and the unconscionable betrayal of working class interests. The division between those who advocated participation in the political system and those who advocated boycott was only the first of many that was to fracture the doctrinal and organizational unity of French socialism.

After the Congress of St. Etienne in 1882, the socialists divided into two major organizations, one led by Guesde and the other by Paul Brousse. Guesde's *Parti Ouvrier Français*, centralized and effective, sought the overthrow of the state and the creation of a transitional "dictatorship of the proletariat," preliminary to the final dissolution of all things bourgeois. Guesde and his followers rejected the notion that any reforms could materially alter the life circumstances of labor, dismissing all such efforts as "shams."[6]

For their part, the *Broussists*, members of Brousse's *Parti Ouvrier revolutionnaire socialiste*, accepted the possibility of effective reform, and were disposed to tolerate wider doctrinal differences among themselves. As a consequence, Marxist orthodoxy was a matter of relatively little concern. More than the *Guesdists*, the *Broussists* concentrated on the peaceful infiltration by the representatives of labor into municipal, departmental, and national legislative bodies in order to affect their reforms.

By the end of the decade, French socialism further subdivided itself into *Allemanists*, the followers of J. Allemane, who sought direct appeal to the workers in the effort to mobilize for revolution. The *Allemanists* were convinced that the primary responsibility of revolutionaries was to educate the proletariat to their historic responsibilities.

"Independent socialists," in turn, led by Benoit Malon, advocated, among other reformist measures, the gradual nationalization of public services, laws protecting the rights of labor, and local self-government for the communes. In fact, the independents provided the intellectual setting out of which some of France's most notable parliamentary socialists—Jean Jaures, Etienne Millerand, and R. F. Viviani—were to arise.

Finally, among the smaller socialist organizations, there were the Blanquists, held together by experiences shared in the Paris Commune of recent memory, and committed to a revolutionary program, both conspiratorial and violent, that would result in anticipated communist outcomes. They were the advocates of all and any means necessary to accomplish their purpose.

Parallel to these doctrinal developments, economic conditions fostered the growth of workingmen's associations. Not only the prevailing conditions of labor, but the very organization of employers' *syndicats*, recommended collective self-defense by all parties involved in productive enterprise. By the mid-1880s, French law allowed the formation of workers' syndicats, and at the same time, the creation of a *Fédération des Bourses du Travail de France*—a Federation of Labor Exchanges—that would provide workers, in each locality, with information, foster contact with others, and serve as employment agencies. These evolving institutions soon became the objects of political competition by the various Marxist and quasi-Marxist groups. Each sought to control the resources and the membership of the Labor Exchanges.

Within this dynamic environment various workingmen's groups emerged that saw the laying down of tools, work stoppages, as among the most effective weapons available to them in their struggle against the bourgeoisie. The leadership of those syndicats sought to persuade their members that perhaps employing the strategy of a general strike might serve to dramatically affect their purposes. Already invoked by some British and American workers in pursuit of their interests, the idea was welcomed by the French syndicats. Work stoppages directly mobilized workers to the struggle for the rights of labor. For some, the very occasion of laying down tools to attain one's rights suggested the possibility of a "general strike," universal in scope and overwhelming in its implications. It suggested the possibility that a general strike might serve not only as a mobilizing and pedagogical instrument in preparing the proletariat for, but a weapon to be employed in the achievement of, revolutionary purpose.[7]

As a consequence, for years following the development of the *Bourses*, efforts were made by the various leaders of workingmen's organizations to agree on the *political* functions of what were essentially *economic* institutions. Some of the politically active socialists urged the use of the *Bourses* as staging areas for the revolutionary general strike. At the same time, there were many workingmen who sought to avoid overt political activity as threatening to their immediate well-being.

By the beginning of the twentieth century, out of that difference, those workingmen's organizations that saw the general strike as the most effective insurrectionary tool available, began to put together a generic doctrine that became known as "revolutionary syndicalism,"[8] to distinguish their revolutionary enterprise from simple trade union activity. One of the first major works that attempted to provide the emerging movement an account of its own development and doctrine was *L'Avenir socialiste des syndicats* by Georges Sorel—originally published in 1898.[9]

THE REVOLUTIONARY DOCTRINE
OF GEORGES SOREL

By the time Sorel published his *L'Avenir*, he was already an acknowledged "gifted Marxist."[10] Born in 1847, Sorel came to Marxism relatively late in life.[11] When he wrote *L'Avenir*, he was over fifty years of age and already retired from civil service. Before *L'Avenir*, he had written two major works, one devoted to an analytic account of the Bible, and the second a critical treatment of the trial of Socrates.[12] Both are important because they provide some insight into Sorel's thought—which was broad gauged and wide ranging, at once brilliant and loosely structured, often ill expressed, yet immensely penetrating. Together with the two volumes, Sorel had written and published a plethora of articles and reviews in French and Italian journals during the last years of the nineteenth century. In general, Sorel's prodigious literary legacy has been spoken of as a "great disordered and disorderly encyclopedia."[13]

Whatever else his work represented by the mid-1890s, it contained essays that clearly gave expression to Sorel's explicit commitment to what he took to be the orthodoxy of classical Marxism. His long essay, entitled "L'Ancienne et la Nouvelle Métaphysique," which appeared in *L'Ere nouvelle* in 1894, contains a clear statement of adherence to Marxism as a doctrine and as a program.[14] At that time—particularly between the years 1894 and 1896—Sorel had not the least hesitancy in identifying Marxism as one of the "greatest philosophical innovations in many centuries."[15]

For all that, the period of Sorel's Marxist orthodoxy was drawing to a close with the 1897 publication of his Preface to the French edition of Antonio Labriola's *La concezione materialistica della storia*.[16] Sorel held that the author's account was an accurate representation of the thought of Karl Marx and Friedrich Engels.[17] In his volume, Labriola dutifully reported that Marxism was a "model philosophy of history" that identified the "underlying economic structure which determines all the rest of social organization"—including all the human responses that were the subject of conventional accounts.[18]

According to Labriola's rendering, understanding the economic foundations of history allows one to anticipate a future that "is necessary and inevitable, whatever may be the vicissitudes and the successive phases that cannot yet be foreseen." He spoke of history as being "all of a piece," the end result of processes "altogether objective and independent of our approval or disapproval." Like Marx, Labriola spoke of revolution as the necessary and objective consequence not of human will or determination, but of the "rebellion of . . . productive forces against the conditions (juridical and political) of production."[19] All of which simply reiterated much of what passed at the time as the orthodox account of Marxist historiography.

In the work reviewed by Sorel, Labriola described Marxist historical method as incorporating the prevailing conception of science that others spoke of as "positivistic." Labriola had reservations about identifying Marxism with positivism because of positivism's association with "bourgeois" thinkers such as August Comte and Herbert Spencer.[20] Whatever his reservations, however, it was evident that Labriola's conception of historical method largely conformed to that which characterized positivism.

Labriola spoke of the "material conditions" understood to "determine" the motives that govern the individual and collective will of human beings. "In the last analysis," Labriola concluded, the most complex human behavior was explained by looking to the material conditions in which human beings found themselves struggling to survive. Like the positivists, Labriola spoke of the most intricate historical sequences having "been actually produced by their own necessity without care for our free will and our consent." Ethics and morality were characterized as "the necessary result of the conditions in which [persons] live and of the circumstances which surround them." Material life conditions explained the course of history, Labriola argued, and in so doing accounted for human ethical deliberation and moral choice. Human decisions were epiphenomena, functions of "material life conditions." Having divined all that, Marxism, he maintained, had become an "exact science" capable of revealing all the "secrets of history" that had hitherto confounded the pundits.[21]

In terms of the history of ideas, the conviction that standard science could accomplish all that was at the core of nineteenth-century positivism. Whatever the reservations Labriola had about the "bourgeois" thought of luminaries like Comte and Spencer, the fact was that classical Marxism was as "scientistic" as traditional positivism—claiming to explain all human behavior employing the strategies made familiar by the natural sciences. As such, Marxism was positivistic, however "dialectical" it may have pretended to be.[22]

It was precisely that kind of reductionism to which Ludwig Woltmann and a number of his Marxist contemporaries objected. Philosophical and ethical concerns occupied a distinctive domain of discourse—that moral truths rested on entirely different grounds than the truths of empirical claims—were convictions that animated those Marxists who recommended an antipositivistic "return to Kant." They argued that human thought, deliberation and choice, could not plausibly be reduced to a "reflex" of "material life conditions." The conduct of human beings involved issues of grave intellectual and reflective concern that could not be resolved by pretending to see them disappear in any account, however complex, of economic conditions. That Sorel might have overlooked all of that, to endorse the reductionism of some "orthodox"[23] interpretation of classical Marxism by writing a laudatory preface to Labriola's volume, is counterintuitive.

In fact, in the volume reviewed by Sorel in 1897, Labriola's treatment of individual and collective human behavior left some latitude for a more generous interpretation of the talk of "necessity" and "determinism" that peppered his account. There were places in Labriola's exposition where he spoke of it being "reasonable" to "subordinate the sum total of human events in their course to the rigorous conception of determinism . . . which would substitute automatism for voluntariam"—but then again, he granted that "the process . . . is very complicated, often subtle, tortuous and not always legible." In fact, he fully conceded that in the effort to account for human behavior, one must accept the fact that any process under scrutiny is invariably influenced by idiosyncratic "ignorance, passion, brutishness, corruption, falsehood, baseness and presumption"—features that make prediction hazardous at best. Moreover, Labriola readily granted that it is the case that the connection between overt conduct, moral deliberation and ethical reflection, presumably determined by a specific "underlying economic structure," is "not always legible."[24]

It seems reasonably clear that Labriola entertained the determinism and automaticity of Marxism only with reservations. He granted that Marxism had not fully explained the "mechanism of that formation and development" by virtue of which humanity makes its own history.[25] In his treatment of Marxism as a theory of history, Labriola appeared somewhat reluctant to assign to a community's economy an absolutely determinant role in the complex history of its members' conduct. He seemed prepared to allow that neither economic determinism nor the derivative role of human will were so clearly established as to warrant the immediate dismissal of alternative interpretations.

It was the measure of reservation concerning the determinism of classical Marxism that allowed Sorel to argue, in his preface to Labriola's volume, that it was a mischaracterization to argue that Marx held that "all political, moral, and aesthetic phenomena are determined (in the precise meaning of the word) by economic causes." Sorel held that such a suggestion was meaningless. "What might such a formula mean? To say that one thing is determined by another without indicating, at the same time, any precise idea of how they might be related, is to utter a foolishness that has made vulgar Marxism a thing of ridicule. Marx can hardly be made responsible for such a caricature of his thought."[26]

Nor did Sorel stop there. He went on to argue that Marx had sought to understand the course of history by making appeal to some obscure principles of psychology that he never chose to explicate. Marx nowhere gave those principles explicit form. Sorel held that the psychology of revolution forever remained only half articulated in Marx's work.[27] Sorel argued that the inherited doctrine required an explication and a more adequate reformulation. He maintained that it was the obligation of Marx's followers to attempt just such amendments and elaborations. That would certainly include reworking the original conceptions, the logic of their relations, as well as the psychological notions that specifically lay at their foundation.[28]

What was clear was that even during the period of his most enthusiastic adherence to Marxism, Sorel, like many Marxists of the period, held that the effort to reduce ethical deliberation and moral judgment to antecedent material causes was entirely unconvincing. As early as the publication of *Le procès de Socrate* in 1889, Sorel reminded his audience that human choice and human behavior could not be reduced to the externalities of material phenomena. He argued that the effort to reduce human psychology to quantitative, exclusively "scientific," measure was intrinsically flawed. He held that the disposition to so understand human activity was an unhappy consequence of the scientific preoccupation with the astronomic universe, with the notion that human conduct obeyed a causal pattern analogous to that which governed the movement of sidereal bodies.[29] He objected to the entire notion that "moral problems might be dealt with employing a deductive method, . . . as one might in physics."[30] One could not explain human conduct, nor the moral commitment that supplied its impulse, by simply providing an account of surrounding material circumstances.

In 1892, four or five years before writing the preface to Labriola's Marxist text, Sorel made very clear his commitment to a notion of ethics that necessitated its relative "autonomy." He had already assumed an epistemological position that allowed for diverse domains of discourse, by virtue of which the rationale that sanctioned moral choice and human conduct was clearly distinguished from the truth conditions governing specifically scientific and logical claims.[31]

Sorel held it to be intrinsically impossible to move from one truth domain—ethics and morality—to another—matters of fact and logic—without acknowledging the different acceptance criteria governing each. Each required a separate procedure for its respective vindication, verification, or validation—quite independent of whatever speculative associations were imagined to obtain between them. One entirely misses the point in dealing with ethical considerations and moral choice when one seeks to account for all the deliberations involved by simply making recourse to individual and/or collective class membership or material interests. Sorel correctly dismissed that kind of determinism as philosophically "vulgar."[32]

Like many Marxists of his time, Sorel was concerned with moral behavior across two distinct dimensions: one was essentially sociological—what causes persons to conduct themselves in one or another fashion; the other was essentially epistemological—what might constitute, under whatever circumstances, an ethically acceptable rationale for any particular moral behavior. Years before his adhesion to Marxism, Sorel had written an account of Socrates' conduct in which he sought to assess its merits against ethical criteria that were essentially historic in character.[33] While he was to refer subsequently to fundamental economic factors in characterizing historic periods, he never sought thereby to account for the philosophical and moral content of human reflection. All the Marxist categories, the introduction of instruments of production and the exchange relations to which they gave rise, functioned as "factors" in the process, but were never *determinant* in accounting for human thought, volition, or performance.

In 1892, in a long essay on the thought of Pierre-Joseph Proudhon, Sorel reflected on the pluriform character of human reasoning, distinguishing between (1) the formal reasoning characteristic of logic and mathematics; (2) the evidentiary basis of factual claims; and (3) the peculiar historicity of ethical reasoning and moral justification.[34] Whatever reservations Sorel had concerning Proudhon's views turned on issues outside the scope of the present account, but what he took away from those deliberations remained central to his political and philosophical views throughout the remainder of his life.

What Sorel found in Proudhon, enhanced by his own studies of antiquity, was the conviction that human beings could attain virtue only in well-ordered association, sustained by coherent pedagogical efforts to instill in them defensible moral principles. Sorel argued that such circumstances obtained when individuals, as productive citizen soldiers, were charged with the obligation of the ethical and physical defense of their community.[35] Already apparent before his conversion to Marxism, they were themes he was never to abandon. Morality was governed by ethical principles that were taught in given historical—but not exclusively economic—circumstances.

When Sorel chose to pursue moral purpose by accepting Marxism, he had already rejected the individualism that animated the industrializing society of his time. He saw that form of individualism toxic to moral purpose. Conversely, Sorel chose to see in Marxism the promise of a rational and organic order of things in which each individual would find a proper place, in which all would be expected to manifest commitment, responsibility, selflessness, and sacrifice in a heroic struggle to protect virtue against the moral relativism of the increasingly dominant bourgeoisie.[36]

Sorel saw reflected in Marxism the Aristotelian conception of man as a social animal, and ethics as a function of communal, not exclusively economic, life.[37] It is clear that as a new convert to Marxism, Sorel did speak of morality as a "system of sentimental illusions," largely a "reflex of an economic system." That did not preclude, as will be seen, the existence of moral decisions and ethical principles that are other than simple reflexes.

Sorel understood that moral choice is necessarily undertaken within a complex economic reality "fabricated, worked, and continually refined." Moral conduct does not take place in a social, political, or economic vacuum. As a consequence, one must necessarily consider the context in which human conduct finds expression.[38]

All of that granted, several things appear reasonably clear in attempting to trace the development of Sorel's ideas. By the time Sorel committed himself to Marxism he had settled on several problems that he held to be of significance. It was evident from both his general approval of Proudhon, as well as his writing through that date, that Sorel opposed the individualism that typified the philosophical and moral dispositions of the rising merchant and industrial bourgeoisie of his time. Moreover, he understood that the individualism that grew out of those dispositions resulted in a "great disorder to be found among the ethical ideas of the day," which Sorel traced to the fact that the moral principles of antiquity, translated into theological doctrine, were no longer persuasive for a significant number of contemporary actors.[39]

Sorel acknowledged an imperative in all of that. He charged himself with the responsibility of advocating a rebirth of virtue, a reformulation of ethical principles. He anticipated his opportunity growing out of the circumstances surrounding the emergence of a new world of industry. Marx, Sorel insisted, had sensitized the time to the ethical implications of an environment no longer natural, a world uniquely different, artificially constructed by the inventive genius of humans, a world of machines.[40]

Sorel reminded his readers that Marx had signaled the significance of the fact that the modern world had been largely created by the inventive genius of human beings. Marx had made the point that while Darwin concerned himself with the "history of nature's technology," real history turned not on the activity of nature, but on that of humanity. Marx reminded us that Darwinism did not capture the real history of humankind. That history turned on technology—the "material basis of all social organization"—and technology was the product of the genius of human beings.[41]

Like Ludwig Woltmann at about the same time,[42] Sorel sought to draw out some of the implications of such an acknowledgment. Both Woltmann and Sorel saw history as a human product—the result of creative actions undertaken by human beings in concert. Instances of creativity—technological advances, organizational strategies, inventiveness—while manifest in individuals, are all collective products, the cumulative result of a collaborative history stretching back over generations. Both Woltmann and Sorel insisted that the history of humanity was a history made by human beings. Woltmann settled on a preoccupation with the biological endowments that made individual and group creativeness possible, while Sorel pursued what he saw as clear ethical implications.[43]

In retrospect, what becomes evident is the fact that by the last years of the nineteenth century, there was little that might count as a single and definitive "orthodox Marxism." So rich in ambiguity and discontinuities was it that by that time at least four principal variants of Marxism could be identified: that of Bernstein and Woltmann in Germany,[44] the critical deconstructionism of Benedetto Croce in Italy,[45] and the ethical reformism of Sorel in France.

By 1896, it was evident that the kind of orthodoxy represented by the Marxism of Karl Kautsky could not contain Sorel. Sorel's Marxism became increasingly antipositivistic, rejecting the notion that any descriptive account of material conditions, however complex, could explain human ethical deliberation or fully account for human choice. In that year he published his "Etude sur Vico," a study that he fully acknowledged helped him with his interpretation of Marxism as well as shape his evolving revolutionary convictions.[46]

Thereafter, Sorel consistently cited the influence of Giambattista Vico on his own thought. It was an influence that revealed itself in Sorel's increasing emphasis on the role of human deliberation and choice in making history.[47] Sorel reminded his readers that Marx himself had turned to Vico in order to insist on the differences between natural and human history.

Marx did that by reminding us that human beings are not responsible for the former, while actively responsible for the latter. As a consequence, in referring to Vico, Marx urged that we must understand history in a fashion different from the manner in which we understand nature. That is because we ourselves are the architects of human history.[48] Like Woltmann, Sorel had commenced his reinterpretation of Marx's work by attempting to resolve some of its intrinsic ambiguities and implicit qualifications.

In 1897, Sorel wrote a long review of Severio Merlino's critical *Pro e contro il socialismo*. It was about the time Sorel began a long and intense correspondence with Benedetto Croce.[49] Both Merlino and Croce were to influence his understanding of Marxism. Both had identified features of Marxism concerning which they entertained grave reservations. In retrospect, it seems evident that their assessments were to contribute to Sorel's ultimate interpretation of Marxism as a philosophical, normative, economic, and revolutionary doctrine.

While Sorel undertook a careful reexamination of Marx's economic analyses during this period,[50] by 1899 his preoccupation with human beings as moral agents came to dominate his reflections.[51] It is in that context that Sorel began to draw together the ideas that might serve as a guide to what was transpiring among workers organized in syndicats. His first self-conscious formulation of revolutionary syndicalism appeared in the 1898 version of his *L'Avenir socialiste des syndicats*.[52]

During the final years of the nineteenth century, Sorel reviewed all of those Marxist tenets that had become "orthodox" in the minds of many. He began to reflect on human psychology, and how human conduct is influenced both by circumstance and moral choice. By the turn of the century, he explicitly abjured the notion of determinism and fatalism governing human history. He saw history as the varied product of intersecting choices undertaken by innumerable individuals each following his or her own moral imperatives.

It was in those circumstances that Sorel began to speak of labor as a school of virtue, with emphasis on the necessity of commitment, self-sacrifice, discipline, and solidarity in any productive enterprise. He found such virtues particularly evident among workers of the land, peasants and smallholders. Where Marx saw only the "idiocy of the countryside," and Labriola the "stupidity" of peasants,[53] Sorel saw devoted, industrious, sacrificial, family- and community-oriented agrarian workers whose sense of personal autonomy was fostered by the sovereign ownership of property and whose productivity sustained the urban working masses.[54]

In none of this is there any suggestion that Sorel sought a return to a preindustrial yeoman's economy. Rather, he anticipated a modern economy in which both urban and rural workers found their fulfillment in increasing productivity. In that, he echoed many of the sentiments of Pierre-Joseph Proudhon[55]—dismissed by Marx as never having transcended the "standpoint . . . of a French small-holding peasant."[56]

By the time he had compiled his *Introduction à l'économie moderne* in 1903,[57] Sorel was calling for a "true" socialist revolution, one having little affinity with that proposed by professional intellectuals. Sorel argued that Marxist intellectuals, as a subset of intellectuals in general, were so impaired by the disabilities of their manner of thinking that they sought to impose a revolution on the working classes that could only result in injury to individual liberty as well as massive erosion in productive potential. Sorel argued that the revolution anticipated by the "orthodox Marxists" who led the various European socialist parties in the pursuit of seats in parliament would inevitably result in a "dictatorship of ideologues"—with all the negative consequences attendant upon such an eventuality.

In parliament, intellectuals, as the ideologues of such a dictatorship, would perform the function of courtesans. They would serve to palliate, in a fictive, artificial, and indecent manner, the needs of those they represented. They could not offer satisfactory solution to the most fundamental of human needs: moral fulfillment. Sorel was entirely convinced that intellectuals who serve the interests of political power, undermine the intrinsic stability and moral integrity of any community.

By that time, Sorel saw intellectuals, with all their pretended detachment and objectivity, as villains in his morality drama. Intellectuals, never having to face the reality of significant choice, were incapable of serving as moral counsel for society. Sorel argued that this was particularly true of the intellectual in what are termed "democratic circumstances"—for the intellectual in such circumstances attempts to present a plausible rationale for a social order not based on family, or community, but on the rootlessness and self-absorption of unrelated individuals.[58] Like the intellectuals who would provide the rationale for the anticipated "dictatorship of the proletariat," the intellectuals who fabricate the vindication for parliamentary democracy, serve only to corrupt humanity and undermine the capacity for true moral choice.

By 1903, Sorel had begun to search for some system of political authority that might responsibly react to the increasing wretchedness of his time. He was convinced that the system fostered by the middle classes of Europe had produced an antinomian, feckless, and irresponsible individualism that augured ill for all Europe. He sought *ricorso*,[59] a reactive rebirth, some remedy to the ethical confusion and moral decay that typified, in his judgment, the increasingly decadent Europe of his day. Like Vico, he anticipated a return to the virtues of a bygone time, to those of the era of the Greek city states, to those of Rome at its zenith, and to those of the early Christian communities. Sorel sought the restoration of precisely those conditions through which individuals had, in the past, found the fullness of self—communities in which leadership was founded on the virtues of heroism, commitment, and good sense—communities in which, as a consequence, obedience, self-sacrifice, labor, and identification with the collectivity followed as a matter of course.[60]

Sorel had early made very clear that he had very little, if any, confidence in what passed as political democracy in the nineteenth century. In his *L'Avenir*, he spoke of "government by all the citizens" as a transparent fiction.[61] He characterized his ideal political system as that which prevailed in antiquity, in the Greek city states and imperial Rome. The very character of political authority in those circumstances could hardly pass as democratic in any modern sense of the term. The reality was that Sorel, as early as the first years of the twentieth century, spoke of a form of political authority that had features that would become increasingly familiar in the course of the emerging century. By the first years of the twentieth century, Sorel had entered into full intellectual maturity. Thereafter, he was to produce those works that were to exercise influence over revolutionary thought throughout much of the twentieth century.

THE REVOLUTIONARY SYNDICALISM OF GEORGES SOREL

Sorel published the works that would define his Marxist heterodoxy at about the same time that Ludwig Woltmann was putting together his own interpretation of Marxism. In that interpretation, Woltmann insisted that any comprehensive ontological "materialism" would necessarily include the "biological materialism" of Darwinism—from which he drew the racist consequences that were to influence the thought of the National Socialists of the twentieth century.[62] Sorel's heterodox Marxism, destined to have equally far-reaching sway, was fundamentally different from that of Woltmann. Both thinkers, each convinced that his thought was firmly rooted in the doctrines of Marx, led revolutionaries in radically different directions.

In 1905 and 1906, Sorel published in Italian and French a series of articles in *Il divenire sociale* and *Mouvement Socialiste*, later to appear as *Réflexions sur la violence*,[63] a volume now considered critical in any effort to come to understand the revolutionary thought of the last century. We are advised not only that we will find in its pages "a deep and constant preoccupation with ethical standards," but that such a preoccupation was to become increasingly common, by the turn of the century, particularly among revolutionary socialist thinkers in both France and Italy.[64]

Between 1904 and 1910, Sorel put together in a single volume the opinions in which his Marxism found its most mature expression. First as a series of articles and then as a single work, his *Réflexions sur la violence* quickly became part of the sustaining convictions of many socialist revolutionaries.

Réflexions sur la violence was different from some of Sorel's earlier works insofar as the volume attempted to supply readers with a very general account of the nature and function of revolution within the context of a decadent and failing civilization.[65] During the last years of the precedent century, employing the insights of Renan and Proudhon, Sorel had devoted his attention to civilizations both in ascent and decline. He went on to outline what he held to be the social and specifically moral functions of revolutions in such circumstances. In the *Réflexions*, all those considerations came together, drawing out all the implications of his earlier work.[66]

Sorel's work was singularly notable because it cast itself athwart the thought of some of the most formidable interpretations of then contemporary Marxism. Most of those Marxist thinkers of the first decade of the twentieth century who found merit in the orthodoxy of Karl Kautsky were convinced that socialism represented a kind of "moral historicism"—with history automatically resolving the most fundamental ethical problems then troubling humanity. Socialism was simply the fulfillment of a kind of moral destiny. History, through the mechanisms made familiar by Marx, would automatically end in an all-embracing moral crescendo in which humankind would find all physical and spiritual needs satisfied.

In Sorel's *Réflexions* we find an entirely different conception of history, morality, and the possibilities of a restoration of individual and collective virtue. In *Réflexions*, morality is not something delivered by the automatic workings of history. It is something that is won in conflict through individual and collective effort. Virtue is the result of mortal challenge. It is something won by *groups* in fatal contention. Collective virtue is the consequence of the spontaneous acceptance of a set of ethical principles by the denizens of a community, living in peril, led by heroes in epic battle against decadence and moral cowardice. Only those circumstances can ensure the victory of morality, and the sublimity, valor, and personal dignity that would inevitably follow.

What emerges from Sorel's prose is an image of a Manichean world in which the forces of light find themselves forever in mortal combat with those of darkness—in which good is eternally at risk, requiring perpetual defense. Sorel provides an image of a world in which good and evil are forever in uncompromising contention—in which the survival of virtue is never assured, but ceaselessly subject to challenge. For Sorel, true virtue surfaces only on rare occasion. He found such virtue in the poor, warlike tribes of yesteryear, filled with "an enormous aristocratic pride," in incessant struggle against their enemies.[67] It makes its appearance, once again, in the Greek city states; then in the march of the legions of ancient Rome; then in the survival of the first Christian communities; and then in the recesses of some medieval monasteries. Other than that, humankind lives in a cursed creation, forever threatened by the prospect of a life to be endured without honor, dignity, rectitude, or purpose.[68]

Sorel's exposition is suffused with an almost unrelieved pessimism.[69] The modern world is decadent because the rationale sustaining almost all its institutions is predicated on an abiding and grasping individualism, an uncritical conviction that community is the result of the voluntary coming together of individuals in order to achieve personal happiness.[70] Individual happiness is conceived an inalienable right, something to be obtained automatically, without the cost of sacrifice, discipline, labor, or commitment. The inevitable consequence of such notions, for Sorel, was moral decay.

Contemporary parliamentary, representative democracy typified, for Sorel, the intrinsic disabilities featured by the modern world. In contemporary democracies, individuals came together only in order to struggle in concert, each in pursuit of individual ends, to the total neglect of organic, collective interest. For Sorel, modern democracy "shared a great resemblance" with the stock exchange, where self-serving egoists labor in the same space, but not in union, to satisfy selfish interests.[71]

Sorel saw his time beset by the intersection of several negative trends: there was the increasing dominance of the merchant and industrial bourgeoisie, animated by an insistent individualism and materialistic scientism. There was expanding political democracy, predicated on the hedonism and selfishness of the self-absorbed heirs of the Enlightenment and the French Revolution. And then there was the narrow opportunism and crass thirst for power that irresistibly drove the political leaders of reformist, meliorist socialism to compromise in parliament with the enemies of rectitude and seemliness. In Sorel's judgment, all these trends came together to create an atmosphere entirely devoid of any saving grace.

For Sorel, the "new socialism," of which he was advocate, was a movement of moral regeneration for a civilization mortally ill. While he was convinced that his "new school" fully represented the spirit of Marx, he acknowledged Marx's errors, as well as the "rubbish" broadcast by some of his followers.[72] As distinct from the orthodoxy of Kautsky's Social Democracy, the clear intent of Sorel's Marxism was to create the conditions that would foster the moral regeneration of a lost humanity.[73] Sorel's new socialism sought a total renewal of the human spirit, a moral rehabilitation that would require the employment of a number of very specific instrumentalities for its realization. Revolution would have to be the first order of business, and that would necessarily entail the mobilization of "inert masses . . . who are not accustomed to thinking."[74] That would demand mentoring, since masses are both totally unaware of the threatening circumstances in which they find themselves as well as how such threats might effectively be met.[75]

All of that would necessitate the selection and preparation of "rather small bodies whose members [would be] rigidly selected by means of tests designed to confirm their vocation." Those selected would serve as an "elite," the most "vigorous and virile" among those committed to salvific revolution. They, "less numerous and well selected, [would] lead the . . . struggle." They would "create the ideological unity" among the masses required "to accomplish . . . revolutionary work."[76]

The ideological unity necessary to effect revolution would be a function of the employment of a mobilizing *myth*—by virtue of which persons would be called to revolutionary responsibility. In itself, Sorel understood the myth to be a linguistic artifact composed of a set of convictions, secure from all refutation, and unaffected by criticism. On the occasion of its invocation in socialism's war against decadence, such a myth would be made up of "a body of images which, by intuition alone, and before any considered analyses are made, is capable of evoking as an undivided whole the mass of sentiments which corresponds to the different manifestations of the war undertaken by socialism against modern society." In general, such a mobilizing myth is a "framing of the future"—that encloses within itself "all the strongest inclinations of a people . . . which recur to the mind with the insistence of instincts," thereby supplying the energy necessary for revolutionary enterprise.[77]

It was clear that Sorel did not conceive myth to be a cognitive product. He held that it was not reason that moved masses to action. Reason, alone, does not inspire; it is devoid of the emotive energy that stirs human beings to combat, and to victory at whatever cost. Sorel argued that it was myth, as an integral whole, that projected itself into the future as a goal—and inspired human beings to sacrifice. Myth functions as motive, as an inspirational idea that fosters and sustains those noble sentiments that inspire epic virtue, virility, and heroic conduct. Sorel insisted that "as long as there are no myths accepted by the masses," there will be no revolution. The myth, in effect, must not be judged as a creature of intelligence, gauged against some measure of abstract truth, but "must be judged as a means of acting on the present. Any attempt to discuss how far it can be taken literally as future history is devoid of sense," and misses the point of the myth's function. Through myth, ideas are recognized not as "scientific" truths, but as motive forces.[78]

Sorel offers instances of myths that have shaped history. He speaks of the myth of deliverance that animated the saints and followers of the Church militant as one historic instance. He cites the instances of those myths that inspire dissident religious sects to combat—in which each of the contending groups conceives itself an army of truth fighting the legions of evil.[79] He writes of the Italian *Risorgimento* as shaped by the nationalist myths of Giuseppe Mazzini.

For Sorel, the myth of his time was the myth of the general strike, the universal laying down of tools calculated to overthrow the oppressor regime beneath which workers would otherwise forever languish. The general strike, inspired by mythic energy, would be "a phenomenon of war," which "like the Napoleonic battle," would seek to "annihilate a condemned regime." The myth would galvanize masses to epic conflict out of which emerge "the elements of a new civilisation" and a new, more sublime, and lofty morality.[80]

The attempt to understand Sorel's notion of social and political myths, together with their role in mobilizing masses in the service of revolution, takes one to the very core of his variant of Marxism. To understand something of his revolutionary strategy requires that one address epistemological issues of fundamental significance. In making his case for the role and nature of myth in social life, Sorel himself turned to the contemporary philosophy of Henri Bergson. He held that any serious effort to understand the character and function of social and political myth might well require "the enlightenment" to be found in "Bergsonian philosophy."[81]

SOREL AND THE PHILOSOPHY OF HENRI BERGSON

Sorel was apparently familiar with the work of Bergson as early as 1889, when Bergson's *Essai sur les données immédiates de la conscience* appeared. We know Sorel read Bergon's *L'Evolution créatrice* as soon as it became available in 1907.[82] Taken together, Bergson's writings were understood to give expression to a "life philosophy"—an attempt to interpret all reality in terms of life—to distinguish it from the physicomathematical empirical researches of the last decades of the nineteenth century that tended to reduce everything to matter in motion. Through the last half of that century, the success of natural science had been arresting. By coming to understand reality through the parsing out of discrete components interacting in lawlike fashion, science had come to understand the world in uniquely mechanistic and deterministic form. Its predictive success had convinced the nineteenth century that the complexity of the object world, and everything in it, could be reduced to objective and analytic components, in terms of atoms, ergs, electromagnetic waves, and other nonobservables. All of which could then be reordered in accordance with fixed laws.

In the final analysis, everything was reducible to "matter" in various configurations and permutations. Human consciousness, courage, passion, will, commitment, sacrifice, and every property of a life lived, was ultimately nothing other but the epiphenomenal product of bits of primordial matter interacting in accordance with the fixed laws of an evolving universe devoid of spirit.

The successes of standard natural science in terms of general utility convinced many that the process could reveal all the "truths" of "reality," both physical and psychological. Everything was conceived reducible to law-governed, discrete, and measurable units in space. The result, as has been suggested, was a form of *scientism*, in which both the subject and object world were understood to be fully explicable in accordance with determinate lawlike processes.

Bergson objected, in principle, to such an attempt to understand living organisms as though they were machines functioning in conformity with predetermined, calculable regularities. He rejected all its attendant implications. He maintained that reality was not to be understood in terms of measure, particularity, and causal determinism. There are those qualitative features of life lived that escape quantitative measurement. One does not understand life and living by pretending that they are to be captured through the measurement of discrete material particles traversing successive locations in space in equally discrete instances of time. Bergson argued, instead, that *consciousness*, not matter, was at the center of reality, and consciousness was not to be measured in independent units reconstructed in time via causal connection. For Bergson, it was consciousness as duration, as life, that lies at the center of reality. Life, like consciousness, was organic, and like life, consciousness was a continual becoming—and becoming had precedence over discrete and discontinuous being.

Bergson refused to speak of consciousness in terms of "states"—of discrete segments. To him, all of that suggested stasis, immobility. He rather spoke of a conscious life, lived in continuities—in which all the states, to which empirical psychologists allude, merge into an enduring sense of awareness, uncertain, indistinct and moving, a surge and flow, a "certain restlessness." Life, Bergson argued, seeks survival and is instinctively moved to manipulate its environment—it is possessed of an urgent tendency to attempt to "act on inert matter."[83] The idiom through which that tendency finds expression is geometric, mathematical. The functional agency that gives it shape is the intellect. The intellect imposes geometric, mathematical measure on the generous flow of experience. Beyond and prior to the intellect and its products, Bergson isolates that which he identifies as "intuition"—an appreciation of the dynamics of life that invokes in us an immediate sense of duration and becoming, a sense of continuous and evolving life that transcends the intellect and its discrete and measurable representations. The immediate truths of intuition are independent of, and antecedent to, the truth conditions governing physical science.[84]

Bergson argued that out of the immediate awareness of life, human beings, finding it necessary to adapt to the demands of a challenging environment, proceed to isolate out of that sensed reality those measurable, abstract, and general aspects of things that allow them to be functionally useful. To meet their needs, human beings reduce the qualitative flow of consciousness, of life, into the discrete and serviceable being of quantitative units.

In effect, Bergson argued that there are two spheres of coming to know: on the one hand, that of space and rigid matter, the proper domain of practical intelligence; on the other, that of vital impulse, enduring awareness, and intuition. The latter, we are told, transcends intellect and reason, and offers communion with the vital reality that is the ground of all things— even if that communion can be appreciated only in fleeting fashion.[85]

Bergson was to contend that the practical intellect was sterile without the impulse of intuition. Human beings pursue practical knowledge because they are moved by the demands of life. Intuitive awareness, charged with vital impulse, informs the will to act. Intuition becomes one with the act of willing. It delivers the occasion for choice, for "free will," for human freedom. For Bergson, as for Sorel, freedom to choose is the very essence of meaningful life.

The mistake made by contemporary thinkers, Bergson contended, is to attempt to force life, the very consciousness of life, into the static units and measures natural to the intellect. The mistake becomes most emphatic when empirical psychology attempts to understand consciousness and life in terms of physicomathematical formulae. The consequence of that mistake is a conception of life in which there is no will, no free choice, no purpose, and ultimately, no comprehensible meaning. For materialists, living is subject to an overarching determinism, a law-governed array, in which organisms are conceived to be the analog of machines that function in conformity with fixed and calculable regularities. The practical intellect is called to service in an effort to comprehend life itself—as though the part might understand the whole.

These were the ideas that Sorel was convinced would illuminate his "theory of myths more thoroughly."[86] In fact, the relationship of Bergson's views to those of Sorel do afford considerable insight into the nature of the mobilizing myths to which Sorel made appeal in his effort to understand the complex processes involved in social and political revolution.

Bergson's philosophy of the nature of science and understanding supplied the specific context for Sorel's discussion of the nature of physical science and its relationship to the human disposition to act. As early as his "Etude sur Vico," Sorel insisted that human beings conjure up mathematical formulae in order to survive in a threatening universe. Like Bergson, he went on to argue that mathematics was an instrumentality employed to our immediate material purposes. Beyond that, human beings suffer a profound and abiding need to act in a living space that is nonmathematical. That space demands moral judgment of human beings—and there the scientific method is of no direct avail.[87] Standard science, in and of itself, is only of ancillary assistance in the articulation of moral judgment and its defense.

It is largely around these issues that all the discussion of the "irrationalism" of Bergson and Sorel collects itself. Sorel is regularly spoken of as an "irrationalist"—as someone who simply renounced reason. Just as often it is said that he rejected science. In fact, Sorel, like Bergson, rejected neither reason nor science. Both renounced the vulgar rendering of science in which science is understood to do more than establish the truth of the laws of force, mass, and velocity—it reduces the sum of human behavior to nothing other than similar mechanical and measurable regularities.

As a man of his time, whatever his reservations concerning mathematicological reasoning, Sorel was inextricably a man of science. As an engineer in government service, he was a scientist in the most practical sense of the word. A substantial part of his published work, in fact, was addressed specifically to scientific questions.[88] Like Bergson, Sorel rejected neither the empirical, nor the mathematicological, methods of science. What he refused to countenance was their application, without qualification, to the entire range of human conduct. Sorel regularly alluded to precisely that when he complained of Marxism's inability to account for the moral constituents of the individual and collective human will to act.

Worse still, in Sorel's judgment, was the utilitarian materialism that Engels attempted to impose on Marxism as a philosophic system. Sorel complained that however vague and ambiguous Marx's own doctrine might have been, it was Engels who sought to make of Marxism a vulgar materialism that was irremediably deterministic.[89]

Like Bergson, Sorel contended that consciousness, the psychological life of human beings, could not be reduced to the lawlike regularities of matter in motion. Bergson argued that, in the final analysis, it was human consciousness and human choice that established what would count as evidence conditions for truth claims. And whatever scientific truths might result, it was ultimately and exclusively the will that inspired action. In and of itself, science cannot inspire acts of devotion to duty, the willingness to suffer in order to participate in the defense of virtue, the acceptance of material loss in the course of fighting for others, or the submission to martyrdom solely "for the honor of taking part in immortal deeds."[90] The intellect, in and of itself, does not inspire one to such enterprise. Intuition and will are critical, "nonrational" constituents of the process.

It is not clear to what extent the thought of Bergson shaped Sorel's revolutionary conceptions. It seems certain that Sorel knew of Bergson's analysis at the time he gave expression to his first intimations of the role of myth in the mobilization of masses. It is equally clear that Sorel welcomed Bergson's support. By the time *Réflexions sur la violence* appeared, Bergson's views on the role of intuition and will were well established and were compatible with those of Sorel. Both the role of myth, as well as the motive force of action in intuition, finds a rationale in Bergson's metaphysics.

Granted that, it is nonetheless true that Sorel remained a qualified Marxist throughout the entire period from the mid-1890s until the time of the appearance of the *Réflexions*. Neither his Bergsonianism nor his defense of Bernstein constituted a rejection of Marxism. Like Bernstein, Sorel argued that to be true to Marxism one was required to be critical and reflective of the inherited philosophical and economic doctrine. Unless wedded to an archaic notion of what philosophy and science might entail, those true to Marx were obliged to critically assess the cognitive merits of the principal propositions of the system Marx left as a legacy.[91] Equally clear is the fact that Sorel intended to divest Marx's thought of the misinterpretations and the distortions that, over time, obscured its most important features. In that effort, he refers more and more frequently to insights found in Bergson's work.

That is not as unusual as it may seem. There were some credible affinities between Bergson's work and that of Marx. There was, for example, Bergson's readiness to acknowledge the fact that the human intellect possessed the unique "faculty of manufacturing artificial objects, especially tools." He was, in effect, thereby satisfying the Marxist conviction that human beings were uniquely tool-making animals—a faculty that shaped their material and spiritual environment.[92] At least in such measure, Bergsonianism was compatible with Sorel's Marxism.

Beyond that, Bergson supplied Sorel with an account of intuition and will that made the determinism of the then regnant positivism no longer defensible. By the turn of the twentieth century, Sorel was convinced that science had grown out of the mechanical positivism that inspired so many during the mid and late nineteenth century. By the first years of the new century, many behavioral scientists had forsaken any notion that human conduct might be fully understood as the result of the intersection of law-governed biomathematical sequences. The corollary of that was the conviction that "there is no process by which the future can be predicted scientifically"—given that human behavior, in essence, is subject to moral choice and contingent decision.[93]

By the time he had written *Réflexions*, Sorel's heterodox Marxism took on some of the properties that had become common among those critical Marxists in Western Europe relatively independent of the constraints of German Social Democratic orthodoxy. Like the neo-Kantians, Sorel raised ethical and moral issues that the orthodox refused to, or were incapable of, answering. Sorel spoke of the general vagueness and ambiguity that made the inherited system difficult to interpret. He questioned the plausibility of the materialist metaphysics that sustained Marxism as a cognitive enterprise.

That final reservation was related to his conviction that a consistent materialism could hardly account for the role played by ethical deliberation and moral choice in individual and collective behavior. He found that those who considered themselves orthodox Marxists were unequal to the task of accounting for the psychology of human beings in association. Like the revisionists, Sorel raised questions concerning the economic and social preconditions of revolution and what that might imply with respect to the mobilization of masses. Finally, he sought to identify the specific instrumentalities involved in moving masses to revolution—and he spoke of those special agents, those elites, whom history had charged with the responsibility of both shaping and marshaling warrior producers to the salvage of a decadent world.

By the first decade of the twentieth century, in the years before the First World War, classical Marxism had already suffered some of those modifications that were to make it an instrument for an unanticipated variety of revolutions. In the course of that same decade, in the East, one of those varieties was to inspire yet another heterodoxy. Before it ran its course from triumph to tragedy, it was to impact the lives of millions upon millions—and would forever be associated with the name of Vladimir Ilyich Ulyanov—Lenin. It was said of him that he must have carefully thought over the work of Georges Sorel and proceeded to apply some of its central principles "with the most terrifying logic."[94]

CHAPTER FIVE

The Heterodox Marxism of V. I. Lenin

The heterodox Marxism of Georges Sorel was to have documented impact on the thought of many European Marxists. Where it could not be documented, there was intrinsic evidence of its influence. There were those, in fact, who argued that V. I. Lenin's revolutionary strategy was a derivative product of revolutionary syndicalism.

In the immediate aftermath of the Bolshevik revolution, serious Marxists sought to understand what had transpired. Not a few among them spoke of Lenin's variant of Marxism as sharing unmistakable theoretic and practical affinities with the revolutionary syndicalism so popular in France and Italy. Like the syndicalists, Lenin's Bolsheviks rejected efforts at social reform within the existing structure of industrial capitalism. Like the syndicalists, the Bolsheviks ultimately came to reject parliamentary democracy and electoral politics. Like the syndicalists, the Bolsheviks were advocates of violent class struggle. Both rejected politicians and professional labor leaders. They both advocated direct action by the proletariat in demonstrations, work stoppages, sabotage, and boycotts culminating, ultimately, in the insurrectionary general strike—to result in the revolutionary overthrow of the "bourgeois state" and its entire institutional infrastructure.[1]

Whatever the ideological similarities shared by the thought of Georges Sorel and Lenin, however, there is no convincing evidence that Lenin ever consciously accepted any of the doctrinal elements of revolutionary syndicalism. It is unmistakable that the Leninism which inspired the Bolshevik revolution displayed features of the revolutionary thought of Sorel. How that came to be involves considerable speculation. Certainly the similarities shared find their origin in something more than simple doctrinal mimicry.

However cosmopolitan Vladimir Ilyich Ulyanov—Lenin—may have been, everything we know of his revolutionary education indicates that his thought was shaped largely, if not exclusively, by Russian Marxists, whose opinions were those of central European orthodoxy.[2] That orthodoxy, during the last years of the nineteenth and the first years of the twentieth century, was to have a unique history in the lands subject to the rule of the czars. Originally finding expression in the stolid orthodoxy of Georgi Valentinovich Plekhanov's Emancipation of Labor Group, it was to evolve into the heterodox Marxism known to history as Bolshevism.

Originally a student of Plekhanov, Lenin was to become prophet of a moralistic, dogmatic, and intolerant Marxism that, like Sorelianism, repudiated parliamentarism and representative democracy. It was a heterodox Marxism that proclaimed, for the first time in history, the legitimacy of elite dominated, single party, ideological dictatorship. That there were features of Sorelianism in all of that is undeniable. As the heterodox thought of Ludwig Woltmann was to go on to influence Hitler's National Socialism, that of Georges Sorel was clearly to survive in Bolshevism.

GEORGI PLEKHANOV AND
THE EDUCATION OF V. I. LENIN

Plekhanov, born in 1856, originally occupied with social and literary interests in his youth, turned to Marxism during the first years of the 1880s. In 1882 he translated *The Communist Manifesto* into Russian, and in 1883 published his *Socialism and the Political Struggle*, qualifying him as czarist Russia's first serious Marxist. In that same year, he became one of the founders of the Emancipation of Labor Group, Russia's first explicitly Marxist organization. It was committed to the mobilization and organization of the revolutionary Russian proletariat.

It was Plekhanov who laid the theoretical foundation for Marxist Social Democracy in Russia. In that enterprise he clearly benefited from the guidance of both Karl Kautsky and Friedrich Engels with whom he entered into correspondence during the 1890s. As a consequence of those influences, Plekhanov published his *The Development of the Monist View of History* in 1895, an unreflecting, entirely orthodox rendering of Marxism as a deterministic philosophy of history.

In that volume his audience was informed that only in the writings of Karl Marx might one find the cognitive strategies necessary for the establishment of a true social science. That was accomplished, Plekhanov argued, by revealing that the flow of history was determined primarily by the invention of "implements of labor." Tools, the implements of labor, were critical to the "development of the means of production," a development that necessarily "brings about changes in the social structure." The "social relations into which the producers enter with one another, the conditions under which they . . . participate in the whole act of production, will naturally vary according to the character of the means of production. . . . Thus social relations . . . are transformed with the exchange and development of the material means of production, the productive forces."[3] The "development of the productive forces," Plekhanov insisted, is "decisive" in the formation and stability of "social relations." Taken together, productive forces and the dependent social relations constitute the "mode of production" which "always determines" the "psychology of society," out of which arise all "ideologies, . . . every literary movement, every philosophical idea," all "legal conceptions." In effect, all "human thought," according to Plekhanov, is determined by the same kind of lawlike regularities governing the mechanical regularities of all matter.[4] For Plekhanov, it was Marx who discovered all those deterministic laws governing the history of humankind. As Darwin revealed the laws of biological evolution, Marx outlined the laws of historical development.[5]

Within that general context, and echoing the orthodoxy of German Marxists, Plekhanov understood revolution to be a function of changes in the mode of production. When the forces of production outgrow extant social relations, revolution is the result. "Struggling social forces" are the necessary consequence of emerging "real economic relations." Out of "a certain economic basis there invariably arise certain ideological superstructures . . . law, justice, morality, equality and so forth" which inform revolutionary conviction.[6] Classes, representing each of the struggling social forces, express their group interests in ideological terms. Those classes that represent the material productive forces that have outgrown existing social relations rise up in rebellion. Revolution happens, and that class, representing the emerging productive forces, inevitably triumphs. In that triumph, humanity prevails over necessity in the sense that "knowing the peculiar inner laws" of socioeconomic development, one can act in conformity with them. In our times, that class, destined to triumph by acting in conformity with the peculiar inner laws of social development, is the proletariat. The inner laws of development produce the bourgeoisie, and the bourgeoisie in obedience to those same inner laws, must necessarily call forth the factory proletariat destined to replace them. Given the unimpeachable fact,

Plekhanov argued, that Russia had embarked, irreversibly, on the "path of capitalist development," as had England and Germany before it, its future was inevitable.[7]

Given such a catalog of convictions, it was evident that by the turn of the nineteenth, and the first years of the twentieth century, Plekhanov had pledged Russian Marxism to an orthodoxy no less insistent than that of Kautsky and the intellectuals of the German Social Democratic Party. Plekhanov renounced the revisionism of Bernstein, the racial materialism of Ludwig Woltmann, the philosophical antimaterialism of Bergson, and, by implication, the historical moralism of Sorel.[8] History, and the derivative human behavior that provided its surface detail, were determined, in the last analysis, by the development of the material productive forces that lay at the foundation of collective life. Neither biological race nor moral conviction served as factors in human performance. The ontological and sociological materialism Plekhanov embraced allowed no room for Bergsonian or Sorelian philosophical alternatives nor for factors, other than those economic, in the shaping of history.

It was to that arid Marxism that Lenin first gave his full allegiance. It was that Marxism he was to transform into Bolshevism.

In tracing the development of Marxism into Bolshevism as an ideology, it is relatively simple, in retrospect, to identify the crucial junctures at which a singular clutch of ideas came together to give shape to Leninism as a variant. It is generally agreed that one of those junctures can be located at the point in time when Lenin wrote his *What is to Be Done? Burning Questions of our Movement*.[9]

In 1901, at 31 years of age, at a time when both Woltmann and Sorel were publishing their own variants, Lenin wrote *What is to be Done?* Published in Stuttgart, the work provided the first elements of that heterodox Marxism subsequently to become the rationale of Bolshevism. The Bolsheviks were to serve as the executive agent of a revolution that was to not only fatally influence Russian, but world, history as well.

What is to be Done? was a work that grew out of the vaguenesses and ambiguities inherent in the works of the founders of revolutionary Marxism. For all of Plekhanov's efforts at explication, so much of classical Marxism remained, at best, uncertain in expression, fragmentary in delivery, analogically reasoned, and empirically suspect, that it was logically impossible for its most gifted followers to decide specifically what all its claims, much less their entailments, might be. So many interpretations of classical Marxism were possible at the beginning of the twentieth century, that some critics could find only contradictions in its doctrines, while its enthusiasts could insist on its illuminating consistencies. In effect and in fact, there were Marxists who insisted that there could only be one Marxism. At no point in time, however, was that ever true.

Since the death of Friedrich Engels in 1895, Marxist variants proliferated. Which of the subsequent Marxisms were "creative developments," which heterodoxies, which heresies, and which apostacies, is impossible to determine with any intellectual confidence. One can only attempt to document changes in doctrine and allow others to render judgments concerning their orthodoxy.

One thing seems evident in all of this. There is no objective standard against which departures from Marxist orthodoxy might be measured. As has been suggested, both Woltmann and Sorel made persuasive arguments that Engels's own departures from classical Marxism, following the death of Marx, constituted, in themselves, heterodoxies.[10] All that notwithstanding, it was clear that Engels was convinced that everything he had written was Marxist in inspiration, and entirely Marxist in content.

The theoretical legacy left by Marx was so rich in content, so vast in its possible implications, and sometimes so obscure in formulation, that there really were very few ideas, no matter how curious, that it would be impossible to find within its compass. Woltmann provided evidence of that—as did Sorel. Woltmann found a singular Darwinism and an implied racism within the doctrinal abundance that was Marxism.[11] The implications of that Darwinism and that racism were carried forward as a Marxist heterodoxy, for a quarter of a century, into the ideology of National Socialism. Sorel, for his part, found an implicit moralism in the writings of Marx that freighted a transformative heterodoxy in its train.

Like all the others, Lenin was to find in the writings of Marx and Engels, the elements out of which he would fashion his own variant—a variant with which the twentieth century was to become familiar. In the years following the death of Engels, from the vantage point provided by Kautsky and Plekhanov, out of a tangle of uncertain interpretations, Lenin was to put together an assorted collection of ideas that were to take shape as Bolshevism.

DARWINISM, MARXIST ORTHODOXY, AND THE PSYCHOLOGY OF REVOLUTION

With the passing of Engels, there were several theorists who could reasonably be considered Marxism's intellectual heirs. Eduard Bernstein and

Karl Kautsky were certainly among their number. For whatever reason, Bernstein's heterodoxy was almost instantly established to almost everyone's seeming satisfaction.[12] Kautsky, on the other hand, was generally considered a spokesman for orthodoxy. For present purposes, it is not necessary to establish that orthodoxy—something that would be impossible—given the essential vagueness and indeterminacy of the original doctrine. That need not be a problem. It cannot be part of the obligation of this account to determine the measure of orthodoxy or heterodoxy of any of the variants of the original Marxism. Still less is it an obligation to explore the distinction between any orthodoxy of Kautsky's theories, and the real or fancied "revisionism" of his political practice. That is not of central interest to the present discussion.

More important is an assessment of some of the specifics of Kautsky's thought: How ethical theory figured in his orthodoxy, and how his interpretation of ethics and moral behavior functioned as components in his understanding of historical materialism. It was that measure of orthodoxy that transferred directly into the publications of Plekhanov, who quickly emerged as Russia's premier Marxist.

It was clear to Kautsky, as it was to Plekhanov, for example, that human volition played a role in history—and that human volition was influenced by moral considerations, ethical precepts, and political prospects. That issue had fueled much of the controversy out of which doctrinal "heterodoxies" were to arise among credentialed Marxists. What was uncertain was how ethical reflection and moral imperatives were to be understood in all their intricacies and effects.

A few years after the publication of his *Ethik und materialistische Geschichtsauffassung*, Kautsky felt called upon to once again address the question of the place morality, ethics, and human volition occupied in classical Marxism as a science of society. In 1909, he published his *Der Weg zur Macht*,[13] a fairly comprehensive survey of what he conceived to be a "maturing socialist reality" in advanced industrial nations. According to his views, the maturation of industrial economies was directly correlated with the increased probability of anticapitalist revolutionary success. Like most Marxists of the period, he held that not only would full industrialization render socialist revolution more probable, but that it would, in a clear sense, render it inevitable. He was convinced that as capitalism achieved full maturity, the sustaining human will necessary for the success of socialist revolution would manifest itself.

The general argument was that the socialist revolution, of which Marx had spoken, was inevitable—because capitalism, as an economic system, was condemned, by the laws governing its own dynamics, to produce the millions of exploited victims who would serve as its "grave diggers." That having been affirmed, what was required was an intellectually satisfying account of how all that might transpire. The assurance that revolution would be inevitable required an argument of some considerable sophistication to render it credible.

Kautsky regularly alluded to the ineluctability governing society in general and revolution in particular. Like Plekhanov, who shared his views, Kautsky essentially repeated the claims that lay at the core of the work of Marx and Engels. What was missing, as both Woltmann and Sorel argued, were those connecting propositions that plausibly related changes in the economic base to the moral decisions that governed the behavior of revolutionaries.

One of the problems on which critics regularly focused was that Marxism seemed to characterize historic processes as *deterministic*, and revolutions as *fatalistic*.[14] As such, human intervention was, in a significant sense, *automatic*. While seemingly the consequence of conscious choice, intervention was a lawlike response to externalities. No real choice was involved.

In coming to grips with some of those issues, Kautsky, and Plekhanov who was to follow, were scornful of critics who imagined that Marxism was a belief system that saw only economic factors active in history—as though history, in effect, proceeded independently of the will of man. Once again—as had any number of Marxist theorists before them—both Kautsky and Plekhanov reaffirmed that *no* serious Marxist ever believed that the flow of history was automatic, advancing without the conscious participation of human beings. That having been said, it was not immediately evident what the practical implications of such assertions might be.

Kautsky, with much more specificity then Plekhanov, went on to attempt an explication of what he understood was involved. He argued that human volition is a function of the interaction of *instinct*, *custom*, and *conscience*. Just as he had argued in his *Ethik und materialistische Geschichtsauffassung*, he spoke of the Darwinian "instinct of survival" as providing the psychic energy that infilled human individual and collective will. So moved, human behavior was characterized by an instinctive defense of life. More than that, the instinct, in more complex circumstances, prompted a disposition to seek not only survival but gratification in increased measures of satisfaction. As an illustrative case, Kautsky cited the fact that beyond their Darwinian instinct to survive, capitalists seek personal advantage, the maximization of profits—just as one would expect workers, once immediate survival was as-

sured, to assiduously seek wage increases. It was out of just such predispositions that an "inevitable" class conflict was predictable. Kautsky's interpretation of Darwinism rendered class struggle both inevitable and voluntarily
chosen—given their instincts—by the participants.

At a more theoretical level, Kautsky argued that the instinct to survive
and attain satisfaction, among the higher primates, is systematically influenced by prevailing group custom. Individual behavior is adapted to existing social circumstances by peer group and situational constraints until conforming behavior becomes habitual. For the individual, the consequence is
that behaving in a conventional fashion, complying with group pressures
to conform, becomes comfortable—and the conforming individual is spoken of as being "good" or "proper." To act in accordance with group norms
is to act "morally." Once the behavior becomes habitual, one is said to act in
accordance with one's "social conscience." To act otherwise would be to act
contrary to social norms and would typically result in an uneasy conscience
and group rejection.

To change instinctual and habitual individual and collective behavior,
according to Kautsky's account, requires that the motive force of instinct,
and habitual conformity, be modified by powerful external influence. Such
influence, Kautsky maintained, could only come as a consequence of major
changes in surrounding "life circumstances"—which meant, essentially, a
change in the manner in which individuals and society met their survival
and welfare needs.

Kautsky went on to argue that meeting those needs directly involves
production. According to the orthodox Marxists of the beginnings of the
twentieth century, changes in human behavior, *in the final analysis*, were
understood to be the consequence of changes in that very economic activity: how things are produced and how they are distributed.

Given the uncertain dynamics involved in the original empirical claims
advanced by its founders, Kautsky was compelled by his responsibilities as
an advocate to catalog the external influences Marxism held to be capable
of affecting individual and collective human conscience. As part of his argument, Kautsky engaged the standard Marxist account of social dynamics.
As long as the forces of production remain compatible with the relations of
production, the patterns of social conduct remain essentially unchanged—
they "reflect" the functional economic base. In such circumstances, individual and collective behavior remains essentially habitual, routine. Only
when the existing productive relations can no longer accommodate the
changing productive forces do tensions emerge that move society to seek a

new equilibrium—and both individuals and groups are forced to alter their conduct.

At such a point in time, the economic base of society is no longer unambiguously "reflected" in prevailing social norms or in the behavior of group members. The "contradiction" between productive forces and productive relations *somehow* generates an effective revolutionary will among those elements of society that will restore equilibrium once more. Human *conscience*, as the most flexible of the factors governing conduct, serves to suitably alter habitual, to provide the rationale for revolutionary, behavior. That change is the consequence—once again, in the final analysis—of the tensions wrought by the technologically developing material productive forces within the confines of what increasingly becomes dysfunctional class relations.

The increasing incompatibility of productive forces and productive relations is spoken of as part of a revolutionary "ripening" of society. In the case of industrial capitalism, it means that society has created conditions conducive to systemic social change. That revolutionary ripening is described in standard Marxist terms as the result of a series of interlocking effects: technological improvements alter society's manner of producing goods; the new technology, because of its very nature and requirements, renders impossible its employment by individual artisans; instead, workers are drawn together into expanding industrial sites to labor at machines as cost effective "wage slaves"; they are paid subsistence wages and live in a state of threat and increasing penury; in times of abundance, their wages do not rise as rapidly as prices; in times of economic contraction, they lose the opportunity to work for their subsistence and are menaced by starvation; the maturing of industrial capitalism draws more and more individuals into its labor force; as a consequence of the rapaciousness of major capitalist enterprises, the middle classes increasingly are reduced to the level of wage workers; ultimately, as a consequence of its intrinsic nature, unable to profitably empty its inventories, the maturing industrial system gradually collapses into stagnation and final crisis. The entire sequence is unavoidable—the result of a law-governed process. The socialist revolution becomes inevitable. Given some specific set of special circumstances for each locality, one can predict the transformative outcome with the full assurance of science.[15] Individual and collective choice is dictated by developments at the productive base of society.

In all of this, as both Kautsky and Plekhanov insisted, individual and collective human conscience has played an integral part. One intuitively expects individuals and groups of individuals to seek to avoid exploitation.

One intuitively imagines that individuals and groups of individuals nurse a sense of moral grievance in such circumstances. That sense of outrage can be expected to fuel revolutionary enterprise.

Social processes so conceived, Kautsky could confidently maintain that "the breakdown of the present social system [is] unavoidable, because we know that . . . economic evolution inevitably brings on conditions that will compel the exploited classes to rise against this system of private owner-ship."[16] The system, he went on, necessarily multiplies the number and strength of the exploited, and diminishes the number of the exploiters, par-ticularly those of the middle classes, so that ultimately only two classes, the grand bourgeoisie and the proletariat, face each other with increasing hos-tility and increasingly disparate capabilities. The outcome of the struggle is fully predictable.

Why all this should take place *inevitably* is predicated, in the last analy-sis, on the economic theories of Karl Marx—his "labor theory of value," his "theory of necessary and surplus value," his "laws" of the increasingly high rate of "organic composition" of capital, the related "declining rate of profit," capital concentration, and so on. Together with the predictable loss of more and more members of the impoverished lower middle class to the growing proletariat, industrial capitalism creates, with the escalating misery that attends its expansion, all the necessary conditions for revolution.

Among other things, such an account all-but-eliminates the possibility that "great men," uniquely gifted individuals, could have any significant in-fluence in the process[17]—any more than great men could influence the rate of free fall of objects in a vacuum, or might influence the predictable eclipse of the sun. Kautsky, like Plekhanov, believed that society evolved in accor-dance with what were held to be confirmed empirical regularities. There was hardly a place in the unfolding of such regularities for the "arbitrary" intercession of "unique" individuals, or groups of such individuals.

After providing his account of the inevitability of the process,[18] and the nature of the role of individuals in it, Kautsky went on to tell his audience that while the conditions of capitalist production ineluctably produced a revolutionary disposition among the relentlessly increasing majority of cap-italist society's exploited masses, one had to recognize that the process was not "automatic." As has been suggested, both he and Plekhanov insisted that the entire process depended on the willed participation of individuals and groups of individuals. However glib the account, it was surrounded by an unmistakable scent of paradox. Kautsky certainly seemed fully aware of the problems.

Kautsky proceeded to attempt a satisfying resolution. He supplemented his account of instinct, custom, and conscience with a further analysis of that "free will," of which "metaphysicians" spoke—that free will that critics imagined was essential to the successful mobilization of workers for revolution. Kautsky distinguished between an arbitrary will and that will that was the product of a determinate environment. A "determinate will" is "free," but the actions it inspires are not "arbitrary"[19]—they are the result of the influence of all the factors cataloged in standard Marxist recitations.

What Kautsky sought to deliver, in effect, was a *psychological theory* that pretended to explain voluntary action. Unlike Woltmann or Sorel, he did not attempt a *philosophical analysis* of normative claims. He sought, rather, to deliver a law-governed, sociological account of normative choice. Moral choice was not to be vindicated; it was to be explained.

Kautsky consistently describes human action as being given initial impulse by the will to survive. Behavior is then shaped by custom, and then differentially inspired by conscience. The will to survive is an evolutionary by-product. Habit is the result of social reinforcement. Habituation to patterns of behavior has survival advantage in a Darwinian world of group competition—consequently, we expect human beings to be creatures of habit. Conscience, in turn, allows tactical adjustments in instinctive or habitual behavior. Those adjustments are functional in communities regularly undergoing changes in "life conditions." Individuals and groups involved in the process act freely, yet in a determinate fashion.

Using that line of argument, Kautsky sought to explain "free" will in the context of what he believed to be a law-governed determinate sequence. In that context, he treated conscience as though it were an adaptive mechanism, functional in an environment that demanded some fundamental change in individual and group behavior at specific intersections in time and development. Such changes would be the result of deliberation involving economic imperatives—the satisfaction of substance, protection, and welfare needs. As the economic system evolved, human beings acted "freely," as conscience dictated—with those dictates emanating from determinate realities.

Kautsky fully accepted the general Marxist understanding of the nature and causes of revolution. According to Marxist theory, revolution was the result of changes in the economic base of society. As the forces of production evolved, the relations of production were compelled to adapt. That adaptation became manifest in the voluntary behavior of humans—with conscience as its lever. Conscience was one of those "phantoms in the mind" through which economic needs found idiom.

All of that having been said, there clearly was something more to conscience and will than had been suggested by their depiction, in the foundational literature of Marxism, as simple "reflexes" or "phantoms" of an economic base. That was the theoretical insufficiency with which orthodox Marxists struggled.

Satisfied with his version of the relationship between human choice and the economic base, Kautsky dismissed the entire discussion concerning the nature of ethical discourse initiated by critical Marxists, neo-Kantians, and Sorelians at the turn of the twentieth century. Neither Kant nor Sorel was taken seriously. They were "bourgeois spokesmen"[20] who pretended that individual human beings were free to make moral decisions based on ethical precepts having little, if anything, to do with prevailing economic conditions.

When critics spoke of moral choice and an informed consciousness influencing human behavior, individual and collective alike, orthodox Marxists seemed content to argue, with Kautsky, that "we consider the breakdown of the present system to be unavoidable, because we know that the economic evolution inevitably brings on conditions that will compel the exploited classes to rise against this system of private ownership."[21] "Free will" certainly could neither independently alter human conduct nor the course of events. History proceeds as a consequence of human actions, but those actions are "free" only in the sense that they are undertaken by conscious persons who deem them proper. Kautsky's argument was that they are willed actions that result from determinate conditions, conditions that themselves are the inevitable consequence of the "laws" discovered by Marx and Engels and embodied in the nineteenth-century orthodoxy of historical materialism.

What all this suggests is that should there be individuals unaffected by the impact of the social laws discovered by Marx, they would remain eccentrics in their environment. History would simply pass them by. They would be ineffectual passengers on an historic journey governed by natural processes over which they had no influence. However initially persuasive such an account may appear to be, the difficulties that crowd around it quickly become evident.

If Marxist theory is to account for the behavior not of eccentrics, but of normal participants in historic action, Kautsky is required to deliver some insight into how changes in the economic base of society alter human behavior so that the entire sequence is entirely predictable. For all the analytic machinery invoked, and the persuasive language employed, the relationships between the economic base and the psychology of participants in the historic process are nowhere specified with testable precision. The plausibility of the assertion that the anticipated, or actual, breakdown of the economic system would compel entire classes to act in a *specific* manner is less than self-evident. To rely on intuitions concerning processes that "compel" individuals, and groups of "exploited" actors, to undertake revolution of a specific kind suggests reliance more on faith than science.

It is well documented that Kautsky believed that while it appears that ideas, moral convictions and ethical precepts, "cause social development," the fact is that "ideas spring from material wants," and that if ideas change from age to age, "the changes were the results of alterations in economic conditions, that is, in the system of production."[22] While such ideas influenced the account found in Plekhanov's *The Development of the Monist View of History*, they do not tell us much. To argue that changes in economic conditions are correlated with changes in ideas does not establish that the latter are simply reflexes of the former. To proceed from economic conditions to ideas, moral convictions, ethical conscience, and active choice would seem to require a great deal more persuasive evidence than is available in the formulations of either Kautsky or Plekhanov.

The reality of that is suggested by Kautsky's recurrent attempts to more successfully address the issue of how human beings become infused with the determinate will that makes revolution a predictable certainty. By the beginning of the twentieth century, Kautsky complicated his original delivery by informing his readers, in more than one place, that ideas, in and of themselves can, in fact, influence individual and collective behavior. In his emendation of the original account, the direction of causal influence sometimes appeared reversed.

As his argument matured in time, Kautsky argued, for example, that different groups among the proletariat, all of whom suffered the same exploitation at the hands of capitalism, manifested significant differences in behavior dependent upon whether they had, or had not, been exposed to Marxist social and economic theory. He cited the notable differences in the behavior of those labor organizations imbued with Marxist theory when compared to the behavior of those groups that were not.

Innocent of Marxist theoretical insights, proletarian elements, in response to economic realities, do indeed oppose their oppressors, but proletarians possessed of Marxist theory succeed not only in opposing their oppressors, but in organizing themselves more effectively. Moreover, they succeed in inculcating in their members a more certain sense of class-consciousness.[23] Apparently in some circumstances, ideas, in the form of Marxist theory, did seem to make some sort of difference in mounting the forces necessary for revolution.

Kautsky seemed convinced that there were intermediate steps in explaining the correlation between the economic system and human behavior—and those steps involved pedagogical responsibilities on the part of revolutionary leadership. With the passage of time, Kautsky seemed prepared to argue that in the course of discharging its pedagogical responsibilities, revolutionary leadership influenced the conduct of the proletarian masses in a fashion that affected individual and group conscience—to alter, to whatever degree, the "ineluctible" course of history.

Such an account introduced the possibility that, somehow or other, within all the inevitabilities, the choices made by individuals, singly or in groups, sometimes make a difference. How much impact that difference might make is difficult to determine given the expository texts available.[24] Nonetheless, in the effort to explain how changes in the economic base of society might be reflected in the consciousness of revolutionaries, it became eminently clear to Kautsky that all the presumed relationships were far more complicated than any Marxist theorist had anticipated.

It is clear that in attempting his explanation, Kautsky was prepared to acknowledge the role of ideas, morality, and conscience in somehow influencing human conduct. "Reflecting" the economic base in consciousness was beginning to appear to involve very complicated procedures.

At the time Kautsky wrote *Der Weg zur Macht*, it was uncertain what might count as Marxist orthodoxy with respect to the issue of the role of ideas (moral or otherwise) in influencing the behavior of a sufficient number of individuals to actually modify the "inevitable" collective responses required by the Marxism of Marx and Engels. By the beginning of the twentieth century, various Marxist theoreticians were to attempt to provide a satisfactory answer to such questions. In the years that were to follow, such questions rose more and more insistently among revolutionary theorists. They are questions that arise as a consequence of any serious inspection of the claims made by Marx and Engels as early as the 1840s.

In his effort to account for the role of ethics and morals in the history of humanity, what Kautsky provided was, at best, a highly speculative, and only partially formulated, psychological theory that attempted to explain individual and collective choice. It is intuitively clear that, in almost any given situation, human beings are faced with options. Compelled to allow for human choice, and a role for morals and conscience in making those choices, Kautsky attempted to limit the discretionary scope of human behavior to parameters dictated by Marx's theories. In the final analysis and actual fact, his account provides for little more than the semblance of choice.

To be told that Marxist theorists are compelled to inculcate proletarians with their beliefs, and that proletarians have no choice but to accept such beliefs, is to make a mockery of human deliberation and human responsibility. What appeared to be, at times, an allowance for the influence of ideas in the unfolding of events, seems to have been sufficiently hedged about so that Kautsky actually denied the substantive reality of choice. It is an interpretation that would render human choice not much more than a shadow of that expected by moral philosophers. Choices become, once again, implausible "reflections" of economic realities. In one place, even after all of his elaborate speculations concerning instinct, custom, and conscience, Kautsky could still insist that the most "beautiful dreams of well-meaning enthusiasts," concerning social goals to be attained, are really not much more than reflections of "economic development."[25]

In some places, Kautsky goes so far as to depict human choices as sharing all the determinism of natural laws. His rendition could not have been satisfying to those, like Sorel, specifically interested in ethics and morality—nor to those, like Woltmann, who sought a serious psychological theory of human choice. It clearly was not satisfying to all those Marxists who advocated a "return to Kant"—or those, like Sorel, who saw moral choice the critical center of human virtue.

Kautsky's treatment did not attempt to explain the imperative character of normative injunctions. At its best, what Kautsky left to committed Marxists was an empirical explanation sketch, speculative at best, of individual and collective psychology, a fragmentary outline of what he thought might account for seemingly voluntary human behavior. To speak of that behavior in a fashion that makes choice little more than a reflection of economic conditions is to neither explain that behavior nor account for its moral character.

Kautsky did speak of intelligence influencing choice. Allowing that, it is evident that the properties of intelligence can hardly be captured by conceiving them "reflections" of anything. When we speak of human beings "reflecting," what we mean is that they are deliberating. The decision by revolutionaries to become Marxists is a result of conscious calculation involving not only an assessment of the empirical truths of historical materialism, but the inescapable influence of qualitatively distinct moral principles. The only possible manner in which human intelligence can be voluntarily mobilized to Marxist enterprise is by establishing the truth and moral persuasiveness of its theories. That, it would seem, requires at a minimum, a commitment to truth, as well as the availability of scientific criteria of truth determination, together with ethical precepts that contribute to the making of the ultimate choice.

In the course of all this doctrinal deliberation, during the last years of the nineteenth century, and the first of the twentieth, a young Lenin rehearsed, without apparent reservation, the entire catalog of standard Marxist tenets concerning social dynamics and the mobilization of revolutionary masses. He was to speak of revolutionary theory and its importance, and the responses made by human beings in a multiplicity of circumstances. He spoke with great confidence of the fact that Marx referred to his "economic law of motion of society" unequivocally as a "law of nature." He insisted that "social laws" were nothing less than those invariant regularities with which science had made us all familiar. Like Plekhanov, he informed his audience that Marx had discovered that of all the "spheres of social life," *productive relations* were basic and primary, "determining all others."[26]

At that stage in the development of his thought, Lenin insisted that the conviction that "the course of ideas depends on the course of things is the only one compatible with scientific psychology." That was true in his judgment because "only the reduction of social relations to production relations and of the latter to the level of the productive forces, provides a firm basis for the conception that the development of . . . society as a process of natural history." That, in turn, eliminates any notion that "modifications" of human behavior, and any attendant moral choices, are governed by "free will." Lenin, perhaps less sophisticated than Kautsky, simply contended at the time, that Marxism was predicated on the scientific truth of "determinism, which postulates that human acts are necessitated and rejects the absurd tale about free will."[27] He had not yet become fully cognizant of the kinds of problems that had collected around that account.

It was not long before Lenin was compelled to reconsider that interpretation of human behavior, in general, and revolutionary behavior, in particular. Driven by immediate concerns having more to do with party politics than philosophy or social science, Lenin's reconsideration was to have as much impact on the modern world as would the deliberations of Ludwig Woltmann. Even as Kautsky was putting together his most elaborate interpretation of the relationship of a society's economy and the moral choices of its denizens, Lenin embarked on an interpretation of Marxism clearly heterodox in substance and portentous in possibilities.

V. I. LENIN AND THE "CREATIVE DEVELOPMENT" OF MARXISM

By the end of the twentieth century, with the passing of Soviet hagiographers and acerbic anti-Marxist critics, it was generally accepted that Lenin was hardly an "orthodox" Marxist. Most historians and analysts seem prepared to grant that his modifications of the Masters' teachings were as substantial and theoretically important as those of Bernstein, Woltmann, or Sorel. In terms of political realities of the twentieth century, Lenin's revisions were to change the face of revolution, the nature of socialism, and the history of the twentieth century.[28]

Lenin's first major works, written before the death of Engels and the scandal over the revisionism of Eduard Bernstein, were characterized by the conviction that the works of the founders of Marxism were not to be altered in any fashion. Lenin was a person of unshakeable conviction. Once possessed of an opinion, he defended it against all objections and all evidence—until he fixed on an alternative—which he then proceeded to defend with equal inflexibility and conviction.[29] Lenin had convinced himself that he was the spokesman for an unyielding Marxist orthodoxy.[30]

Among his very first publications, written in 1894, about the time that Plekhanov was preparing his *The Development of the Monist View of History*, Lenin insisted that the dialectical method of Marx and Engels was nothing other than "the scientific method in sociology, which consists in regarding society as a living organism in a state of constant development," involving a process of successive stages, with one "growing inevitably . . . out of the preceding one regardless of whether men believe in it or not, whether they are conscious of it or not. Marx," he continued, "treats the social movement as a process of natural history, governed by laws not only independent of human will, consciousness and intentions, but, rather, on the contrary, determining the will, consciousness and intentions of men."[31]

The young Lenin imagined that such formulations were those to be found in the writings of Kautsky, to whom he appealed, at that time, for doctrinal guidance. Lenin recognized Kautsky as an intellectual leader among the heirs of the founders of Marxism. Kautsky had written a draft of the Social Democratic Erfurt Program of 1891—under the direction of Friedrich Engels—to thereby fix his orthodoxy in the minds of all Social Democrats.[32] In effect, Lenin had reason to fully identify Kautsky with the classical conventions of the founders of revolutionary Marxism.[33]

At the same time, political developments in Germany required appropriate response, and Kautsky, as one of the major intellectual leaders of the party, was charged with the obligation. One of the most persistent questions the party faced was what the role of the party and its leadership might be in the course of the anticipated inevitabilities.

Party doctrine consistently maintained that science had assured the ultimate victory of socialism. As part of the process involved, it also predicted a proper revolutionary response on the part of the "vast majority of proletarians." There was an emphatic air of automaticity about the anticipated revolution.

Everything the party had insisted upon for decades involved a conviction that socialist revolution was ineluctable. Given such convictions, it was not intuitively clear what purpose the party or its leadership might actually serve in such a sequence. As has been indicated, half a century before, Engels had written that "revolutions [are] . . . everywhere and always . . . the necessary consequence of conditions which were wholly independent of the will and direction of individual parties and entire classes."[34] If such were the case, what was the role of political parties, their leaders, or their members, in what was seen as an inevitable progression?

With time, even sympathetic commentators were troubled by the inevitability of the anticipated revolutionary process.[35] As has been indicated, by the turn of the century, Kautsky was compelled to address the entire complex issue. An adequate answer would have to resolve not only the issue of the place ideas, theoretical claims, ethical principles, and voluntary conduct occupy in the dynamic of the entire historic procedure, but more specifically what the role of the Social Democratic party and its leadership was understood to be in what was conceived to be an inevitability.

It was counterintuitive, therefore, that for decades, Marxist theoreticians insisted on the importance of theory in the conduct of revolutionary agitation. However inevitable the sequence, Marx himself had made the defense of theory central to his entire enterprise. Both he and Engels had assiduously fought those both inside and outside the revolutionary ranks in order to defend the integrity of their theories. Even though Marxist theory contended that true revolutionary theory simply had to be discovered—to be necessarily accepted by the proletariat—it was somehow essential that Marx's doctrine be rigorously defended. Somehow or other, the issue had become: how was one to explain the functional importance of theoretical truth in a revolutionary struggle whose outcome was predetermined?

It was evident that the founders of Marxism were convinced that correct theory was a necessary component of successful revolution. Revolutionaries were required to defend its integrity. After the passing of Marx, Engels understood the German Social Democratic party to be the purveyor of orthodox Marxism as well as its special champion. Somehow, the inevitable revolution required both.

Engels joined Kautsky in the effort to provide a rationale for the existence, maintenance, and perpetuity of the Social Democratic party. It was not enough for the party to perform an essential function; it must also be perceived as doing so. However inevitable the socialist revolution, the party must be seen as performing a nonsubstitutable service in the process. In a discussion of precisely those issues, written at the very commencement of the twentieth century, Kautsky maintained that "many of our revisionist critics believe that Marx asserted that economic development and the class struggle create, not only the conditions for socialist production, but also, and directly, the *consciousness* of its necessity." Such a notion obviously left little role for the revolutionary party.

Kautsky's response was to argue that such a conception of revolution was "mechanical." Mobilizing the proletariat was hardly that. It necessitated communicating to them the truths of Marxism—and that required effective organization. Both were party responsibilities in the linked chain of anticipated inevitabilities.

In making his case, Kautsky added still further complexities to his account of the fashioning of revolutionary consciousness—with its instinctual, conformist, and deliberative components. He insisted that the notion of a revolutionary consciousness necessarily manifesting itself automatically in the course of events was grievously misleading. The required consciousness, he went on, could not be expected to arise *spontaneously* (*urwüchsig*). "Socialist consciousness," independent of all its other complexities, he maintained, "is something introduced into the proletarian class struggle from without [*von Aussen Hineingetragenes*]." Introducing, defending, and propagating that consciousness was the peculiar responsibility of the party.

In the course of earlier discussions, Kautsky had maintained that the availability of correct theory influenced the behavior of revolutionaries. By the time he delivered his commentary on the draft program of the Austrian Social Democratic party at the turn of the century, he was prepared to insist that only the Social Democratic party, of all the extant political parties, could deliver just such theory and thereby assure "socialist consciousness" to the entire class of revolutionary proletarians. The *bourgeois intellectuals* of the party, he indicated, would educate the proletarians to their historic responsibilities.[36]

It is not at all clear, at the time, that Kautsky understood the full implications of his contentions. Certainly he, as had all committed Marxists, consistently maintained that true doctrine was essential to their purpose — although it had not been made clear why that should be the case. Within that context, by the turn of the twentieth century, Kautsky was prepared to recognize that it was the responsibility of "declassed" bourgeois intellectuals to produce it.

Marx, Engels, and Kautsky were all declassed bourgeois intellectuals. In the body of *The Communist Manifesto*, Marx and Engels had spoken of "a portion of the bourgeois ideologists, who have raised themselves to the level of comprehending theoretically the historical movements as a whole . . . go over to the proletariat."[37] In affirming that, they were clearly alluding to themselves. The founders of Marxism maintained that at some stage in the preliminaries leading to revolution, some bourgeois intellectuals would defect to the proletariat. How that happens — when the "principles, ideas, and categories" that motivate such intellectuals change from being reflections of existing social conditions to reflections of an alternative future — was uncertain. Proletarians presumably entertain the principles, ideas, and categories they do because those principles, ideas, and categories reflect *their* life circumstances — but why renegade members of the bourgeoisie should similarly cleave to those principles, ideas, and categories is left unexplained.

Neither Engels, Kautsky, nor Plekhanov undertook to explain the choices made by the bourgeois intellectuals who provided theory for the German or Russian Social Democratic party. The issue hung over Marxists without satisfactory explanation throughout its history. However the presence of bourgeois intellectuals in the party was to be explained, Engels, in his time, and Kautsky and Plekhanov in theirs, insisted on the existence of the party, armed with the orthodox truths of Marxism, as necessary for the mobilization, organization, and control of potential proletarian revolutionaries.

What was new was the clear insistence that without the theoretical activity of committed bourgeois intellectuals, and the availability of a party to effectively disseminate their products, the inevitabilities of the revolution might somehow be altered. That gave every appearance of making the inevitable revolution, in some measure, *contingent* on the cerebral activity of some select intellectuals leading a specific political party.

Kautsky had already argued that revolutionary ideas were essential to the inevitability of revolution; by the turn of the twentieth century, he was prepared to see the revolutionary party as an essential vehicle for the transmission of those ideas. While Kautsky may not have fully appreciated the implications of his position, it was not long before someone did make it all abundantly clear—to draw out implication almost entirely unanticipated by either Kautsky or Plekhanov.

In 1902, while Kautsky was still struggling with the issues, the thirty-two-year-old Lenin published his *What is to be Done?* In that single essay, he committed himself, and his followers, to the basic precepts of what were to become, and forever remain, the political fundamentals of Bolshevism, the single party state and its implied totalitarianism.[38]

In writing *What is to be Done?* the young Lenin echoed much of the assessment found in the earlier accounts made available by German Social Democrats. What perhaps distinguished his discussion was his absolute outrage at any evidence of "ideological instability and vacillation" among revolutionaries. He disdained those given to "unprincipled eclecticism"—for he held that only an orthodox "revolutionary Marxism," as he understood it, could "guide the world struggle of the proletariat."[39] It was self-evident that he was convinced that there was only *one, true* revolutionary Marxism and he was its spokesman. More than that, he was convinced that without correct theory, and its inculcation in the thought of the masses, none of the "ineluctibilities" of Marxism would mature.

Granted that, Lenin went on to argue that any ideologist "worthy of the name," must be responsible for solving "all the theoretical, political, tactical, and organisational questions" that the revolutionary movement might encounter, for in his view history had charged the movement's ideologists with the responsibility of guiding the proletariat on its "inevitable" course. To contend otherwise, he wrote, would be to surrender the entire enterprise to "spontaneity," and to the "opportunism" and institutional anarchy it brought in its train. The task of the revolutionary intellectual is neither to "worship" nor be "servile" with respect to any spontaneity that might manifest itself among the masses, but to "point out [its] dangers and defects," and *elevate* whatever spontaneity might be found among workers to the level of full revolutionary consciousness.[40]

Both before and after he wrote *What is to be Done?* Lenin made a distinction between the "material" ingredients of revolution and the "consciousness" that provided direction. He argued that "revisionism" arose out of the failure, on the part of revolutionary leaders, to appreciate the critical role played by *ideological truth* in the process. If the revolutionary intellectual, inspired by doctrinal truths, does not *lead* the proletariat in its spontaneous reaction to capitalist exploitation, the movement will be deflected from its course. Lenin lamented that there were those among the revolutionary intellectuals who "have elevated the worship of, and servility towards, spontaneity to the dignity of a theory and are preaching that Social Democrats must not march ahead of the movement, but should drag along *at the tail-end.*"[41] Thereafter, for Lenin, "tailism" was to remain one of the most grievous "revisionist" tendencies to afflict revolutionary Marxism. Revolutions were not spontaneous—leadership was required.

The revolutionary party, and the intellectuals who supplied its social theories and formulated its tactics, were responsible for leading the mass membership and converting those still uncommitted. Invested with such responsibilities, party intellectuals assume the historic obligation of creating and sustaining "a strong and centralised organisation," staffed exclusively by determined and resolute defenders of party ideology. Only in such fashion might party intellectuals effectively serve the inevitable revolution. Out of all that one sees the outlines of the single party state and the totalitarianism that follows.

For Lenin, the role of ideologists in the party, and the integrity of the party itself, required that party ideologists and all party organizations would have to be periodically "purged." Anyone guilty of doctrinal "diffuseness and the blurring of clear demarcations" would have to be excommunicated. Only through "internal party struggles" might a revolutionary party ensure its "strength and vitality."[42] Only then might "tailism" and "opportunism" be neutralized, and a "strongly welded," rather than a "diffuse," party emerge.[43]

In all of this one cannot help but see the features of the hero in history—the role of the committed, moral, sacrificial leader of masses, without whom, all the inevitabilities of history come to nought. Whatever the pretended rationale, Sorel's warrior elite makes its appearance and shapes the course of history.

Sorel had discovered all of this in Marxism even as Lenin was maturing to his responsibilities. In retrospect it is possible to unearth much of it in the writings of some of the principal luminaries of Marxism. Kautsky had said things that resembled those found in Lenin's *What is to be Done?*—which, in turn, seemed to echo things said by Sorel. The difference was that Lenin had drawn out all the theoretical and practical implications that had remained largely interred in previous accounts—to produce his own unique variant of Marxist "orthodoxy."

By the time Lenin published *What is to be Done?* his central theses were eminently clear. Any spontaneous, automatic revolutionary response by "masses," to whatever stimuli, would serve no purpose without the direct intervention of party intellectuals at several levels and during a variety of stages in the process. In the first instance, "without revolutionary theory there can be no revolutionary movement"—and the provision of theory involved inordinately more than might have been otherwise expected. Without the conscious intercession of a revolutionary elite, "inevitability" looked more and more like a contingency.

Lenin insisted that "without German philosophy, which preceded it, particularly that of Hegel, German scientific socialism—the only scientific socialism that has ever existed—would never have come into being."[44] He seemed to be saying that without the theory of scientific socialism, the inevitability of revolution would be compromised. Without those thinkers who produced German philosophy and German scientific socialism it seems that there would be no socialist revolution.

Granted all of that, there was something specifically "Leninist" in Lenin's account. Sorel had rejected the mathematicological character of social science. For Sorel, there could be no determinism governing human behavior. For Lenin, on the other hand, Marxism was a positive social *science*, sharing all the features of physical science. Lenin insisted that Marxism, as a social science, delivered itself of impeccable truths that did not require the kind of review the Sorelians and Kantian revisionists were advocating. Science, Lenin held, does not forever scrutinize claims, whether simple or complex. Science establishes truths, and makes no progress if it allows "old ideas" to coexist "side by side" with new ones. For Lenin, it was the unimpeachable scientific content of Marxism that certified the inevitability of revolution. So critical was its scientific credibility, its having been "proved," that Lenin insisted that only revisionists sought further review. Marxism, firm in its convictions, needed only to be adequately "studied."[45] Thereafter, for Leninists, there could be only one true, scientific Marxism—whatever the revolutionary party said it was. The party, and its leadership, were possessed of "Truth."

The revolutionary intellectuals, upon whom the revolution depended, had the responsibility not only of reaffirming the scientific truth of Marxism, jealously protecting it against dilution or contamination, but of dispensing it, in pure form, to the revolutionary masses as well. Without the truths of scientific socialism, the entire working class movement would remain confined to simple trade unionism. Workers would never mature to the political, and truly revolutionary, level of consciousness. In effect, "class political consciousness can be brought to the workers *only from without*," through the direct intercession of the party's declassed bourgeois intellectuals, the analog of the revolutionary elite of which Sorel spoke.[46]

Should all that be accepted, several considerations immediately thrust themselves forward. If revolutionary truth is one and impeccable, and is to be dispensed only with the insistence that it not be altered in any fashion, then those selected to perform that service must be forever under scrutiny. That implied that periodic purging would be institutionalized. In fact, at the commencement of his essay, Lenin quoted, with approval, Ferdinand Lassalle's comments on party purges: "Party struggles lend a party strength and vitality; the greatest proof of a party's weakness is its diffuseness and the blurring of clear demarcations; a party becomes stronger by purging itself."[47]

The "ideological leadership" of which Lenin spoke in both *What is to be Done?* and *One Step Forward, Two Steps Back (The Crisis in our Party)* implied a kind of control inescapably *hierarchical* and *centralized*—ultimately invoking a caesaro-papal authority to maintain coherence and integrity. Throughout his delivery, Lenin insisted on just such institutional features for his proposed revolutionary party. Equally explicit in his proposed reorganization of Russian Social Democracy was the need for *discipline* and *obedience*—all of which prompted cries, by the opposition, of an attempt by Lenin to impose a "theocracy" on the party, a "monstrous hypertrophy of centralism," which would require "blind submission" by its members, together with "a suppression of individuality" and an insistence on only *one* interpretation of Marxism and the tactics that interpretation implies.[48] These were the same charges leveled against Sorel.

Lenin consistently spoke of those who objected to his program for the hierarchical reorganization of the Social Democratic party as "anarchists," "opportunists," and "individualists," insisting that they were undisciplined and selfish in their resistance to the "formulated expression of the will of the whole." They refused to accept the revolutionary imperative that the revolution required party discipline and self-sacrifice.[49]

By the time he wrote *One Step Forward, Two Steps Back*, Lenin made a clear distinction between radical ideologists, who represented Marxist theory, and simple intellectuals. He understood ideology to be the exclusive responsibility of "revolutionary ideologists," and, like Sorel, expressed unqualified disdain for liberal "intellectuals." He spoke of such intellectuals, advocates of liberalism and parliamentary democracy, as "unstable" and singularly "opportunistic." Unlike the declassed bourgeois ideologists who served the party, simple intellectuals were essentially bourgeois in disposition, given to "vagueness, amorphousness, [and] elusiveness," as well as "aristocratic anarchism" and "opportunism."[50] Like Sorel, Lenin saw intellectuals as given to compromise and irresolute in judgment.

When he wrote *What is to be Done?*[51] in 1901, Lenin had been content to refer to the theoreticians and ideologists who provided the working class with a revolutionary conscience as "intellectuals." He was clearly more reluctant to speak of party ideologues as intellectuals in 1904. In the later work he seemed ill disposed to invest confidence in intellectuals, *per se*, whom he tended to see, as did Sorel, as self-serving and vacillating members of the bourgeoisie.[52]

A case can be made that his increasing estrangement from intellectuals, as an identifiable social segment, may have been a result of intraparty struggles after 1901. Whatever the case, Lenin seemed to have reservations concerning intellectuals after 1904 that he had not entertained prior to that time.

In 1901, Lenin still sought to "efface" all "distinctions" between workers and intellectuals, although he did acknowledge that there were fundamental differences between the tasks for which each group was responsible. Their respective tasks required markedly different talents. Moreover, Lenin believed that those who are both born with the talents necessary for intellectual work, and possessed of the appropriate revolutionary focus, are so few that they must necessarily constitute a "vanguard *elite*." Everything said by Lenin in his *What is to be Done?* indicates that he was, like Sorel, absolutely convinced that only such a select vanguard elite was capable of successfully leading the proletarian masses to Marxist victory.[53]

Predicated on the possession of impeccable truth, staffed by those responsive to no other truths, Lenin understood the single party elite as possessed of a terrible legitimacy to which no other leadership could aspire. Inspired by a doctrine of impeccable truth, the revolutionary party has a warrant to educate "immature" masses to the higher levels of revolutionary consciousness.[54] The truth serves the ultimate interests of all—even if that truth remains obscure to the majority it will benefit. As a consequence and in principle, the "epistemarchic" party can demand discipline and obedience of its followers. Any lack of discipline and any disobedience is evidence of ill will, ignorance, or stupidity. In whatever case, the transgressor becomes the object of political and social sanction. The party purges heretics and demands obedience and discipline from all members of the political community. Sharing major attributes with the most exclusivist religions, such modern revolutionary parties have been identified as "theurgical instruments," and "political religions."[55]

LENINISM AND MARXIST ORTHODOXY

It is not the case that such an involution of what had been an essentially rational and democratic revolutionary persuasion was only perceived in the long years between the Bolshevik revolution in 1917 and the "cold war" that followed the termination of the Second World War. Many in the very ranks of socialism foresaw the implications of Lenin's heterodox Marxism as early as its first expression in *What is to be Done?* Shortly after its appearance together with *One Step Forward, Two Steps Back*, Rosa Luxemburg published a long article in *Neue Zeit*, under the title, "Organisational Questions of the Russian Social Democracy"—only later to be entitled, "Leninism or Marxism?"

In her article, Luxemburg recognized all the ominous potential contained in Lenin's heterodoxy. In proper Marxist fashion, she pointed out that Russian Social Democracy lacked the maturity of working class movements that had arisen in advanced industrial environments. Russia's urban proletarians were few in number and scarcely inured to the productive responsibilities that Marxist theory held would render them proper denizens of an emerging socialist society. As a consequence, Luxemburg argued, one could hardly expect the workers of Russia to possess a social consciousness adequate to the discharge of revolutionary obligations.

In this instance, it seems clear that Luxemburg recalled Engels's admonitions to revolutionaries everywhere. In his discussion of the peasant war in Germany, for example, and his reflections on the fate of revolutionary Thomas Münzer, Engels reminded his audience that nothing worse could befall such a leader than to attempt to further a radical social program for which the necessary material preconditions had not yet matured. "The social changes of his fancy," Engels warned, would have "little root in the then existing economic conditions." The result could only be frustration. His "aspirations" would be "distorted in the crude minds of his mass of followers." His would be a "premature" attempt to put together a society possible only at a later period.[56]

In Luxemburg's judgment, these were much the circumstances in which Lenin found himself. In Russia, she reminded her readers, "Social Democracy must make up by its own effort an entire historic period." Russian workers remained "atomized" and socialists were compelled to attempt the building of suitable organizations with just such unresponsive members. It was easy to understand why the aspiring leaders of such a mass might insist upon "centralization," authoritarian, and hierarchical controls.

Luxemburg argued that Lenin was simply a product of the primitive conditions prevailing in czarist Russia. As a consequence of its circumstances, Lenin's Bolshevism must be, of necessity, equally primitive, opposed to any semblance of democratic "spontaneity" on the part of Russia's workers. Any loss of central control was conceived a threat to revolutionary purpose, allowing the potentially revolutionary mass to dissipate its energies in purposeless pursuits. That was the reason, in Luxemburg's judgment, why one of the principles to which Lenin committed the party was "the blind subordination, in the smallest detail, of all party organs, to the party center, which alone thinks, guides, and decides for all."[57]

In her relatively brief commentary on Lenin's proposals concerning the organization of the Social Democratic party, Luxemburg clearly perceived the first outlines of a new political party that would dominate the revolutionary history of the twentieth century. It was a party that for the first time in history would base revolution on the hierarchical organization and the direct mobilization, by an elite, of society's masses.

It was an elite-centered party, with a small minority of leaders, who, because armed with the most perfect knowledge about the world and everyone in it, are authorized to rule those who have not yet been raised to the same level of competence. Because of the lack of competence on the part of the masses, a Leninist revolutionary party would have but little confidence in a representative parliamentary system based on universal suffrage. For Lenin, the masses require informed and determined leadership. To fail to provide that leadership would be to fail in one's Marxist responsibilities.

Luxemburg perceived the Leninist party as one having assumed pedagogical obligations unlike any other. Ideally, Marxism sought the voluntary identification of masses with the ideology of the party. In Luxemburg's judgment, given the backwardness of Russia, that could only be a forlorn hope. Short of its accomplishment, Luxemburg argued, the revolutionary party expected the masses to simply submit to the "will of the center." She fully anticipated that under conditions short of pedagogical success, the system would become a party dominant, and perhaps personalistic, dictatorship over supine masses.[58]

Luxemburg's prescience was limited to Lenin's preoccupation with party organization and the consequences of that organization. Behind that preoccupation, and Luxemburg's analysis, a number of other issues remained almost entirely neglected. While it was evident that Lenin believed that the revolutionary consciousness of the working masses must be brought to them through the medium of a specially gifted vanguard, it remained unresolved how that vanguard itself acquired the requisite consciousness. As both Woltmann and Sorel had suggested, there was no simple causal relationship between the economic base and human psychology.

Lenin had argued that the proletariat, if left to its own devices, would develop nothing other than a "trades union mentality." Only the intercession of a fraction of the bourgeoisie, declassed and learned, animated by the revolutionary consciousness that had somehow failed to find a place among proletarians, could make of trade unionists, true Marxists. Revolutionary consciousness would have to be delivered to the proletariat by revolutionaries not of their own class.

How all this was supposed to take place is not in the least evident. It is difficult to imagine how the economic base of society could be reflected not in the consciousness of the proletariat, but in the consciousness of a few declassed members of the bourgeoisie.

Clearly there were difficulties with Lenin's conceptualization of how the entire process might work. Luxemburg was not obliged to deal with the same complexities. For Luxemburg, revolutionary consciousness arose quite spontaneously among the proletariat. Marx and Engels regularly suggested some sort of spontaneity in the development of class-consciousness. They often spoke of the activity of the proletariat being directly related to economic factors—being more manifest, for example, where there was "more developed industry, greater wealth, [as well as] a more significant mass of productive forces."[59]

The spontaneity of revolutionary consciousness to which Luxemburg appealed was in the tradition of many socialist theoreticians, Marxist and non-Marxist alike.[60] It was Lenin, in this case, who was a revisionist. While it is perfectly true that one can find allusions, in the many, many pages of the Marx corpus, to a multitude of possible interpretations of how the revolutionary proletariat comes to mature consciousness, Lenin's conceptualization of the process was clearly distinctive, if not unique, among the orthodox Marxists of his time.

The "vanguard elite" played a very special role in Lenin's revolutionary agenda. However one chooses to interpret Lenin's views concerning proletarian consciousness, a major question remains: how does the vanguard elite acquire the consciousness and will requisite to its historic purpose?

To attempt any answer at all, it is necessary to return to some of the same issues that occupied Dietzgen, Woltmann, Sorel, and Kautsky throughout the years before the turn of the century. Like them all, there are places in his writings where Lenin alludes to the *moral* considerations and party *ethics* that influence elite revolutionary judgment.[61] In fact, virtually everything Lenin wrote was quick with moral sentiment. He was consistently outraged by the behavior of his class enemies as well as any undisciplined conduct of members of his own party. All that notwithstanding, he refused to allow ethical judgment or moral choice any effective role in his account of how revolution proceeds. He affirmed, without qualification, that "in Marxism there is not a grain of ethics from beginning to end."[62] One is left to puzzle as to the source of his moral sensibilities.

LENIN'S ETHICS

If there is no ethics to be found in Marxism, it is difficult to understand how one might provide justification for the individual and collective decision to invoke violence, not to speak of terror, in the pursuit of revolutionary purpose. In one place, Lenin simply dismisses the issue as lacking substance.

To make his case, Lenin quoted a characterization of the generation of consciousness and the determination of will that Marx himself had found "absolutely correct." In the Afterword of the second German edition of *Capital*, we find Marx approving the following account: "Marx treats the social movement as a process of natural history, governed by laws not only independent of human will, consciousness and intelligence, but rather, on the contrary, determining that will, consciousness and intelligence."[63]

Lenin fell back on the tradition that took that to mean that the "ideal is nothing but the reflection of the material." The source of consciousness and the determination to act were understood to be a "reflection" of things taking place in the external material world. He repeated the notion that "ideas" of morality and ethics are epiphenomena, reactive products of "external, objective phenomena"—apparently unaware of all the failed efforts to make such an interpretation in the least credible.

However odd it sounded, given his views concerning the delivery of revolutionary consciousness by the vanguard elite, Lenin simply repeated some of the formulations of the Masters. He maintained that, irrespective of how deeply felt the conviction that one's behaviors are determined by moral ideas and conscious conviction, the truth was that neither ethics, will, nor consciousness was responsible for individual or collective conduct. The real causes were to be found in the impact of material life conditions on consciousness—following the patterns made familiar by those regularities governed by natural law.[64] It was a thesis that was more than familiar.

By the time Lenin wrote his first essays, many questions had already crowded around such notions. They were never to be really resolved by Marxists. They continually resurfaced in the reflections of revolutionaries throughout the twentieth century. As has been suggested, some traced the sources of lawlike human behavior to Darwinian imperatives, others to one or another form of utilitarian individual or collective judgment, and still others made recourse to a "return to Kant." None fared particularly well—a fact that is not surprising, considering the difficulties of distinguishing the differences between instinct, custom, and ethical judgment in informing the will.

Lenin's first treatments of ethics, moral conduct, and political will were deceptively simple. The initial forays were very quickly abandoned and he undertook more sophisticated analyses. One of his more comprehensive treatments of the subject appears in his attempt to deal with the thought of his political opponents.

In his critique, Lenin grappled with his opponents' understanding of both modern science and "moral ideas." In the course of the discussion, reference was made to class morality, i.e., bourgeois and/or proletarian morality, but also to an "abstract philosophical morality" that seemed to have neither as its reference. The concept of a morality that is not an immediate reflection of class interests thus made a brief, and suggestive, appearance in one of Lenin's earliest efforts to analyze the nature and function of normative decision. He was not to develop the idea of a morality independent of class interests any further, and it was not to play a substantive role in any of his discussions that followed. Thereafter, more or less consistently, the "object of the individual's spiritual life" was spoken of only as a "representation of the interests of one social class or another."[65]

The possibility of an "abstract philosophical morality" disappeared in the deliberations that followed. Lenin attempted to render a credible account of the role played by consciousness, ethics, and will in the course of history using only those concepts commonplace in the accounts provided by Marx and Engels. Unlike Dietzgen, Woltmann, Sorel, or Kautsky, Lenin made no consistent effort to provide an independent, compelling analysis either of the nature of morality or normative discourse.

Elsewhere in his critique of his opponents, Lenin fleetingly refers to another important notion that would influence all his subsequent revolutionary deliberations concerning loyalty, commitment, and self-sacrifice. In outlining Marxism as empirical sociology, he made recourse to the concept "group." It will be argued that like the notion of an "abstract philosophical morality," Lenin's special acknowledgment of the role that "groups," as distinct from "classes," might play in history was to prove of singular significance.[66] If there can be a morality that transcends class interests, and a group other than class to which that morality can be attached, the outlines of an entirely altered political ideology makes its appearance.

In his analysis, Lenin recognized that individuals, per se, were of little historical consequence. It was the behavior of *collectivities* that found expression in the "natural laws" that governed societies. Some of that was implicit in the writings of Marx and Engels.

Marx regularly referred to human beings as "group animals (*Gemeinwesen*)"—and Engels, in his *The Origin of the Family, Private Property and the State*, spoke of group life before the existence of classes. Before there were classes, human beings had organized themselves in communities of limited compass, and as Dietzgen, Woltmann, Sorel, and Kautsky had already suggested, their behavior, in substantial part, if not entirely, was a function of Darwinian social instinct and life lived in association. Those associations that existed through geologic time were not *classes*. Through much of prehistory, and all the stages of savagery and barbarism, human beings lived in collectivities that could hardly be identified as classes. There was, in effect, moral behavior long before there were classes.

In such a context, it becomes immediately apparent that Lenin's description of moral behavior as actions exclusively determined by specific class interests is less than convincing.[67] Together with the evident fact that there was morality and ethical conduct before there were classes, it seems manifest that the range of moral ideas prevalent in any society extends far beyond the number of possible class distinctions. Coupled with the reality of moral behavior and ethical concerns in society, before there were classes, is the acknowledgment that there are more moral divisions among the members of almost any society than there are class differences.

Most Marxists attempt to conceal that latter reality by obscuring the differences between divergent moralities. Anything other than Marxism is simply categorized as "bourgeois." Christians, Jews, social Darwinists, logical positivists, utilitarians, situational ethicists, pragmatists, and narcissists are all somehow "bourgeois moralists," representing an omnibus "bourgeois morality."

As though such problems were not enough, there are places where Lenin recognizes that Marxists share ideals with members of the *petit bourgeoisie*.[68] In fact, he speaks without embarrassment of common normative goals that appear to transcend class differences. He speaks of the development of "individuality," for example, as a positive goal more general than any that might be considered class specific. He deplores any conditions that "cramp," "suppress," and "stultify" the full development of self—conditions not limited to the capitalist epoch.[69] There is an intimation that self-fulfillment, as a value, is accorded a transclass and transhistorical validity—all of which suggests the possibility of a revolutionary doctrine that might address interests of a recruitment base that was multiclass or transclass in character.

It is clear that Lenin conceived self-fulfillment both as a moral goal, independent of class, as well as a realistic project only in an environment of full industrial maturity and the collective ownership of property. But the fact that he imagined self-fulfillment a realistic goal only under specific conditions does not diminish its transhistorical and transclass qualities. Self-fulfillment appears to have all the features of an intrinsic value against which all other values become instrumental. It would seem that behind Lenin's overt moral and ethical relativity there is the structure of a very different normative system that is universalistic, rather than class based.

Should such be the case, Leninism, as a variant of Marxism, might be construed the advocate of a society that provided the necessary conditions for individual development. It would be a creed that conceived revolution as instrumental to the realization of intrinsic, universalistic normative values. While some Marxist-Leninists were to attempt to articulate such a rationale in the long years after the establishment of the Soviet state, the effort was never convincing. Nonetheless, the recognition that there are features of Leninism that suggest different moral and ethical alternatives than those immediately orthodox is important for understanding the Marxist heterodoxies that were to follow.

Both Woltmann and Sorel pointed out that human beings have entertained universalistic values as long as human beings have had historic memory. Major Marxist theoreticians, including Friedrich Engels, seem to have recognized as much. They may have spoken of such values as premature, and as utopian, insisting that they were values that anticipated, rather than reflected, reality, but they did seem to acknowledge their real existence. For Marxists like Sorel, such values are an important component in any attempt to understand normative discourse and moral deliberation.

Sorel pointed out that it was clear that communism existed as a generic human ideal long before Marxists anticipated that it might become a reality. The ideal did not exist as a reflection of the maturation of the productive forces available to humankind—it preceded it. Unless one can talk coherently about the source and nature of these "premature" and "utopian" ideals, in and of themselves, one can hardly claim to have persuasively resolved some of the most basic normative problems that attend human individual and collective behavior.

Most of Lenin's discussion, like that of most Marxists, is occupied with how ideals are to be attained, not the moral or ethical quality of the ideals themselves. It is one thing to address the material conditions requisite to the achievement of ends and another to address the essential nature of those ends themselves.

Woltmann, Sorel, and the neo-Kantians emphasized those distinctions. Throughout the twentieth century, Marxist-Leninists continued to dismiss them as though they lacked consequence. They were mistaken. The fact that there are universalistic values that are not class specific, means that there are values that attach themselves, or can be attached, to associations other than those of class.

The fact remains that there are many values for which human beings have sacrificed throughout history that cannot be identified with any specific class interests. Moreover, human beings have chosen to sacrifice for such values whether those values might be realized in their lifetimes or not. It may or may not be true, as Lenin insists, that only by representing the interests of an emerging economic class might one effectively participate in real social change[70]—but that is a problem in applied social science and tactical politics, not an intrinsically ethical issue. Lenin sometimes seemed to understand that—and apparently felt that it was one of Marxism's merits that it evoked in its followers a willingness to self-sacrifice. For all that, he went on to tell his readers that Marxism "subordinates the 'ethical standpoint' to the 'principle of causality'"—a suggestion that one's sacrifice is not moved by ethical considerations but by is caused by the lawlike regularities of economic determinism.[71]

The best that one can make of the position assumed by Lenin was that there are universal human values quite independent of class interests, but that it becomes possible to realize them in practice only when society achieves a peculiar stage in social evolution. Only then does a social class appear that is compelled to make those values its own. Clearly Lenin deplored exploitation, in and of itself. He no less deplored violence and war, in and of themselves. He approved of multifaceted individuation, peace, compassion, fellowship, freedom, and justice—but, in his judgment, all such values were nothing more than "claptrap" as long as they were impossible of realization in circumstances of productive backwardness and the exploitative productive relations that necessarily result.

In the midst of the avalanche of writings of the period between the turn of the twentieth century and the First World War, Lenin touched upon themes that were to transform his Marxism. He spoke of the role of ethics and morality in human behavior—and of the role of mass mobilization—and that of a special elite of revolutionary intellectuals in the process. He spoke of groups other than classes as the objects of commitment and sacrifice. He directly or tangentially addressed almost all the themes found in the heterodox Marxism of Woltmann and Sorel. And he spoke obliquely of a political system totalitarian in character that would bring true humanity and fulfillment to the entire world.

What that clearly implies is that Lenin entertained a much more complicated system of political beliefs, group dynamics and normative convictions than he was prepared to explicitly acknowledge. Had he pursued their implications, he would have had to acknowledge the intellectual poverty of much of that which he pretended to make his own. In the making of history, he would have had to acknowledge the role of human associations other than class. He would have had to acknowledge the role of universalistic moral principles in the shaping of conduct. Lenin seemed forever unwilling to pursue his analyses to their ultimate conclusions. As the world teetered on the brink of the First World War, there were others prepared to go where Lenin was not. Among them was another heterodox Marxist, who was to put his stamp on our time.

CHAPTER SIX

The Heterodox Marxism
of Benito Mussolini

The only evidence of the presumptive influence of the thought of Georges Sorel on Bolshevism is found through a content analysis of the publications of V. I. Lenin—and speculation on his familiarity with some of the works of revolutionary syndicalists.[1] That influence can be traced without question, on the other hand, in the case of the doctrinal deliberations of Benito Amilcare Andrea Mussolini. We know, with documented assurance, that by the age of twenty-one Mussolini had read and reflected upon at least some of the works of Sorel.[2]

Mussolini was born in Romagna, in northern Italy, in 1883, and had early identified himself as a revolutionary socialist. His father had been a well-known "internationalist" (as socialists identified themselves at the time), and the young Mussolini never concealed his Marxist proclivities. In 1901, at the age of eighteen, he published his first essay, abandoned the Catholic faith, and made public declaration of his socialist convictions. At almost the same time, he departed Italy for Switzerland to avoid conscription into military service.[3]

In Switzerland, Mussolini undertook the study of social science with singular application, and at one point enrolled in the University of Lausanne, to audit a course on political economy conducted by the internationally celebrated Vilfredo Pareto. During that period, he published a review of Pareto's *L'Individuel et le social*. At the same time he translated manuscripts from German and French for publication.[4] By then, he had become familiar with Sorel's first essays on the role of revolutionary violence in history. Soon afterward, he identified himself with the thought of revolutionary syndicalism—that radical Marxism inspired by Sorel.[5] Before he came under the influence of Sorel, Mussolini had established his Marxist orthodoxy in a number of publications. The most important of them was an antireligious tract, written in 1904, that was clearly inspired both by the Marxism of Marx and Engels, and the scientific skepticism of nineteenth-century positivism.

THE MARXIST ORTHODOXY OF
THE YOUNG MUSSOLINI

At the very commencement of the twentieth century, the young Mussolini, thirteen years Lenin's junior, embarked on a career as a socialist intellectual[6] and agitator. He was a convinced Marxist, thoroughly committed to the notion that capitalism would inevitably suffer the catastrophic collapse inherent in the deterministic "laws" that governed the system.[7] He was as persuaded as the most orthodox of Marxists that the entire "superstructure" of society—its religious beliefs and morality, as well as the individual and collective behavior it sponsored—were simple "reflexes" of its economic base.[8]

Barely having turned twenty years of age, Mussolini's Marxism was inflexibly "orthodox"—as orthodoxy was understood by German Social Democracy. He had absorbed the doctrine well. He advocated the overthrow of the entire capitalist system and the destruction of the "bourgeois state." Like other Marxists, he imagined that, with the revolution, the bourgeoisie, as a class, would disappear. All that would be accomplished by assiduously pursuing the class struggle. The expropriation of "bourgeois property" would necessarily follow—to be administered and productively employed by the working class, already competent to the task.[9]

It was during that time that the young Mussolini, as a socialist revolutionary, took it upon himself to publish a pamphlet on Marxism and religion. For a small publishing house, established by himself and his friends—grandiloquently called The International Library of Rationalist Propaganda—Mussolini wrote a brief antireligious pamphlet entitled *L'uomo e la divinità*, in which was recorded his public response, in Lausanne, Switzerland, to an account advanced by a now forgotten Christian evangelist.

It was basically a compendium of what had become standard antireligious, rationalistic, and positivistic arguments against the existence of a supernatural creator—as well as a diatribe against the organized church that pretended to represent him on earth. For current purposes, the pamphlet is interesting because it contained some reflections that have relevance in terms of the evolution of Marxist thought in the twentieth century.

In his essay, Mussolini refers to many of the issues that had collected around Marxism by the turn of the century. Among them, the issue of a Marxist ethics occupied some space in this, his first extended discussion of his revolutionary convictions.

Like most of the orthodox Marxists of his time—Karl Kautsky and V. I. Lenin among them—Mussolini stated unequivocally, "for us 'morality' is nothing other than one of the elements of the ideological superstructure of human society, product of the actual substratum of economic conditions; it changes as the economy changes"[10]—which, like other such formulations, actually says very little of substance. Upon any inspection whatever, it might mean a variety of things.

In one place, for example, Engels suggested that to say that morality is the product of economic conditions might mean nothing more than that before men can philosophize or moralize, "they must eat, drink, have shelter and clothing."[11] Human beings can think, and entertain moral reflection, only if they survive. In order to survive, they must nourish themselves. In that rather trivial sense, their thought is *dependent* upon an available economic base—a "product of the actual substratum of economic conditions." If that is what the young Mussolini meant, it really tells us little if anything. It said little more when it was memorialized by Engels.

To be told that morality changes as economic conditions change is not to be told anything much more substantive. That moral behavior, and its ethical rationale, may change in a variety of fashions as a consequence of changes in the economy, is hardly a revelation. "Applied morality" sometimes appears very different from the "pure morality" from which it derives—none of which tells us anything illuminating concerning the origins of ethical principles or the moral conduct they vindicate.

All of that is perhaps too demanding when one considers the thought of the young Mussolini, or the thought of Lenin, both of whom framed their discussions concerning ethics and moral behavior in essentially the same fashion. Both, at approximately the same time, simply reiterated and reaffirmed, without the pretense of analysis, some of the apparent core beliefs of classical Marxism. Without an effort to unpack such familiar claims, one is left with the clear impression that the young Mussolini believed that moral, ethical, and philosophical consciousness, in general, was composed of nothing other than "reflections" and "phantoms in the brain"—epiphenomena of the economic base of society.[12] Mussolini spoke, for example, of bourgeois morality being "modeled" after the circumstances in which the rising bourgeoisie found itself in its economic, and subsequent political, struggle against the traditional nobility and the ensconced clergy of post-medieval Europe. Somehow or other, the moral principles that governed the lives of human beings were understood to be a function of their class circumstances. Ethical behavior was conceived to be a simple reflex of the specific economic interests of a select number of human beings.

Together with the recitation of some of the commonplace features of classical Marxism found in Mussolini's tract on religion, there were some oblique references to issues not so easily classified—but which brought to mind some of the questions concerning ethics and morality unintentionally raised by Josef Dietzgen and specifically emphasized by Ludwig Woltmann. They were questions alluded to only indirectly by Lenin and Engels.

Like Lenin and Engels before him, Mussolini made recourse, in his exposition, to a specifically "human morality," that he opposed to that which was religious—a morality that apparently transcended class interests and which addressed itself to "universal humanity, universal brotherhood, and the free development of self, employing all the energies intrinsic to the human personality." Mussolini spoke of a morality whose critical imperative was: "Obey your conscience and render yourself fully human [*sii uomo*]!"[13] Such a morality could hardly be, in and of itself, exclusively Marxist. In its universality, it could hardly be seen as a simple reflex of any economic conditions. Its themes could be found in the enjoinments of all religions, in all economic circumstances, and in all the writings of all the philosophers of all times and places.

The young Mussolini spoke of the revolutionary effort to assure the "harmonic development of humanity, understanding life . . . as a free expansion of active and living energy." In itself, it was a "revolutionary" injunction already recommended before the beginning of the Christian era, by both pre-Christian Greek and Roman thinkers. It was evident that the young Mussolini hardly reflected on the fact that such aspirations antedated Marxism by millennia and could hardly "reflect" any specific economic base. None of that deterred him from fancying himself a Marxist advocate of a newly discovered creed that gave expression to "a hallowed, human ideal capable of bringing true humanity to the humankind of tomorrow."[14]

Just as Lenin made a brief allusion to an "abstract, philosophical morality" that stood above class interests—Engels, in the late 1870s, had made ready reference to a proletarian morality that was "a really human morality which [stood] above class antagonisms."[15] No one seemed prepared to address the fact that however such universal morality might be conceived, it could hardly be seen as a reflex of class interests or economic conditions—which suggests that morality might have a source independent of society's material base.

Having acknowledged the existence of a "really human morality" that could not be understood to be a simple reflection of economic conditions, Marxists were left with a conceptual muddle. The fact is that the notion of a "really human morality" existing in mind before the existence of the "material life conditions" of which it was supposedly the "reflection" creates, at the very least, an analytic conundrum. The existence, in consciousness, of a morality that is something other than a reflection of economic conditions suggests the possibility that human beings might be capable of class independent deliberation concerning philosophical and ethical issues. Should that be the case, it would be difficult to account for that ability within the inflexible determinism of the inherited Marxist system.

What the existence of a morality that transcends economic interests seems to suggest is something Woltmann had already brought to the attention of thinking Marxists some years before.[16] If morality, and its consciousness in mind, are older than the existence of classes—and would survive their disappearance—one could not dismiss the possibility that ethical judgment and moral concerns might influence contemporary human behavior independent of prevailing economic circumstances.

Like Woltmann, Mussolini made ready reference to common elements of a moral universality to be found in the thought of Plato, Cicero, and Buddha[17]—that could hardly be plausibly attributed to a common class membership or a common economic base—and on at least one occasion, Mussolini spoke of an "autonomous morality," independent of obedience to anything other than conscience.[18] While he acknowledged, as had other Marxists before him, that such a morality could not be fully attained in practice until requisite material conditions had matured, it was clear, for all intents and purposes, that Mussolini seemed to grant that moral and ethical principles might influence the behavior of actors independent of a specific "material base."

The "new morality" of which Mussolini spoke, at the time, drew attention, directly and indirectly, to some of the problems at the center of Marxism as a comprehensive philosophical system. Unlike Lenin, the issue was to prove of considerable ideological importance to the young Mussolini and some other critical Marxists of his time.

That the possibility of a morality that transcended both time and class occupied Mussolini's attention was probably the consequence of his un-common familiarity with socialist thought and the socialist literature of the period. He read and reviewed Werner Sombart's *Der Sozialismus und die soziale Bewegung*, for example, that contained an extensive critical discussion centered on Marx's treatment of moral and ethical thought.[19] By that time, already familiar with the writings of Georges Sorel, Mussolini made a point of insisting that the commitment to revolutionary socialism, while predicated on scientific considerations, was essentially *moral*—a commitment to a morality that could not simply be reduced to a reflection of the material circumstances in which the proletariat, as a class, found itself.[20]

By 1908, Mussolini had come under the influence of some of the major exponents of revolutionary syndicalism. As a consequence, by his mid-twenties, unlike Lenin, he devoted an uncommon measure of attention to the role of ethics and morality in human behavior. Mussolini began to make regular reference to moral incentives as critical in politics and revolution. Thus, he spoke of socialism as a reasoned belief composed of "three elements, one doctrinal, one practical, and a third ideal."[21] How one was to understand that third component remained uncertain. It was equally unclear throughout those early years just how Mussolini understood not only the origins and influence of moral judgments, but the philosophical status of ethical principles and ideals as well.

What was evident, by the time Mussolini conceived himself a syndicalist in 1904, was the fact that theoretical syndicalism reflected some of the central convictions of Sorel. Sorel had argued that the revolutionary goals of Marxism stood independent of Marxism's theoretical frailties. Whether Marx's notion of the labor theory of value, or his convictions concerning the remorseless concentration of capital, or the inevitable catastrophic collapse of capitalism, were true or in error, was not critical to the responsibilities of social revolutionaries. What was central to the revolutionary enterprise was the lifting of the burden of exploitation from the majority of human beings—the creation of an environment in which all might realize their human potential—an exquisitely moral purpose. For Sorel—in effect and in the last analysis—ethics and morality, and not science, lay at the heart of revolution.[22]

More than that, for many revolutionary Marxists of the period there were associated problems that featured an ethical or moral component. They turned on human motivation and the role of leadership in revolutionary episodes. Probably influenced by both Sorel and the Italian social science of his time,[23] Mussolini had begun to put together a collection of notions about how a socialist revolution might proceed. Like Lenin, the young Mussolini was quick to remind his various audiences that revolutions seem to be invariably led by minorities—and only when such minorities provide the first initiatives would masses follow.[24] Like Lenin, Mussolini spoke of "proletarian elites" active in mobilizing masses—and of the "people" as "always ingenuous and childlike," burdened by a "torpid consciousness"[25]—unless led by just such elites. As early as the first decade of the new century, Mussolini anticipated the advent of an antireformist, revolutionary "authoritarian socialism." It would be led by socialist revolutionaries who, taken together, Mussolini saw as a "vigilant vanguard of the proletariat"—a "new elite" having all the properties described by Pareto.[26] It would be an elite possessed of properties similarly described by Lenin—as well as by Sorel and the principal spokesmen of revolutionary syndicalism.

For the purposes of discussion, it is interesting to note that during his exposition in *L'Uomo e la divinità*, Mussolini developed yet another theme that was to influence the evolution (or devolution, as the case might be) of Marxism—a matter of some sociological importance. Like Engels and Woltmann before him, Mussolini spoke, at critical times in his exposition, of generic "communities," or "groups" of human beings, as historic actors. On those occasions, Mussolini spoke of groups rather than economic classes. He spoke of such groups as being "associated by blood, locale, sexual affinity . . . and intellectual interests," as well as economic concerns.[27] There was more to group affiliation than economic interest—a consideration, it will be argued, that would transform Marxism as a system.

In the same context, like Engels and Woltmann before him, Mussolini spoke of such communities in terms of hundreds of thousands of years of evolutionary time. He spoke of *pithecanthropoid*, of humanoid, and of human groups, existing in savagery and barbarism long before anything akin to economic classes existed. Like Kautsky and Woltmann, Mussolini spoke of human beings, through evolutionary time, eons before specifically class interests could have affected them, living in associations governed by instinct, mimicry, sentiment, moral principle, and conscience.

Woltmann had drawn some of the obvious implications of such an account. Engels had not. Nor had Mussolini—at that time. Only later, in the critical years leading to Italy's involvement in the Great War, did all these threads of argument come together to fashion some of the fabric of the first Fascism. In the interim, it was revolutionary syndicalism and the thought of Sorel that was to influence Mussolini's more immediate reflections.

MUSSOLINI, SOREL, AND
REVOLUTIONARY SYNDICALISM

In 1909, Mussolini published a review of Giuseppe Prezzolini's *La teoria sindacalista*.[28] It was an essay that remains essential if one would understand Mussolini's progression from the orthodoxy of German Social Democracy to what was to become one of Marxism's most fateful variants.

In the course of his review of Prezzolini's book, Mussolini indicated that, by that time, he had been of syndicalist persuasion for about five years.[29] Years later, Renzo De Felice argued that the fact that he had been a revolutionary syndicalist during those years was central to Mussolini's intellectual development. De Felice held that "the most important influence upon Mussolini's development . . . was that exercised by revolutionary syndicalism. Even after Mussolini concluded his [initial] socialist phase, the influence of revolutionary syndicalism revealed itself in the . . . manner he conceived social relations and political struggle."[30] What was not said, and yet was equally important, was the fact that Mussolini's relationship with Prezzolini, the editor of the iconoclastic journal *La Voce*, was to be of similar, if not equal, importance. The influence of Prezzolini, and the authors that collected around *La Voce*, helped shape Mussolini's heterodox Marxism into what it was to become.

In writing his review of Prezzolini's volume,[31] Mussolini outlined the basic elements of the syndicalism to which he subscribed. It was a rendering that remains important insofar as it revealed a great deal about Mussolini's own political views. In his review, Mussolini spoke of syndicalism as future directed and action oriented—as identified wholly with the proletariat to the exclusion of bourgeois influence—as antiparliamentarian and opposed, in principle, to the politics of popular elections. He emphasized the differences between the meliorative, parliamentarian, and party-based socialism of German Social Democracy, the tentative reformism of what was taken to be Italian Marxist orthodoxy, and the revolutionary radicalism of syndicalism. In the course of his exposition, Mussolini proceeded to identify the major differences between the socialism of party adherents and the socialism of revolutionary syndicalism. For syndicalists, Mussolini insisted, socialism was nothing less than an epic conflict between two fundamentally opposed visions of the future. Like the great struggles of antiquity in which the destiny of the world was determined, the class struggle between the proletariat and their antagonists, each led by their respective elites,[32] would be of historic significance.

In images like those that found favor in the prose of Lenin, Mussolini spoke of an historic struggle that would require "new characters, new values, new men." It would involve conflict between groups of human beings, each possessed of an entirely different ethical consciousness. The warriors of the social revolution were tasked with obligations that would demand discipline, selflessness, and sacrifice of them. "The social revolution," Mussolini said, "would suffer a period of violence, an heroic, insurrectionary interlude . . . for which one must prepare the protagonists." He anticipated an epoch which would have as its fatal responsibility "the development of human character . . . [and] the economic and moral shaping of a new human being."[33]

Those charged with making revolution could no longer escape into that form of "economic determinism" that promised automatic social change as a consequence of "inscrutable laws poorly understood." Mussolini insisted, "Syndicalism understands history to be the result of the willed action of human beings . . . who leave the impact of their transformative power on things and institutions. . . . Syndicalism does not deny 'economic necessity,' but supplements that necessity with a willed 'ethical conscience.'"[34]

In the contest between protagonists, Mussolini contended, revolution takes on the features of armed conflict, a conflict that demands a heightening of moral sensibilities and selfless commitment. The struggle demands violence, "simple, ingenuous, primitive, traditional violence," directed against the bourgeois state and all its associated institutions. Revolution requires that its ideas not remain "on the shelves of libraries," but actively engage the will and energies of determined human beings. The general strike, the preferred weapon of revolutionary syndicalism, provides the occasion for engaging in that violence. It also affords the opportunity for the training of the proletariat in order that they might assume those "heroic" responsibilities that would flow from the defeat of their class enemy and the conquest of the means of production.

Out of that victory would emerge the "new society of producers" that had become the inspirational ideal of the movement. The workers' syndicats, composed of those transformed in the process of revolution, would become the cells of the emerging producer society.

All of that had become familiar in the Marxist works of Sorel. Perhaps more important for the present account is the fact that there were elements in Prezzolini's treatment of Sorel's work that, while not appearing prominently in Mussolini's review, are particularly relevant in coming to understand the relationship of Marxism to the emergence of that future Fascism that was to be one of its major variants.

In his treatment, for example, Mussolini briefly alluded to the fact that Prezzolini argued that the thought of Henri Bergson was not essential either to the formation, or to the plausibility, of Sorel's syndicalism. Actually, there was more to Prezzolini's discussion of Bergsonian thought and its possible relationship to syndicalism. Prezzolini made a point of the failure of Bergsonianism to provide a coherent philosophical foundation for syndicalism.

Prezzolini argued that Sorel, for a variety of easily understood reasons, sought to emphasize the "spiritual" qualities of humankind. What that meant was that Sorel had raised objection to the then prevalent positivism and its intrinsic "scientistic materialism." Sorel opposed the popular scientism of his time because he argued that such a conception of the world could only foster political quietism among the thinkers of the late nineteenth century. Positivism's determinism and its reduction of all the issues involving ethics and morality to material causes necessarily enfeebled the will and left no incentive to struggle. If history was nothing other than a complex fatality, with events the necessary consequence of the "laws of historical development," humans were nothing other than marionettes in a drama over which they had no control. Sorel rejected the positivistic pretense that any such determinism was dictated by "objective science."

In order to make his case, Sorel articulated fairly sophisticated arguments that sought to distinguish the truth conditions governing social science from those appropriate to mathematicophysical disciplines. As has been argued, in making that distinction, Bergson's "spiritualistic" philosophy—his emphasis on the role of intuition, creativity, conscious reflection, and moral concern—seemed supportive to Sorel. In response, Prezzolini undertook to demonstrate that Bergson's "life philosophy" was actually poorly equipped to deal with serious epistemological and deontological questions.

Prezzolini pointed out that Bergson's thought harbored within itself an unresolved and troubling dualism: with human "spirit," life, consciousness, and "vital impulse," somehow opposed by external "matter." Prezzolini maintained that it would be very difficult for "spirit" to bridge the distance between itself and a preexistent matter. If consciousness and vital impulse were somehow primary in the entire process of coming to know the world, how does one proceed from the immediate reality of consciousness to that external materiality with which it must contend—without making appeal to a host of indefensible intellectual presuppositions?

It is clear that Bergson argued that consciousness is possessed of a form of intelligence designed to assist human beings in their efforts to adapt to the world. It is that intelligence that gives us the measure of the material world. Positivists and materialists of all sorts had said nothing less. But there is another form of intelligence that Bergson speaks of as "intuitive," that reveals the artificiality of the reality measured out in time and space, in logic, in geometry, and in simple mathematics. Given Bergson's argument, what could be the epistemological and ontological status of that material and "artificial" reality, exposed by intuition?

Prezzolini argued that given Bergson's views we are left uncertain which reality is ontologically true—the "practical world, made up in geometric form and tied together with abstractions," provided by functional empirical science, or that world of flow and dynamic change found in intuitive awareness?[35] Prezzolini argued that the resolution of such fundamental philosophical issues required a far more sophisticated treatment than any found in the works of either Sorel or Bergson—or, for that matter, in the works of Marx or Engels. Prezzolini recommended recourse to some form of modern Hegelianism, an epistemological and perhaps ontological idealism that would address such concerns at a more fundamental level than any evident in Bergson's intuitionism and "anti-intellectualism."[36]

By the time he wrote *La teoria sindacalista*, Prezzolini had transitioned through philosophical pragmatism and given himself over to that Italian form of philosophical idealism that found expression in the works of Benedetto Croce and Giovanni Gentile.[37] In effect, Prezzolini afforded domestic Marxists, Mussolini among them, the occasion of a specifically Italian "return to Kant" in their efforts to resolve some of the philosophical and theoretical questions that were clearly part of their intellectual inheritance. Prezzolini held that only some form of philosophical idealism could address some of the most demanding ontological, epistemological, and ethical problems that afflicted Marxist thought. It was a contention that was later to surface among those Marxists who followed Mussolini into Fascism.

In 1909, Mussolini made only oblique allusion to Prezzolini's specifically philosophical arguments in his review of *La teoria sindacalista*. He either chose not to address the entire complex business, or he felt incompetent to do so at that time. In any event, Prezzolini had raised a number of critical issues that were to become increasingly influential to the evolving Marxist heterodoxy with which Mussolini was to become identified.

There were other important subjects that Mussolini chose not to address on the occasion of his review. In his text, for example, Prezzolini made a point of arguing that syndicalism advocated an integral collectivism—dismissing the "bourgeois individualism" that Sorel conceived both threatening to group survival and destructive of virtue and moral conduct. Prezzolini, like Sorel, went on to indicate that such a saving collectivism might arise in communities other than economically defined classes. Once again, the argument in support of the existence of vital communities other than classes made their appearance—just as they had in the works of Engels and Woltmann—and briefly in that of Lenin.

In his book on syndicalism, Prezzolini suggested that, in Italy, the entrepreneurial bourgeoisie might well host an open national community—composed of individuals who shared ethnic, linguistic and cultural affinities—tapping into generic group, rather than a specifically class, sentiment. Such a community, Prezzolini maintained, infilled by a sense of solidarity and mission, might provide the structured environment in which the proletariat might be educated to moral purposes. Prezzolini went on to argue that the very need to industrialize the Italian peninsula, three-fourths of which remained, at that time, economically retrograde, might well constitute the mission that could render the community capable of fostering and sustaining individual and group morality. It would be a community in which a sense of collective mission would provide the demanding atmosphere of high moral tension and self-sacrifice that would produce the future "warrior producers" of whom Sorel spoke.[38]

Given his interpretation of Sorel's intent, it seemed evident to Prezzolini that Marxism, as it was understood by its advocates at the beginning of the twentieth century, lent itself to a number of perfectly consistent, if opposed, theoretical and practical formulations. Prezzolini argued that German socialists, moved by group sentiment, however orthodox their Marxism, might well be prepared to identify with their nation as a "community of destiny" should it be threatened from without—to produce a kind of "national socialism."[39] While it seems clear that he held that such a posture might be seen by others as "insincere," it is equally evident that it would not necessarily appear so to Sorelians. In general, Sorel had argued that group solidarity, the basis for much of virtue and moral conduct, was essentially generic, without any intrinsic connection to any specific class or community. History had demonstrated that the sense of group solidarity might well be attached to the nation as well as any alternative. Given the appropriate circumstances, it was evident that Sorel conceived that any collectivity might, with equal right, lay claim to the allegiance of individuals.

Sorel had argued that tribal communities, city states, religious sects, as well as modern nations might serve as communities of solidarity, offering the circumstances in which human beings would be challenged to lift themselves above their narrow interests and aspire to greater purpose than the simple satisfaction of material needs. Sorel understood solidarity to be a condition for the moral elevation of humankind.

Given his review, it appears evident that Mussolini read Prezzolini's text with considerable attention. While not prepared at the time to address some of the more difficult questions raised, he did undertake to begin to analyze the issue of which specific "community of destiny" might properly engage the commitment of the proletariat as a class.

In his review of Sorel's *Reflections on Violence* that appeared shortly after that of Prezzolini's account of syndicalist theory, Mussolini repeated his positive judgments concerning revolutionary syndicalism. All the themes that made up the substance of his review of Prezzolini's *La teoria sindacalista* are found in the subsequent text. Mussolini continued to identify himself as a syndicalist,[40] and reiterated his commitment to the moral conceptions of Sorel. He continued to speak of the "new men" who would emerge from the revolutionary struggles of syndicalism—and insisted that Sorel's vision provided revolutionaries with "a more certain comprehension of Marxism that had originally arrived in Italy in an unrecognizable state."[41]

Beyond that, and perhaps of more interest to the present account, Mussolini touched on the issue of nationalism and the role it might play in the revolutionary politics of Marxism. In the course of his discussion, Mussolini acknowledged that no one could deny the existence of the love of country as a sentiment.[42] What he proceeded to maintain was that the patriotism of socialism could only be "equivocal." The proletariat, whatever its sentiments might be, had no material interests in the survival of Italy as a nation. The Italian bourgeoisie denied the Italian proletariat property; the lack of education among Italy's workers denied them pride in the nation's cultural achievements; and the reactionary politics of class dominance in Italy left the proletariat without any form of expression. Whatever the basic patriotic sentiments of the proletariat might be, the bourgeoisie left them bereft of a fatherland.[43]

The discussion leaves the reader with a sense that Mussolini, in some measure, deplored the alienation of workers from their nation. Almost immediately after his review of Sorel and the discussion of unrequited national sentiments, Mussolini wrote, at some length, of the glories of Italy—of the political and cultural achievements of ancient Rome, of the commercial and civilizing accomplishments of Venice and Naples, of the beauty and universal humanizing influence of that Italy that he identified as "the common fatherland of genius."[44]

Perhaps more significant than that in putting together a connected account of his emerging Marxist heterodoxy, Mussolini wrote of the Italy of his time as an Italy awakening from a long sleep. "Where once lovers dreamed and nightingales sang," he wrote, "now factory sirens blow. Italy is accelerating its pace in the great marathon in which the world supremacy of nations is being decided."[45] The relationship of nations among themselves was a matter of concern.

In his discussions of the period, Mussolini addressed some of the critical issues that had arisen among revolutionary Marxists at the turn of the twentieth century. He alluded to philosophical, scientific, and moral concerns that were to remain unresolved among Marxists throughout the century.[46] He obliquely alluded to the alternative communities—class, racial, or national—with which Marxist revolutionaries might identify themselves in the modern world.[47]

What is clear in all of this is the fact that the young Mussolini was attempting to address and resolve matters that were then, and were to forever remain, at the intellectual center of Marxism. How science and philosophy were to be understood; what role morality played in human history; how might national sentiment influence the role of revolution in modern times—were questions that remained unresolved among Marxists however orthodox, heterodox, or heretical.

Independent of the more profound intellectual problems, it was evident that as a young Marxist revolutionary, the young Mussolini took pride in his nationality and his fatherland.[48] More than that, he applied Sorel's appeal to productivism and industrial development to the historic conditions in which retrograde Italy found itself. Equally clear is the fact that, at that juncture, Mussolini held that the revolutionary proletariat, because of the exactions of the bourgeoisie, could neither share his national pride nor his enthusiasm for Italy's accelerated economic and industrial growth.

Much of the discussion that arose out of these issues was to be found in the contemporary pages of Prezzolini's *La Voce*—and in retrospect, it seems evident that at least some of the impetus for Mussolini's intellectual development found its origin in Prezzolini's treatment of the same subjects that engaged Sorel and the syndicalists. Mussolini's familiarity with *La Voce*, and the intellectuals who gathered around it, helps account for many of the features of that variant of Marxism we now speak of as Fascism.

SOREL, MUSSOLINI, AND THE *VOCIANI*

During the first fifteen years of the past century, Giuseppe Prezzolini and Giovanni Papini were young intellectuals who managed to influence political thought in Italy to a degree that hardly could have been anticipated. Independently or together they edited a number of periodicals, some more durable than others, which succeeded in shaping the thought and politics of several generations of Italians who were to go on to help govern events for a quarter century. The journal, *La Voce*,[49] was only the most prominent of those founded by them in the course of the first years of the twentieth century.

Not long after the founding of *La Voce*, Mussolini identified himself to its editor, Prezzolini, as already one of the journal's "assiduous readers."[50] *La Voce* had been a lineal descendant of the journals *Leonardo* and *Il Regno*. In its time, *Leonardo* had been a vehicle for the discussion generated by a variety of contested issues. Among those issues, one finds those that turned on emerging political nationalism, philosophical idealism, and developmental economics. Mussolini informed Prezzolini that he had been as assiduous a reader of *Leonardo* as he was of *La Voce*.[51]

For our purposes that fact is of some importance. It was as editor of *Leonardo* that Papini raised some of the same philosophical questions that engaged Sorel. The materialism of what had become standard philosophical positivism no longer satisfied Papini—and he became one of the first spokesmen in Italy to reject positivism and broadcast the alternative merits of American pragmatism.[52] Like Sorel, Papini sought a more satisfying answer to epistemological and moral questions than those found in the various materialisms that dominated the intellectual community of the time.

As editor of *Leonardo*, Papini came to the attention of Enrico Corradini, leader of an Italian political nationalism then only beginning to find itself. The Italian nationalism of the time was little more than partially articulate and coherent. In 1903, Corradini asked Papini to put together an intellectual rationale for Italy's emergent nationalism—and in February 1904, Papini presented his ideas to a political audience for the first time, to repeat them at various sites throughout Italy during the months that followed. For our purposes several things are significant in the published account of his speech.[53]

First of all, Papini articulated a clutch of ideas that were to regularly resurface in the pages of *La Voce*. For the purposes of reconstructing the development of Mussolini's Marxism, some of those ideas are important. Papini insisted, for example, that it is sentiment, passion, that moves persons to political activity. He was to argue that feelings animate the will, and that it is the will that gives rise to action. He went on to maintain that socialism in Italy possessed the sentiment and the will that finds outlet in action—but he proceeded to contend that because socialist orthodoxy made *class* the exclusive basis of group identity, Marxist revolutionaries could neither understand nor undertake contemporary revolution with any hope of success.

For Papini, the identification with one's class hardly provided the grounds for historic undertakings. Identification with one's class was an expression of a very narrow, and equally unappealing, materialism. Moreover, when the apologists for Marxism sought to furnish some sort of altruism to offset the selfish interests of class, they almost invariably appealed to "humanity." The attempt to move from narrow class identification to one with an abstract "humanity," simply revealed how few options were actually available to revolutionary Marxism. To identify with one's class is to identify with one's most immediate material concerns. To identify with "humanity" is to identify with an empty and insubstantial Platonic idea. Papini held that to attempt to inspire human beings to sacrifice required something more.

In the modern world, Papini went on, it is the nation, embodying the immediate interests of individuals and their class, but extending far beyond that to include shared culture and history, that serves as an historic actor. It is the nation, interacting with other nations in both amity and enmity, that, all taken together, constitutes the substance and story of humanity. Any doctrine that rouses the nation to such endeavors is the product, not of "reflections" of the economic base, but of the philosophic and moral deliberations of mature human beings. Understanding that, Papini went on, one begins to appreciate that history is made only with "heroic intensity" and a readiness to suffer "supreme sacrifice."

The passions of life, and the demands made upon the individual in the course of meeting collective responsibilities, necessitates leadership by those specially gifted by nature and circumstances. Life, Papini insisted, imposed arduous demands on individuals living in committed association—that could only be discharged under the leadership of a dedicated elite. He reminded his readers that we learned as much from social scientists in France and Germany and from Gaetano Mosca and Pareto in Italy. Beyond that, he went on, such a commanding elite must emanate from the bourgeoisie—the Italian nobility being effete, and the proletariat lacking the background and training necessary for such responsibility. In effect, by a different route, Papini had come to some of the same conclusions concerning revolution as had Lenin.

Lenin, like Papini, argued that revolutions are made by an elite leadership drawn from the bourgeoisie—mobilizing uncertain and unreflecting masses. Lenin's "declassed" elite clearly shared some features with that bourgeois elite to whom Papini appealed. Like Lenin's revolutionary elite,[54] Papini's elite was expected to be independent of narrow class interest in order to serve a more generous purpose. At the time, what distinguished the notions of Papini and Prezzolini from those of Lenin turned on their recommendation that the revolution would require the industrial development of the economically retrograde peninsula.[55]

For Papini, the goals of any serious revolution would be shaped by the circumstances in which the nation found itself. In Italy's case the revolution would respond to the meanness of Italian life—its manifest inferiority in the modern world. It would be a revolution that would address the nation's dearth of raw materials for the effective development of industry. It would be a revolution predicated on the need for space that might support a burgeoning population—on a need for markets for emergent domestic industries—on the need for popular literacy—and on the need of an infrastructure of transportation and communication.[56] All that would be required to make of revolution something glorious—and of collective life something more generous, more vast, more heroic.

In 1904, that was the vision of revolution common to many *vociani*.[57] One does not have to search far to recognize the overlap between just such ideas and those of the Sorelians. That explains something of the appeal of *Leonardo* and *La Voce* for the young Mussolini. At the same time that he was reading Sorel's publications, Mussolini found in *La Voce* many of the same themes that made up the substance of revolutionary syndicalism. An unknown political activist in his mid-twenties, Mussolini found the journal of sufficient importance not only to subscribe to it, and submit articles for publication in its pages, but to volunteer his time and effort to solicit subscriptions in its service.

The very fact that the journal attracted his attention is important in any effort to reconstruct the course of Mussolini's Marxist heterodoxies. *La Voce* was founded and edited by Giuseppe Prezzolini—with Giovanni Papini so serving on occasion. Both Prezzolini and Papini were supremely independent thinkers and exchanged correspondence with a roster of notables including Pareto, Benedetto Croce, Giovanni Gentile, and Roberto Michels. All were to contribute something to the substance of *La Voce* and, as a consequence, to the evolution of Mussolini's thought. When he wrote his review of Prezzolini's book on syndicalist theory in 1909, Mussolini had already adapted to his own system of beliefs some of the major themes found in the pages of *La Voce*.

All those issues we have considered, the community with which one might expect the proletariat to identify,[58] the nature of philosophical inquiry and normative assessment,[59] the role of science and morality in revolution, and the nature and composition of revolutionary leadership, all continued to work their way through the revolutionary thought of the young Mussolini.

Personal circumstances and world events would subsequently influence Mussolini's thoughts on these issues, as they would his judgments concerning the ultimate interests of the revolutionary proletariat. They were not questions that could be easily resolved—and they were to influence the ongoing discussions among the major intellectuals of syndicalism and revolutionary radicalism in Italy at least until the outbreak of the Great War. Before the coming of that war, the discussion that turned on all these issues became particularly intense in the turbulent period leading up to Italy's conflict in the Mediterranean involving the Ottoman Turks.

SYNDICALISM, NATIONALISM, AND MUSSOLINI

In the years immediately preceding the war in Tripoli, Mussolini chose to accept a position as secretary for the socialist secretariat of labor in the Austro-Hungarian province of Trent. While there, he was to work intensely with Cesare Battisti, to assume the responsibility of editing his socialist daily, *Il Popolo*.

More than simply working with him, much of Mussolini's prose of the period reflected much of Battisti's political thought—and turned on issues that were to remain important to Mussolini's political evolution throughout the interval leading to the advent of the First World War. That is not to suggest that Battisti inspired Mussolini's ideological development. It seems perfectly evident that before they came together both shared a roster of opinions concerning the nature of association and the character of human sentiment. By his own testimony, Mussolini had been an avid reader of *Leonardo* and *La Voce* before his sojourn in the Trentino. He entertained some of the views that found expression in their pages—including the suggestion that national sentiment might be a powerful incentive to revolutionary association.

In effect, Mussolini brought with him a complex set of ideas about social revolution, bearing on the issues involved in the mobilization of masses. He was to find that he held many of those ideas in common with Battisti with whom there was to be sympathy and an enduring mutual regard.[60]

During the nine months spent in the Trentino, Mussolini worked with Battisti who—while as firm in his internationalist convictions as was Mussolini—had never abandoned his sense of Italian identity. As a student, Battisti was a member of a society of students who insisted on maintaining that identity in a region that had been separated from the motherland by treaty since 1815—after the defeat of Napoleon. By treaty, the Trentino was transferred to the Hapsburg Emperor of Austria-Hungary.

The Hapsburgs chose to rename the Trentino the southern Tyrol. Neither the earlier transfer nor the later change of name extinguished the sense of being Italian among members of the resident ethnic population. At almost the same time that the Hapsburgs chose to change the name of the region, there was the archeological discovery of the *Tavola Clesiana* that recorded the fact that the Emperor Claudius had, in antiquity, extended Roman citizenship to the inhabitants of the Trentino. The Italians of the region cited that fact as evidence of the historicity of their identity—and persisted in distinguishing themselves from other ethnic communities within the Austro-Hungarian empire. The agitation for a measure of autonomy, the preservation of the Italian language, and the establishment of Italian language schools for the defense of Italian culture, continued throughout the last decade of the nineteenth and the first decade of the twentieth centuries.

With the beginning of the new century, Battisti and the ethnic Italian socialists led the struggle for Italian autonomy in the Trentino. It was that struggle that Mussolini was later to identify as "one of the most beautiful pages in the history of the socialist party in the Trentino."[61] It was that atmosphere, charged with national sentiment, into which Mussolini was thrust in 1909.

Mussolini was to ally himself with Battisti who, as a convinced socialist, was nonetheless an ardent advocate of Italian rights in a politically unresponsive environment. As such, Battisti was an articulate opponent of both the regional liberal democratic party as well as the political representatives of the Catholic church. He held the first to be vacillating and irresolute in the defense of ethnic Italians, seeking only the interests of their class. In turn, he saw the clerics as far too accommodative to imperial rule.

As a socialist, Battisti sought to defend the rights of nationality as well as foster the general renewal of morality and integrity. All of that could be accomplished only by invoking the national sentiments of the subject community. "Nations," he argued, "represent an affirmation of a grand solidarity and a necessary step in the unification of humankind."[62] Out of that sense of national solidarity, a new morality of human fraternity was expected to grow. Like many Marxists of the period, Battisti held that the defense of nationality did not contradict his most fundamental socialist and ethical convictions.

Battisti led the struggle for national autonomy in the Trentino. He went so far as to argue that socialists were prepared to struggle for such recognition united with their class opponents, the bourgeoisie—if the bourgeoisie would remain resolute in the face of the Hapsburg government.[63] It was clear that as a socialist, Battisti was prepared to undertake struggle, allied with those who were theoretically class enemies, in the service of their inclusive nationality.

In Austria, the issue of nationality had emerged as a critical problem for the *Gesamptpartei*—the official Austro-Hungarian socialist party—as early as its founding. During the last years of the nineteenth century the party faced serious internal dissention because Czechs, Slovaks, and other Slavic groups, together with Romanians and Italians, all mistrusted the Germans, who occupied almost all the leadership roles in the party. The Germans, in turn, demonstrated profound national and ethnic prejudices. Because of that, on the occasion of the biennial party conference in Vienna in 1897, the non-German minorities sought to create a federated organization in which the various ethnic communities would have adequate and responsive representation. The issue remained unresolved until the end of the century—and it was clear that, among Marxists, the nationalities issue would never find complete resolution.[64]

The issue clearly involved group identity. Austrian socialists were prepared to acknowledge that among the candidates for group identity nationality was evidently as important as economic fraternity. Under some set of conditions, Battisti, as a socialist, was prepared, among the options available, to extend priority to the defense and enhancement of nationality.

These were the circumstances in which Mussolini found himself during his sojourn in the Trentino. During this period, he had occasion to specifically address some of the concerns that would occupy him his entire political life. Among other things, it was manifest that, like Battisti and the *vociani*, he never abandoned the nation as a possible object of attachment, however preoccupied one might be with class conflict.

Like Battisti, and as a socialist, Mussolini insisted that any "universal solidarity" required by the revolution he advocated, could neither "can-cel the fatherland" nor detract from its "ideal integrity."[65] In fact, and once again like Battisti, among his complaints against the functionaries of the Catholic church in the Trentino, Mussolini included the charge that they were prepared to deny their national loyalties in a compliant and submis-sive accommodation with their Hapsburg rulers.

Mussolini went on to applaud the special sobriety, courage, and tenacity of Italian workers, who employing "Latin genius," would one day create the "new man" of the anticipated future society—"who would act, produce, dominate matter, enjoy that triumph that multiplies life's energies, and move on, as one, to other goals, other horizons, and other ideals."[66] Those accomplishments, however international in ultimate scope, would be Ital-ian in essence.

Within that context, and again like Battisti, Mussolini deplored "chau-vinism," and the "narrow" and "stupid nationalism" of "proprietors" or clerics, who exploited the sentiment of "patriotism" for personal or institu-tional gain. He lamented the invocation of national sentiment in order to obstruct the free passage of international cultural exchanges or fuel those hatreds calculated to accomplish nothing more than abet the class interests of the bourgeoisie.[67]

In a complex interplay of national sentiment and workmen's identity, Mussolini's thought during his respite in the Trentino reflected the influ-ence of an entire constellation of social science luminaries and revolutionary thinkers—including syndicalists[68] and *vociani*. Battisti had already settled on a similar collection of convictions—and both he and Mussolini were in substantial agreement on the role national sentiment might play in the revolutionary transformation of the modern world.

While he was in residence in the Trentino, Mussolini was urged by Prez-zolini to write an extended essay on the region, and Mussolini agreed. Upon his expulsion from the Trentino by the Austro-Hungarian govern-ment, Mussolini took up the preparation of his study for the series pub-lished by *La Voce*.[69] The work is interesting for several reasons.

In the first place, Mussolini's long essay provides evidence that he was well informed concerning the available social science, and Marxist relevant, literature of the period. More than that, in his discussion of the "chauvin-ism" of the German socialists in the Trentino, he cited the racism of Ludwig Woltmann as the foundation of "theoretical pangermanism"—the rationale for the efforts undertaken by those socialists of German origin to seek do-minion over the multiethnic Trentino. Acknowledging Woltmann's Marxist ideological convictions, Mussolini recognized that whatever orthodoxy might mean to fellow Marxists, it could be significantly stretched into a variant that was to most grievously impact the twentieth century.[70]

The pangermanists advocated the dominance of Germans in the region by appealing to the racist conjectures of a number of scholars other than Woltmann. Mussolini cited A. de Gobineau, V. Lapouge, and H. S. Chamberlain among them. As advocates of German mastery, they, like Woltmann, argued that Germans, sometimes as "Aryans," and other times as "Nordics," were especially gifted creators of culture. For the German Socialists, Germans were creators of the modern world. Slavs and Italians were creatures of lesser order, destined by biology and evolutionary history to a secondary role in modern society.

Mussolini's discussion of racial theory is surprisingly sophisticated. He pointed to the evident lack of definitional clarity concerning the concept "race," as well as the absence of identifiable anthropological evidence unequivocally distinguishing the major European races. He dismissed racism as an impaired effort to gather sentiment behind a kind of racial socialism calculated to assure Germans that their nation would be accorded a privileged place among the "great powers."[71] As objectionable as racism might be as a variant, Mussolini was prepared to recognize that classical Marxism might supply the elements for just such a curiosity. As has been indicated, both Kautsky and Lenin had been prepared to recognize Woltmann as a theoretically gifted Marxist.

Mussolini's treatment of the sentiment of nationality among the Italian workers of the Trentino was very different from anything to be found in the work of Woltmann. Mussolini conceived national sentiment devoid of specifically racist implications—and dealt with the phenomena in exclusively political and sociological terms.

In the text of *Il Trentino veduta da un socialista*, Mussolini speaks with evident pride of the enduring "psychological and linguistic ethnic unity of Italians" in the politically repressive surroundings of the Trentino.[72] He went on to speak of any effort on the part of Italians to free themselves from the "Austrian yoke" as intrinsically revolutionary—but adds that most Italians had resigned themselves to their then current circumstances—largely because the dominant elements among them, the land owners, the churchmen, the owners of small manufactories, and the merchants, were all timid and self-seeking, finding more evident benefits in accommodating themselves to the Austrians than any alternative.[73] The Italian socialists alone, among all the Italian elements in the Trentino, pursued a defense of Italianità, of nationality. But in that inauspicious environment, one only found separatist, anti-Austrian tendencies, rather than specifically nationalist sentiment among the workers.[74]

Mussolini spoke candidly of the possibilities of a return of the Trentino to Italy. He dismissed it. The bourgeoisie of the Trentino were neither modern nor active, incapable of sustaining political efforts that had any promise of success. The agrarian sector was passive, even in the face of provocation. Even the workers of the region, irrespective of their many virtues, were mostly involved in artisan trade, wedded to small enterprise and ill disposed to political assertiveness. The military was loyal to its Austrian overseers. Mussolini concluded that the preconditions for substantial social change did not exist in the Austria of 1909. As an aside, he spoke of only one possibility for restoring the province to Italy: a war between the two monarchies.[75] However casual the comment, it was a clear commitment to war as the possible occasion of revolution.

That was the Marxism with which Mussolini returned to Italy, to take up once again his tasks as an agitator and organizer for revolutionary socialism. By that time, the Italian Socialist Party had expelled its syndicalist members for ideological heterodoxy—and Mussolini, once again subject to the peculiar orthodoxy of the national party, denounced Sorel for having given himself over to monarchism and political nationalism.[76]

What seemed evident to everyone, except those most intimately involved, was the fact that Sorel's "defection" to the nationalism and monarchism of the "class enemies" of the proletariat was not the consequence of inconsistency or weakness of conviction. It reflected Sorel's reasoned belief that the moral rehabilitation of Europeans, the creation of a "new man," both as socialist producer and warrior, could just as easily be accomplished by mobilizing masses to the service of a community other than class. In fact, the issue of which association might qualify as a "community of destiny" for the revolutionaries of the twentieth century was to engage Marxist revolutionary thought throughout the subsequent decades.

During the period immediately after his denunciation of Sorel, international developments began to intrude into the complex reflections of Mussolini. He continued to entertain the syndicalist convictions that had earlier begun to influence his thought while conducting an increasingly intense correspondence with Prezzolini.

What was clearly in evidence was an increasing sophistication and subtlety of reflection on the part of the youthful Mussolini. The simple reiteration of notions that had become "orthodox" among German Marxists certainly no longer made up the substance of his writings and speeches. In the Trentino he had begun to articulate notions of a different sort of socialism, one in which national sentiment would occupy a critical place.

MUSSOLINI, AUSTRO-MARXISM, AND NATIONALISM

As international issues began to cloud the future of Europe at the beginning of the second decade of the twentieth century, the young Mussolini had just concluded his involvement in the ethnic politics of Austria-Hungary. It was an experience that would expose him to a number of ideological issues that were to more and more test the relevance of the orthodox version of his inherited Marxism.

In Austria-Hungary, Marxists faced a number of special concerns to which they devoted a great deal of attention. There were philosophical issues—epistemological and moral—that German Social Democrats pretended not to acknowledge after the passing of Josef Dietzgen and Ludwig Woltmann. There were contested matters, economic and historic, and questions concerning the real factors that inspired human beings to sacrifice and revolution.

As citizens of a Hapsburg empire that was host to a multitude of nations, fragments of nations, ethnic communities, and populations, the Marxists of Austria-Hungary found themselves obliged to consider all those issues attendant upon that diversity. Austria-Hungary was partially developed economically, with a large traditional, and a rapidly expanding industrial, sector—which provided a context in which the applicability and coherence of Marxism as a theory of revolutionary political conduct might be tested.

All of that seems to have made Austro-Hungarian intellectuals, Marxist and non-Marxist alike, more sensitive to all those questions German Marxists managed to neglect without particular misgiving. Once German "revisionists" had identified themselves, the remainder of the Social Democratic Party followed the somewhat stilted orthodoxies of Karl Kautsky. The Austro-Marxists, like their French counterparts, found it increasingly difficult to remain within the confines of an orthodoxy defined by German rigidities. Max Adler and Otto Bauer were to pursue some of the major issues of Marxism as a philosophy, a theory of history, and a revolutionary strategy into the intensity of the twentieth century. Intellectually active at a time when systematic social science was making its fulsome appearance, they were to produce some of the most interesting works in the tradition.

More often than not neglected by intellectual historians, more occupied with the dubious orthodoxy of notable "Marxists" such as Josef Stalin, Mao Zedong, and Kim Il Sung, the thought of Adler and Bauer remain nonetheless, extremely important in any serious consideration of Marxism as a system of revolutionary reflection. Perhaps more than any of its other aspects, Austro-Marxism's careful reassessment of the epistemology of the young Marx and the mature Engels, together with their treatment of national sentiment and political nationalism, are critical to understanding the evolution of Fascism out of the uncertainties of classical Marxism.

One fails to find reference to the impact of Austro-Hungarian thinkers on the development of Fascism, and yet their names are to be found in the works of many of the most important revolutionary syndicalists—that we know contributed to the ideology that would be Fascism. Some of the most immediate themes that were to characterize Fascism: nationalism, voluntarism, elitism, and developmentalism, already made their appearance in the years before the Italian war in Tripoli in 1911. Many of those themes engaged the attention of Austro-Marxists in a fashion that helps us understand their role in the making of Fascism.

Retracing the influence of the thought of Marxists such as Otto Bauer and Max Adler on the development of that variant of Marxism we identify as Fascism requires a return to their works—and those collateral works that appeared at essentially the same time, in the same political and historical environment. There is little serious doubt that the work of both Marxist and non-Marxist Austrian theoreticians found its way into the arguments of the *vociani*, the syndicalists, and ultimately those of Mussolini himself. The work of such thinkers is intrinsic to an understanding of Fascism as a variant of Marxism.

CHAPTER SEVEN

The National Question and Marxist Orthodoxy

In the years immediately preceding the First World War, Marxism, as a revolutionary belief system, was subject to intensive reassessment and extensive modification by any number of committed theoreticians—V. I. Lenin and Benito Mussolini among them. However orthodox they might imagine their reflections, each contributed to the ongoing modification of the uncertain system. The fact is that the Marxism that survived the death of its founders underwent significant change throughout the period—whether acknowledged or not by those responsible.

Lenin, who insisted on his orthodoxy throughout his political life, had early introduced conjectures concerning the role of elites in the mobilization of revolutionaries—that changed the character of Marxism—conjectures that could hardly find sure source in the writings of Marx or Engels. He also had begun to attempt reformulations of Marxism that might address the issue of revolution in less developed environs. The changes he introduced were important in a variety of ways. In all of this, he was only one among many.

French and Italian syndicalists, who insisted on their unwavering commitment to the Marxism they had inherited, introduced questions concerning some of the most fundamental epistemological and moral arguments at its core. They considered philosophical reductionism—tracing the thought and behavior of human beings to some external, material source—unconvincing. There was objection, in principle, to the notion that some sort of "scientific" determinism governed all human behavior—ranging from moral deliberation to act, to ideological commitment. The confidence with which the claim that human beings simply "obeyed" natural laws that escaped their control was increasingly seen as unwarranted. The automaticity of the original system became more and more systematically qualified.[1]

The entire question of how human beings came to know "matter" through simple and complex sense perception was reviewed with particular intensity. Even among committed Marxists, there were protests against the "vulgar materialism and self-sufficient positivism" that pretended that empirical science might reveal everything about all aspects of existence. In an argument that shared some elements of that to be found in the work of Georges Sorel, the Austrian socialist Max Adler argued that a sophisticated Marxism recognized that, in the last analysis, "the complete reality of our being actually resides only in the will." In that final analysis, he maintained, it was only the conscious readiness on the part of human beings "to admit truth as an obligation" that made science a meaningful undertaking. Granted that, Adler argued that it was the sense of obligation with which human beings pursued the truth that made science an enterprise "serving the ends of morality, as a value to be realized."[2]

In Austria, Adler was prepared to reopen the entire discussion concerning the role of will and morality in science and human history. In France, Sorel undertook the reconsideration of those Bergsonian arguments that turned on will and moral incentives—and imagined them liberating Marxism from that "vain and false positivism" that conceived all human behavior "subsumed" under "deterministic laws."[3]

Perhaps more than that, in the course of the discussions among Marxists, there were critical issues that turned on the nature of human sociality. As has been suggested, Engels had precipitated the discussion. He had alluded to human association in terms of families, tribes, gentes, kinship systems, and confederations that endured during long epochs—long before the existence of economic classes. Throughout prehistoric times, throughout savagery and barbarism, human beings knew nothing of class differences—all of which indicates to many that until relatively recent time human beings had adapted themselves to living life in communities other than classes.[4] This suggested, in turn, that Marxism's original claim that "the history of all hitherto existing society is the history of class struggles" could not be true—without important qualification. There were "primeval communities," innocent of class distinctions, in which human beings evolved for millennia before the emergence of any groups that might undertake "class struggle."[5] Implications followed from such assessments.

Woltmann had made a point of just such considerations in making his case for the priority he accorded race.[6] He pointed out that Engels, in granting the reality of prehistoric human communities in which human-kind housed itself for geologic epochs, had changed Marxism as a theory of history in fundamental fashion. It was Engels who spoke of a struggle for existence between "hordes, tribes, and races" that long predated class warfare. Woltmann went on to argue that it was within those alternative associations that human beings evolved. He proceeded to argue that such could be the case only if humans had been possessed of all the properties of group animals while denizens of such communities. Through the Darwinian struggle for existence, and the natural selection of suitable psychological types, members of such groups would have evolved into "collective beings" with a disposition to identify with fraternities ranging from face-to-face kinship groups to historic empires. More than that, it was within those primordial communities that humans took on all those traits that distinguish them from lesser species. All that, Woltmann argued, had to be more important than any contemporary struggle between economic classes.

By the first decade of the twentieth century, there were Marxists who were attempting to render inherited Marxist doctrines compatible with the latest discoveries concerning the evolution of human beings. Engels had done no less. He had revised the Marxism bequeathed to him by its founder in order to have it accommodate human *reproduction* as a dynamic element of human history. Alongside the material *production* with which Marx made several generations of his followers familiar, Engels insinuated biological reproduction—propagation of the species—as an equally important historical determinant. Engels introduced the modification as though it would make no difference to the integrity of the doctrine.[7]

That human descent, and human genetic modification, implicit in biological evolution required that human beings be organized in self-regarding communities—long before there were economic classes—raised a number of critical problems for Marxists. It seemed implausible to argue that it could only be class membership that fashioned human consciousness, human beliefs, and human commitment. Everything about evolutionary history suggested that other associations might be as important as class in the making of human beings.

By the beginning of the twentieth century there were Marxists prepared to consider race or nationality, rather than class, as associations in which humans might pursue their social and historic destiny. For Woltmann it was race. For many other Marxists it was to be nationality. By the beginning of the twentieth century—for a variety of reasons, both theoretical and practical—national sentiment and political nationalism came to occupy the attention of many Marxist revolutionaries. By 1910, the Sorelians spoke of critical human associations in terms of the tribes and city states of antiquity—and in terms of modern nationality. The seamless identity of the individual with any of these associations could produce all the virtues with which revolutionary syndicalists occupied themselves.

In the flood of problems that beset Marxism at the beginning of the twentieth century, nationality, national sentiment, and political nationalism surfaced with particular insistence. Since that time, Marxists have attempted to resolve the problems intrinsic to the vague and ambiguous intellectual legacy left them by the founders of their system. The problems became increasingly arresting among the Marxists of Austria-Hungary and czarist Russia—before everyone was overwhelmed by the Great War.

CLASSICAL MARXISM AND NATIONALISM

Karl Marx and Friedrich Engels left very little that might qualify as a "theory" of nationalism. Whatever they left as an intellectual legacy was intricate and confusing and gave every appearance of being hopelessly inadequate to the understanding of political nationalism—that perplexing phenomenon that was to exercise devastating influence over the history of the world in the twentieth century.

Classical Marxism's inability to deal competently with the entire question of popular nationalism as a political reality has been identified specifically as its "great historical failure."[8] By some of its most sympathetic critics, classical Marxism has been spoken of as being unable "to come to grips with the national phenomenon. . . . European Marxism's inadequate understanding and conceptualisation of the national question is acknowledged by most contemporary writers on the subject." Most have recognized the "recurrent inability of the European Marxist tradition adequately to conceptualize the national question."[9]

At the very commencement of their treatment of the subject, neither Marx nor Engels had very much to say about national sentiment or political nationalism—or their potential impact on then current events. In *The Communist Manifesto*, Marx and Engels were content to simply announce that "workingmen have no country." In their judgment, by the middle of the nineteenth century, the very activity of the manufacturing bourgeoisie already resulted in the rapid extinction of "national differences and antagonism." They went on to insist, with equal conviction, that "national one-sidedness and narrow-mindedness [had] become more and more impossible," and that by 1848 the industrialization of the major nations of Europe had "stripped [the proletariat] of every trace of national character."[10]

Thereafter, national sentiment and political nationalism were treated as nothing more than the transient consequence of developments at the productive base of society. At the time, as has been argued, Marx consistently spoke of the overt political features of any political system as "reflections" of its "economic base."[11] In discussing some of the most complex features of society, Marx would cast them as simply "flowing" from, and in conformity with, the productive forces at its base. Social relations, however complex, were somehow understood to arise in "conformity with . . . material productivity"—which, in turn, would produce equally "conforming . . . principles, ideas and categories."[12] Within such a conceptual framework, national sentiment could only be seen as the epiphenomenal by-product of developments at the productive base of society. In general, Marx appeared to conceive nationalism as conforming to felt need on the part of industrial capitalists to secure a domestic market for their commodities. National sentiment was no more than the simple by-product of economic determinism.

The founders of Marxism went on to affirm that "the ruling ideas of each age have ever been the ideas of its ruling class." Nationalism was conceived a political sentiment produced and disseminated by the bourgeoisie. Nationalism thus arose in Europe only because it reflected the felt needs of the ruling industrial classes.[13] The needs of the bourgeoisie were somehow "reflected" in the political sentiments of the working classes through a process that neither Marx nor Engels ever chose to fully explicate.[14]

The very porosity of the original Marxist conceptual scheme allowed Marxists to produce the most diverse understandings of what nationalism was—with each Marxist insisting that, whatever the case with respect to other Marxists, his or her own variant was really faithful to the original system. The necessary consequence was that there was no single "true" Marxist notion of political nationalism. The result was that throughout the entire twentieth century, the issue of nationalism continued to torment Marxists.

A number of other issues collected around the mobilizing properties of nationalism and the sentiment it invoked. In one fashion or another, concepts such as "biological race," "imperialism," "culture," "morality," "voluntarism," and simple "psychological determination," alone or together, were associated with nationalism in one or another sense. Of all the contested concepts that made up the substance of traditional Marxism, it was nationalism that was to prove one of the most mercurial.

LENINISM AND THE NATIONALITIES QUESTION

It has been argued that Lenin, as early as the turn of the twentieth century, had modified the Marxism he had inherited by assigning a special place to vanguard elites in the process of making revolution. Rather than repeat the orthodox conviction that "life" would make the "vast majority of proletarians" revolutionaries, Lenin insisted on the nonsubstitutable role of minoritarian leadership in the process—however inevitable the process, in its entirety, may have been conceived to be. More than that, Lenin proceeded to argue that revolution might be undertaken within the confines of a "backward" productive system rather than being limited to the advanced industrial nations. That realization made leadership by a knowing elite all the more necessary.

The question that has haunted Marxism since that day has been: could revolution in a less developed industrial economy, were it successful, be conceived "socialist" in any meaningful sense? Both Marx and Engels understood history to be replete with revolutions of various kinds. They also recognized that their specific sort of revolution—socialist and/or communist—could only transpire at the conclusion of the growth sequence of industrial capitalism. Both Marx and Engels had systematically and regularly rejected the notion that "their" revolution might be undertaken in primitive economic circumstances. When Marx was asked, for example, if revolution might overtake Russia while it still remained industrially retrograde, he responded that the issue was whether one might anticipate a "socialist," rather than a generic, revolution, in an economy incapable of producing the abundance that theoretically would render class conflict unnecessary. His answer was negative. Both Marx and Engels were convinced that only the material abundance of mature industrialization would break the recurrent cycle of revolution and the reconstitution of hierarchically arranged "class society." Any revolution that inherited an economy of inadequacy would leave human beings struggling for survival—to reconstitute the invidious distinctions that probably precipitated revolution in the first place.

Classless socialism would be possible in retrograde Russia only if such an uprising were a "signal for a proletarian revolution in the West."[15] Only under the condition that the nation inherit, from the industrialized West, the material prerequisites of socialist revolution—might a revolution in Russia pretend to satisfy the theoretical strictures of Marx and Engels.[16]

These were the issues faced by Lenin as he sought to engineer revolution in a Russia he himself identified with an economy that was in a state of "shocking general backwardness."[17] Initially, Lenin had papered over the difficulty by arguing that revolution in Russia would precipitate revolution in the West, thereby restoring the integrity of Marx's original prescription. That notwithstanding, history was to isolate revolution in backward Russia[18] and, as an inevitable consequence, transform Marxism into something it had never been.

It was not immediately clear how Marxism would be transformed, but it was evident that the immediate question was how Leninists might address the national sentiment that was evident among the ethnic communities that made up the working masses of czarist Russia. The sense of community that inspired ethnic workers in Russia was unmistakably apparent. They favored those who spoke their own language and who shared their common culture. To simply dismiss such sentiments as "bourgeois" was not only unconvincing, it was counterproductive.

Clearly, one could hardly have expected all of Russia's ethnic minorities to have been "internationalist" in the sense expressed in the major works of the founders of Marxism. According to the original thesis, the internationalist consciousness of the proletariat was a function of the maturity of the economic system. The consciousness of the Russian working classes could not "reflect" the maturity of the productive system at the base of Russian society. Russian workers were not "mature" in the traditional Marxist sense. They labored in an economy that was backward. Under such circumstances, it was uncertain what sense of group identity they might be expected to have.

LENIN AND STALIN ON THE NATIONAL QUESTION

In the years before the First World War, given the peculiar conditions that obtained in czarist Russia, both Lenin and Stalin had been forced to address the "nationality issue." They saw the issue as one of critical ideological and organizational significance for Russian revolutionaries. They were compelled to deal with a political reality that required that the revolutionary leaders of Russian socialism deal with proletarian groups of a variety of national origins ranging from the Jewish Bund to Muslim associations. Until the time of the Great War, given the complexities involved, Lenin never succeeded in resolving his difficulties with political nationalism. Throughout much of his intellectual life he grappled unsuccessfully with the concept as it had been left by the founders of classical Marxism.

However inept his treatment, Lenin saw the issue of nationalism as of fundamental importance for the Russia of his time. Perhaps as many as fifty "nationalities"—depending on how one chooses to define "nationality"—were "prisoners" within the political boundaries of the czarist empire. If one anticipated making revolution with "masses," it would hardly do to have those masses divided along the lines of their constituent national loyalties.[19] As early as 1913, fully conscious of just such considerations, Lenin had framed his convictions concerning the role of national sentiment in the course of historical development. Lenin made very clear that in his judgment, the "Marxist view" was that nationalism was a transient and evanescent sentiment, originally employed by the first capitalists to undermine the disabling feudal constraints that hindered the growth and territorial expansion of an industrial and commercial economy. The emergent bourgeoisie invoked national feelings in order to free the path for capitalist development of an adequate domestic market. Somehow or other the self-serving bourgeoisie inspired masses of peasants and urban workers with nationalist sentiment in order to satisfy capitalist purpose.

Modern capitalism, Lenin contended, required a large market and extended territory in order to profitably distribute its commodity production. All of that he deemed "progressive." Like Marx and Engels before him, he conceived any effort to sustain and/or foster national peculiarities that might serve to reduce the extent and adequacy of that intended market as "retrograde," and ultimately, "counterrevolutionary." In the historic sense, given Marxism's unidirectional conception of industrial development, "progress" meant the acquisition and maintenance of the largest possible territorial arena to sustain steady increments in commodity production and profitable distribution. Since socialism required the fullest development and territorial extension of the industrial base, "progress" in manufacturing served the ends of the ultimate socialist transformation of society.[20] Local "nationalisms" and parochial sentiments that limited the territorial extent of such development mitigated against all of that.

For Lenin, Marxist doctrine legitimated the "awakening of the masses from feudal lethargy . . . for the sovereignty of the people, of the nation" at a time when the consolidation of the nation was the necessary condition for the rapid development of industrial capitalism. "But," he continued, that was "the limit the proletariat can go to in supporting nationalism."[21]

Lenin maintained that once industrial capitalism had "matured"—that is to say, when it gave evidence of being "ripe" for socialist revolution—any manifestation of regional national sentiment was intrinsically counterrevolutionary. That was because Marxism knew of no nationalism appropriate to the needs of the *international* proletariat. Nationalism was intrinsically divisive at a time when the international revolution required a unified revolutionary class. The responsibility of Marxist revolutionaries was to "break down national barriers, obliterate national distinctions, and to assimilate nations"—following the secular trends of industrial capitalism itself—trends that were seen as "transforming capitalism into socialism."[22]

Those realities, Lenin insisted, left ultimately only two alternative "world outlooks" available to revolutionary leaders: reactionary "bourgeois nationalism" as opposed to progressive "proletarian internationalism."[23] There could be no third alternative.

Given Lenin's logic, as long as the advanced industrial nations had not matured to the point at which socialist revolution had become inevitable, one could expect capitalists to exploit nationalism in order to help create the conditions for further economic growth and industrial development—and nationalism, under those circumstances, might even be legitimately considered "revolutionary." When capitalism had reached maturity, and was "rotten-ripe" for revolution, the appeal to nationalism, in Lenin's judgment, was irretrievably reactionary. Given such an interpretation of national sentiment, Lenin seemed to remain theoretically uncertain on how to deal with political nationalism in less than "mature" economic conditions. There seemed to be but two possibilities. National sentiment represented either the reactionary or immature dispositions of peoples gulled by finance capital to serve its immediate purpose, or it appealed spontaneously to those peoples still lodged in economic and specifically industrial underdevelopment. It would be hard to imagine what theoretical insight would lead one to imagine that they might be internationalist in orientation.

Given such notions, it is difficult to anticipate how responsible Marxists might deal with the predictable nationalism of economically retrograde populations. And yet, for years prior to the First World War, Lenin was compelled to deal with just such considerations. His policy recommendations made up what has come to be known as the Marxist-Leninist position on the "nationalities question."

While unalterably convinced that proletarian doctrine must be international in essence, Lenin recognized that the populations of many of the real or imagined nations of economically retrograde czarist Russia, by virtue of their very backwardness, still clung to nationalist sentiments. In order that they not be alienated, Lenin advocated a policy of "self-determination" for any and all of them. He argued that prior to the revolution, the various nationalities in Russia would be required to remain united so as to advance a unified front against capitalists, landowners, and the dynasty. After the anticipated revolution, the "oppressed nationalities" of Russia were to be granted self-determination. There clearly was a measure of duplicity in the Bolshevik nationalities program. At best, the nationalism that was to be allowed the minority nationalities in postrevolutionary Russia was to be a doctrinal nationalism that was "strictly limited" to what was considered "progressive." It was not to be allowed to bourgeois ideology "obscuring proletarian consciousness."[24]

For Lenin, there was nothing substantial in nationalism. In principle, nationalism was an ephemeral form of public expression that was born of, and served exclusively, instrumental purpose. When the bourgeoisie was consolidating "nations" in order to serve its resource, productive and distributionistic requirements, nationalism was productive—compatible with the course of history that would culminate in the proletarian revolution. When the bourgeoisie sought to employ nationalism to its own specific advantage—to profit, to pillage primitive communities all over the world, to mobilize the working class against its fellows across the border—national sentiment was counterproductive. All of which Lenin understood to be entailed as "tendencies" in the "universal law" of cosmic capitalist development.[25]

During the period immediately preceding the First World War, Lenin conceived nationalism as little other than a "reflection" of prevailing circumstances. In the imperialist nations it served finance capitalism. In the retrograde regions on capitalism's periphery, it was the necessary consequence of a peculiar state of economic backwardness. It would inevitably disappear with economic maturity. In the interim, Lenin recommended its tolerance. For Lenin, *class* had historic substance, *nation* did not. His theoretical understanding of nationalism, as a political phenomenon, was reductionist—seeing it exclusively a by-product of class and economic interest. It was understood as nothing other than a transitional product of maturing industrial capitalism.

Almost a decade before, J. V. Stalin, as a political worker in the field, formulated very much the same instrumental view of nationalism as sentiment and political movement. Like Lenin, Stalin saw both as epiphenomena. He conceived national sentiment and nationalism serving specific class interests and assuming distinctive expression in the course of historical development.[26]

Closer in time to Lenin's work, in 1913, Stalin expressed his concern with a "mounting wave of militant nationalism" that was "threatening to engulf the mass of the workers."[27] He had earlier clearly expressed the conviction that "if the proletariat is to achieve" its anticipated socialist victory, "*all* the workers, *irrespective of nationality*, must be united."[28] In the period immediately preceding the First World War, that unity appeared to be in jeopardy.

In the course of his exposition, Stalin undertook to do something not undertaken by Lenin. Stalin offered a lexical definition of what he understood a "nation" to be. He told his audience that "a nation is a historically constituted, stable community of people, formed on the basis of a common language, territory, economic life, and psychological make-up manifested in a common culture." He went on to argue with considerable confidence that should "a single one" of those properties be missing, "the nation ceases to be a nation."[29] He conceived nations as transient, having a beginning and ending sometime in history. More than that, Stalin conceived the nation, an historical artifact, as belonging to a definite epoch—that of emerging capitalism.

Like some of the major German theoreticians who preceded him, Stalin interpreted nationalism, and its attendant sentiment, to be the singular product of the "young bourgeoisie," seeking to "secure its 'own,' its 'home,' market." Before industrialization sharpens class antagonisms, the emergent bourgeoisie can rally the peasants and proletarians to its cause. They become nationalists by default. Even under such circumstances, the enterprise serves essentially bourgeois interests. The fact, Stalin argued, is that nationalism, at whatever stage it manifests itself in the process of capitalist development, always serves the bourgeoisie. It is, Stalin insisted, "in its essence," an exclusively bourgeois contrivance.[30]

Prior to the Great War, both Lenin and Stalin made very clear their total rejection of nationalism as a political vehicle for the mobilization of revolutionary masses in the service of socialism. Neither ever completely abandoned that conviction. Within the conceptual notions of Marxism-Leninism, nationalism could never serve "proletarian" purpose.[31] At its very best, and under whatever guise, nationalism served only bourgeois interests. Lenin did approve the invocation of nationalism, however, in order to mobilize masses for revolution in the regions peripheral to the advanced industrial nations—only because such revolutions impaired the survival capacity of international capitalism. Nonetheless, however much such uprisings might further the world proletarian revolution, they were understood to have been undertaken in the immediate interests of the bourgeoisie.[32] Nationalism was conceived a bourgeois device, serving direct or derivative bourgeois purpose.[33] In general, Lenin argued that nationalism could only divert "the attention of large strata from social questions, questions of the class struggle, to national questions, questions 'common' to the proletariat and the bourgeoisie"[34]—thereby deflecting revolutionary energies. For Lenin and Stalin, the proletariat, in principle, could never legitimately be mobilized around anything other than *international* appeals—for international objectives. National sentiment, both insisted, could never give expression to the *true* interests of the proletariat as a revolutionary class.

In the years leading to the First World War, both Lenin and Stalin were insistent in rejecting nationalism as part of Marxism-Leninism's revolutionary strategy because both saw the local nationalisms of the many ethnic groups that made up the Russia of their time depleting the collective energies of the international proletariat. Both sought a unified, centralized association of workers, loyal to their class, rather than to any "abstract" national, interests.

For his part, Stalin had articulated a notion of political nationalism that was considerably more nuanced than that of Lenin. However much Stalin agreed with Lenin's overall revolutionary convictions, it remained evident that he considered nationalism a much more substantial political product than one might have suspected. Why that should have been the case is interesting.

Stalin's definition of the nation shares remarkable similarities with that advanced by another of his Marxist contemporaries: Otto Bauer. In 1907, half a dozen years before Stalin wrote his study, "Marxism and the National Question," Bauer produced a major work of Marxist analysis in an effort to come to understand the phenomenon of "proletarian nationalism."

One of the principal reasons for the emphatic insistence by Lenin and Stalin on the explicitly international focus of the proletariat was in response to Bauer's book. Bauer's work was to influence the debate devoted to the revolutionary role of national sentiment and nationalist convictions in the politics of the early twentieth century. It was a book written by an intellectual who had witnessed the sway of national sentiment on the proletarian communities of his native Austria-Hungary. Bauer was convinced of the importance of coming to understand national sentiment and political nationalism if Marxism was to effectively channel the real and potential energies of the "oppressed classes" to the service of proletarian revolution.

In his work, Bauer sought to systematically address the issue of national sentiment as it clearly found expression among the multinational membership of the working classes of Austria-Hungary. Like Russia, Austria-Hungary was a dynastic state, a political entity composed of the most diverse ethnic elements, held together by a hereditary monarchy. Given the reality of the national consciousness expressed by workers of the most disparate ethnic communities, Bauer sought to construct a suitable Marxist theory of national sentiment and national consciousness that would both account for their behavior and suggest future policy.

Marx and Engels had originally argued that the workers of Europe had no sense of nationality. They anticipated the disappearance of the nation state with the worldwide expansion of industrial capitalism. They saw no need to provide a more expansive theoretical account of what they held to be a transient phenomenon. Bauer had lived enough and experienced enough to realize that they had been mistaken.

At the beginning of the twentieth century, Bauer acknowledged that nationality remained a critical issue for the working class. He reluctantly applied himself to the production of a satisfactory rendering—absent from the doctrinal heritage left by Marx and Engels. He attempted to account for the continued influence of national sentiment on the political behavior of the working class at the beginning of the twentieth century.

As a result of his efforts, Bauer produced an account that has been spoken of as "a major contribution to the general development of Marxist theory in this area."[35] It was a response, however cautiously expressed, to the explicit, and uncompromising, stance taken by Marx and Engels against the national sentiment of those "historyless" Czechs, Serbs, and other Slavic national communities, referred to by the founders of Marxism as the "wreckage" of peoples inevitably destined to be absorbed into the "great German empire."[36]

It was precisely among those peoples that Bauer recognized an abiding sense of national identity that could not be dismissed by insisting that they were without a national history. They were the peoples of Austria-Hungary, and time had made evident the strength of their national sentiment. Bauer was persuaded that they entertained a true sense of nationality. Whatever they were, Bauer was convinced that revolutionary socialism could muster them to its cause only by respecting their national integrity.

Bauer recognized a certain kind of legitimacy in national sentiment, and argued that Austrian Marxists were obliged to understand the intense feeling conjured up by national cultural identification. Whatever revolutionaries chose to make of the sentiment of nationality, it was evident to him that it was an issue badly dealt with in the works of the founders of revolutionary Marxism. Even before the First World War revealed the hollowness of the socialist slogans of international solidarity, Bauer had argued for the genuineness of national sentiment and the reality of nationality.

Some time before the war, both Lenin and Stalin appreciated the importance of the issue. It was both a confirmation of the importance of the subject and the theoretical significance of Bauer's work that prompted both Stalin and Lenin to undertake to write on the "national question" years before nationalism shattered the Second International and effectively neutralized internationalism as a revolutionary creed.

OTTO BAUER AND PROLETARIAN NATIONALISM

Years before the coming of the First World War, Otto Bauer published his *Die Nationalitätenfrage und die Sozialdemokratie*,[37] a book that was to provide dimension to Marxist discussion on the national question. Until that time there was little serious Marxist literature specifically devoted to nationalism, and how it was to be understood. Most of the preceding discussion had been unrelenting in its economism and reductionism. Nationalism was presumed to be the simple product of capitalist interests. Born of the capitalist need for a large domestic market, nationalism was an invention of the self-serving bourgeoisie—a rationalization of business interests.[38] Development of the material productive forces determined its appearance, and class interest shaped its ideological expression. It was conceived a modern product, the fruit of emergent capitalism.

The treatment of nationalism, reflected in the work of both Stalin and Lenin, was to perceive it as something to be thwarted. In principle, nationalism was not to be recommended under any circumstances. Socialism's primary task was identified as "regrouping the proletariat of all countries into a living revolutionary force [having] only one conception of its tasks and interests"—abjuring national sentiment and rejecting any association with political nationalism. The "immediate mission" of socialist agitation was understood to be "the spiritual liberation of the proletariat from the tutelage of the bourgeoisie, which expresses itself through the influence of nationalist ideology."[39] Nationalism, in all its formulations and expressions, was seen as nothing more than a bourgeois snare and subterfuge, a cover for antiproletarian machinations. Through some occult process, the bourgeoisie managed to instill national sentiments in the proletariat. Such unreal sentiments could only work against the interests of the working class.

Bauer was to argue a substantially different case. He was to bring to the issue both subtlety and a rich acquaintance with the social science literature of his time.

That was true in large part because of the environment of which he was a product. The Austria-Hungary in which he was nurtured gave the international intellectual community such philosophical and social science luminaries as Sigmund Freud, Ludwig Gumplowicz, Ernst Mach, and Ludwig Wittgenstein. Bauer reached intellectual maturity at a time of intense intellectual activity in Austria, when the nascent social sciences began to have an impact on theoreticians of every persuasion.

Bauer was to become one of the intellectual leaders of what came to be called "Austro-Marxism," and shared in the respect accorded Max Adler, Julius Deutsch, Gustav Eckstein, Karl Renner, and Rudolf Hilferding.[40] All were to be spokesmen of a Marxist variant that was to have measurable impact on leftist intellectuals before and after the First World War. Of them all, for our purposes, Otto Bauer was perhaps the most important. The doctrinal developments he fostered were to impact, directly or indirectly, the lives of millions in the subsequent history of Europe.

Even the most superficial inspection makes immediately evident the sophistication of Bauer's analysis of nationalism. Compared to the treatment that was subsequently provided by Lenin and Stalin, Bauer's account is a model of careful social science explication. He undertook a conceptual analysis that documents not only his knowledge of inherited Marxist doctrine, but confirms his familiarity with the burgeoning non-Marxist sociology of his time. It was evident that Bauer's work was inspired, at least in substantial part, by serious scholarly concern—a concern that distinguishes his work from that of Lenin. Lenin's interests were almost always singularly and exclusively political, dismissing as "bourgeois" any thought that, in his judgment, was not sufficiently revolutionary. The difference is made evident at almost every point in Bauer's treatment of nationalism and national sentiment.

In the introduction to his work, Bauer speaks of his motivation. He recognized as early as the beginning of the twentieth century that the national question would be central to the political thought and policy recommendations of revolutionary Marxism in the immediate future.[41] He seems to have known that, at least in part, because he had experienced the durability and the intensity of national sentiment among the peasants and the workers of his native Austria-Hungary. Among working class organizations, he had observed the national tensions that readily manifested themselves.

As a consequence of his increased sensitivity, he clearly was not persuaded by the generalities concerning the national question that seemed to satisfy some Marxist theoreticians of his time. He conceived national sentiment as having a more profound and compelling source than simple inculcation at the hands of the bourgeoisie.

It was not that he denied the contention that nationalism, in fact, was originally inspired by bourgeois interests. Bauer was fully prepared to acknowledge that nationalism was an expression of emergent capitalism's need for a "generous, densely populated economic region," controlled by its agencies, in the effort to satisfy capitalism's implacable need to profitably distribute its expanding productivity and invest its surplus capital. Elsewhere, he speaks of the "development of nations" being a product of "the history of the mode of production and of property"[42]—satisfying at least the rudiments of the Marxist interpretation of social evolution. But he clearly felt it implausible that a sentiment so pervasive and so resistant to change could be the simple consequence of bourgeois inspiration.

Bauer's account differed from the "orthodoxy" common among German theoreticians in that he recognized that whatever bourgeois motives there may have been behind the emergence of national consciousness, in order for it to become a political reality, there must have been a susceptibility among workers and peasants. The bourgeoisie could hardly impose a sense of nationality on a population; there had to have been a ready receptivity that could account for its acceptance and persistence. Nationalism must have found a ready response among people quite independent of the specific content supplied by transient economic circumstances. It seems reasonably clear that Bauer found the standard Marxist explanation for the rise and significance of national sentiment simplistic. His work is dedicated to advancing an explanation with greater inherent plausibility.

Bauer saw national sentiment rooted in the Darwinian history of humankind. Like Dietzgen, Kautsky, and Woltmann, as well as many of the lesser Marxist intellectuals of the period, Bauer sought to trace the continuities between Darwin's convictions concerning human descent and Marxism as a conception of historical development. He sought to link national sentiment to the evolutionary history of humanity. He sought a credible explanation of why the mass of workers and peasants would become possessed so readily of a sense of national identity. Whatever the influence exercised by the bourgeoisie, it could not alone account for the broad-based national passion exhibited by members of the working class.

Like many Marxists of the period, Bauer saw human society growing out of those of animals, sharing the properties common to all social creatures. All displayed heritable differentiation that arose in the course of selection, territorial isolation, and inbreeding. He spoke of the genetic traits that came to distinguish endogamous, isolated breeding communities as the overt, physiological, biological foundation of group differentiation. His interest in these "natural communities (*Naturgemeinschaften*)" was limited—introduced only in order to satisfy the intellectual demand for comprehensiveness—an account of the relationship between biological and social evolution. It was a response to the positivistic search for a "unified science" that was a preoccupation among intellectuals at the close of the nineteenth century.

Bauer's real interests were not with such generic "natural communities." His real concern was with the specifically human "culture communities (*Kulturgemeinschaften*)" erected upon them. Moreover, his interest was not in providing a descriptive rendering of how particular cultural communities emerged from history, but rather to account for the fact that communities of humans acquired an identifiable and entrenched "national character" in the process.[43]

Bauer began his account by tracing national origins back to autochthonous breeding circles, communities of blood kindred (*Blutsgemeinschaften*), that shared not only common physical properties, but common destinies as well—born of the fact that all members shared common labor, common social relations, common law, common religious beliefs, common customs, and a common language.[44]

He went on to characterize these primordial communities, addressing himself to the general psychological dispositions that apparently animated them. He spoke of the general disposition of the members of such communities to feel comfortable in the presence of members of their community—and diffident when confronted by outgroup members. He spoke of an ingroup amity that ended at the boundary of each "natural community"—and of the individual's spontaneous identification with the community. It was identification so thorough that the one merged entirely with the other. Each individual saw in the community the essence of him- or herself.[45]

Bauer traced national consciousness back to just such general psychological dispositions—formed in the evolutionary past. In his judgment, long before there was a bourgeoisie or a proletariat, all the psychological components of a generic national consciousness were evident among human beings distributed in prehistory as "communities of destiny (*Schicksalsgemeinschaften*)."

Out of common descent, a common history, and common culture—a common destiny—a common "national character" emerges, and nations begin to make their appearance. "The nation," Bauer informed his audience, "is a collection of human beings bound together in a common destiny that shapes them into a community of character (a *Charaktergemeinschaft*)."[46]

Bauer reminded Marxists that long before there were modern nations, there were communities of destiny, distinct in their origins and durability from the occupational and class associations, the citizenship and membership in voluntary groupings, with which they were familiar. Bauer argued that the essentially economic associations and groupings of which Marx and the Marxists spoke, while predicated on more fundamental communities of destiny, were fundamentally different. The class and occupational associations with which Marxists concerned themselves were founded in relatively recent times. They were products of immediate outcome potential—material considerations that influence immediate life circumstances. Classes involve their members in the pursuit of economic interests and material comforts. They are only indirectly related to those communities of destiny that through language, law, belief, and faith create the very spiritual essence of the individual as a "species-being (*Gemeinwesen*)."

For Bauer, it was clear that the economic associations with which Marxists generally concerned themselves could not and would not command the depth of commitment one finds characteristic of membership in more primary communities of destiny. It was in life lived in primeval communities that Bauer saw the origins of national sentiment.

Thus, while Bauer acknowledged all the international obligations implicit in revolutionary Marxism, he made clear that national sentiment had a politically significant immediate priority over class membership. In the course of its development, industrial capitalism succeeded in making education a national enterprise. To service its own needs, it introduced the working classes to the historic and cultural patrimony of the nation. With rapid communication and the mass production of books, masses were increasingly drawn into an awareness of nationhood. Motivated by its search for profit, capitalist enterprise made contemporary members of the community increasingly familiar with the thought of their antecedents and the history of their community. More and more members of the general population came to share the character traits of the historic nation.[47] All of that was constructed on the reality of psychological properties rooted in the evolutionary history of humankind—properties already disposed to accommodate the deepest of community sentiments.

By the beginning of the twentieth century, Bauer contended, the elements of national sentiment had become so intrinsic to the psychology of the proletariat, that one could hardly expect them to be surrendered for a "naive cosmopolitanism" that entertained no distinctions whatever between communities. He insisted that there was every evidence that the internationalization of the industrial means of production did not mean the disappearance of a sense of national differences.[48] For the members of many communities, in fact, the realization that they were perceived "backward," economically and culturally retrograde, by those nations industrially sophisticated, prompted a response among them that could only be characterized as reactive nationalism. As a consequence, Bauer anticipated that nationalism might well become a significant political force to be reckoned with even in those nations that lacked an industrial base or an effective bourgeoisie.

In such circumstances, the pursuit of international proletarian unity could hardly be a simple matter. In Bauer's judgment, international working class collaboration could be attained only with the promise of the continued cultural autonomy, intellectual integrity, political freedom, and unity of each constituent nationality.[49] Bauer argued that the sense of community that united workers to their nationality was no less binding than their sense of association as workers. Their consciousness of nationality was stoked by a deep sense of common descent, common culture, and shared destiny, rooted in dispositions that could be traced to the life circumstances of humans at the dawn of the birth of *homo sapiens*.[50]

More than that, Bauer argued that the proletarian struggle in the service of the principle of nationality was, in essence and fact, profoundly revolutionary. For Bauer, it was only socialism that held forth the promise of the full and free development of individuals of whatever class. Only socialism would create the conditions in which each individual could fully identify, without obstacle, with his or her respective community of destiny. With that would come the sense of individual worth, rooted in identification with one's *Gemeinschaft*. Only socialism anticipated a worldwide federation of free nations growing to full flower, independent of the parochial and divisive interests of capitalists.

For Bauer, it was capitalism that distorted the sense of uniform community membership that thwarted the sense of personal worth implicit in identification with one's community. It was capitalism, by fabricating class differences, that denied workers full membership in their respective communities of destiny, those communities that provided them history, culture, and moral purpose. Only socialism, with its abolition of class distinctions, would allow workers to fully identify with those communities in which they would find not only material, but spiritual fulfillment. Those who obstructed all that were the class enemies of the proletariat.[51]

Beyond that, Bauer contended, the masters of capitalism systematically offended national sensibilities by fostering the dominance of the "civilized" over the "lesser" nations. The advanced industrial nations, he argued, sought to impose their language, their law, their customs and usages on those they considered less "civilized"—those peoples deemed, even by some Marxists, to be without history (*geschichtslosen Nationen*).[52] Socialism could only oppose all of that in the service of national sensibilities.

While Bauer was fully prepared to acknowledge the dynamic role played by the material productive forces in the history of communities, he insisted that national sentiment, as one of the realities of the twentieth century, could not be discounted as a simple "reflection" of their development. The will and intention of human beings who participated in that development could not be construed convincingly a simple reflection of that development itself.[53] In his emphasis on the role of that directed will, Bauer constructed an analytic framework that altered much of the doctrinal legacy left him by Marx and Engels.

Bauer argued that the twentieth century had not found the proletariat bereft of a fatherland. Proletarians were not devoid of national sensibilities. It was not true that they were indifferent to group distinctions. They took conscious pride in their own national culture as well as their own national history. They gloried in their nation's past achievements and dreamed of future accomplishment. As a consequence, Bauer objected—in principle and for pragmatic reasons—to any effort made to amalgamate all proletarian groups into one centralized and bureaucratized internationalism on the pretext that it was required for world revolution.[54]

The importance of Bauer's variant of Marxism can be measured by the venom with which it was attacked by Lenin and Stalin in the years that were to follow. Both charged Bauer's interpretation with major responsibility in socialism's subsequent failure to meet the challenge of the Great War. In an uncritical sense, they were right. On the occasion of the war, the working masses of Europe chose to identify with their several nations—employing arguments that shared a significant similarity with those advanced by Bauer. In fact, some of Bauer's central convictions were to serve as a bridge between nineteenth-century Marxism and the Fascism of the twentieth.

BAUER, MARXISM, AND LUDWIG GUMPLOWICZ

While the prime motivation for Bauer's work arose out of his recognition of the importance of national sentiment among Europe's proletariat, some of his intellectual strategies can be traced to that preoccupation among Marxists, at the end of the nineteenth century, to link the materialist conception of history to Darwinian notions of evolution. Years later, Karl Kautsky could still insist on their shared continuities.[55] He reinvoked the memory of Ludwig Woltmann, and agreed with him—with reservations—in seeing Darwinism as an essential part of the "material foundation" of Marxism. Bauer was of similar persuasion. In his judgment, Darwinism was an intrinsic part of the rationale of the materialist interpretation of human history. In attempting to provide the most comprehensive scientific basis for Marxism, Marxists in general, and Bauer in particular, invoked Darwinism and advanced an account of human history that proceeded from biological, to social, evolution.

Engels had originally tendered the claim in a variety of publications and with a variety of qualifications.[56] Whatever their qualifications, Marxists like Dietzgen, Woltmann, and Kautsky embraced Darwinism as an essential part of Marxism as a theory of history. While acknowledging Darwinism as a material prologue to Marxism, Kautsky complained that Woltmann had pursued Darwinism into racism.[57] And of course, Kautsky was correct.

Of course, there was something more in Woltmann's heterodoxy than simple exaggerations or misinterpretations of the relationship between Darwinism and Marxism. Woltmann recognized that the Darwinian struggle for existence, the mechanism behind the evolution of species, implied a secular process involving geologic time. That, in turn, suggested a catalog of psychological dispositions that might have become fixed, through natural selection, among human beings struggling to survive.

Throughout his exposition, Bauer made confident references to a similar process. He was candid in identifying the sources that contributed to his interpretation. In identifying those sources, he did not hesitate, in general, to cite non-Marxist social science as collateral confirmation of his views, views he considered entirely orthodox. In one place, at the very commencement of his account of the rise of nations, Bauer specifically referred to the supportive social thought of non-Marxist Italian sociologists.[58] That allusion was arresting for a number of reasons, some of which are important in the effort to trace the gradual devolution of Marxism as a revolutionary doctrine.

While Bauer's reference to Italian sociologists was generic, it was important. He used it as an introduction to his discussion of nationality and its origins—the theme of his work. It is strange that he should make recourse to Italian social thinkers, when, as has been suggested, his native Austria-Hungary was the home of some of the most innovative thinkers on the subject.

In speaking of Italian theoreticians, Bauer attributed to them the availability of a list of elements that, in their relationship, gave rise to nationality and a consciousness of nationality.[59] In fact, one readily finds such lists in the works of Gaetano Mosca, who, as one of Italy's foremost social scientists of the period, seemed to speak to all the relevant categories immediately addressed by Bauer. In addressing the issue of the "principle of nationality," Mosca identified a "community of descent," a *comunità di sangue*, a *Blutsgemeinschaft*, as one of its significant constituents. He spoke of common beliefs, laws, customs, and history, and of a "social type," a *Charaktergemeinschaft*, that results. He alluded to a dispositional sense of ingroup amity and outgroup enmity among such communities—as well as the isolation that such dispositions necessarily foster.[60]

The discussion in Mosca clearly anticipated, in substance, that of Bauer. What is curious, once again, is that Bauer used "Italian sociologists" to introduce his discussion. Years before Mosca or any other easily accessible Italian thinker, a prominent co-national of Bauer, Ludwig Gumplowicz, had provided a similar list of constituent elements that contributed to the formation of national consciousness. Mosca himself cited Gumplowicz as either the source of, or the support for, his own generalizations concerning the factors that foster group building, and lie at the foundation of nationality.[61]

Why Bauer failed to mention Gumplowicz in the course of his discussion concerning national consciousness remains, to this day, something of a puzzle. Gumplowicz has been judged to have been a sociologist of prominence, an intellectual equal of Emile Durkheim. His work, in fact, is "ranked among the most important statements of sociology in its formative period."[62] He was well known among the social theorists of his time. He was cited in a great deal of the social science literature of the period—and he was an Austro-Hungarian, a co-national of Bauer. And yet, although he refers, in his work, to an entire inventory of non-Marxist social theorists of a variety of nationalities, Bauer nowhere mentions Gumplowicz—a prominent theorist at the nearby University of Graz.

Certainly Gumplowicz's work was familiar to Marxists by the turn of the twentieth century. Why that should have been so has already been indicated. Many, if not most, Marxists were interested in the relationship of Darwinism and historical materialism. Like the Marxists of the period, Gumplowicz, as a monist and a positivist, sought to unify the social and natural sciences. His general epistemological orientation was fundamentally compatible, therefore, with that of most Marxists.

Ludwig Woltmann, as one of the Marxists of the period, seeking the union of Darwinian evolutionary science with the materialism of Marx,[63] made ready recourse to the work of Gumplowicz.[64] The impact of Gumplowicz's theoretical tenets on Woltmann's reflections may well suggest the reason why Bauer may have been reluctant to employ them.

Gumplowicz had spoken of social development being the consequence, throughout human history, of the struggle, among themselves, of "heterogeneous social elements (*heterogener socialer Elemente*)"—whether hordes, tribes, phratries, moieties, clans, ethnic communities, or religious groups. In one of his major works, Gumplowicz spoke of such conflict as involving "race war (*Rassenkampf*)"—an unfortunate characterization.[65] His work was directly concerned with the explanation of the social behavior of groups—and how that behavior provided the energy for social change.[66] Gumplowicz made the clash of heterogeneous groups the centerpiece of his conception of social change.

By 1900, Woltmann made allusion to the nature of those conflicts between heterogeneous social elements of which Gumplowicz spoke as being more primitive and fundamental than any struggle between economic classes. Not acknowledging the careful distinctions offered by Gumplowicz, Woltmann was prepared to speak of "racial strife (*Rassenkampf*)" as more elemental than class warfare.[67] Given that conviction, he thereafter was to reduce the "class struggle," so critical to Marxist political strategies, to a matter of secondary historical and political concern—to finally abandon class conflict as a serious historical determinant.[68] While Bauer was prepared to acknowledge the role played by primitive group impulses, he never renounced the immediate historical and political significance of the class struggle.

Gumplowicz's entire argument rested on a conception of historical and social dynamics predicated on the existence of mutually exclusive and contending heterogeneous human groups (*heterogener Menschengruppen*). Such groups were understood to be a legacy of humankind's evolutionary past—possessed of psychosocial properties fixed by the circumstances of the millennial struggle for existence. In the effort to survive, such social groups, through arduous selection, were understood to have become essentially homogeneous in terms of their own interests, and united in purpose by those group-building factors—consanguinity, local association, and common culture—of which Bauer later was to speak.[69]

For both Gumplowicz and Bauer the prehistory of humanity was composed of a quilt of social groups sometimes called "races," and at other times, "nations." However these groups were identified, for both Gumplowicz and Bauer the fact was that the history of humankind was written in the evolution of a multiplicity of different "social elements." Gumplowicz conceived those social elements in perpetual conflict, and in that conflict the dynamic source of adaptive social change. Strife, for Gumplowicz, was simply the surface manifestation of the universal law of development.[70] Bauer, as a Marxist, seemed to be equally prepared to speak of strife as a lever of development. Such conflict was scheduled to be resolved only through society's final socialist transformation.

Marx had understood the development of society to have been a function of class struggle, ultimately culminating in that final catastrophic engagement in which classes would be abolished and universal peace would be attained. For Marxists like Bauer there was the conviction that there would be an ultimate harmonization of class interests by virtue of which all conflict would be disarmed.

There was no place, within that final solution, for national or generic "group," conflict. For Gumplowicz, on the other hand, to suggest that the universal law of conflict between heterogeneous social groups (whether races, tribes, clans, federations, or nations) might be abridged by time, or in response to circumstances, was illusory. He counted it a piece of idealistic and essentially utopian wishful thinking.[71]

Gumplowicz's sociology rested on the conviction that the irreducible elements with which social theorists would have to deal were groups, that throughout evolutionary time, gradually took on the form of tribes, phratries, clans, city states, nations, and/or empires. Only in the course of social evolution, in complex social structures, do subsidiary castes, estates, and classes arise. They are the result of the growing diversity of material and moral interests that collect in complex communities around which ancillary groups create a peculiar identity. As long as there are societies, and group-building propensities among humankind, there will be mutually exclusive communities. Within those communities, as they become more complex, classes will articulate themselves—and like the relationships between all and any groups since the beginning of history—they too will be essentially antagonistic and potentially violent.[72] However their subsidiary relationships are negotiated or resolved, the intrinsic conflicts between the self-sustaining communities of which they were part—as nations, confederations, or empires—would persist. In substance, Gumplowicz, as Woltmann after him, did not conceive class conflict as anything other than a phenomenon episodic, limited, and peripheral to the general history of human struggle.

Bauer, on the other hand, consistently refers to all the essential social elements with which he concerns himself as the proper objects of attention only insofar as they contribute to our understanding the nature of "nations." Rarely, in the course of his account, does Bauer ever refer to alternative social groups. It is evident that his primary purpose is to address modern nations and the role played in them by economic classes. He clearly wishes to occupy himself with the failure of society's dominant classes to provide for the full incorporation of subordinate classes into the national community. For Bauer, class struggle remains critical to his rendering, both in terms of explanation of humankind's social history as well as important in the then contemporary political strategy.

For Bauer, the working classes evince an abiding desire to be fully incorporated in an historic community of destiny. They are heirs of a history that has made them irretrievably "collective beings (*Gemeinschaftswesen*)." Socialism's task, he argued, was to relieve all members of the community of the burden of class oppression, and invidious class distinction, so that all might achieve fulfillment through identification with their fellow nationals. Within his sociological rationale, as well as his policy recommendations, the only social groups with which Bauer was prepared to deal, with any application, were nations and classes.

All the properties with which Bauer identified "communities" were attributed almost exclusively to "nations." All the dispositional traits and relationship intricacies associated with elemental social groups that one finds in the works of either "Italian sociologists" or Gumplowicz, Bauer assigned almost exclusively to the nation.

Bauer seemed determined not to associate his assessment of nationalism and class relationships with anything to be found in the work of Gumplowicz. The fact that most of the substance of Bauer's account of premodern social life can be found in Gumplowicz's major works did not deter him. What he seems to have sought is to disassociate himself from Gumplowicz's fixed notion that given the universal laws governing social life, one could not expect that social life between self-conscious "elements" could ever be harmonious. Before the turn of the twentieth century, Gumplowicz had dismissed socialism as empty utopianism. In his considered judgment, the social world would forever be beset by the "universal laws of group conflict."[73] It seems reasonable that as a socialist—irrespective of how fascinating he found the substance of Gumplowicz's work—Bauer would choose to conceal any overt association. Bauer insisted that socialism would ultimately deliver universal harmony to all of humanity. A documented association to the work of Gumplowicz could only be an intellectual embarrassment. That having been acknowledged, Bauer remained convinced that national consciousness and national sentiment were active factors in the collective behavior of the working classes. While both Lenin and Stalin treated the associated phenomena as transient and ephemeral, Bauer anticipated their persistence in the world that would follow the international proletarian revolution.

The doctrinal differences between the variants of Marxism, that became increasingly emphatic in the years antecedent to the Great War, were to contribute to the creation of an alternative and heretical Marxism. All the lines of argument that were evident in the works of Marxists at the turn of the twentieth century were to come together before the First World War to supply the logic of the rationale for intervention. At the core of that rationale was an appeal to the sentiment of nationality. In Italy, as war loomed on the horizon, it became increasingly apparent that both nationalism and the notion of class struggle contended for pride of place in any discussion of revolution and social dynamics. In the doctrinal struggle that occupied Marxists of every stripe during those years, revolutionary syndicalists came to play a central role in the exchanges that were destined to shape the subsequent history of Europe. In that dispute, one found traces of contentions bruited by Otto Bauer and Ludwig Gumplowicz—and around them one can identify themes that find their original impetus in the previous ideological thought of Josef Dietzgen and Georges Sorel. One can read their impact in the revolutionary thought of Benito Mussolini.

It was in the course of that dispute that Mussolini, under the documented influence of theorists like Bauer, Gumplowicz, Sorel, and Prezzolini, identified himself with the thought that insisted that the "universal solidarity" required by Marxist revolution would neither "cancel the Fatherland" nor detract from its "ideal integrity."[74] In fact, there is more than a suggestion of the work of Bauer in Mussolini's reflections on the role of the Italian proletariat in the contested Trentino.[75] Rapidly, over the next few years, more of the thought of Gumplowicz began to surface in the prose of Mussolini—and one caught the first clear intimations of Fascism.

It was Gumplowicz who supplied the evidence of those psychological group traits that were to influence the articulation of Fascist doctrine. It was Gumplowicz who spoke of the "unlike social groups," the "heterogeneous social elements," that appeared in history in constant competition—sometimes as swarms, hordes, tribes, sometimes as clans, phratries or moieties, and at other times as city states, nations, or empires—and at yet other times as subordinate economic classes. Whatever manifest form they assumed, they were all animated by a sense of collective identity, as Bauer's "communities of destiny." They were all self-regarding in whatever form they assumed—and forever in conflict. Gumplowicz saw the class struggle, at its most significant, as no more than a relatively minor instance of a complex and varied general phenomenon.

For his part, Woltmann became convinced that *race* was the biological substratum of hordes and swarms, city states and nations, and of all the groups into which human beings sort themselves. For Woltmann it was race consciousness that supplied the psychic energy out of which history emerged. Racism was the motive force of historical development. He came to see class struggle as a relatively insignificant form of the universal struggle for existence with which Darwin had made European intellectuals familiar.

With the substitution of a struggle of races for the struggle of classes, Woltmann had transformed the very essence of Marxism. It seems reasonably certain that the work of Gumplowicz was instrumental to that consequence. More fundamental than that, Gumplowicz's interpretation of social dynamics laid the foundation for a view of history that saw conflict between heterogeneous communities of destiny, however they were defined, serving the purposes of human development. There were those who would see nations, rather than races or classes, as critical to understanding history.

It was among the revolutionary syndicalists that such considerations were to fashion yet another variation of Marxism. Together with the insights provided by Sorel, who conceived life lived in communion to provide the occasion of special virtue, the syndicalists were to address the issue of national sentiment and political nationalism in a fashion reminiscent of the exposition found in the work of Bauer and Gumplowicz. The implications of such treatment would not fully mature until the advent of the Great War.

It would seem that Bauer anticipated some of those developments—but remained ill disposed to extend his speculation to the point where it might impact on the integrity of the Marxism to which he had committed himself.

He was prepared to speculate on the nature of national sentiment, but not ready to hazard such extensive modifications of inherited doctrine as some other Marxists of his time. As a consequence, Bauer was prepared to rummage through the literature of the emerging social science of his time only just so extensively. He was prepared to employ Darwinian insights in the effort to comprehend the dynamics of human social life, but prepared to take his conclusions only just so far. In the last analysis, he chose to protect the Marxism he had inherited. In that regard, he was not unique.

Other dedicated Marxists were employing those same insights in studies they identified as perfectly orthodox. Like them, Bauer had drawn some of the implications here considered in his effort to deal effectively with the nationalities question. Like many others, he would allow his insights to carry him only so far. In the end, he could not abandon the economic reductionism and the centrality of the class struggle of classical Marxism. That was to leave his discussion concerning national sentiment and nationality without conclusion. The remainder of the discussion was left to others—who would then proceed to make history.

CHAPTER EIGHT

Revolutionary Syndicalism and Nationalism

One of the most dramatic, if little appreciated, intellectual developments in Marxist theory prior to the advent of the First World War took place among those theoreticians identified as revolutionary syndicalists. By the first years of the new century, Sorel's ideas came to influence a number of notable Marxist intellectuals, not the least of whom was Roberto Michels, one of the more important founders of modern political sociology. Together with a roster of other gifted social thinkers, including Sergio Panunzio, Paolo Orano, and A. O. Olivetti, Michels was to shape classical Marxism into a modern instrument of revolutionary politics.

Born in 1876 in Cologne, the offspring of German-French parents, Michels was to become a convinced Marxist by early manhood.[1] An Italian by choice, in the first years of the new century, he was one of the more interesting theoreticians of Italian syndicalism. He was described by those who knew him at the time as "a gifted and convinced socialist."[2] As early as 1903, he was one among many Italian revolutionary Marxists who saw in Sorelian syndicalism a regenerate socialism.

Together with his political activism, Michels early became one of the major intellectual historians of the first decades of the twentieth century. In 1909, he published his *Storia del Marxismo in Italia*,[3] which to this day provides one of the more informative accounts of the evolution of early Marxist thought on the Italian peninsula. Primarily an account of Marxism as a theory of history, the work not only catalogs the various interpretations that, by that time, collected around the inherited doctrine, but provides evidence of Michels's own orientation.

The peculiar history of Marxian thought in Italy prior to the turn of the twentieth century would hardly concern the present account except for the influence it would continue to exercise on revolutionary ideas throughout the next decades. It is clear, for example, that the social and political reflections of Mikail Bakunin left traces of anarchism, libertarianism, and emphatic antistatism[4] that persisted in the doctrines of Marxist intellectuals in Italy until the end of the Great War.

Together with anarchism, one found the sometimes decisive influence of social Darwinism in the thought of Italian Marxists. Like the foremost German theoreticians, Italian Marxists early fell under the sway of Darwinian concepts. Before the turn of the century, some of the central notions of evolutionary biology clearly influenced the Marxism of some of the peninsula's most prominent thinkers.[5] As a consequence, biological and anthropological factors became so prominent among some Italian "positivists" that an entire school of "Marxist" criminal anthropology developed, emphasizing the "materialist determinants" of human behavior.[6]

In dealing with the history of revolutionary thought in Italy, Michels identified all the variants of traditional Marxism that had already made their appearance. In his judgment, all of them collected around a set of Marxist convictions that included confidence in the "fatality of the communist revolution" in advanced capitalist economies—predicated on the necessary reality of the concentration of capital in fewer and fewer hands, together with the extinction of the middle classes in the process. Together with those beliefs was the expectation that the proletariat would suffer increasing emiseration until the entire system would end in catastrophic contraction.[7]

Michels maintained that, for Marxists, science had revealed history's "ineluctable" trajectory. The talk was of inevitabilities and absolutely predictable outcomes. As a result, and perhaps more interesting than all that, is the fact that in the first years of the twentieth century, Michels, almost casually, isolated one of the major consequences of identifying revolution with what are held to be the impeccable findings of science.

In outlining the belief system of "scientific" Marxism, Michels remarked that because the "revolutionary party" was conceived to be a unique "repository of truth," its followers were expected to submit to its leadership without reservation.[8] Michels, in the first years of the twentieth century, gave expression to a thought that was to weigh heavily in the deliberations of all revolutionaries throughout the twentieth century. In Michels's account of violent social change, one finds the unmistakable suggestion that successful revolution in our time was destined to produce a most singular system of political rule—the total submission of rank-and-file membership to "enlightened" leadership. It was among the first anticipations of what would one day be identified as "totalitarian rule."

Together with that, Michels proceeded to invoke yet another consideration that had occupied some Marxists since the first articulation of the doctrine. In making the revolutionary doctrine of Marxism "scientistic," to see revolution the automatic outcome of material factors alone, most Marxists of the period failed to assign "ideology" and "moral concerns" sufficient influence in human affairs. Michels insisted that human behavior was a function of the intersection of a number of factors, among which moral and political convictions could hardly be dismissed. Material factors and associated regularities were clearly of practical consequence, but human motivation, Michels was to argue, was no less essential.[9]

One of the results of that conviction was Michels's article documenting the role of moral considerations in the political thought and behavior of Italians.[10] He conceived moral reflection a particularly important factor in shaping the behavior of the Italian working classes and their leadership. While particularly important to Italians, he did not suggest that such concerns were restricted to them alone. His earliest discussions included regular reference to ethical and moral issues present in the deliberations of all revolutionaries, and how those issues contributed to revolutionary conduct everywhere. In 1903, he reminded his audiences that while science must provide the factual guidance for any political movement, the inspiration of conduct must necessarily turn on moral incentive. Goals, however material in character, Michels insisted, inescapably involve ethical calculation.[11] He had taken up a theme that had been recurrent, if unresolved, in the deliberations of the very first Marxists.

Michels was convinced that human deliberation involved both factual as well as ethical assessment in order to provide the rationale for human conduct. He argued that the will must be engaged if human beings were to act. He made the case for the role of moral incentive in the mobilization of those who would make revolution. The decision to act must be infilled with normative energy. In that sense, he was one with many of the late nineteenth-century Marxists who found privative the monofactorial interpretation of historic development. Like them, he found totally unconvincing the insistence that economic factors alone, however artfully defined, fully explained individual or collective conduct.

There were several questions woven into the attempt to address the issue of how human conduct might most responsibly be interpreted. The first question was whether, in fact, human behavior could be explained convincingly through exclusive appeal to economic factors. Marxists like Josef Dietzgen and Karl Kautsky understood full well that human beings act in response to moral imperatives—and that the will is informed by concerns having little, if anything, directly to do with economic interests. Their efforts to provide a reasonable response were not particularly persuasive.

The issue was empirical. It was not conceivable that human beings could be led to sacrifice and labor without an appeal to ethical principle and moral purpose. Other than that, there was the epistemological question of how one might understand affirmations of value. One understands the truth criteria governing logical and empirical claims, but how one establishes the binding character of moral injunctions is not at all clear.

Michels's preoccupation with the empirical, and not the epistemological, question is evident throughout his writings. Nowhere in his work does one find any attempt at linguistic analysis—rigorously distinguishing normative from logical and factual claims. In that, Michels was very much like most of the Marxists of his time. What they, like Michels, wanted to determine was how the world operated. Many, if not most, wanted to know how revolutions were made—not how one might vindicate them. Whatever the case, many doubted that either Marx or Engels, or those who sought to make a dogma of their teachings, had effectively addressed any of those questions.

By the time he wrote his history of Marxism in Italy, Michels had settled many of those questions in his own mind. His familiarity with French revolutionary thought had brought him into contact with the work of Georges Sorel—who made him familiar with one of the more sophisticated interpretations of complex human behavior available at that time. As a consequence, Michels became intensely involved in the emerging social science of the epoch. One finds increasing reference to the works of the major figures of modern inquiry ranging from Gaetano Mosca, through Werner Sombart and Vilfredo Pareto, to Gustav Le Bon. Their thought contributed to that interpretation that was to become integral to a current of Marxism that was ultimately identified as "syndicalism."

Syndicalism, because of the peculiar prevailing circumstances, achieved its most sophisticated and influential expression not in France, but in Italy.[12] Out of syndicalist thought was to emerge one of the most transformative variants of Marxism.

SYNDICALISM, SOCIAL SCIENCE, AND NATIONALISM

Anglophone intellectuals have spent surprisingly little time in the assessment of Italian syndicalism. There is scant substance in much of that which is available in English.[13] Unhappily, without tracing the evolution of syndicalist ideas during the years between 1902 and 1915, it is impossible to understand the transition of Marxism from the form it was received by the ideologues of Italian syndicalism to that in which it found expression in the Fascism that grew out of the Great War.

In fact, the transit can be traced with persuasive precision, involving reference to the works of an intellectually aggressive group of syndicalist thinkers that included Michels himself, together with Olivetti, Panunzio, Orano, Edmondo Rossoni, and Michele Bianchi—in effect, those "syndicalist theoreticians of the first rank" who were to serve among "the hard core of the founders of the Fascist movement."[14]

In retrospect, it is relatively easy to identify the uniqueness of syndicalist thought at its inception. As has been suggested, Michels early focused attention on ethical and moral issues as they served to mobilize sentiment in the pursuit of revolutionary purpose. In that, he continued on the path already traversed by those Sorelians who preceded him. What was perhaps different in his work was the special emphasis given to such concerns.

It was within that context—the concern with moral purpose and ethical goals—that Michels addressed the issue of national sentiment and political nationalism that was to become so critical to the doctrinal interests of revolutionaries. During the first years of the twentieth century, Michels spoke of the revolutionary significance of "ethical nationalism." He spoke of the importance of a kind of "*Kulturpatriotismus*"—a commitment to one's nationality characterized not by an identification with a specific territory, or reigning house, or given symbols, but with a given culture: a language, a religious heritage, an historic tradition, a commitment to others who share one's sense of moral satisfaction in the achievement of the greatest possible physical and spiritual well-being for all, irrespective of class or circumstance.[15]

It was reasonably clear what the young Michels had in mind. He maintained that some then contemporary socialists remained confused concerning critical concepts like "nationalism" and "national consciousness." He argued that nationalism could be understood as an aggressive defense of one's consciousness of group membership—that might manifest itself as hatred and belligerence toward outgroup members. Granted that, he went on to argue that national consciousness was a perfectly natural sense of association that he predicted would persist even after the proletarian revolution forecast by Marxists.[16] That notwithstanding, Michels maintained that nationalities, whatever diffidence was characteristic of each, could live together in harmony under special circumstances. He cited Switzerland as illustration—and proceeded to argue that socialist "internationalism did not require that one abandon national identity"[17]—simply that conditions be created in which self-regarding nationalities could live in harmony. He held that true patriotism did not conflict with socialist commitment nor rule out the persistence of national sentiment. True patriotism did not entail any particular enthusiasm for the political leaders or institutions of one's native land—or for a specific geographic space. True patriotism, Michels maintained, is a function not only of the individual's identification with a community (*Volksgemeinschaft*), but a consequence of a natural human sentiment common to all those who share an historic culture, have lived lives in familiar places, remember collective achievements, and labor in common enterprise.

More than that, Michels argued that true patriotism was expressed in the selfless commitment to those of one's community (one's *Volksgenossen*), a commitment that would gradually expand to ultimately include, in some significant sense, the entire population of the earth, however much cultural distinctions were maintained. True patriotism would one day encompass all of humankind in their natural group associations. Even in that distant world, national differences would remain, and human beings would continue to have every right to persist in celebrating their differences. True socialist internationalism would accommodate national differences and respect national sentiments. In that sense, Michels rejected the notion that the proletariat knew no fatherland. For him, the working class of every nation regularly gave expression to national sentiment. He would expect nothing less.[18]

In substance, Michels anticipated much of the argument concerning national sentiment that is now identified with the Marxist thought of Otto Bauer. As has been indicated, it was Bauer who later was to speak of nationality as a natural product of association, of shared language and shared memories. It was he who spoke of *Volksgemeinschaften* as "communities of destiny." And it was Bauer who spoke of the persistence of a sense of nationality even after the anticipated universal revolution of the working class. Michels earlier had said no less.

What is interesting for the purposes of exposition is the fact that the central ideas of both Michels and Bauer can be traced back directly to the work of Gaetano Mosca and Ludwig Gumplowicz—both major influences on the development of social science at the turn of the twentieth century. As early as 1903, Michels had entered into a collegial relationship with Mosca. They discussed Marxism and revolution with a depth and intensity that could only have profoundly influenced Michels's thought.[19] Together with that, Michels registered the influence of the work of Gumplowicz on his own theoretical development.[20]

More significant than the mechanical citation of the works of Mosca and Gumplowicz in his publications is the fact that one can easily isolate some of the controlling ideas shared by all three. It is clear that for both Gumplowicz and Mosca, social life has always been characterized by the competitive interaction of diverse groups, in struggles for existence and preeminence.[21] For both Mosca and Gumplowicz, "social elements," or "social types,"[22] whatever forms they assume—tribal, national, confederational, or economic class—interact to weave the complex fabric of history.

In the course of that history, groups compete, members develop a sense of ingroup amity, a sense that reinforces their abilities to survive in hazardous circumstances. Correlative to ingroup amity, there is outgroup diffidence—again a disposition that has had survival value throughout the evolutionary history of humankind.[23]

There are features in these discussions that harken back to traditional Marxist doctrine. As has been indicated, where Marx had originally spoken of the universal competition of *classes* as the substance of history, Engels, in his *Origin of the Family, Private Property and the State*, had spoken of hordes, families, tribes, and gens as communities in competition through those long ages before recorded history. These were the group actors—the social elements—in the drama of human history long before the class warfare of which Marx had spoken.

Many Marxists before Michels and Bauer saw in the history of human evolution the origins of the sentiment of association. The entire notion of a "sentiment of community" was understood to be rooted in the mechanics of the competitive struggle for group existence. Human beings were disposed to identify with their primary and derivative associations as a consequence of the conditions governing group survival in the course of biological evolution. The thousands of years occupied in the struggle for survival had made human beings "group creatures (*Gemeinwesen*)"—prepared to selflessly merge with those communities in which they would work out their destinies.

By the turn of the twentieth century, much of this had become implicit and explicit in Marxist discussions concerning group life. One found its clear expression in the works of Dietzgen and more emphatically in the publications of Woltmann. About the same time that Gumplowicz was publishing his *Rassenkampf*, Marxists were already talking about "group" rather than exclusively "class" struggle in the making of history. Kautsky had spoken of "social drives" having been fixed among both animals and humans during the long epochs of biological evolution. In all of this, some Marxists began to argue that human identification with class membership could only be subsidiary to identification with the variety of "heterogeneous social elements" in and through which human beings survived and evolved through geologic time.

As was the case with Engels, Marxists, at the turn of the century, attempted to accommodate Darwinian insights into their belief systems by insisting that whatever predispositions may have been fixed in human psychology in the course of evolution—in the modern world, *class* membership remained the most important. Of all the associations with which human beings have identified themselves in the course of evolution, class, doctrinaire Marxists argued, is presently the most historically significant.[24]

What most of those Marxists did not seem to recognize immediately is that such a construction makes of class membership a *contingent* variable in any account of historical and social development. The identification of individuals with their class could only be the result of class membership being the most important factor in their lives. Should there be persuasive evidence that individual, or collective, destiny is determined, or more significantly influenced, by other than membership in an economic class, one could anticipate changes in loyalty, commitment, and the readiness to sacrifice to follow.

Non-Marxist theorists had made that perfectly clear. Vilfredo Pareto, Mosca, and Gumplowicz were only the most prominent of the social scientists of the period who argued that the identification of individuals with an association was the consequence of a variety of economic, political, and moral influences. Not one of them was prepared to argue that class membership constituted either the only plausible, or the most important, association in which human beings might individually or severally work out their destinies. Woltmann and Sorel, both originally among the more orthodox Marxists, had already acknowledged as much. Once such a possibility was countenanced by Marxists, what followed was not entirely unanticipated.

MICHELS AND NATIONAL SENTIMENT

Roberto Michels was particularly active among syndicalist intellectuals during the first decade of the twentieth century. By 1908, in a long essay on "Cooperation,"[25] Michels argued that human behavior was a function of membership in a collectivity, and was governed by the interaction of a multiplicity of factors. That provided the occasion to speak not only of the importance, but of the complexity of "class identification." In the context of that discussion, he maintained that it was rare, to say the least, that any given collection of individuals all shared a specific, and exclusive, "class interest." Individuals, in any real life situation, more often than not, shared interests with more than one identifiable economic class. Moreover, Michels went on, not only are individuals and groups of individuals moved by a multiplicity, and sometimes, contradictory economic interests, but it is often the case that individuals and groups of individuals are moved by an "immaterial" consideration that conflicts with those more measurable and material. He spoke with easy confidence of the influence of language, religion, and nationality on the behavior of individuals and groups. He went on to insist that among those interests that were not immediately "material," was a subset that engaged the interests of all, irrespective of class identity. He cited the existence of law as one such instance.[26]

While extant law, by and large, may well serve specific class interests, no community would choose to be without any law whatever. One may labor to make law more equitable, more relevant, more available, but there were few who would argue that the existence of law itself was a matter of indifference to any community. Everyone has an interest in the existence of law. In effect, Michels argued that the ultimate interests of any community could hardly be served by material interests alone. There were other interests, more broadly gauged, that governed human behavior. The existence and persistence of law was one.

In Austria-Hungary, he continued, while economic factors were important, it was language, culture, and nationality, more than class, that divided the realm. Human beings, he went on, collect themselves around shared properties—properties that need not be economic. A sense of group identity emerges out of a variety of common traits, and we observe, as a consequence, the regular manifestation of that ingroup amity and outgroup diffidence mentioned by most social scientists of the period.[27]

In his subsequent discussions of "patriotism," Michels made eminently clear that he recognized national sentiment among those group-sustaining affects that unite individuals in viable association. He went on to recognize that national sentiment was often expressed in terms of religious, regional, and dynastic interests. While not the primary source of sentiment, they provided the more specific grounds of self-regarding group membership.[28] Michels was not a "primordialist." He did not imagine that human beings have always been possessed of a sense of nationality. National sentiment was a specific form of a generic sentiment that provides the ground for sustained human communion. For Michels, the sentiment of community was a by-product of human evolutionary history, and made its modern appearance as a sense of nationality under certain conditions—the consequence of the impact of a number of intersecting variables.[29]

National sentiment was but one expression of a modern sense of community, that arises out of a life lived in a "narrower or broader association, in tightly or loosely knit communities, in a certain circle of ideas which renders the individual proud to be a member of this and no other community."[30] National sentiment, "patriotism," was one form that the sense of community might assume in history. Class membership was another. Which sense would prevail would be determined by the prevalence of some given collection of normative and material interests at any given time. In the modern period, it was evident that together with class interests, national sentiment was prominent if not predominant.

In a clear sense, Michels was attempting to answer the question of why Marx would have ever imagined that the history of humanity was to be understood as the exclusive product of class struggle. Already engaged in the work of Dietzgen, Woltmann, and Kautsky, Michels chose to explain class membership by recognizing such membership as only one form group association might assume. He argued that the same psychological qualities that made human beings class creatures, made them tribal, city state, and national creatures as well. What sort of creatures they were to be was determined by some complex set of historic circumstances.

At about the same time that Michels was exploring the complexities of national sentiment, Italy found itself poised to embark on a war against Turkey in the presumed defense of Italian interests in the Mediterranean. In September 1911, Italian naval and ground forces engaged those of Turkey in Tripoli and Cyrenaica. They quickly brought Tripoli under siege, bombarded Derna, and challenged the Turkish fleet in the Dardanelles. Michels, as a socialist, was surprised by the evidence of national sentiment freely displayed by so many of the most unassuming members of the working classes. However knowledgeable he was concerning the properties of group membership, the evident nationalist fervor expressed by the lowliest of Italians left him puzzled. Among Marxists, he was not alone in his perplexity.

Some of Michels's fellow syndicalists were equally surprised by the phenomenon. They were driven to try to understand the behavior of the Italian working class when faced with the prospect of international conflict. The result was public discussion that was protracted and searching.

Prior to 1911, there had been intimations of the role national sentiment might play in the politics of the nation, and when the possibility of war resulted in what doctrinaire Marxists took to be anomalous behavior on the part of workers of town and country, syndicalist intellectuals were driven to undertake a studied analysis. In the months preceding the actual outbreak of war, for example, A. O. Olivetti addressed the question of the role national sentiment might be expected to play in Italy's domestic and foreign politics.[31] Like many syndicalists, Olivetti recognized that national sentiment was perfectly natural, the consequence of the long, evolutionary history of human association.[32] For modern human beings, national sentiment was an essentially cultural product—the consequence of shared language, religion, and historic circumstances. Michels had said as much.

Moreover, Olivetti was echoing Michels when he spoke of national sentiment as supplying "mythic energy" to collective purpose. Michels had long acknowledged that the identification with a defined group produced affect capable of generating selfless, even sacrificial, behavior on the part of individuals. The evolutionary history of human beings affirmed as much. At its best, Olivetti was to maintain, those dispositions might be harnessed to progressive doctrine, to give empirical meaning to a Hegelian conception of a goal-directed unfolding of history.[33]

Olivetti went on to make argued distinctions. He rejected what he identified as "political nationalism" as artificial, calculated only to serve exclusively "bourgeois" interests. Neither syndicalists nor the proletariat could have interest in such a contrived nationalism. Nor could either have interest in the "anthropological racism" produced by intellectuals, such as Woltmann, who sought to make special sense of group sentiment in the context of Darwinian evolution.

Olivetti went on to indicate that the most gifted social theorists of the time—Ludwig Gumplowicz foremost among them—treated biological race as a derivative and subsidiary product of group life.[34] He pointed out that Gumplowicz dealt with race as a group phenomenon, a by-product of associated life. Gumplowicz did not confuse the reality of group life with the attempts by biologists and anthropologists to distinguish one anthropological race from another. Biologists and anthropologists succeeded only in making race an "abstract" classificatory category, capturing under one or another rubric some set of ascriptive properties having little to do with the natural sentiment that animated real human beings. For Gumplowicz, national sentiment, like class sentiment, is not the result of scientific abstraction. Both are spontaneous feelings natural to a life lived in common. "Race," as the abstraction it had become for evolutionary scientists, hardly possessed the mythic energy both Michels and Olivetti were prepared to associate with the sentiment of nationality or class.

Individuals were prepared to sacrifice for their nation or for their class, but hardly for their race—defined as it was by abstractions. Human sentiment could inspire the members of almost any real association. Anthropological abstractions, Olivetti argued, could not provide the psychological grounds for any association that might so serve.

Olivetti concluded his discussion with the recognition that the sentiment of "nationality," however natural, varied in expression throughout history. As both Gumplowicz and Michels had argued, group sentiment was an object specific expression of a general sentiment of association. As such, it was a sentiment that could animate any durable human association. At the beginning of the twentieth century, that sentiment found manifest expression in nationalism and class identification—the two "realities" with which true revolutionaries would have to contend.

At the beginning of 1911, Olivetti was prepared to argue that it was class with which Italy's workers would identify. Conversely, he held that political nationalism addressed itself to, and was a contrivance of, the middle class. He maintained that, like the abstractions of anthropologists, the contrivances of the possessing classes entirely ignored the realities that governed the life of the working masses. Workers could not share in the enthusiasm generated by political nationalism, for workers were innocent of any knowledge of the cultural history of the nation. Illiterate and unschooled, they had no cultural or historic sense of the "fatherland." Opposed to the "bourgeois government" that controlled their environment to their disadvantage, the proletariat could only be mobilized by appeals to their class, rather than their national, interests.

As can be appreciated almost immediately, Olivetti's analysis trafficked on the insights earlier supplied by Gumplowicz and Michels. The distinctions he drew between nationalism and syndicalism were based on what he understood to be the realities of his time. With the actual outbreak of the war in Tripoli, Olivetti continued his line of argument—but that argument unexpectedly, but inexorably, led him to make a case for proletarian support for the nation's war in Tripoli.[35]

In making his argument, in September, for supporting the war against

Turkey, Olivetti argued that reflection had convinced him that the Italian proletariat, in fact, did have a manifest investment in the present and future of their nation. He argued that the war was part of the historic process that Marxism itself had taught revolutionaries to anticipate, and in which they were expected to participate.

Marxism had taught revolutionaries that the anticipated social revolution would be forthcoming only as an accompaniment of the full maturation of industrial capitalism—in the course of which a developing capitalism would be driven to expand over extended regions, introducing the elements of modern production to those places and peoples bypassed by history. Italy had only begun to participate in just that predictable sequence. To obstruct Italy's participation in that historical development would be to deflect proper growth, and consign the peninsula to the "limbo of precapitalism" forever—and foreclose on the revolution.

For Olivetti, it was evident that the nation's bourgeoisie, charged by history with its economic development, had failed to display the properties requisite to the task. For whatever reason, Olivetti maintained, the Italian possessing classes had proven themselves passive and ineffectual, remaining marginal to the process intended to shepherd the nation into the modern era. As a consequence of the very backwardness of the peninsula, the proletariat remained entirely unprepared for revolutionary responsibilities. The most competent and aggressive among them abandoned their retrograde environment in order to immigrate to places where they could better survive and prosper. In Italy, the revolution was faltering.

The war in the Mediterranean provided the occasion for transforming the circumstances of the working classes of the peninsula. Olivetti argued that it would goad the bourgeoisie to once again take up the tasks of an adolescent capitalism—development and expansion. It would force the nation to take on properties with which it was not familiar—a Nietzschean and Bergsonian vitality that was intrinsically revolutionary. To commit themselves to war, the syndicalists would give expression to a manifestation of "force, audacity, and energy . . . infinitely preferable to the stagnant pettybourgeois and reformist notion of life lived without challenge." The war would serve as a "revolutionary propaedeutic," the initiation of a process that would produce a "new civilization characterized by producers," who would be, themselves, "profoundly heroic," to live in an electric atmosphere of "constructive idealism," united "by a robust and intrepid consciousness" in "organic and assertive harmony, steadfast and free, disciplined yet spontaneous."[36]

Animated by the thought of Marx, Sorel, Nietzsche, and Schopenhauer, an "aristocratic syndicalism" would inspire a revolution that would result in the creation of a heroic, economically developed, industrially mature, and "technologically advanced," nation—a nation "stronger, wealthier, and renewed, with an increased respect for itself, . . . at last no longer burdened by the morality of slaves."[37] In substance, by the end of the war in Tripoli—employing all the elements of social theory found in the revolutionary socialist works of Marx, Sorel, Michels, Paolo Orano, and Arturo Labriola—Olivetti had put together the clear outlines of a conception of radical national syndicalism that was to influence the thought of revolutionaries throughout the entire period leading to the outbreak of the Great War.

Olivetti addressed himself to that national sentiment he held to be a spontaneous manifestation of a collective will, shaped by culture, and inspired by memories of a history of achievements that contributed to the uplift of humanity. That sort of nationalism gave expression to a particular "collective personality," moved by a revolutionary vision of a "concrete and progressive reality."

In all those senses, Olivetti saw "integral" nationalism as kindred to revolutionary syndicalism. Both were dynamic doctrines of "energy and will." They both saw political democracy as an expression of passivity and accommodation, of false illusions of universal fraternity and effortless meliorism. Like Michels, Olivetti argued that the achievement of real purpose in the modern world required sober convictions animated by natural, rather than artificial, sentiment. Both rejected the commonplace convictions of what passed as modern "democracy." Both were convinced that masses are incapable of undertaking self-directed and self-sustaining activities. For both, masses must necessarily appeal to leadership to avoid lapsing into total irrelevance.

At about the same time that Michels was finishing his masterwork on the oligarchic tendencies in political systems,[38] Olivetti was making the same point and addressing himself to the necessity of elite intervention in the mobilization of human resources for social revolution. Olivetti spoke of the role of myths, and the invocation of heroes, to instill in masses a sense of the seriousness of life. By the time of the war in Tripoli, the syndicalists shared all these notions with developmental nationalists.[39]

Together with all of that, both revolutionary movements were inspired by an ethos of production. Both saw their revolutions as directed by an "aristocracy of producers," disposed to dissipate the hedonism and selfishness that characterized the shallow and unfortunate world they knew. These were the doctrinal elements that had matured within the ranks of syndicalist intellectuals by 1912. They are to be found in the published works of those most distinguished.[40] The same ideas were to resurface in the arguments advanced by those who would intervene in the Great War. In 1915, they were to arguments that were to be bruited by Mussolini, the leader of Italy's revolutionary socialists.

It was Michels who would formulate the arguments that would bridge the distance between the War in Tripoli and the Great War.

He would gather those arguments together in his *L'imperialismo italiano*—published on the very cusp of the First World War.[41] In the preface to that work, Michels reminded his audience that he had long involved himself in the study of problems that collected themselves around the issues of the fatherland (*patria*), the nation, and nationality. The work he then presented the reader was one that sought to understand the collective psychology that "approved with enthusiasm, and with almost complete unanimity, . . . [Italy's] policy of armed expansion" against the Turks in 1911. For the first time in the modern period, Italians, long held to be an inherently pacific people, had taken up arms. Michels understood all of it as the first appearance of a "proletarian imperialism"—an armed effort to compel the "great powers" to recognize that "proletarian" Italy would no longer serve as tributary.[42]

MICHELS AND "PROLETARIAN NATIONALISM"

The entire, complex argument found in *L'imperialismo italiano* contains all the elements of Olivetti's rationale supporting the war in North Africa. The principal difference between the two resides in the fact that Michels's rendering is a more detached, didactic, and less dramatic, presentation. Other than that, one does not find any effort on the part of Michels to explain the sequence of events leading up to the war by assigning exclusive efficacy to class interests. For Michels, as was the case with Olivetti, the war in Tripoli had other than economic causes. However much some members of the business community profited from the sale of comestibles, uniforms, and ancillary military supplies, for example, and however much entrepreneurs in heavy industry profited from the provision of iron and steel together with the sale of weapons of war to the state, Michels argued that the desire for such gain could not have determined the decision to engage the Caliphate in 1911. There were enough economic interests desirous of peace to neutralize those inclined toward war.[43] Clearly convinced that economic variables could hardly account for Italy's decision to undertake war against the Turks,[44] Michels cited three influences he considered far more determinant: demographic, political, and psychological.[45]

That Italy found itself attempting to support a rapidly growing population created all-but-intolerable political, economic, and moral pressures on its ruling class. Michels dutifully recited the statistics recording the numbers of Italians who had fled their homeland over the preceding two decades to seek opportunity elsewhere. Together with that accounting, Michels recounted the budget of humiliations suffered by those workers who had settled on foreign shores. He reported that the Italians—almost all workers—were regularly demeaned, often assaulted, and not infrequently killed by mobs in the lands in which they sought succor. They were lynched in the Southern United States, and made subject to homicidal assault in France, in Switzerland, in Argentina, and in Brazil.[46]

Michels saw the woes of Italian migrants the result of several factors. Italy was poor, and singularly ill considered by the more advanced countries. Its government was incapable of extending any effective defense for Italian citizens who sought work in foreign countries. Italy had neither military nor economic leverage with those foreign governments that controlled the lives of its translocated citizens.

Michels argued that Italy, because of its retrograde economy, could not support its population—and could not protect them when they sought livelihood elsewhere. The peninsula's population was denser than almost any country in Europe, and its industrial base, while developing, was insufficient to provide employment for all those who made themselves available. Agriculture, centuries old, conducted with the most primitive of methods, largely labor intensive, still found itself burdened with surplus labor.

In the course of his account, Michels, like Olivetti, focused primarily on the retrograde character of Italian industrial development. He spoke of an Italy decades, if not centuries, behind the North European countries.[47] Italy was capital poor, almost half its population illiterate, and ill prepared for tasks in a modern setting. Italy, at the turn of the twentieth century, was something other than a developed nation. Unlike those nations, fully capable of marshaling their own populations to productive enterprise—Italy exported its workers, to consign their present and future to the control of foreigners.

Michels insisted that the ultimate resolution of the problems that attend the massive outmigration of Italians was to be found in the rapid industrialization of the nation's economy, together with the modernization and growth of its traditional agricultural sector. In the interim, a space was sought somewhere that could accommodate the nation's surplus population without abandoning Italians to the uncaring ministrations of foreigners. The war in Tripoli, in his judgment, was an effort to secure that space. Italians from the most impoverished and densely populated regions of the South could make the easy transit to Libya where they might make a better life for themselves under the protection of their own government.

While that appears to have been the intention, what becomes evident in Michels's text is his recognition that the acquisition of part of the North African coast, in and of itself, would do very little to solve Italy's immediate demographic problems. Libya could hardly accommodate the hundreds of thousands of Italians that sought escape from the poverty of the homeland. Most of the available land in the territories acquired by the war against the Turks was owned by long-established Arab proprietors, and was hardly arable without extensive and expensive irrigation. There was little industry in the region, and other than the opportunities created by government services, the prospects of meaningful employment for any new immigrants were not good.

It is not necessary to follow the text very far to realize that while Michels argued that demographic pressures largely influenced the decision to embark on the war against the Caliphate, he did not expect the conquest of Tripoli, in and of itself, to significantly change the dynamic that saw Italy losing workers to the service of others.[48] Nonetheless, Michels supported Italy's decision to wage war against Turkey. Why he did so was interesting in terms of Italy's immediate future.

Michels addressed issues that were far broader than the war itself. While the conquest of a portion of North Africa would do little to solve Italy's immediate demographic problems, it would contribute to the psychological transformation of Italians. Michels argued that the war, and the mobilization for war, would serve to rekindle among Italians the memories of a past that had seen Italy the seat of one of the world's foremost civilizations. The call to arms might recall the onetime grandeur of the nation. The war, and the mobilization for war, might reinvoke that sense of historic responsibility among Italians that had once characterized the Rome of antiquity. Italians would speak, once again, of the Mediterranean as *mare nostrum*, our sea—and of "restoring to the Motherland that which was once hers."[49]

Any reasonable reading of Michels's exposition reveals that his concerns were far more complex and comprehensive than any simple treatment of Italy's war in Tripoli. In that, he followed many of the suggestions found in Olivetti's account. Michels found in the call to armed conflict a call to heroism, and productive creation. It was a call to mobilization around the myth of Roman glory.[50]

Michels fully appreciated the role of evocative myths in the mobilization of masses. Their efficacy, in his analysis, was general—not in the least limited to the gathering of Italians. He argued that political symbolisms, particularly the myths of ancient glories, served to mobilize collective energies in most modern cases of national revolutionary, economic, political, and military undertakings. In effect, generic collective sentiment could be shaped into modern political nationalism through the medium of myth and collective aspirations.[51]

In Michels's text, one finds an account of the specifically political, diplomatic, and strategic interests of Italy independent of the issue of the war in Tripoli. It was clear to Michels that the war against the Caliphate would not resolve all the difficulties Italy would face in the relatively near future. On the one hand, it could provide basing facilities on the North African coast that might challenge the supremacy of Great Britain and France in the Mediterranean. On the other, it distracted Italy from its efforts to restore its control over its "lost lands" in the Trentino and Dalmatia. There was the acknowledgment that Austria had long thwarted the legitimate interests of Italy in the Balkans, in the Adriatic, and in the Mediterranean. It was Austria-Hungary that occupied lands whose populations were Italian. It was Austria-Hungary's navy that threatened the long coast of Eastern Italy, defenseless because of its inhospitability to naval bases that might serve the nation. For Michels, it was evident that victory in the war against the Turks did nothing to address any of those issues.

Michels held all those matters to be of concern for his adopted nation, and that the lack of their resolution contributed to the sense of gathering international tension. The war in Tripoli had made evident to him that a constellation of material and moral issues animated Italians and signaled momentous decisions to be addressed in the not-too-distant future.

All the elements that together made up the syndicalism of the first years of the century reappeared in the "proletarian nationalism" Michels identified in 1913. He made a case for a revolutionary nationalism that would inspire an historic people to restore an ancient grandeur by infusing them with an ethic of labor and sacrifice, calculated to sustain a program of rapid industrialization and economic growth. The moral imperatives would be "proletarian" because Italy, as a nation, suffered all the disabilities Marx had identified with all those who labor. Italy, in its entirety, was "proletarian." Its opponents were "plutocratic."

By the time of the Italo-Turkish War of 1911, the most radical of Italian syndicalists had put together all the components of a revolutionary ideology, rooted in Marxism, but transformed by the thought of Sorel and all those Italians he had swept up in his vision. For all its prefigurations found in the work of intellectuals like Michels and Olivetti, how comprehensive the ideology of revolutionary syndicalism had become only became apparent with the coming of the Great War.

FILIPPO CORRIDONI, THE ARCHANGEL OF SYNDICALISM

There is perhaps no better manner with which to illustrate the doctrinal developments among Italian revolutionary syndicalists in the period between the War in Tripoli and the First World War than to trace them in the thought of the young Filippo Corridoni. He was called, by those who admired him, the "tribune" and the "apostle" of labor, and after his death, the "archangel of syndicalism." In the years following the Great War, it was his name the first Fascists invoked in order to signal something of the character of the revolution they sought.

Born on the nineteenth of August in 1887, in the town of Pausola, in the province of Macerata, he was the son of a foundry worker, from whom he inherited the sentiments that made him a Marxist at the age of seventeen,[52] and a revolutionary syndicalist at twenty. A voracious reader and an ardent orator, he very quickly rose in the ranks of the revolutionary labor movement, to provoke the abiding concern of the authorities. After his first arrest in 1907, he spent the next eight years in and out of Italian prisons and in episodic exile.

His publications throughout this period are distinguished only insofar as they reflected standard syndicalist argument. His *Riflessioni sul sabotaggio* was a rationale for the employment of sabotage in the defense of the interests of the urban proletariat[53]—the publication and distribution of which cost him a period of confinement for the advocacy of violence against persons, property, and the state.

There is nothing in these essays that would distinguish Corridoni's thought from that of any number of other revolutionary syndicalists.[54] Only in the months of Italy's indecision, after the outbreak of the Great War, and before Rome's commitment to the Triple Entente in May 1915, did Corridoni give expression to those doctrinal statements that were to render him the herald of Fascism. However distinctive Corridoni's thought during that critical period, one can trace its elements to the arguments broadcast by those radical syndicalists who were his immediate antecedents and intellectual mentors.[55] Corridoni put those ideas together in so dramatic a fashion that they inspired many of Italy's workers to volunteer their services in the cause of the fatherland.

In the crisis generated by the advent of the Great War, Corridoni's convictions had taken on a particular cast. The form assumed was distinctive, fashioned of continuities that could be traced not only to Sorel, but to many of those syndicalist thinkers with whom Corridoni shared his life and beliefs.[56] As history would have it, Corridoni was not to have much time to fully develop his ideas. As a volunteer in the armed forces of the king, he was to fall in the Great War at the age of twenty-eight—in an attack on Austro-Hungarian defenses in the highlands of Carsico. And yet, he left so inspiring an argument, that long after his death some of its elements were to be invoked and reinvoked by Italy's revolutionaries.

While in prison in April 1915, serving yet another sentence for political subversion, Corridoni wrote his final, and most substantial revolutionary tract: *Sindacalismo e repubblica*. It was to serve as his political testament, to be identified by Fascists, throughout the history of their party, as one of the doctrinal inspirations of their movement.[57] Like Michels's *L'Imperialismo italiano*, Corridoni's *Sindacalismo e repubblica* was a transitional political statement that documents yet another stage in syndicalism's passage from Marxism to Fascism.

That having been said, there is absolutely no doubt that Corridoni conceived his long essay of April 1915 as fundamentally Marxist in substance. He says as much in his exposition.[58] He makes eminently clear that he always was, and remained at the time of his writing, committed to the central convictions of the revolutionary from Trier. He understood himself drawing implications from a complex legacy.

In fact, he proceeded to explain why few, if any, of Marx's predictions had been realized in the more than a quarter century since his death. Corridoni acknowledged that there was little, if any, compelling evidence that Italian industry had undergone the concentration of capital in fewer and fewer hands Marx had anticipated for all capitalist systems. Nor had there been a correlative disappearance of the middle classes, or increasing emiseration among the proletariat.

In his catalog of factors that had influenced the evolving economy of Europe, Corridoni cited those already advanced by both Marxist and non-Marxist analysts ranging from Bernstein, through Kautsky, to Woltmann, and beyond. For his part, Corridoni chose to emphasize the interventions of the state in the national economy as an explanation for the apparent inapplicability of Marx's "laws of capitalist development." The state had conjured up tariff regulations and provided special privileges to industry and agriculture that insulated the capitalist economy from the "natural laws" that Marx had argued ultimately would bring down the system.

For all that, Corridoni continued to invest confidence in the truth of Marx's doctrine. It was the political behavior of the state that interfered with the working out of the process; and then there were technological developments that rendered capitalist production so profitable that industrialists could afford to be somewhat "generous" to workers and thereby, in some measure, relieve the wretchedness of their lives and impair their revolutionary consciousness.[59]

For Corridoni, that helped to explain why there had not been the promised revolution. There was no doubt in his mind that Marx's insights into capitalism, as a modern productive system, had been basically correct.[60] But whatever the merits of his explanation for the failure of Marxist prognostications, one part of his argument was to have critical influence in the development of syndicalist doctrine and the articulation of Fascist ideology.

Like many of the syndicalists before him, Corridoni recognized that Italy was laggard in its economic development and technological proficiency. Not only was Italy economically and industrially retrograde, it appeared "organically incapable" of resolving its disabilities. Italy appeared destined to languish in underdevelopment, suffering all its attendant disabilities. Italy's bourgeoisie had failed to complete their "historic mission"—the industrialization of the peninsula. Marx had clearly indicated that industrial maturation was the necessary condition for revolutionary resolution. Without schooling in a mature capitalist system, the proletariat would never develop either the requisite class-consciousness or the associated competence essential to the assumption of control over the postrevolutionary productive system.[61]

Unlike Lenin, who seemed to see nothing in the fact that he proposed to make "socialist" revolution in an industrially backward nation, Corridoni, like many of the revolutionary syndicalists of his time, was prepared to draw a number of significant consequences from that reality. He advanced some relatively specific policy recommendations from the recognition that Italy remained economically underdeveloped.[62]

While Lenin imagined that the Russian revolution would precipitate a worldwide proletarian revolution that would provide the industrial base for the socialism he advocated, Corridoni and the revolutionary syndicalists of the period recognized that any such eventuality was most implausible.

Instead, Corridoni, and the revolutionary syndicalists, advocated a "revolutionary development" of the economy of the backward peninsula. What became evident was that Corridoni, and the revolutionary syndicalists, had a strategy, radically different from that of Lenin, for addressing the problem of economic backwardness.

Like Lenin, Corridoni spoke of the accelerated and accelerating productivity of capitalist industry in general—with the result that in the advanced industrial economies domestic markets were quickly saturated, making it impossible to profitably clear inventories. What followed was the frenetic search for market supplements. It was within that general context that Corridoni spoke of those features of the modern world that had become commonplace in the revolutionary literature of the turn of the century. Like Lenin, and Hobson[63] before him, Corridoni argued that since capitalism's prodigious yield could not be sold profitably in domestic markets—capitalists were driven to seek market supplements and investment opportunities outside the system. That necessity was considered, by most Marxists and reformers of the period, the "taproot of imperialism."

Corridoni proceeded further with the argument. He drew from it implications seemingly absent from Lenin's *Imperialism*. Corridoni maintained that economically less developed nations suffered very specific disadvantages in the general process precipitated by imperialism. He held that industrially retrograde nations on the periphery of advanced capitalism did not have the capacity to defend either their territorial or market integrity. With too narrow an industrial base, they could not create a military that could protect their physical, financial, or commercial environment. Latecomers to industry were at a serious disadvantage in the modern world. They were demeaned, exploited, and humiliated in their relations with "the great powers"—and frustrated in their efforts at rapid economic growth and industrialization.[64]

Without protective tariffs, domestic industry in less developed countries was overwhelmed by products from more advanced competitors. Less developed communities were literally and figuratively "colonized." Their populations were alienated from their historic past and their native culture. The poor nations on the margins of capitalism could not prosper. Bereft of domestic capital, rich only in population, poisoned by an imported political culture of indulgence and individuality, the latecomers to economic development in general, and industrialization in particular, were threatened by perpetual backwardness, together with cultural and moral decay.

For Corridoni, Italy found itself in just such circumstances. It struggled to survive in what he called essentially "precapitalist conditions." Italian capitalists lacked initiative, resources, and the requisite autonomy for rapid industrial development. The inevitable consequence was the attendant immaturity of the proletariat. Italy's workers could neither make revolution nor effectively direct the economy should such a revolution be successful.[65] In those circumstances, syndicalists could neither advocate nor expect the kind of revolution that required the participation of the "vast majority" of a population composed of "class-conscious" proletarians.[66]

Corridoni argued that the revolution that had begun to cast its shadow over Italy could only be the consequence of the failure of the entrepreneurial bourgeoisie to discharge its "historic mission."[67] Because industry was underdeveloped, there were only few workers possessed of the maturity that might make them true revolutionaries. The classes on the peninsula were not well defined. The only interests that sustained their activities were local, material, and uninspired. Corridoni argued that none of that could initiate or sustain the kind of revolution Marx had anticipated.

Corridoni argued that a retrograde Italy required inspiration. The tasks before the nation, if it ever really aspired to attain the promise of material prosperity, spiritual fulfillment, and equity, required unqualified commitment, discipline, sacrifice, and labor by the entire population—agrarians, artisans, industrialists, and workers alike.[68] He clearly expected some form of "class collaboration" during the process, until industrialization produced the mature working class that might service a syndicalist economy.[69]

During the interim, from economic backwardness to industrial maturity, Corridoni expected the war that loomed on the horizon to result in the final territorial completion of the "beloved nation" that had only recently achieved nationhood with the Risorgimento.[70] In itself, that would stimulate economic growth and industrial sophistication. Other than the immediate effect of resolving the nation's irridentist impulses, a victorious Italy, having successfully conducted itself in a major conflict, would be capable of defending its future economic and commercial interests.

That would be an important consideration, since at the victorious conclusion of such a war, the nation would be at the crossroads of trade between the Mediterranean and Asia. Italy would once again become a mercantile nation—required to defend its sea lines of communication and trade. Its economy would grow and deepen.[71]

Italians would no longer find it necessary to leave their homeland to search for a livelihood in the service of foreigners. The nation would be cured of that "dangerous malady that deprived it of its most youthful and most ardent workers."[72]

Corridoni spoke of all this as part of an "adaptive" or "transitional" revolution.[73] The conditions necessary for the revolution Marx had anticipated had not matured. The revolution that urged itself on Italy would serve as transitional to the economic and industrial maturity of the peninsula.

Until the very day he left to take up arms in a national struggle from which he was not to return, his ultimate purpose remained forever constant. The revolution he anticipated would involve an extensive collaboration of classes—ill defined as classes were in that largely ill-defined economic environment of retrograde Italy.[74] In the future, under the auspices of a developmental revolution, class interests would be more sharply defined. In some future time, Corridoni sought the advent of an "integral" and "organic" republic, arrayed in federated, and confederated, craft and professional syndicates.

For the more immediate future, he went on to propose a people's militia, in place of a standing army, that would involve all citizens in the defense of the nation. That, together with the proposed federation of workers' syndicates to govern the economy, the functions, and hence the prerogatives, of the "bourgeois" political state would be maximally reduced.[75] The bourgeois state would no longer cripple the economy with enactments that succeeded only in dissipating capital and deflecting productivity.

Echoing Sorel and his syndicalist colleagues, Corridoni sought a revolutionary society of combatants and producers. To that purpose, he advocated popular legislative initiative, referendum, and recall in order to achieve and sustain the republic anticipated by the original founders of the movement.

As an activist advocate of Italy's intervention in the Great War, Corridoni recognized the role played by commitment to the national community in the entire historic process that was unfolding. What is equally clear is the fact that Corridoni understood that Italy had only begun the arduous process of economic maturation. If the process were to be successful, it would involve all Italians in a complex and demanding series of responsibilities that promised little in terms of immediate material benefit. There would be only moral satisfactions and personal fulfillment for those animated by the spirit of devotion to a much loved "community of destiny."[76]

As has been suggested, many Marxists at the turn of the twentieth century understood the sentiment of association that inspired commitment, sacrifice, and labor from human beings. As a generic sentiment—the probable product of evolutionary selection—it could infill any number of alternative associations. By the advent of the First World War, many Marxists understood that workers, as a class, could share a sentiment of belonging with all citizens of the national community. Very few, Lenin among them, refused to accept such a possibility or draw out any of its implications.

ITALY, REVOLUTIONARY SYNDICALISM, AND
THE COMING OF THE GREAT WAR

The Great War was the cauldron in which were fused all those elements of traditional Marxism that had sorted themselves out of the body of work left as an intellectual heritage by Marx and Engels. At the core was a recognition that human beings were disposed, by nature, to identify themselves with a community of similars. Long before it became a concern for those who later became known as "mainstream" Marxists, syndicalists had written extensively about the moral and psychological relationship of individuals and the groups with which they identified themselves.

Olivetti and Orano had early written about the psychology of human beings in association.[77] Both acknowledged that human beings have regularly identified themselves with groups as varied as tribes, moieties, clans, religious sects, dynasties, empires and nations—the identification a function of contingent circumstances.

Only those Marxists who were to identify themselves as Bolsheviks denied the analysis merit. In the years before the Great War, both Lenin and Stalin rejected the possibility that members of the proletariat—or peasants, or members of the bourgeois—could identify with their nation. Anything like that could only be the consequence of corruption, venality, seduction, or "false consciousness." Throughout the years that were to follow, that conviction was to create very special problems for Lenin and his revolution.

Those revolutionary syndicalists who opted to support Italy in its war against Germany and Austria-Hungary were to identify themselves as "national syndicalists"—to include in their number some of the most important ideologues of the first Fascism. Corridoni, who, like Mussolini, had opposed the War in Tripoli, decided to support Italy in the Great War—seeing it as a "revolutionary war"—out of which the nation would emerge transformed. Corridoni's decision was not made on impulse. It reflected the thought of Arturo Labriola, one of the principal leaders of revolutionary syndicalism. It was shaped by the reflections of Roberto Michels, and the political convictions of A. O. Olivetti, together with a host of nameless and forgotten radicals who carried the elements of the Marxism of the nineteenth century into the Fascism of the twentieth. It was one of the principal leaders of syndicalism, a gifted and knowledgeable Marxist, who anticipated what the revolution implied for a nation struggling to find its place in a world of advanced industrial powers. On the occasion of Italy's war against the Ottoman Turks, Labriola said that his nation's future inescapably involved "revolutionary purpose." It would involve all that spoken of by Corridoni. But more than that he affirmed, "Let us be clear that we are not only in combat against the Turks in Tripoli or against their naval deployments in the Dardanelles. We struggle against all the intrigues, the threats, the impostures, the wealth, and the weapons of plutocratic Europe—those who refuse to tolerate any actions by the minor nations that might compromise their iron hegemony."[78] However reluctantly, Labriola saw something of Italy's future, when, after the "mutilated victory," the developing nation conceived itself betrayed, confined, and exploited by its erstwhile allies of the Great War. Before all that was to transpire, Italy had to endure the trial of the most calamitous war in human history.

CHAPTER NINE

The Great War and the Response of Revolutionary Marxists

In the years immediately before the advent of the Great War, doctrinal Marxism underwent erratic and pluriform development. Only the institutionalized leadership of the German Social Democrats persisted in their pretended orthodoxy—and even there, on the occasion of war, the majority opted to provide war credits to the Kaiser. By the time of the Great War, Leninists, for their part, had put together the first elements of a Bolshevik variant. Some German radicals, in turn—inspired, in part, by the "racial socialism" of Ludwig Woltmann—advanced the rationale for a pan-German socialism[1]—and Italian syndicalists proceeded to fabricate their own developmental national syndicalism out of Marxist components.

In Italy, the official Italian Socialist party sought to retain an ineffectual orthodoxy that was half German in origin and half indecisive in practice. In these parlous circumstances, Marxism faced the first major crisis of the twentieth century.

Between the time of the Italian war against the Turks, and the coming of the Great War, the complex and competitive strategic, economic, and political interests of some of the major European powers created the tensions that led to overt military conflict. The real or fancied interests of the principal powers, all tangled in a web of treaty obligations, inexorably drew everyone into the greatest conflagration ever experienced by humankind. In the subsequent conflict, massive reserves of men and materiel were put into motion to be thrown against opponents equally marshaled and armed. In the carnage that resulted, not only were millions slaughtered, but Marxism itself as a belief system, was to become a casualty.

It was already clear that after the death of Engels, Marxism began to unravel as a coherent doctrine. Eduard Bernstein was only one Marxist intellectual who raised questions concerning its empirical substance and its predictive competence. Ludwig Woltmann pursued its theoretical implications into areas that were to entirely transform the very character of Marxism, and Georges Sorel was to search out the moral substance of Marxism and reflect on the dynamics of revolution. An entire host of revolutionary syndicalists followed—including major social scientists of the competence of Roberto Michels—to restructure the substance of Marxism as it had been understood until that time. In the course of those transformations, V. I. Lenin introduced his own "creative development"—to make of what had been orthodox Marxism his own singular unorthodoxy.

Within that doctrinal turmoil, orthodoxy attempted to retain its linearity, finding expression in the writings of the stalwarts of the German Social Democratic party. Karl Kautsky continued to insist that industrial capitalism, whatever its variable performance, must inevitably end in the catastrophic collapse foreseen by Marx. There would necessarily be increasing emiseration of the proletariat and an accelerating proletarianization of the middle classes. There would be a regular decline in the standard of living of all working people, with the increasing accumulation of wealth in the hands of an exiguous minority.[2] All this was expected to follow with ineluctable fatality. The Great War was really not much more than irrelevance. Whatever transpired, the inevitabilities of scientific Marxism would determine the future.

For the orthodoxy of German Marxism, the First World War broke out over just this collection of convictions. It was just that orthodoxy that was not destined to survive. Prior to the advent of the war, Kautsky, following the lead of Friedrich Engels, had insisted upon the "scientific inevitability" of the "catastrophic collapse" of industrial capitalism and its "automatic" transmogrification into proletarian socialism.[3] As a consequence, there was very little overt discussion of how organized socialism was to behave on the occasion of an intra-European war. The socialist theoreticians of the Second International were content to lose themselves in the talk of the lawlike process that would lead Europe's proletariat to worldwide revolutionary triumph. There had been no serious discussion of a major international conflict—nor how such a conflict might impact the anticipated world proletarian revolution. When socialists did occupy themselves with the possibility of a major European war, they spoke almost exclusively in slogans and epigrams. Socialist thinkers were typically antimilitary and pacifistic. The very possibility of international war was largely dismissed as an anachronism. One sensed that orthodox Marxists expected that in the most unlikely possibility that such a war would occur, socialists and the entire proletariat would simply choose not to participate.

By the onset of the Great War all that seemed hopelessly inadequate to contend with the reality that threatened to overwhelm the advanced industrial nations. As a consequence, and although not immediately appreciated, Kautsky's orthodoxy became more and more irrelevant. With the passage of time, he was to be rejected by Leninists and syndicalists, and after the war, the Social Democrats would fail to seriously hinder the National Socialist seizure of power in Germany. In Italy, Kautsky's form of Marxist orthodoxy was largely dissipated with that nation's entry into the Great War, and in France his form of Marxism fitfully continued until it flickered out with France's abject defeat in the Second World War. Kautsky himself pursued a fate little different from that of the doctrine to whose defense he had devoted his life. He fled Germany before the advance of Hitler's National Socialism—to proceed to Vienna, to be driven from there, first to Prague, and finally to Amsterdam—where he died in poverty in 1938.

Whatever Marxism was to become in the twentieth century, it was to have very little to do with Kautsky's orthodoxy.[4] It was to survive in the form given it by V. I. Lenin and his heirs, in the variants found in Fascism, and in deviant expression among National Socialists. The Great War proved to be the crucible out of which the viable elements of Marxism were to sort themselves—to change the history of the modern world. The prolix, confusing, and sometimes contradictory doctrines left by Marx and Engels as legacy to their followers in the twentieth century were to be tested by the choices made by Marxists in the face of a European war. When socialists of whatever ideological orientation were compelled to make decisions concerning the war that threatened the future of all humankind in 1914, inherited doctrine proved ineffectual. It was uncertain how Marxists should behave in the face of one of the gravest crises in human history. Little in the body of inherited doctrine seemed unambiguously helpful.

MARX AND ENGELS ON WAR

As their nation moved closer and closer to war, German socialists had no clear guidance as to how they, as "orthodox" Marxists, were to behave. Neither Marx nor Engels left sure counsel. Clearly, internationalism was favored in principle. But what that might mean on the occasion of international conflict was in no wise free of ambiguity. In their time, for example, both Marx and Engels had clearly favored war when war would further Germany's unification and expansion. That would be part of the process that both identified as the "cunning of history"—the process they expected to culminate in the proletarian world revolution.

That conjectured process involved the globalization of industry, with those nations already industrialized, the bearers of development to laggard regions. Thus, both Marx and Engels could insist that the "country that is more developed industrially only shows to the less developed, the image of its own future"[5]—to subsequently imply that the more industrially advanced nations, including Germany, would serve as agents of transformative change.[6] Industrially advanced nations were vehicles of destiny. They would introduce industrialization and economic modernization to those countries that had "not yet participated in history."

In the course of their long intellectual careers, both Marx and Engels had offered a variety of judgments concerning war. About the only thing that was clear was the fact that they were not pacifists. At times they justified one or another war because the defeat of one or another participant would be "progressive" in effect—defeating "reactionaries," uplifting "retrograde peoples," and/or sweeping aside the "miserable remnants of former nations." They consistently spoke, for example, of Slavs as ethnographic "debris," of negligible historic importance. A war fought to remove them as an obstruction to "historical development" would be justified.[7] It also smacked of a kind of "socialist racism."

Of the nonindustrial peoples, those who would be the recipients of the largess of those already industrialized, the choice of the founders of Marxism remained more-or-less consistent throughout their lifetimes. Many of the economically stagnant peoples were seen as the "residual remnants of peoples" who would remain "historyless (*geschichtslosen*)" until and unless salvaged by those more advanced. Both Marx and Engels drew a distinction clearly reminiscent of that entertained by Europeans through much of the nineteenth century. It was a distinction made in terms of "civilized" versus "primitive" peoples.[8] Neither Marx nor Engels hesitated in identifying some one or another "historyless" people as somehow "backward" and/or "degenerate," having little claim on historic significance. They spoke, for example, of Spaniards and Mexicans as degenerate—and indicated that the "more primitive" a nation, the "more 'scandinavian' it must be"[9]—demeaning both Latinos and Scandinavians at the same time.

These characterizations were not reserved exclusively for Spaniards,

Mexicans, or Scandinavians. Both Marx and Engels spoke of "Slavonic nations" as being bereft of "vitality" as well—and destined to be "absorbed by a more energetic race."[10] They also spoke of North Africans in a similar fashion. In speaking of the French colonial suppression of the Bedouin rebellion in Algeria, for example, Engels affirmed that "upon the whole, it is in our opinion, very fortunate that the Arabian chief has been taken. . . . [The] conquest of Algeria is an important and fortunate fact for the progress of civilization. . . . After all, the modern bourgeois with civilization, industry, [and] order . . . is preferable to . . . the barbarian state of society."[11]

Correspondingly, in addressing the expansion of the United States into Mexican territory at the time of the Mexican war, Engels stated that the "Yankee incursion" served the "interests of civilization," for they brought with them "profitable methods of agriculture . . . trade [and] industry." For Engels, it was all a matter of the "influence of the more highly developed nation on the undeveloped one." Engels conceived it part of the "cunning of history" to bind "tiny, crippled, powerless little nations together in a great Empire and thereby [enable] them to take part in . . . historical development. . . . To be sure," he went on, "such a thing is not carried through without forcibly crushing many a delicate little national flower. But without force and without an iron ruthlessness nothing is accomplished in history."[12]

Engels spoke in very much the same fashion of the "small independent states by which Germany is surrounded." He argued that they were entirely devoid of historic consequence. He insisted that the "policy of the revolutionary party" must be to "strongly unite the great nationalities," in order to effect the absorption of those "mongrel would be . . . miserably powerless so-called nations as the Danes, the Dutch, the Belgians, Swiss, etc." Given such a notion, the war of Germany against Denmark in 1850, undertaken to absorb Schleswig-Holstein, was, for Engels, a truly "revolutionary war."[13] Engels insisted that where peoples of "two completely different levels of civilization" confronted each other, the more developed enjoyed the "natural right" of dominion. It is a question, he maintained, "of the level of social development of the individual peoples." Marx had insisted upon the same principle. Wars fought in the service of "civilization" against barbarism and backwardness were fully warranted. Even if such wars were fought in contravention of international treaties, Marx insisted, "progress counts for more than all treaties because such is the law of historical development."[14]

There were times, of course, when for both Marx and Engels, war constituted nothing more than an effort by the bourgeoisie to win some advantage in international competition. Acknowledging that, there remained times when they supported the war of one industrialized nation against another. Their judgments concerning such wars varied with time and circumstance. There was no simple theoretical rule applicable in each and every case. There was no clear measure with which to distinguish "progressive" wars from those that were simply undertaken in the exclusive service of "bourgeois," rather than "historic," socialist interest.

In effect, both Marx and Engels had held some wars, those in the service of "progress" and "civilization," to be warranted—and other wars that were to be disdained. In all of that, there were times when Germany's wars were seen as both progressive and revolutionary. For Marx and Engels, Germany seems to have occupied a prominent place among industrial and industrializing nations. Early in his intellectual career, Marx had favored the creation of the German Empire as a bulwark against reactionary Russia, and he supported Germany in its war against France in 1870 for a variety of reasons—not the least of which was the fact that "his" party had its base in the homeland of the Kaiser. In both 1848 and 1870, when Germany found itself embroiled in military conflict, Marx and Engels expressed their support of the fatherland with only some reservations. Both Marx and Engels conceived the Franco-Prussian war of 1870 as serving their own, as well as universal, revolutionary interests. For Marx a German victory against France would "transfer the center of gravity of the workers' movement from France to Germany . . . and would mean the predominance of our theory over Proudhon's, etc." For Engels, support for a German victory was forthcoming because he understood that victory to be intrinsically "progressive"—uniting the proletariat in common cause with the nation.[15] Marx and Engels extended their support as long as Germany's war against France was "defensive." They proceeded to object when Bismarck sought the annexation of Alsace-Lorraine at the expense of France.

Given all the complexities involved in international conflict, the criteria governing the support of Marx and Engels, as well as its withdrawal, were neither immediately evident nor easily calculable. Engels had not objected to Germany's annexation of Schleswig-Holstein at the expense of Denmark a few years before. It would appear that their readiness to extend support for one or another participant in international conflict was governed, at best, by contingencies not always immediately obvious to others.

Only one consideration appeared constant. Throughout their lifetimes, czarist Russia remained the enemy of Europe and of the anticipated proletarian revolution.[16] As early as 1848, both Marx and Engels argued that a German war against Russia would be "revolutionary," defeating czarist "reaction," while assisting Germans in shaking off "the chains of a long, ignoble slavery." They saw war against Russia as the occasion to free Germans from threat while contributing to the liberation of others.[17] Those convictions were to have particular relevance as the prospect of war between Germany and Russia loomed on the horizon in 1914.

About the time of Marx's death in 1883, Engels became increasingly preoccupied with the possibility of a general European war. Like Marx, he saw that war as a possible "race war," a war of Slavs and Latins—of Russia, France, and Italy—against Germany.[18] He understood that such a war would devastate Europe, lay waste its industries and population centers and render proletarian revolution increasingly unlikely in the "flood of chauvinism" that it would unleash.[19] He feared that the "wretched, ruined fragments of one-time nations, the Serbs, Bulgars, Greeks, and other robber bands" would drag the advanced industrial nations into a nightmare conflict. He articulated the same sense of dread throughout the remainder of his life.

In 1887, he went on to speculate that the Biblical destruction that such a war would wreck on Germany would surely result in "the creation of the conditions for the final victory of the working class."[20] A major European war would either destroy all possibilities of proletarian revolution or ensure its advent. As a consequence of just these kinds of judgment, one really had little sure guidance from either Marx or Engels in selecting a course of action in the event of a major European war.

In 1891, four years before his death, Engels returned to the theme of a catastrophic European war. He spoke to his most intimate friends and affirmed that the German Social Democratic party, on the occasion of such a war, should be prepared to support the fatherland against a foreign foe—"on condition that [the government] would be ready to fight relentlessly and use every means, even revolutionary means [to preserve] . . . the nation."[21] He went on, in 1892, in an article written for the annual *Almanac* of the French socialist parties, to urge Europeans to "realize that if France, in alliance with Russia, should declare war on Germany, she would be fighting against the strongest Social Democratic party in Europe; and that we would have no choice but to oppose with all our strength any aggressor who was on the side of Russia."[22]

Thus, before his death, Engels assumed a position concerning a possible European conflict that appeared entirely unambiguous. In his judgment, German socialists should be prepared to support the fatherland in its fight against any combination of nations that included czarist Russia in order that the fatherland might discharge its historic developmental responsibilities. Engels conceived that to be a socialist and Marxist, rather than a specifically nationalist, obligation.

When, in the late summer of 1914, European Marxists found themselves compelled to face the real prospect of war, they had very little unambiguous theoretic guidance. For all the antiwar slogans repeated in all the socialist conferences for all the years before the First World War, the actual advent of war found Marxists entirely unprepared to effectively respond. Socialists and Marxists throughout Europe dissolved into uncertainty. While it may have seemed clear what Engels expected German socialists to do, it was singularly unclear what might be expected of French or Italian, much less Russian, socialists. That was to be left to their leaders to decide. The result was that individual and idiosyncratic choices were to shape the future of Europe and the world in totally unanticipated fashion. In the course of all that, Marxism disappeared as a single ideology.

V. I. LENIN AND THE COMING OF THE GREAT WAR

By the time the First World War broke over Europe, Lenin had already established himself as one of Russia's major Marxist theoreticians. Within the compass of that recognition, he had already articulated a conception of a Marxist party as one led by an exiguous "vanguard" of professional revolutionaries. Other than that, he attempted to codify the Marxism he advocated in rigidly positivistic terms, having all the features of the scientism of the end of the nineteenth century.[23] Whatever else he was doing, Lenin was remaking Marxism in his own image.[24]

Although the evidence of mounting crisis troubled many Europeans, the outbreak of war apparently took Lenin almost completely by surprise. More than that, the first responses of the various European socialist parties left Lenin incredulous. He could not believe that most of the representatives of the major socialist parties, in Russia as well as the most advanced industrial nations, were extending support to their respective governments in the face of international conflict. He could not believe that socialists had both "betrayed" their prized internationalism as well as their insistent antimilitarism. The German Social Democrats, led by Europe's most determined opponents of war, voted war credits for the Kaiser, invoking the familiar argument that not to do so would mean a victory for the Czar of

Russia, and for reaction in general. Led by Karl Kautsky, many German Marxists conceived their defense of the fatherland to be fully compatible with their socialist responsibilities—and with the enjoinments of Engels in the 1890s.

In France, Jean Jaures, Jules Guesde, and Gustave Hervé, the revolutionary leaders of socialism, rallied around their own government in defense of the fatherland. Guesde explained that French workers were morally obliged to defend their nation against the Germans, who had "betrayed the peace of Europe." In Russia, the "first Russian Marxist," Georgi Plekhanov,[25] supported the fatherland's alliance with France and England in a war against "reactionary" Germany and Austria.

While there was some vacillation in England, ultimately the nation's socialists lent their support for the war. Only in Italy did Marxists resist, demanding absolute neutrality from their government in the face of European conflict.

Most of those Marxists who lent their support for the war cited the positions on war assumed by Marx and Engels in the course of their long lives. As has been suggested, while the criteria employed by the founders of Marxism governing their support for war were often difficult to fully divine, it was clear that neither Marx nor Engels were pacifists—Engels declaring, in a letter to Bebel, that if the "civilized lands" of Europe were attacked by Russia on occasion of the war he anticipated, he would "mount his horse" in their defense.[26]

All of this was enough for most Marxists. They were not prepared to dismiss support for the war on the grounds of some arcane philosophical or sociological principle. They were prepared to calculate how war might contribute to the furtherance of social revolution—and thus justify their support. Most seemed to imagine that the defense of their respective nations would best serve the ends of the "inevitable" proletarian transformation of society.

Among them, it was Lenin who stood apart. Early in September 1914, on the very declaration of war, Lenin declared the evolving conflict to be neither defensive nor revolutionary in character. He saw it as an "imperialist and dynastic war" serving exclusively the interests of the "bourgeois-chauvinists"[27] intent upon the "looting of foreign countries" and the suppression of the "revolutionary movement of the proletariat."[28] He went on to insist that any Marxist who acceded to the wishes of "opportunists" and "chauvinists" in their ranks, and supported their nation's war effort, would betray Marxism. He refused to countenance the possibility that any nation had the moral or revolutionary right to defend itself against any aggressor.

In his judgment, by September 1914 there were many who had vacated their revolutionary obligations. They included almost the entire leadership of the Second International—encompassing those who were the direct intellectual heirs of classical Marxism, and who had achieved political maturity under the tutelage of Engels himself. Lenin insisted that those very paladins of Marxist doctrinal integrity had "succumbed to the blandishments of bourgeois nationalism, to chauvinism"—to defend their decision with "the most hypocritical, vulgar and smug sophistry"—at the expense of their integrity and the survival of proletarian internationalism.[29]

Given the fact that his was a minority position among Marxists, Lenin was obliged to demonstrate that whatever either Marx or Engels may have said with respect to war—that seemingly contradicted his position—did not apply in the then present circumstances. Lenin insisted that what had been said by the founders of Marxism in their time was, somehow or other, no longer relevant. The Great War, for Lenin, was a "bourgeois war"—absolutely not to be fought by the proletariat and its leaders. Instead, revolutionaries were enjoined to "raise high the banner of civil war" with the coming of war. They should resist service in their nation's armed forces, disrupt the manufacture and transportation of war materiel, and attempt to engender revolution on the part of the "masses." Lenin's first and immediate response to the advent of the Great War was to call for the defeat of his country and to advocate a fratricidal civil war.[30] Those whom he himself identified as among the "most eminent Marxists" of his time—including Kautsky and Plekhanov—aligned themselves against him.

By the beginning of 1915, as a consequence, Lenin sought to put together an argument that might support his position against some of the best informed Marxist theoreticians of the new century. Under the pressure of those circumstances, he discovered the specifically imperialist character of the war. The Great War reflected, in his assessment, the needs of industrial capitalism at its "last and highest stage."[31] Lenin had discovered a "new stage" in the evolution of industrial capitalism: imperialism. That new stage explained why his position, and his position alone, was truly revolutionary.

Just as he had discovered at the beginning of the twentieth century why the proletariat in the advanced industrial countries had not undertaken to overthrow the capitalist system as Marx had predicted—by the outbreak of the Great War he had fathomed why the nineteenth-century statements and analyses of Marx and Engels were no longer applicable to his time. History had entered an entirely new stage apparently unanticipated by either Marx or Engels.

By February 1915, Lenin had marshaled his arguments against all those Marxists who had chosen to support the war effort of their respective countries. He began with the contention that both Kautsky and Plekhanov had failed to correctly apply "Marxian dialectical thinking" in their appraisals. Eminent as they were, they had failed to recognize that anything said by Marx or Engels during the time of the consolidation of industrial capitalism was not applicable to the time when the "objective conditions" signaled the final, catastrophic "collapse of capitalism." Of course Engels had called upon the German people to fight in their nation's service. And of course, Marx had supported Germany's war against France and any war against czarism. Lenin was to argue that all that was simply appropriate to the time that was witnessing the consolidation of the European capitalist states. It was irrelevant, however, to industrial capitalist states during their "last and final" phases. In circumstances that then threatened Europe, if not the world, with catastrophe, one must be "truly scientific" if one is charged with the responsibility of making policy recommendations. Lenin insisted that his critics "had distorted" the real meaning of the quotations of the founders of Marxism. He maintained that when Engels called upon the Germans to "wage a life and death struggle against the allied armies of France and Russia," it was at a time—1891—when Germany's bourgeoisie was still "progressive," retaining the potential to further develop the economy's modern forces of production. About twenty years later, according to Lenin's dialectical assessment, Europe had transcended that period, and had entered an "entirely different epoch," one in which the bourgeoisie was no longer "progressive," but "old and outmoded," administering a system that, objectively and scientifically, was moribund.[32] Lenin had discovered that the Great War was a special sort of war. It was an "imperialist war," a war that was being fought by and for "bourgeois states" that had "outlived themselves"—only barely surviving in "the final stage in the development of capitalism." In that last stage, capitalism could only eke out an existence by "plundering" other countries and exploiting economically retrograde peoples.[33]

Lenin had discovered that industrial capitalism was no longer the system that had "created more massive and more colossal productive forces than . . . all proceeding generations together."[34] It had become "stagnant," "decadent," and "parasitic," and rotten-ripe for international proletarian revolution.[35] The Great War was its last, horrific death rattle.

By February 1915, Lenin had put together his argument. His essay, "Under a False Flag," written at that time, contained essentially all the components of his work, *Imperialism, The Highest Stage of Capitalism*, which was to be subsequently identified as "his most influential"—to make of Leninism a distinctive variant of Marxism—"the Marxism of the imperialist epoch."[36]

In "Under a False Flag" Lenin argued that the "epoch" of "progressive national bourgeois movements," during which the bourgeoisie fostered and sustained the development of the industrial forces of production, had passed. The "new epoch," Lenin insisted, saw "social and class content" in the capitalist nations "radically change." Capitalism had entered into a period of "exhaustion," having "outlived itself," condemned to lapse into the grip of "the most reactionary finance capital" and spiral downward "into decay."[37]

All of this bespoke, for Lenin, a conjuncture of "trends": the increasing "internationalisation" of the "working masses"; "class contradictions" were becoming increasingly acute, with "sharper and more bitter forms of struggle arising"; the life circumstances of the proletariat were becoming more and more attenuated; and the "pressure of finance capital was becoming intolerable." Only the fact that exploitation of the backward regions of the world allowed the imperialist powers to accrue "superprofits," with which to suborn the "petty bourgeoisie," and an insignificant minority of working class "aristocrats," permitted a "brief period" of continued survival for the entire system of capitalist oppression and social decay.[38]

For Lenin, all this explained the rise of "opportunism" and reactionary "social patriotism" in the ranks of revolutionary socialists.[39] It also explained why Marx's own analysis of war was inapplicable to the new epoch. In his time, Marx had understood that the "objective conditions" for the "downfall of industrial capitalism" had not yet matured. It "was not surprising," therefore, as long as the conditions conducive to revolution had not yet manifested themselves, that "Marx and the Marxists" of the past epoch "confined themselves to determining which bourgeoisie's victory would be more harmless to (or more favorable to) the world proletariat"—and proceeded to advocate support in its service.[40]

In Lenin's judgment, by 1914, all that had changed. By the outbreak of the Great War, the objective conditions necessary for proletarian revolution were manifest. Lenin had formulated his convictions on the basis of "science, i.e., from the standpoint of class relations in modern society." As a consequence, he had discovered that the bourgeoisie, the owners of the means of production in the modern world, were "senile and moribund." They could no longer "maintain their rule." They had lapsed into a crisis that opened a "fissure through which the discontent and indignation of the oppressed classes [would] burst forth." Lenin was convinced that his modified Marxism was the "last word in historical science." His "dialectical science" had confirmed the "objective truth" of his analysis. Capitalism had entered into its final revolutionary crisis. The "imperialist war" itself was evidence of that. More specifically, the fact that the European powers, under the control of finance capitalism, were prepared to consume human and material resources in profligate fashion to protect the profits extorted from the backward economies of the world by exploiting their markets and affording the opportunity for the export of surplus capital was, in Lenin's mind, compelling proof of the morbidity of the capitalism of his time.[41]

He gave didactic expression to all this in his *Imperialism, The Highest Stage of Capitalism: A Popular Outline*, which first appeared in pamphlet form in St. Petersburg in 1917. In that pamphlet, Lenin drew together all his theoretical insights—including his conviction that the proletariat, whose consciousness had been subverted by capitalist gold, could not make revolution, thus requiring the dedicated leadership of a small elite of professional revolutionaries. At the same time, he offered a rationale for a Marxist opposition to supporting one's country in wartime. He called, instead, for an uprising against one's government—to initiate civil war. His argument was straightforward.

CAPITALISM IN ITS HIGHEST AND FINAL STAGE

There was absolutely no ambiguity in Lenin's position. As he understood the history of the world, industrial capitalism had matured to the point at which all of its productive assets were controlled by monopolies and cartels. So aggregated, the entire system fell under the control of a financial hierarchy—*finance capital*—itself monopolized and cartelized.[42]

Rummaging through a collection of statistical tables, Lenin pretended to establish, as fact, that productive capital no longer played a major role in the dynamics of mature capitalist systems. That role had been preempted (apparently some time around the turn of the twentieth century[43]) by a gaggle of money changers. So indifferent were they to production that technological innovation—so important to Marx in his analysis of capitalist competition—stagnated. As a consequence, small enterprises, much of the

source of productive innovation and managerial efficiency, were systematically undermined—to be "forced out."[44] Lenin insisted that in the advanced
industrial states, small enterprises and the middle class they supported, declined in number. With their decline, there was a failure to innovate. Without that impetus, there was stasis in agricultural production. The predictable result was the failure of agriculture in the advanced industrial nations
to meet the most elemental food needs of their respective populations.[45]
Lenin insisted that widespread malnutrition and persistent starvation had
become endemic to those countries—part of his evidence that the most
mature capitalist societies were "retrogressing" and "moribund." Given all
that, Lenin concluded that imperialism had already created the conditions
requisite for the "inevitable" proletarian revolution.

In the world context, imperialism had become "parasitic." Incapable of
stimulating and sustaining its own technological development, the financial oligarchy that had acceded to control in advanced capitalist environments, had become a class of unproductive usurers. Finance capitalists lent
money to impoverished nations in order to exploit them and pad the profits
of "coupon clippers." Those profits produced and sustained a subclass of
rentier capitalists prepared to support the policies of their imperialist governments. Thus, the "superprofits" Lenin had identified as the cause of the
subversion of what should have been a "revolutionary" working class was
also the material cause of the conversion of major elements of the declining
middle class to ideologies of "opportunism" and "social chauvinism."[46]

For Lenin, the superprofits of imperialism not only deflected the proletariat from its revolutionary course, but also fueled the opportunism and
chauvinism to be found among the "pseudo-proletarian" Marxist leaders
of the social democratic movement.[47] Enough of the enormous profits extorted by finance capital from the peripheral economies filters through to
the working class elite and members of the petty bourgeoisie to provide a
"social base" for imperialism.

Rather than employ capital for technological and productive improvements, imperialists exported it for profit. That, according to Lenin, renders
imperialism "parasitic." The selective distribution of rewards among some
elements of the working, and middle, classes, makes imperialism "reactionary." Its failure to provide for its domestic population—with the decline of
living standards throughout the bulk of the working classes—generates the
necessary psychological preconditions for proletarian revolution.

Lenin—at least since the first years of the twentieth century—had argued that the working class would mindlessly follow the lead of an elite

suborned by the ruling classes. Only dire economic circumstances might provide the occasion for a Marxist leadership to substitute itself in a leadership role. He argued that the generic failure of capitalism to provide for its workers, together with the horrors of mass immolations to which whole populations were made subject in the wake of the Great War, had made the system "rotten-ripe" for social revolution.

Since the turn of the twentieth century, the finance capitalists sought to seize the territories of others, and exploit resident populations, for their own profit. The world had resolved itself into exploiter and exploited nations. Those communities that had accrued enormous reserves of capital employed their wealth to exploit those bereft of assets and economic defenses. The international community had become an arena of a kind of competition entirely unanticipated by Marx. The advanced capitalist nations battened on the backward communities on their periphery. Lenin appeared, in effect, to abandon Marx's entire conception of the predictable expansion of modern capitalism to the less developed "ahistorical" regions of the globe.

Marx had argued that with the accrual of profit in the advanced capitalist nations, the export of capital to the less developed communities was both predictable and would serve to stimulate their industrial growth and economic modernization. He expected that the rate of return on investment in capital poor regions would be attractive to those who were capital rich. The consequence would be a flow of investment capital to backward economies, resulting in productive growth and industrial development. Territories that had found themselves "outside of history" would thence come to participate in its flow.

Lenin's account of the "highest stage of capitalism" is notable in the absolute assurance with which it is delivered. Nonetheless, it is not clear how much of it is really an empirically convincing rationale for the program of defeatism for his native land and his attendant call for immediate social revolution in the course of the First World War.

Behind all his conviction, and the eloquence of his delivery, there were serious issues left unresolved. For all his insistence, it was evident almost immediately that Lenin was prepared to grant that, in some sense or other, imperialism was something more than simply parasitic and moribund. His seeming rejection of Marx's notion of the progressive role of advanced capitalism in the backward regions was more apparent than real. In the course of his discussion, Lenin recognized that the advanced capitalist countries, given their abundance of investment capital, have and would continue to provide funds for fostering infrastructural development and agricultural productivity in less developed economies. In places, he tells his readership, for example, that "capitalism is growing with the greatest rapidity in the colonies and in overseas countries."[48] In those instances, Lenin appears prepared to acknowledge that the advanced capitalist countries, in fact, foster the modern development of the retrograde economies of backward nations. "Finance capitalism" would seem to be something more than simply "parasitic."

In several places Lenin, like Marx, speaks of the "export of capital" underwriting the development of an industrial infrastructure in less developed economies on the periphery of advanced capitalism. The predictable result could only be the introduction of modern productive enterprise into those territories. In fact, in places Lenin held that "the export of capital influences and greatly accelerates the development of capitalism in those countries to which it is exported." Thus, Lenin continued, while the export of capital "may tend to arrest development in the capital exporting countries, it can only do so by expanding and deepening the further development of capitalism throughout the world." As a consequence of the export of surplus capital from the advanced industrial regions, modern industry was taking root in the most backward regions of the globe. Lenin warns his readers that as a consequence of that development some of those dependent nations are becoming increasingly competitive—and he speaks, as a consequence, of "the struggle among the world imperialisms . . . becoming more acute." In that context, he specifically mentions Japan.[49] Finance capitalism would seem to be in the business of creating its own competition—something Marx argued more than half a century before[50]—and which Lenin's *Imperialism*, on occasion, seemed disposed to deny.

At the same time that he recognized the "progressive" consequences of the export of capital by the advanced capitalist states, Lenin insisted that the result is a division of the world into "a handful of usurer states and a vast majority of debtor states."[51] Somehow or other, industrial capitalism develops rapidly in the colonies as a consequence of finance capitalism's export of surplus capital, while at the same time condemning itself to stagnation and those colonies to hopeless indebtedness. All that, according to Lenin, changes the entire dynamic of world revolution.

In that regard, he quotes Rudolf Hilferding when he reports that the intrusions of imperialism into the colonies stimulates a "growing resistance" on the part of the peoples in the less developed regions—presumably a consequence of their growing awareness of their nation's indebtedness. A "national consciousness" grows among them. In finance capitalism's expansion into the economically backward regions of the globe, "capitalism itself gradually provides the subjugated with the means and resources for their emancipation."[52]

Finance capitalism thus sponsors and fosters the emergence of industrial capitalism in the economically backward regions of the world while, at the same time, providing the "means and resources" for the emancipation of the peoples in those regions. Revolution, it would seem, would be initiated by the peoples of backward regions at the same time they were enjoying accelerating economic modernization and industrialization. For Marx, revolution would be the product of an uprising of proletarians of the advanced industrial countries. For Lenin, that was no longer the case.

His special insight into the Marxist dialectic prepared Lenin to stand classical Marxism on its head. He argued that "parasitic or decaying capitalism" was no longer subject to revolution at the hands of its proletarian masses. It would seem that finance capitalism exported both capital and nationalist revolution to the peripheral, less developed nations of the world system. And yet, in another place, Lenin argued that the superprofits collected by the "rentier states" from the less developed regions permitted the continued "rapid growth of capitalism"—in fact, Lenin argued, "capitalism is growing far more rapidly than before," however "uneven" he conceived it to be.[53] On the one hand we have capitalism "decaying" into finance capitalism, while still "growing rapidly," staffed by a working class suborned by an "aristocracy" in the pay of those dispensing the "superprofits" extorted from the peripheral backward economies. On the other hand, we have the less developed peripheral economies growing under the stimulus of export capital flowing in from the advanced economies, at the price of incurring debt—which apparently gives rise to nationalist resistance on the part of their resident populations.

Lenin's vision of the world, often touted as providing revolutionary clarity to the Marxist movements of his time, seems hardly that. It is clear that his new interpretation of Marxism put revolution on the agenda for a Russia that he understood to be "most backward economically."[54] Revolution was to come to those backward economies that both Marx and Engels conceived "unripe" for socialist transformation. Where Engels had insisted that any "communist" revolution undertaken in an economically backward region was destined to fail, to revert to the exploitation characteristic of essentially agrarian systems,[55] Lenin was to insist that the "proletarian revolution" would occur in just such backward environments. At the same time, he allowed that finance capitalism, "exploiting" colonies while itself "decaying," might continue to grow "rapidly" for some unspecified time—rendering "proletarian revolution" unlikely in the advanced industrial countries—those countries considered by Marx and Engels the only places where real socialism might take root.[56]

In effect, Lenin attempted to resolve the political difficulties of his time—by radically modifying inherited doctrine. His discovery of a "new epoch" of industrial capitalism—unanticipated by either Marx or Engels—was intended to explain the failure of the proletariat to rise up in rebellion against its oppressors. The peculiarities of capitalism's "final stage" were expected to account for the "defection" of working class leadership on the occasion of the European war. All of that was understood to supply the reasons for capitalism's continued survival, irrespective of the insistence in Marxist theory that it was destined to suffer imminent and catastrophic collapse.

The "Leninism" that resulted was clearly fundamentally different from the doctrine Lenin had inherited. It was soon to become evident that Lenin's Marxism was to be an attempt to bring socialism to a retrograde economy—something both Marx and Engels insisted could not be done.

The effort to achieve socialism in a country burdened by a backward economy and ravaged by war, made of Leninism something far different than anything found in Marxist orthodoxy. Leninism was to ultimately provide a rationale for political rule predicated on all the austerities of all the authoritarianisms and despotisms long familiar to primitive economies. Ultimately, Leninism was compelled to impose productive discipline on an essentially peasant people. That discipline was administered by a single party that conceived itself possessed of impeccable truths about society and history. Those truths were delivered and implemented by a charismatic leadership, a leadership armed with a "dialectical science" subject to no control other than that of the transcendental insight of a self-selected, "vanguard" aristocracy. To cement the commitment of populations only partially industrialized, Marxist-Leninists, armed with the "new Marxism," were to invoke collective sentiment and discipline that was to look very much like the sentiment and discipline that was to be enjoined by totalitarians everywhere.

Lenin had teased "Leninism" out of the complex system of beliefs that survived the passing of Engels in 1895. It was one of the variants of Marxism that would transfigure revolutionary politics in the twentieth century. Another variant was to take form among revolutionary Italians at almost the same time. To the political, social, and ideological crisis generated by the

First World War, revolutionary socialists and Sorelian syndicalists in Italy were to respond with their own variant of Marxism. Benito Mussolini was to be their principal spokesman.

THE BACKGROUND IN ITALY

When the Italian government chose to enter into armed conflict with the Turks in 1911, one of its most consistent and irrepressible opponents was Benito Mussolini. In the provinces of his birth, he led the socialist opposition to the war. He had made his generic opposition plain some time before. He reminded Italians that before Italy embarked on the "conquest" of the Trentino, Trieste, or Tripolitania, it should conquer illiteracy, undertake comprehensive rehabilitation of the nation's soil, pipe fresh water to the Southern provinces, and provide elementary justice for all Italians.[57]

When Italy became embroiled in the War in Tripoli, Mussolini mobilized opposition, advocated and supported a general strike directed against the conflict—to suffer denunciation and endure confinement as a result. His responses were those of an "orthodox" socialist. Consistent with that orthodoxy, he argued that militarism and capitalism were somehow intrinsically connected. "Militarism," he argued, "has become a typical, fundamental and necessary expression of bourgeois society. Capitalism and militarism are two aspects of the same phenomenon. . . . One is unthinkable without the other. No sooner had capitalism emerged from its primitive phase of development but it gave birth to militarism. To reject the one is to reject the other."[58]

Radical Marxists like Lenin and Mussolini had consistently maintained that militarism and war were inevitable products of industrial capitalism.[59] It is not clear what such contentions might imply in terms of the international conflict that cast its shadow over all of Europe in 1914. Surely there had been wars—presumably one of the manifestations of militarism—long before there was capitalism. Clearly aware of that, both Marx and Engels had given support to a variety of armed conflicts between and within nations, both capitalist and precapitalist, both European and non-European. Whatever the relationship between capitalism, militarism, and war, the founders of Marxism were clearly prepared to lend their support for at least some wars.

That notwithstanding, by the time of the First World War, socialist orthodoxy seemed prepared to proclaim that no war was justified. War was conceived exclusively a bourgeois enterprise, calculated only to profit the rich. In those circumstances, it seemed evident that Mussolini's posturing at the time of the War in Tripoli was neither more nor less than an expression of socialism's official concern on the occasion of the gathering of war clouds.

By 1914, Mussolini had acceded to the intellectual and political leadership of the Italian Socialist party. That leadership involved assuming the editorship of the party daily, *Avanti!* — and made Mussolini an official spokesman of the party's integrity in terms of socialist orthodoxy.

As well as a leader of the party, Mussolini was the leader of its "intransigent" and radical wing. He had only recently wrested leadership from the reformists of the party. Lenin had followed the intraparty struggle on the Italian peninsula and had welcomed the advent of the Mussoliniani to positions of leadership. In retrospect, there is every reason to argue that at the outbreak of the Great War, "Mussolinism" shared many of the doctrinal properties of "Leninism."[60]

Mussolini clearly favored the elitism of Lenin's *What is to be Done?* Inspired by Sorel and the syndicalists, Mussolini, like Lenin, spoke candidly of the "struggles within human society" as "being and have always been a struggle of minorities."[61] Like Lenin, Mussolini was convinced that a minority of intransigent revolutionaries bore the special responsibility of informing the "masses" of their historic obligations and of inspiring them to their discharge.

The difficulty Mussolini had was that as an official spokesman of a party of mixed opinion, rather than a spokesman of a faction, he was not free to speak with candor. Unlike Lenin, Mussolini felt compelled by his party obligations to tailor his public utterances to the party's official position. Within those constraints, he clearly felt the need to explore policy alternatives as an independent Marxist. To satisfy that impulse, he founded a theoretical journal in 1913, *Utopia*, in which he might speak in the first person, independent of the organizational restraints inherent to his party responsibilities.[62]

In the introductory issue of his journal, Mussolini spoke of the intellectual responsibilities of Marxists. He spoke of the intellectual complexity of the system of beliefs they had made their own, and of the variety of interpretations to which that complexity had given rise.[63] He spoke of the failed positivistic interpretation of inherited doctrine; and of the inability of its orthodox interpretation to account for human will and commitment in a convincing fashion. He alluded to the Darwinism that had confounded the system, and to the political reformism to which the very complexity of the system contributed.[64]

At the prompting of Giuseppe Prezzolini, Mussolini undertook to locate his thought among all those currents that made up the body of Marxism. In response, he first made a distinction between the empirical realities of his time and their ideological and doctrinal "reflections." He sought to make a clear contrast between the realities of his time and their expression in revolutionary formulations. The distinction was important for him. He chose to occupy himself with observed realities and not their doctrinal "derivations."[65] He pursued the distinction in order to speak of the doctrinal "derivations" that made up much of the substance of orthodox Marxism. He argued that some of the convictions expressed as then contemporary orthodoxy were really reflections of the realities to be found in the England of the 1870s.

Mussolini argued that Marx, in the course of his lifetime, had managed to capture a cross section of capitalist reality in his work. It was a reality, he reminded his audience, that was, by then, a quarter century old. Mussolini held that classical Marxism had fixed that reality in locutions that many Marxists imagined would forever remain true—like prehistoric flies in amber. Actually, Mussolini argued, what classical Marxism had captured was "a reality in motion."

Mussolini argued that the distinction between the theory of revolution and the realities, in time and circumstance, to which revolutionaries must respond was sometimes critical. He held, for example, that the Marxists of the late nineteenth century, following Marx's exposition in *Das Kapital*, conceived capitalism as having exhausted its potential. Some socialists, he went on, deceived themselves into believing that, in fact, industrial capitalism had completed its historic trajectory. They were prepared to imagine that the formulations provided by Marx, decades before, had captured some sort of immutable reality that carried in its train an inevitable outcome.[66]

In Mussolini's judgment, all of that involved serious error. Reality, he insisted, had a way of baffling those who attempted its capture. To those who believed that industrial society had concluded its trajectory, he maintained that "capitalism" had given evidence of "its ulterior development. It has not yet exhausted its potential transformations."[67] Marx's *Das Kapital* captured but a momentary cross section in the history of a dynamic system.

Mussolini was to argue that reality was far more subtle than any doctrine. To illustrate something of his case, he went on to speak of the fundamental duality at the theoretical foundation of Marxism: the contention that society was composed of two opposing classes, the bourgeoisie and the proletariat. Mussolini spoke of the complexities that made that contention anything but convincing. He spoke of the intractability of attempting to objectively characterize the meaning of "class"—or, however defined, how one might pretend to understand the psychology of entire classes and subclasses. He spoke not only of the "heterogeneity" of the ill-defined classes that presumably shape history, but of the diffuseness of their imagined psychology. He reminded his audience, for example, that one could speak of the "youthful and ardent" industrial and intellectual bourgeoisie, and then of the calculating finance and commercial capitalists—and then of the diverse "subspecies" one might isolate—the small and large property holders, as well as of artisans and the self-employed technicians. While all members of these classes and fragments of classes, as capitalists, might well be motivated by the desire to accumulate profits, they are all conceivably animated by a diversity of immediate interests. As a consequence, there is little that one can say, with much assurance, concerning their overt political conduct in any given circumstance. A "modest rentier" might be close, in terms of material interest, to those of unlimited wealth, but may be religious as opposed to others of his economic fraternity who are atheistic. Members of the subclass may differentiate into those who are democratic in terms of political persuasion, while others might be of more conservative bent. Still others might be reformist or radical—as their spirit moved them. One might say no less concerning any extant bloc of proletarians.

Mussolini's theoretical position was clear. The articulated doctrinal reflections we tend to so much admire, often follow, rather than precede, reality. With respect to experienced reality, one must forever be prepared for novelty, for unanticipated events and unanticipated complexes of events. "Social revolution," in the final analysis, Mussolini contended, grows out of "an act of faith," not a "mental scheme or simple calculation."[68] Marxism, as theory, was neither necessary nor sufficient to make social and political revolution.

In all of that one cannot mistake the echo of the contentions of Edward Bernstein, Georges Sorel and Henri Bergson,[69] of Giuseppe Prezzolini and A. O. Olivetti. The revolutionary Marxism with which Mussolini was prepared to face the crisis of the Great War distinguished itself from the apparent theoretical intransigence of Lenin. Lenin pretended that all his systemic changes in the body of inherited Marxism constituted its one true rendering. Mussolini, on the other hand, granted that a variety of legitimate interpretations of the inherited doctrine were to be expected—his among others. He argued that his was perhaps the most responsible in a dynamic and changing reality.

BENITO MUSSOLINI AND THE COMING
OF THE GREAT WAR

In July of 1914, after the assassination of the Archduke Franz Ferdinand by a Serbian nationalist, the Austrian government presented an ultimatum to Belgrade—with which Belgrade refused to comply. By August, Vienna was at war with Serbia. By the end of the month, Russia, Belgium, and Germany had ordered a general mobilization in anticipation of a continent-wide conflict. In the flurry of threats, recriminations, mobilizations, and troop movements that darkened the future of Europe, the Italian Socialist party announced its "absolute neutrality." It insisted that socialism was antithetical to armed conflict, recognizing that conflict between nations only militated against the most fundamental class interests of the proletariat.

At first, it was not difficult to maintain the party position. Mussolini was its spokesman. He threatened that in the event of a declaration of war by the Italian government, the proletariat class would mobilize all its resistance against it.[70] It was not entirely clear what doctrinal reasoning lay behind such a response. As has been indicated, both Marx and Engels, in their time, had supported one or another side in the national wars that had erupted on the continent.

In the circumstances surrounding the then present war, Italy was bound by treaty to Germany and Austria-Hungary, a treaty to which most politically sensitive Italians objected for a variety of different reasons. First of all, few in Italy were well disposed toward the Central Powers. There was a long and painful history of Austro-Italian conflict in the Udine and Trentino. Italians had long-standing and heartfelt territorial claims on Trieste and the Dalmatian coast—areas held by the Hapsburgs. As early as July, for his own reasons, Mussolini made his objection perfectly clear to any activation of the treaty with Germany and Austria-Hungary. Both countries represented retrograde and repressive monarchies, opposed in practice to the socialism he championed. He threatened that should the government of Rome undertake any move to meet its obligations under its mutual defense treaty with the Central Powers, the "Italian proletariat" would have only one recourse, "to rise up in rebellion."[71]

Beyond that, Mussolini conceived the war a conflict between "imperialisms"—German and English—a conflict that served the exclusive interests of the bourgeoisie.[72] It was a war that grew out of the environment of "armed peace" created by capitalism, that economically competitive bourgeois governments finally ignited into an armed conflict.[73] It was a war, he argued, in which the proletariat had no discernible, immediate investment.

Irrespective of his convictions, Mussolini made his sympathy for the Triple Entente—Britain, France, and Russia—apparent. That clearly distinguished his position from that of Lenin. Without question, from its very commencement, Mussolini was not indifferent to the war or its outcome. While he rejected the war as violative of socialist principles, he did distinguish between wars. He did not insist that should the government enter the war on the side of the Entente that the proletariat would rebel.[74] More than that, he announced that should Austria attack Italy because of Rome's failure to honor its treaty obligations to the Central Powers, the proletariat would take up arms in defense of the common fatherland.[75]

He pointed, with apparent approval, to the response of the French and Belgian proletariat in defense of their respective homelands on the occasion of the German invasion. The immediate costs of war, Mussolini reminded his audience, always fell most heavily on peasants and workers. As a consequence, a war initiated by the ruling classes in order to serve the interests of the bourgeoisie might precipitate any one of several responses, ranging from a proletarian defense of the homeland to a social and political revolution by the working classes.

Between August and November 1914, Mussolini remained spokesman for a socialist policy of "absolute neutrality," and an unflinching opponent of war. Equally clear was the fact that he was not entirely comfortable with a posture that allowed no room for flexible response. More than that, he was not, like Lenin, an advocate of defeatism. He explicitly rejected defeatism as an antiwar strategy.

In his journal, *Utopia*, Mussolini reviewed the options available to socialists on the occasion of a war involving their nation. In August, without identifying the author of defeatism as a Marxist strategy, he spoke of those who proposed to "martyr their nation" in their principled opposition to the "capitalists' war." Instead of defending the nation against armed aggression, it would seem that they proposed to "throw open their frontiers to invaders."[76] Mussolini pursued the logic of such a tactic.

He reminded Marxists that the congress of the Bourses du Travail of 1911 had recommended that in the event of war the proletariat should express its opposition in the form of a general strike. That, Mussolini argued, could only result in one of two alternatives. Either the general strike would result in a revolutionary collapse of the government, or the government would suppress the action as an act of treason against the nation—and the workers' organizations would be vigorously dispersed. In either case, the nation would still face the threat of armed invasion. If the workers' revolution succeeded, the workers' government would face the same threat—and would be compelled to resist invasion with a nation and a defense force in total disarray. Should the government have suppressed the workers, the nation would face invasion equally divided and disabled. In effect, by the first week of August 1914, Mussolini had considered, and dismissed, Lenin's proposed antiwar strategy that urged civil war and revolution as the proper Marxist response to the impending European war.

Beyond that, it seems evident that between August and November 1914, Mussolini remained uncertain as to the proper strategy Marxists should adopt in the face of the events that had overwhelmed Europe. He was outraged by the brutality of the German invasion of Belgium and heartened by French resistance—and acknowledged that war, falling as it would most heavily on the working classes, might well precipitate social revolution.[77]

In fact, compared to Lenin, Mussolini had a much more nuanced and uncertain notion of the genesis, conduct, and consequences of the war. While generic capitalism was identified as primarily responsible, Mussolini, like Roberto Michels and some of the major syndicalists, attributed some of the immediate causes of the war that had broken over Europe to dynastic rivalry, domestic problems, and popular prejudice. He alluded to the fact that history had parsed industrial capitalism into nations, and each nation sought its own advantage in its competition with others. He added further dimension to the analysis when he proceeded to refer to the diverse interests of the component classes in each peculiar national environment.[78] He was clearly prepared to entertain the influence of a variety of factors in shaping events. He spoke of domestic economic considerations, of mass psychology, and of national enmities as contributing to the outbreak, as well as the subsequent conduct, of the war.

As early as the first weeks of August, Mussolini acknowledged that the socialist International had failed in the face of the crisis. For all the reasons intimated, some of the most committed Marxists of Europe had opted to defend their respective "bourgeois" nations against the "bourgeoisie" of other nations. Marxists, he argued, had no clear theoretical appreciation of what had, and what was, transpiring. The socialists of the International were bereft of a uniform and specifically doctrinal response. By and large, each national socialist political organization tended to support its respective government. None of the major socialist organizations chose to "martyr" their own country on the altar of Marxist principle.[79]

Throughout September and October, Mussolini found himself in a series of debates with those who advocated Italy's intervention in the war on the side of the Entente. They pointed out that he clearly favored the Entente; and that he was prepared to countenance a war in the defense of France and Belgium; and they pointed out that the socialist position on the war, which was absolute neutrality in the face of international conflict, looked remarkably like that assumed by the principal spokesmen of the bourgeoisie.

On the 13th of October, Mussolini intimated that he was prepared to consider Italy's involvement in the burgeoning conflict "entirely and simply from a national point of view—a point of view that did not exclude that it would be both national and 'proletarian' at the same time."[80] On the 18th, he wrote the article that would ultimately sever his ties with the official party position, and herald the appearance of his own specific Marxist heresy.

On that occasion, Mussolini made the argument for "active and operant neutrality" rather than the "absolute neutrality" officially demanded by the party. He indicated that the "absolute" neutrality of the party had never been absolute in fact. Socialists, in general, had systematically and consistently favored the nations of the Triple Entente. They sought the defense of independent and largely defenseless nations like Serbia and Belgium against the feudal militarism of Germany and Austria-Hungary.

Mussolini argued that he was no longer sure what "absolute" neutrality entailed. Clearly it could not mean an indifference to the fate of the nation. That would be to sacrifice not only the bourgeoisie, but the interests of the proletariat as well. The entire nation would be consigned to an entirely uncertain future. The entire nation, with all its constituent classes and subclasses, would be made subject to the feudal domination of Germans and Austrians. He could not convince himself that socialism required the party leadership to sacrifice the interests of Italy's working classes to any such loathsome outcome.[81]

In effect, on the 18th of October 1914, Mussolini argued that, for reasons that had become eminently obvious, the socialist party was not in any position to make revolution. To make revolution in time of war would leave socialists facing the dilemma he had reviewed in the opening weeks of the conflict. Unless all the proletarians of all the warring nations simultaneously undertook revolution, Italy faced the real prospect of invasion by its erstwhile allies. It would then have to abjectly submit to "Teutonic fury," or defend itself. The revolution made to oppose war would find itself compelled to fight a war.

Mussolini went on to consider the possibility that the socialists might support a war on the side of the Entente. That could conceivably shorten the war, thereby saving the lives of an untold number of workers in all the major nations of Europe. Furthermore, the outcome of that war would shape the environment in which the workers of Europe would have to fashion their subsequent destiny.

Mussolini argued that none of those options were attractive, but history had forced Marxists to choose. To remain immobile in the face of movement everywhere clearly would be to fail one's responsibilities. It was evident to him that the socialists of Italy had allowed themselves to be overcome by events, to assume a posture that rendered them observers, rather than shapers, of events.[82]

Almost immediately afterward, the directorate of the Socialist Party called a meeting to consider Mussolini's changed position. On the nineteenth and twentieth of October, at the conclusion of a clamorous conclave of party leaders, Mussolini submitted his resignation from the editorship of *Avanti!* For days after, he continued to argue his case, to no avail. The party was prepared to accept his resignation as editor of the party newspaper, and Mussolini went on to seek support among "revolutionary socialists."

Shortly thereafter, in repeating the arguments that led him to contest the party's position with respect to the war, Mussolini emphasized a point that he had made before but which had remained less than central to his discussion: he said he wished to address the issue of the war "from a national point of view, one that incorporated that of the revolutionary proletariat."[83] Finally, on the tenth of November, he spoke candidly of the failure of most socialists to have ever come to a serious understanding of the historic, political, economic, and revolutionary role of *nations* in the contemporary world.

On that date, before an audience of Milanese socialists, Mussolini rehearsed the fact that traditional Marxists had never fully come to grips with the issue of nationality, and national sentiment, and their role in the course of events. In saying that, Mussolini carefully distinguished his proposed analysis from the agenda of "bourgeois nationalism." He argued, as had Filippo Corridoni, that he spoke as a socialist—and that the socialism that had become orthodox in Germany had not addressed all those issues that the war had made vital. The orthodox in Germany had simply repeated the slogans of the International without thought and critical distinction. He spoke of the critical interests of the proletariat that were invested in the nation, and then went on to remind his audience that both Marx and Engels had recognized the indelible influence of national sentiment on human association.[84] The "orthodox" in Italy, following the leadership of foreign orthodoxies, had failed to make anything of it.

He went on to cite those instances in the Marx-Engels correspondence that documented the support of both Marx and Engels for Germany's war against France in the Franco-Prussian war—and Engels's special enthusiasm for the efficacy of German arms. He insisted that even the founders of scientific Marxism understood the role of nationality and national sentiment in historic evolution—and at critical junctures argued for the compatibility of national and proletarian interests. On the same day that he reaffirmed his decision to resign his public offices in the party, and announced the appearance of his own daily, *Il Popolo d'Italia*, Mussolini maintained that if socialism were to survive as a meaningful political movement, it would have to settle its account with the reality of national sentiment.[85]

In affirming that, Mussolini focused on the single most critical issue that Marxism would face throughout the revolutionary twentieth century. It was the issue in which all of the variants of Marxism would seek their ultimate resolution. It was an issue that was to help define the central heresy of V. I. Lenin and bring together all the threads of theoretical dissidence that had become evident by the time of the First World War. Out of the cauldron of the first world conflict, a transmogrified nationalism was to emerge that in its varied expressions was to make up the ideological substance of most of the social, political, and economic revolutions that were to shatter the equanimity of the twentieth century. Nationalism was to become the issue upon which Marxist orthodoxy was to founder. It was nationalism that was to provide much of the doctrinal substance for all the Marxist variants of all the revolutionary movements that were to be of significance in the twentieth century. It found expression in the "nationalism" of Adolf Hitler's National Socialism, and in the "patriotism" of Marxism-Leninism and Maoism. The notions of national sentiment and nationalism provided much of the doctrinal substance that inspired the revolutionary zeal of millions upon millions throughout the century—and it received its first full and frank intellectual treatment among the Marxist ideologues of the first Fascism. They were the Marxist radicals of revolutionary syndicalism.

CHAPTER TEN

The Great War, Revolution, and Leninism

The First World War was midwife to the fulsome appearance of both Leninism and Fascism. Out of the doctrinal legacy left by the founders of Marxism, V. I. Lenin and Benito Mussolini each fashioned a system of beliefs that were to mobilize millions to service—to commitment, obedience, sacrifice, and violence.

As has been suggested, such invocations are animated by normative injunction—that in the twentieth century characteristically took on ideological form. Ideologies are a compound of empirical and moral claims, all calculated to shape voluntary behavior. Such ideologies addressed a representative collection of themes: the community identification of participants; the critical values that presumably characterize the community with which persons identify; the imputed mission to be discharged by that chosen community; as well as the instrumentalities employed in the fulfillment of purpose. By the time of the Great War, the variants of traditional Marxism that were to dominate the century had already been supplied their ideological essentials.

For most of the twentieth century, it was argued that Leninism and Fascism, in some real sense, were fundamentally antithetical in terms of ideological goal culture. Leninism was of the "left," and Fascism was of the "right." In many instances, the contention was accompanied by an insistence that Fascism was essentially "antihuman," fundamentally irrational, and given to only two "absolute values": violence and war.[1]

Only with the final collapse of the Soviet Union have commentators more frequently spoken of Leninism's "fundamentally conflictual . . . view of social reality"—and of communism's "messianic foreign policy," sustained by "an enormous military." All of that was understood to be infused with a "shared sense that the Russian people are superior and have a unique role to play in the world."[2] By the end of the twentieth century, many had arrived at the judgment that Leninism had been a most singular kind of left-wing internationalism.

It is not odd that judgments concerning Leninism should have changed over time. What is odd is that it had taken so long.

The twentieth-century variants of Marxism, given their common origin, shared many features. All the issues raised by Marxists like Dietzgen, Woltmann, and Sorel—like Michels, Olivetti, and Corridoni—came together during the First World War to produce the ideologies that made our time what it was. In retrospect, the process through which that was accomplished is reasonably clear.

LENINISM AND THE TRANSFORMATION OF MARXISM

Traditional wisdom would have it that Lenin rejected any form of nationalism in defense of an unqualified internationalism. Nationalism was of the political right, and reactionary—while internationalism was of the left, and revolutionary.

It is not difficult to lapse into just such an interpretation of Leninism. Lenin's call for the defeat of his own homeland at the very commencement of the Great War seemed to establish his antinationalist credentials. His denunciation of "chauvinism" and "social patriotism" seemed its confirmation.

Lenin's thought, actually, was complex and "dialectical"—anything other than transparent and rectilinear. A clear and unambiguous interpretation of its intent could not always be forthcoming.

For a very long time it was easy to pretend to see in his doctrine an exclusivistic "internationalism," that abjured any form of nationalism. He was understood to have been a champion of "proletarian internationalism." It was said that Lenin, like Marx before him, imagined that the working classes had no "fatherland." As though all that were not sufficient, after the October revolution, Soviet theoreticians went on to insist that "nationalism is the worst enemy of the working class." What that seemed to mean was that Lenin had "definitively solved" all the theoretical issues that had collected around nationalism, national sentiment, and the "nationalities question," and had opted for an unmitigated internationalism.[3] Actually, the purported resolution of all those problems was achieved more in pretense than fact.

Granted that Marx understood nationalism to be a transient phenomenon, sometimes progressive and sometimes not, it was not at all evident how that might provide policy guidance to revolutionaries in 1914, faced as they were with the reality of a conflict that would involve all the major powers. As has been indicated, before the Great War, many of Marxism's foremost theoreticians saw nationalism, both as a political concept and as a sentiment, involving a very intricate set of empirical and normative considerations. Given the emerging crisis, it was not at all self-evident how an "orthodox" Marxist might deal with nationalism.

With the outbreak of the Great War, most Marxists opted to support their respective nations in the armed conflict that threatened them all. Lenin's advocacy of defeatism for one's own nation was clearly a minority response—and most commentators understood that advocacy to be idiosyncratic rather than evidence of doctrinal integrity.

Actually, the notion that Lenin was, in principle, antinationalistic rests on a very privative conception of what "nationalism" might be taken to mean—neglecting to take into account much of the critical thought that had collected around the term in the two decades before the advent of the Great War.

Careful consideration of Lenin's public posturing during the first years of that war reveals some critically important qualifications to the position he had assumed in 1913. The reality was that Lenin's views on nationalism and national sentiment were only seemingly simple and straightforward. In fact, they were quite complex and subtle. Mikhail Agursky has made a case that Lenin was, in some fundamental sense, a Great Russian nationalist—granted a nationalist of an uncommon sort.[4]

About a year after Lenin wrote his "Critical Remarks on the National Question"—with the insistence that "Marxism cannot be reconciled with nationalism, be it even of the 'most just,' 'purest,' most refined and civilised brand"—he asked his audience, "Is a sense of national pride alien to us, Great-Russian class-conscious proletarians?"—to which he himself immediately replied, "Certainly not! We love our language and our country."[5]

Lenin went on to expand upon that acknowledgment. He spoke of the humiliation suffered by his "fair country" at the hands of those who had reduced Russians to the status of slaves. He proceeded to affirm that "We are full of a sense of national pride, and for that very reason we *particularly* hate *our* slavish past"—a past that was the product of domestic despotism, misrule, and exploitation by capitalists both domestic and foreign.

"The *worst* enemies of our country," Lenin continued, were precisely those forces—and they were enemies that only the class-conscious, Great-Russian proletariat could defeat. "Full of a sense of national pride, we Great-Russian workers want, come what may, a . . . proud Great Russia"—the restoration of "Great-Russian national dignity." That required the defeat of the domestic and foreign class enemies of the Great-Russian proletarian—to be achieved by recognizing that the "interests of the Great-Russians' national pride . . . coincide with the *socialist* interests of the Great-Russian (and all other) proletarians."[6]

Lenin argued that the "true" nationalism of the Great-Russians found ultimate expression in international revolution. Great-Russians were "full of pride because [their] nation [had] created a revolutionary class . . . capable of providing mankind with great models of the struggle for freedom and socialism."[7] In such fashion, Lenin had succeeded in combining revolutionary nationalism and internationalism in a single revolutionary program. The *Great-Russian* proletariat could take national pride in the fact that they, and not the Germans or the French, would lead the international revolution.

Lenin's notions were by no means unique in the history of revolutionary Marxism. Marx and Engels had argued in very much the same fashion. Their support for Germany in its regional wars, and their insistence that the German proletariat bore special historic responsibilities, arose out of a similar set of convictions.

As has been indicated, both Marx and Engels supported Bismarck's war against France, for example—largely because Germany's victory would transfer leadership of the international revolutionary movement from France, with its "bourgeois" Proudhonists and Blanquists, to "their" Social Democratic party in Germany. That would make the *German* proletariat leaders of the imminent world revolution.

For Engels, "the German working class" was "clearly superior to the French both theoretically and from the point of view of organization. The predominance of the Germans," he went on, ". . . would mean the predominance of our theory . . ."[8] Germans would provide both the brains and brawn of the world revolution.

Marx and Engels both saw Germans as the natural leaders of the world revolution. The German Social Democratic movement would provide the international proletariat its theoretical leadership, and German industry would supply a substantial part of its material base. Associated with that was the conviction that the revolution required that all the small and "historyless" nations on Germany's periphery be "absorbed" in the process.

That conviction was part of the general understanding the founders of

Marxism entertained concerning what they held to be the pattern of history. Both Marx and Engels consistently maintained that the anticipated proletarian revolution necessitated the worldwide expansion of the advanced industrial nations. They both supported the expansion of the United States into Mexican territory, for example, and the French conquest of North Africa, on just such grounds. Great Britain, in turn, was doing "history's work" in conquering South Asia and bringing to those backward nations the benefits of a modern economy.[9] The consolidation of lesser nations into those more industrially advanced was part of history's plan.

Classical Marxism's conception of international proletarian revolution was explicit. The revolution required the appropriate material preconditions—a productive base that was industrially mature and an urban population that was essentially proletarian. In their judgment, the revolution that was anticipated was to be led by Germans, who were theoretically and organizationally better prepared than any other candidates. The other revolutionary nations would collect around German leadership. None of that, of course, would imply German dominance—the "historyless" and "primitive" peoples drawn into the vortex of revolution would simply become, without prejudice, one with the economically advanced, revolutionary community—to be lifted to the level of promised fulfillment.

That kind of Marxism would seem to satisfy both German nationalist sentiment and the demands of revolutionary internationalism.[10] And that seemed the kind of Marxism Lenin had in mind. Just as Marx had decided that the revolutionary baton had passed, in the course of time, from the French and British to German workers, Lenin decided that, in the imperialist epoch, revolutionary responsibilities had been transferred from the German, to Great-Russian, workers.[11]

That the thought of the founders of Marxism lends itself to such a construction suggests a great deal about the nature of ideology and the role it might play in the policy crises that tested the integrity and the sense of responsibility of all Marxists in 1914. Lenin entertained many of the same general notions found in the works and letters of Marx and Engels. Like the founders of revolutionary socialism, Lenin insisted that the imminent world revolution required for its success the most advanced theory—to be supplied by Bolshevism alone. Lenin argued that all the socialist parties of Europe had shamelessly betrayed the revolution by supporting their respective governments in the Great War. That was the consequence of the failure of theory. They did not appreciate the fact that industrial capitalism had entered its final stage—imperialism—nor did they understand all the attendant implications. Only Bolshevism had been true to the cause—and only because Lenin had supplied its leaders with his theory of imperialism.

To explain the defection of revolutionary leadership in all the advanced industrial countries, Lenin made recourse to his "theory" of imperialism—his "creative development" of Marxism. Without his "advanced theory," European socialists had allowed themselves to be misled by bourgeois nationalism and social chauvinism. Without understanding the necessity of a highly specialized, professional, elite leadership, the social democrats had succumbed to "bourgeois democratic" impulse, "opportunism," and class betrayal. Only the Great-Russian proletariat, armed with the advanced theories of Bolshevism, could lead the world revolution. Bolshevism would gather to its cause all of its neighbors, sharing with them "the human principle of equality."

Lenin quickly qualified that promise of equality with the insistence that Bolshevism did "not advocate preserving small nations at all costs; *other conditions being equal*, we are decidedly for centralisation."[12] In effect, the Great-Russian proletarian would lead the world revolution, gathering to itself, through "centralisation," all those nations not possessed of "advanced theory."

Lenin's argument was admirably coherent, although not often fully appreciated. Because other social democrats had not understood all the implications of modern imperialism, they could not possibly appreciate what might count as responsible revolutionary strategy. In 1917, in his "Revision of the Party Programme," Lenin chose to emphasize a number of features of the modern world that would become increasingly important in the time following the conclusion of the Great War.

He told his followers to "more vividly" emphasize the fact that a "handful of the richest imperialist countries" were prospering "parasitically by robbing colonies and weaker nations." That was important because among the consequences of that reality was the "rise of powerful revolutionary movements in countries that are subjected to imperialist plunder." Conversely, "that plunder, by imperialist methods, . . . tends to a certain extent to prevent the rise of profound revolutionary movements" in the imperialist nations—"a very large (comparatively) portion of their population" have been compromised by participating "in the division of the imperialist loot."[13]

An entirely new conception of world revolution emerged out of Lenin's notions of imperialism. His explication of those notions took form as a programmatic strategy of international revolution that would influence modern history to a degree totally unanticipated at the time. In retrospect, some of its implications should have been immediately evident.

For Lenin, given the dynamics of the "new epoch," the world was divided into "imperialist" and "oppressed" nations. Revolution was largely precluded in those nations that were imperialist—their populations having been suborned by the profits obtained by imperialism's exploitation of peripheral communities. For those exploited communities, on the other hand, revolution is fostered by their very exploitation. Where Marxism anticipated revolution in advanced industrial circumstances, Leninism saw revolution manifesting itself first in economically primitive conditions.

For Lenin, the populations of the imperialist countries tend to behave as capitalists would have them behave. They batten on profits extorted from the weak and defenseless—those who find themselves in less developed communities. The proletariats of the imperialist nations, living "bourgeois" lives, led by an "aristocracy" of workers, become "social chauvinists," and nationalists.

The populations of the exploited communities, on the other hand, become revolutionary. One sees in them the harbingers of the future. Because of their subjection to systematic and protracted exploitation, Lenin anticipated critical revolutionary energy emerging among the denizens of less developed, marginal economies. He anticipated that the peoples of the "periphery," mercilessly exploited by the capitalists of Western and Central Europe, would be driven to revolutionary response. The Bolsheviks, the vanguard of the revolutionary masses of Great Russia, armed with the most advanced theory, would lead the anticipated world revolution and gather the revolutionary populations of the less developed periphery into the fold. Great Russia, through the Bolsheviks, would assume the leadership of world revolution.

What was not clear at that juncture was precisely how Lenin expected world revolution to proceed. Marx had anticipated that modern industry, with its cheap commodities and effective communications would "batter down all Chinese walls," to compel all nations on the margins of machine capitalism to embark on a process of economic modernization and industrial development. He expected that such an eventuality could not be conducted without generating a sense of inefficacy and impotence among native peoples. He cataloged the humiliations and the deprivation suffered by the peoples of China and India in the course of the expansion of Western capitalism. He spoke of their increasing resistance to the impostures of the advanced industrial states. He saw their populations taking "active, nay, a fanatical part in the struggle against foreigners. . . . They kidnap and kill every foreigner within their reach. . . . What," Marx asked, "is an army to do against a people resorting to such means of warfare?"[14]

All that notwithstanding, Marx did not confuse the issue. What he anticipated was not a proletarian uprising in Asia, but a "popular war for the maintenance of Chinese nationality"—and, at best, a *bourgeois* revolution that would see the Chinese Great Wall adorned with the call to "Liberty, Equality and Fraternity."[15]

Marx maintained that given the impact of European incursions into Asia, with the attendant demand for product, and the inflow of capital, together with the articulation of a modern infrastructure, one could predict the emergence of an enterprising Chinese bourgeoisie. Economic and industrial growth would follow. That process would be largely independent of the maturing proletarian revolution in Europe—but as a consequence of emerging Asia's increasing competition for market share and investment, it would serve as an accelerant.

With the proletarian revolution in the advanced industrial nations, socialism would extend itself in assisting the less developed communities, still in the first phases of development, to complete the process of economic modernization. The anticipated world revolution would thus involve an interactive phased series of events. The proletariat in the advanced industrial nations would undertake revolution once that economic maturation had been attained. Marx understood that to be the necessary, if not sufficient, basis for proletarian liberation. Once the proletariat had established itself as dominant in the advanced industrial nations, it would have the resources to assist the less developed countries to achieve economic maturity and complete the creation of the material substructure of world socialism.

The revolutionary process was much more uncertain in the thought of Lenin. While it was clear that he was convinced that the socialist revolution was imminent everywhere,[16] it was not clear how the revolution would proceed. Granted he spoke of the "revolutionary struggle of the proletariat" and the "smashing of the state machinery," and so forth, it was not evident *where* the revolution would commence, or which class or classes would bear its associated responsibilities.

It seems evident that Lenin expected the world revolution to commence in Russia—which he himself identified as economically retrograde. Because of the dependence of imperialism on such backward economies for market supplements and investment opportunity, their loss was expected to precipitate the international revolution. Losing its market supplements, raw materials, and investment opportunities would hasten the final collapse of capitalism.

Revolution in industrially retrograde environments implied, at the very least, multiclass collaboration. In Russia, Lenin sought the mobilization of the peasants, who made up the vast majority of the empire's workers and soldiers. Bolshevik leadership was largely, if not exclusively, composed of those of bourgeois, and petty bourgeois, origins.

For their part, Marx and Engels had generally spoken of the masses that would make up the foot soldiers of their anticipated revolution as "proletarians." They understood that with the maturation of machine industry, the "vast majority" of the subject population would have become "class-conscious" urban workers. They would make the revolution and assume its responsibilities.

Lenin argued that because imperialism had deflected revolution from mature to immature economic environments, and transformed the urban proletariat into "labor lieutenants of the capitalist class, real vehicles of reformism and chauvinism," the dynamics of revolutionary activity had changed in fundamental fashion. Without fully exploring all the implications of such an eventuality, Lenin continued to insist that "imperialism is the eve of the social revolution of the proletariat."[17] The implications involved very quickly became apparent.

According to Lenin's thesis, revolution would probably commence in economically underdeveloped circumstances. Revolutionary leadership would originate among nonproletarians. The ranks of the revolutionary armies would be drawn from peasant masses. And yet, somehow, the revolution would be "proletarian."

Apparently, what made such a revolution "proletarian" was its guidance by "correct theory." This was made evident by the fact that Lenin denounced and proceeded to persecute all non-Bolshevik Marxists in the Russia that emerged from the October revolution. Mensheviks, Social Revolutionaries, independent Marxists—none were spared his wrath. In the course of his early rule, many non-Bolshevik Marxists were silenced, denied the right to participate, in almost any fashion, in the politics of revolutionary Russia. Ultimately, they were incarcerated, frequently exiled, and often put to death.

Lenin had created a very singular Marxism. Many, if not most, Marxists did not recognize its contours. Beginning with Rosa Luxemburg, who objected to the first formulations of Leninism at the beginning of the century,[18] to Karl Kautsky, the dean of German Social Democracy, the theoreticians of the left had difficulty recognizing any Marxist orthodoxy in Bolshevism.

By the end of the Great War, all the problems that had beset Marxist intellectuals in the long years before its coming, resurfaced with an intensity borne of cataclysmic human conflict and the revolutions it engendered. Even before the Great War had come to its end, in the summer of 1918, less than a year after the Bolshevik seizure of power in St. Petersburg and Moscow, Kautsky wrote his *The Dictatorship of the Proletariat*, a critique of some of the central concepts of Leninism as they had manifested themselves in the behaviors of the leadership in revolutionary Russia.[19]

In Kautsky's studied opinion, whatever had transpired in Russia with the October revolution, had very little to do with Marxism. Bolshevism had transformed Marxism into something it was not. That was clear to Kautsky in Bolshevism's treatment of several critical Marxian concepts—among them, "democracy," the "revolutionary masses," "revolutionary leadership," "class," the "state," and the "dictatorship of the proletariat." The treatment of all those concepts negatively impacted on what Kautsky held to be the "truth" of "the teachings of Marxism."[20]

Kautsky's objections to Leninism rekindled all those discussions that had fueled controversy at the turn of the twentieth century. Once again, but with greater intensity, all those contested concepts resurfaced. Kautsky's *The Dictatorship of the Proletariat*, written after the Bolshevik seizure of power, and before the end of the Great War, returned, once again, to some of the most critical issues that divided Marxists after the passing of Friedrich Engels.

MARXISM, DEMOCRACY, AND THE STATE

Over the years, the discussion that has surrounded Kautsky's critique of Leninism, as it appears in his *The Dictatorship of the Proletariat*, has sometimes taken on the properties of an attempt to determine "what Marx really meant" when he spoke of the "dictatorship of the proletariat." In trying to determine Marx's precise meaning, such an enterprise seems futile. So many plausible interpretations can be imposed on the wealth of theoretical reflections to be found in Marx's writings that to pretend that *one*, and only one, interpretation is correct, seems, at its best, unconvincing. Scholars are left with a clutch of competing plausibilities and very few certainties.

Kautsky commenced his critique of Bolshevism by identifying Leninism with the same ends sought by all Marxists: "to free the proletariat, and with it humanity, through socialism."[21] He certainly did not argue, as many did at the time, that Leninism was something other than Marxism. Rather, Kautsky conceived himself warning Marxists, specifically Leninists, that any tactical policies undertaken in the course of revolution that would impair *democracy* would threaten the ends of the revolution itself. Kautsky maintained that his argument with Lenin did not turn on ends, but involved a concern that the invocation of improper means might jeopardize those very ends to which all Marxists were committed. The socialism Kautsky was prepared to defend was "unthinkable" without democracy.[22]

Kautsky contended that not only was socialism to be attained using parliamentary democracy as a necessary institutional instrumentality, but that any established socialism could not be socialism without being intrinsically democratic. His critique did not necessarily turn on the "true" interpretation of Marx's thoughts about proletarian revolution. His argument was predicated on what he understood to be the very logic of revolutionary Marxism.

Kautsky unpacked his argument by referring to a "revolutionary will to socialism" as necessary to the accomplishment of Marxian purpose—and that such a will could, and would, only be created by "great industry." It was industry that educated what had been rural labor to the responsibilities of governance. Large-scale industrial production cultivated cooperation among producers, and elicited recognition among them of the complexities involved in advanced commodity manufacture, marketing, and distribution—all competencies required of proletarians if they were to manage socialist enterprise after their accession to power.[23]

Kautsky maintained that according to the materialist conception of history, only capitalist enterprise could transform "reactionary" peasants, propertiless vagabonds, "harmful parasites . . . without education, without self-consciousness, [and] without cohesion," into those equipped to assume modern responsibilities at "the indispensable economic foundations of production and therefore of society."[24] Only by discharging their responsibilities as workers in modern industrial production might all the "non-revolutionary" elements of society be transformed into "truly revolutionary proletarians." Only then would the modern proletariat constitute itself an army of "self-conscious, independent movement of the immense majority, in the interest of the immense majority."[25]

Workers trained to productive responsibilities in developed industry become the knowledgeable agents of revolution, possessed of the skills necessary for mobilization, and the organizational talents necessary to manage socialized industry after the revolution. That, Kautsky argued, could only be the case if the subject workers had the opportunity to be educated and to educate themselves to such purpose. That would require not only training in an advanced industrial setting, but a liberal political environment in which a free exchange of ideas was possible and in which the proletariat had the opportunity to assume specifically political responsibilities. The alternative would find a "proletariat . . . too ignorant and demoralised to organise and rule itself."[26] In such circumstances, workers could hardly find liberation. The central issue for Kautsky was not the peculiarities of the "dictatorship of the proletariat," but the essential nature of the proletariat whose dictatorship it was to be.

Kautsky's argument was that Marxism had taught its followers that socialism's liberating revolution could only follow the full maturation of society's economic, particularly industrial, base. That maturation would provide not only the material abundance necessary for the abolition of classes, but would furnish the mass of skilled, responsible, educated, and self-conscious proletarians who would assure the creation and maintenance of a tolerant, nurturing, and democratic system.[27]

Kautsky's point was that a society that has traversed the "inevitable" stages of economic development, would necessarily host an "immense majority" of self-conscious, skilled, and benevolent proletarians who probably could establish socialism "without violence and bloodshed"—and certainly without political dictatorship.[28] The immense majority of self-confident workers would have little to fear from that small minority of capitalists who would survive the winnowing of the final stages of capitalism's senescence.

In the circumstances of full maturity of the economic base, the former exploiting class could only constitute a residual minority. Marx had taught that a mature industrial system would be characterized by the concentration of wealth in few hands, the vast majority of smallholders having been jettisoned into the proletariat—the consequence of competition in an environment in which the overall profit rate of enterprise approximated zero. The inevitable collapse of the system would literally compel the proletariat to assume control of production. Constituting, as they would, the vast majority of the population, the proletarians would hardly find it necessary to suppress their former oppressors with violence, or to deny them civil and political rights after the revolution, in order to secure and retain power. Whatever Marx and Engels imagined the "dictatorship of the proletariat" to have been, it could not have meant elite rule, the abolition of civil or political rights, or the invocation of mass violence and terror.

All Marxists were committed to the proposition that social and political revolution, and the victory of the proletariat, was inevitable. They differed on whether that revolution would be violent.

In a speech delivered to the Congress of the International at the Hague in 1872, Marx held that it was inevitable that the proletariat would one day seize political power in order to create the anticipated new economic order. He went on to say, "We do not assert that the way to reach this goal is the same everywhere. . . . We do not deny that there are countries like England and America . . . where the worker may attain his object by peaceful means."

Twenty years later, while Engels was still his mentor, Kautsky repeated something of the same judgment. "Because we know nothing about the final decisive battles of the social war," he declared, "we cannot anticipate if they will be bloody, if physical violence will play a significant part—or if they will be conducted exclusively with economic, legislative and moral pressures."[29] What Kautsky did suggest was that as industrial capitalism matured, the likelihood that physical violence would be necessary would correspondingly decline.

Once again, the reasons for such a judgment were clear. As the machine economy of a community matured, the increase in the proportion of the population that would be class-conscious proletarian would rapidly overwhelm the numbers that made up the oppressing classes.[30] Kautsky argued that the prospects of a peaceful transition from a ripe industrial society to one that was socialist were good. Conversely, should social and/or political revolution manifest itself in an industrially less developed environment, it could hardly be either "proletarian" or "socialist." The best that could happen would be its rescue by an attendant revolution in an appropriately mature economy.[31] Revolution in a retrograde environment could only conclude with a restoration of the old class strife. Only if revolution in an advanced economic environment provided the appropriate human and material resources might the situation be salvaged. Thus, when Marx was asked if a revolution in the backward Russia of his time could possibly result in Russia "skipping the stages," that typified the economic evolution of the West, to immediately achieve socialism, he replied, "only . . . if the Russian Revolution becomes a signal for the proletarian revolution in the West, so that both complement each other."[32]

It was within that context that Kautsky invested so heavily in the role that parliamentarism might play in the general runup to proletarian revolution. As early as the time of the Erfurt Program, while Engels still guided his arguments, Kautsky held that voting for members of the German parliament provided important educational opportunities for the proletariat. They came to understand political life in ways simply not available in non-democratic and nonparliamentary circumstances. For the working class, the situation created by parliamentary elections increased the opportunities for active association, free communication, and mutual support. On such occasions, urban workers learned to assume responsibilities and developed skills necessary for their future tasks.[33]

Parliament, Kautsky argued, was a product of the revolutionary industrial bourgeoisie in its struggle against monarchial absolutism. The "absolute state" of that time constituted a "fetter" on the emerging productive forces. In their effort to reduce the controls exercised by the state, the bourgeoisie sought to make public power subject to the control of the public. To accomplish that, they struggled to create a functioning parliament, calculated, in whatever measure, to "control the government."[34]

To accomplish their purpose, according to the thesis, the bourgeoisie allied itself with other classes anxious to escape exploitation by the nobility. The result was the creation of a representative institution that, at least to some degree, was responsive to the demands of the citizenry. Given such views, Kautsky conceived the state subject to the influence of a citizenry composed of diverse classes. In such circumstances, he told his audience, "every class will endeavor to shape the . . . state in a manner corresponding to its particular interests." Parliament becomes the institutional means for effecting that purpose.[35]

In the course of things, the attempt to influence parliament leads to a struggle over the conditions governing the franchise, voluntary association, and the freedom of advocacy. All classes develop an interest in these political rights in their effort to influence parliament and through parliament, the permanent bureaucracy and the executive state itself.[36] Thus, in Kautsky's judgment, the state does not "stand above" classes, is not the exclusive organ of class rule, but constitutes a public agency that can be influenced (however little or however much) by diverse classes. He argued further that given the character of parliamentarism in a democracy, there is "no franchise . . . which would secure to the possessing classes a lasting monopoly."[37]

Several things are revealed in Kautsky's discussion. He does not believe that the political state is in the unqualified service of an identifiable class; it can be influenced by a variety of classes and subsets of classes. More than that, the state cannot be an agency in the unique service of a given class because the entire notion of "class" rule is difficult to fully understand. The meaning of the term "class" is not transparent. Kautsky told his readership that any class that is "not organised as such is a formless fluctuating mass, whose exact boundaries it is quite impossible to mark." Unless a given class is "organized as such," it cannot function as an agency of control. Kautsky went on to maintain that "in capitalist society, with its constantly changing conditions, the classes cannot be stereotyped in fixed grooves. All social conditions are in a state of flux." Therefore, "class membership is always changing" together with their respective interests.[38] Control of the state by a single class becomes impossible.

Kautsky carried the logic of his argument further. Even after the proletarian revolution, society would still be host to all the complex and changing interests of the various components of the "fluctuating mass" of workers themselves. Whatever the organization of the state, it would still have to respond to those varied interests. And the best conceivable vehicle for the expression and resolution of those diverse, and sometimes conflicting, proletarian interests would be some form of democratically elected parliament.

Kautsky argued that the proletariat did not constitute a monolithic entity, each member sharing interests indistinguishable from others. He held that the proletariat, because of its divided and varied interests, could only manifest unanimity if housed in an authoritarian political party that imposed obedience and conformity. That could only result not in "the dictatorship of the proletariat, but a dictatorship of one part of the proletariat over the other."[39]

Kautsky's case did not turn on the issue of what Marx "really meant" by invoking the notion of the dictatorship of the proletariat. It turned on the conviction that if Lenin were correct in his views about revolution and the attendant dictatorship of the proletariat, then Marx could only have been wrong. According to Marx, class-conscious proletarians can only make their appearance, and the ideological superstructure representing their fundamental interests could only be forthcoming, when "productive forces" had matured to the point where "social relations" constituted a "fetter" on their further development.[40] Kautsky argued that it was at that juncture that society might ease into social and political revolution without violence and terror to effect and sustain it—and parliament might serve as the democratic expression of the popular will in a socialist state. For Kautsky, that was what Marx, given Marxism's entire theoretical structure, "really meant" in conjuring up the image of a "proletarian dictatorship."

LENIN AND THE "DICTATORSHIP
OF THE PROLETARIAT"

Lenin's response to Kautsky was dictated by a number of imperative political concerns only indirectly bearing on basic ideological issues. Nonetheless, his response was typical of all those he directed against his ideological opponents; it was personal, vituperative, uncompromising, and couched in studied theoretical terms.

It was evident that from the position he had assumed at the very commencement of the Great War, Lenin could only have considered Kautsky an "opportunist." Kautsky had extended passive support for the "imperialist war." As a consequence, in Lenin's judgment, Kautsky had irretrievably compromised himself. For Lenin, Kautsky's position with respect to the dictatorship of the proletariat was a "lucid example of . . . utter and ignominious bankruptcy . . . [and a] complete renunciation of Marxism." He spoke of Kautsky as articulating a "Marxism . . . stripped of its revolutionary living spirit"—nothing other than an "unparalleled vulgarisation of the theories of Marxism."[41]

Lenin immediately identified Kautsky's criticisms in *The Dictatorship of the Proletariat* as an "opportunistic" rationale for "bourgeois democracy," something Lenin dismissed as either the result of incompetence or betrayal. He scorned Kautsky's arguments in support of "bourgeois democracy" as "liberal"—as being vastly different from anything that, in any sense, might qualify as Marxist. Lenin identified himself as an advocate of "proletarian," rather than "abstract, democracy."

Lenin was prepared to argue that "proletarian democracy" was "true" democracy, something fundamentally different from the democracy of the bourgeoisie. "Proletarian democracy," in Lenin's opinion, was nothing other than the "dictatorship of the proletariat," so cavalierly dismissed by Kautsky. He proceeded to expand on the operational meaning of that dictatorship for revolutionary Marxists.

Lenin maintained that the term "dictatorship," when employed in the phrase "dictatorship of the proletariat," "does not necessarily mean the abolition of democracy for the class that exercises the dictatorship over other classes; but it does mean the abolition . . . of democracy for the class over which, or against which, the dictatorship is exercised." In fact, "proletarian democracy" meant, for Lenin, proletarian "dictatorship . . . based directly upon force and unrestricted by any laws. The revolutionary dictatorship of the proletariat," he went on, "is rule won and maintained by the use of violence by the proletariat against the bourgeoisie, rule that is unrestricted by any laws."[42] Given his interpretation, "democracy," for Lenin, meant coercive rule by the "proletarian majority" at the expense of the "bourgeois and petty bourgeois minority."

The forceful suppression of the bourgeoisie, and the denial of their civil and political rights, grew out of the conviction that only violence and dictatorship could assure and sustain the political victory of the proletariat over their tormentors. Only the forcible destruction of the bourgeois state machine, and the subsequent denial of civil and political rights to those it had served so effectively, could assure the survival of proletarian victory.

One of the premises upon which Lenin constructed his interpretation was that the advent of socialism necessarily entailed violent revolution. For that reason, Lenin felt compelled to address the notion, entertained by many Marxists, that a peaceful, democratic transition to socialism might be possible.

It was common knowledge that Marx had suggested that Great Britain, the United States, and Holland might make the transition from mature industrial capitalism to socialism without violence. Kautsky had made much of the fact. Given Lenin's convictions, such a view was unacceptable. In response, he argued that Marx's suggestion had been expressed at a time in history before the age of imperialism—which "finally matured only in the twentieth century."[43] Lenin was prepared to contend that Marx's suggestions were made at a time when the economic and political properties of the world were undergoing rapid change, and imperialism had not yet made fulsome appearance. Neither Marx nor Engels could appreciate any of that. For Lenin, the possibility of a peaceful transition to socialism had been precluded by the advent of imperialism.

Once again, at a critical theoretical juncture, Lenin's analysis turned on the conviction that the modern world had entered a "new stage." Pivotal parts of Marxism, in terms of tactical policy, as well as socioeconomic and political theory, had to be revised in order to accommodate the changes imperialism brought in its train. Lenin maintained that between the time in 1872, when Marx suggested that socialism might come to the advanced industrial nations without violence, and the turn of the century, the capitalist powers had undergone fundamental change. They had made the transition to capitalism's most advanced stage: finance capitalism. At that stage, the entire capitalist system was subject to the "complete domination of the trusts [and] the omnipotence of the big banks"—all insulated from revolution by massive bureaucracies and defended by standing armies.[44]

Given those circumstances, proletarian revolution could only attain and "maintain its rule . . . by means of . . . the terror which . . . rifles, bayonets and cannon . . . inspire in the reactionaries." All of this, Lenin went on, could only be "highly authoritarian"—abolishing, of necessity, "parliamentarism," and its attendant "parasitic excrescence, the state."[45]

To emphasize his point, Lenin quoted Engels's 1891 introductory essay to Marx's *The Civil War in France*. There, Engels affirmed that "the state is nothing but a machine for the oppression of one class by another, and indeed in the democratic republic no less than in the monarchy."[46] All of the civil and political rights advertised by bourgeois democracy were, according to Lenin, entirely without substance. Every bourgeois democracy retains "loopholes" in its constitution, affording the ruling class the opportunity to dispatch troops against workers, to suspend the rights of assembly, and to move against anyone who might threaten its dictatorship. "The more highly developed a democracy is," Lenin went on, "the more imminent are pogroms or civil war in connection with any profound political divergence which is dangerous to the bourgeoisie."[47]

Lenin proposed that instead of representative parliamentary democracy, the Russian revolution of October 1917 brought with it "true" proletarian democracy—a "*million times* more democratic than any bourgeois democracy"—the organization of the exploited workers and peasants in "soviets," the "direct organisation of the working and exploited themselves, which *helps* them to organize and administer their own state." In less than a year after the revolution, Lenin could insist that the old bureaucratic machine of the bourgeois republic of Alexander Kerensky had "been completely smashed, . . . the old judges . . . all been sent packing, the bourgeois parliament . . . dispersed."[48] Proletarian democracy had made its appearance in what had been czarist, and briefly, "bourgeois democratic," Russia.

In all of that, the meanings accorded commonplace notions like the "state," "democracy," "parliamentarism," and "dictatorship" were transmogrified. Lenin provided all those concepts with idiosyncratic content—thereafter to influence, for more than half-a-hundred years, the political and economic history of Russia in totally unanticipated fashion.

For Lenin, proletarian democracy finds expression in a "state" that is not really a state. The proletarian "nonstate," for Lenin, was understood to be a "democracy for the exploited, and a means of *suppressing the exploiters*; and the suppression of a class means inequality for that class, its exclusion from 'democracy.'" He then proceeded to agree with Engels: "so long as the proletariat still needs the state, it does not need it in the interests of freedom, but in order to hold down its adversaries." In some final sense, "the interests of the revolution are higher than the formal rights" of bourgeois democracy or the appeal of "abstract freedom." Lenin further agreed with what he understood Engels to have said in dismissing the notion that elections might provide the proletarian state some sort of "moral authority." Only the "armed people" could deliver such authority. Bourgeois elections could contribute nothing to the process; they had been one of the deceptions that allowed the "bourgeois dictatorship" to exercise its dominance.

Lenin made it perfectly clear that the revolutionary state, "i.e., the proletariat organised as the ruling class," was nothing other than "a machine for the suppression of one class by another."[49] There was nothing other than force, and the threat of force, governing the state's behavior or informing its authority. This was as true for the proletarian, as it was for the bourgeois, state.

Central to all that was a significant issue. If Lenin's revolutionary state is understood to be nothing other than the dictatorship of the proletariat—with civil and political rights reserved exclusively for proletarians—the question of how it might be determined who was, and who was not, a "proletarian" became an issue of fundamental importance. In addressing that issue, Lenin was forthcoming.

No one, other than those committed to Bolshevism, qualified as "proletarian." Lenin was very specific. Of course, none of the bourgeois parties qualified. But then again, neither did most of the revolutionaries—neither the Socialist Revolutionaries, the Mensheviks, nor any of the Social Democratic followers of Plekhanov.[50] As Kautsky had anticipated, the dictatorship of the proletariat turned out to be a dictatorship of part of the proletariat—led by a self-selected bourgeois vanguard—over the remainder.[51]

Perhaps more interesting than anything else is the fact that Lenin had articulated his position with regard to the dictatorship of the proletariat some considerable time before Kautsky published his critique.[52] In the fall of 1917, before the October revolution, Lenin wrote his *State and Revolution*—which, with some significant changes in emphasis, argued the same case to be subsequently found in his response to the "renegade" Kautsky. In effect, Lenin's contentions concerning the dictatorship of the proletariat were not afterthoughts.

What is perhaps most interesting in the account made available in the *State and Revolution* is Lenin's acknowledgement that, after the revolution, the political state, as a "semistate," would continue to exist as the dictatorship of the proletariat. In opposition, Russian anarchists were advocates of the complete and immediate dismantling of the state directly following the revolution. Lenin's response was unequivocal and emphatic.

Lenin maintained that unlike anarchists, Marxists—however much they deplored the old state—advocated the fabrication of a successor after the revolutionary destruction of the old. For Lenin, the state was a necessary instrument in the suppression of enemies—and would continue to serve in just such capacity—until the time when class differences no longer obtained. Until that time, the proletariat that "won political power . . . [would] completely destroy the old state machine and replace it by a new one consisting of an organisation of the armed workers."[53]

For Lenin, the state was "a product and a manifestation of the *irreconcilability* of class antagonisms. The state arises where, when and insofar as class antagonisms objectively *cannot* be reconciled. And, conversely," he continued, "the existence of the state proves that the class antagonisms are irreconcilable."

In effect, Lenin *defined* the state as essentially a control agency. It necessarily appeared wherever irreconcilable differences appeared between classes. Conversely, the fact that there was a state was evidence of irreconcilable differences. If after their revolution, the proletariat reconstructed the state, there would be evidence of irreconcilable differences. And that would justify the reconstruction of the state!

Because Lenin conceived the state the inevitable product of irreconcilable differences, it followed that the state, any state, would be literally unconstrained by law—in order that it might effectively impose its will on the fundamentally antagonistic classes. In that fashion, the state would prevail in order to control those "conflicting interests" that threatened to "consume society."

Lenin maintained that according to Marxist theory, the state, by definition, is an instrument of oppression—the only variation turned on which class was being oppressed at any given time. There can be no state that is anything other than a weapon in the interminable war of classes. Where there are classes there will inevitably be war. Where there is class warfare, there must be the state. Even in the most "democratic" of "bourgeois" republics, the "most powerful, economically dominant class" becomes the "politically dominant class"—exercising its power through the state. That exercise of power may manifest itself "indirectly, but all the more surely," either by the "direct corruption of officials" or through "alliance of the government with the Stock Exchange."[54] For Lenin, the state is always and everywhere an apparatus of control and suppression—it can never be abstractly "democratic."

For Lenin, in the course of that interminable war between classes, the state is, and could only be, an agency of class suppression and exploitation.

Moreover, once entrenched, the state is resolutely resistant to any change that might threaten its dominion. As a consequence, Lenin could argue that once a bourgeois democracy was established *"no* change of persons, institutions or parties . . . can shake it." The bourgeoisie even manages to make universal suffrage serve as an "instrument of [its] rule." For Lenin, "bourgeois democracy" was nothing other than "democracy only for the rich, for the minority," disposed, by its very nature, to defend itself everywhere with the "utmost ferocity and savagery." All of that had been implied in Lenin's original definition of the state, *any* state. As a consequence, it followed that only by means of "violent revolution" might the "armed workers" destroy the bourgeois state—the agency of their oppression. By making class exploitation part of the definition of the state, Lenin made the recourse to violence an inevitability.

In place of the exploitative bourgeois state, the workers were enjoined to establish the "proletarian semistate," that "centralized organisation of force," that would assure the suppression of its antagonists. More than that, given the circumstances, the proletarian semistate was a necessary instrument in assuring the security and success of the revolution.

In drawing out all the implications of his position, Lenin was admirably candid. Beyond the suppression of class enemies, proletarian rule would require an entire catalog of powers. He informed his audience that "so long as the state exists there is no freedom. When there is freedom, there will be no state"—for it was evident to him that "until the 'higher' phase of communism arrives, the socialists demand the *strictest* control by society *and by the state* over the measure of labor and the measure of consumption."[55]

Lenin was explicit. Bolsheviks were not "utopians." They did not "'dream' of dispensing *at once* with all administration, with all subordination." The required administration would become "a splendidly equipped mechanism" to be "set going" by the "iron hand of the armed workers . . . establishing strict, iron discipline." Subsequent to the seizure of power and the confiscation "of the means of production in the name of the whole of society," the proletarian semistate, that "voluntarily centralized" organization of force, would assume the responsibility of leading "the enormous mass of the population—the peasants, the petty bourgeoisie, and semiproletarians—in the work of organising a socialist economy." This was the dictatorship of the proletariat that Lenin spoke of as being only a "temporary" requirement. The length of time involved was unclear. There were times when he apparently conceived it casting a long shadow over an entire historic epoch.[56]

Such a coercive, centralized agency of management and administration, however characterized, would have to "control" and/or "suppress" potentially "antagonistic" classes. In *The Communist Manifesto*, Marx had identified only the proletariat as a "truly" revolutionary class. Peasants and the petty bourgeoisie, while sometimes in temporary alliance with the proletariat, were understood to be essentially "reactionary."[57] If the state is to "wither away" only in "a society in which there are no class antagonisms"[58]—real or potential—the state could only be expected to disappear when classes had entirely disappeared. Before that resolution, the state, as the dictatorship of the proletariat, would be obliged to control and/or suppress its real and/or potential class enemies.

All of this constituted the principal components of what Lenin understood to be the "Marxist theory of the state." It was the commitment to just that "theory" that, in his judgment, distinguished true, from pretended, Marxists. It was a conception of political power that understood the dictatorship of the proletariat, the proletarian semistate, "necessary not only for every class society in general, not only for the *proletariat* which has overthrown the bourgeoisie, but also for the entire *historical period* which separates capitalism from 'classless society,' from communism." Throughout that historical period, the proletariat would need the state (that was really not a state), "not in the interests of freedom, but in order to hold down its adversaries." Beyond that, throughout that historical period, it would need the state to lead the masses in the organization of socialist production.[59]

LENIN, THE STATE, AND THE POSTREVOLUTIONARY ECONOMY

Lenin's discussion of the "proletarian semistate" was anything but casual woolgathering. His views governed Bolshevik rule in postrevolutionary Russia. Throughout the turmoil of war, counterrevolution, and foreign intervention, it was easy to ascribe to circumstances the homicidal violence, and the massive denial of civil, political, and human rights, that characterized Lenin's rule.[60] But it soon became evident, with the end of the Great War, and effective termination of the civil war, that the pattern of Bolshevik rule was hardly the product of circumstance. It faithfully reflected Lenin's notions of the role of the state in the governance of the proletarian nation and its economy.

It was after the destruction of their domestic opponents that the Bolsheviks embarked on their most exacting experiments. They sought to "militarize" labor, for example, by conscripting workers into "armies of labor," that they imagined had been recommended by Marx in *The Communist Manifesto*. To feed the cities, peasant agriculture was pillaged by arbitrary and inefficient "requisitions" that produced famine and provoked resistance in many regions. Where organized defiance was mounted, a policy of mass murder was pursued.

Granted the impact of revolution, war, foreign intervention, and civil conflict, it was evident that the behaviors of the "dictatorship of the proletariat," with its imposed "unconditional and incontestable obedience," and its "militarized production," all sustained by "coercion and repression," were not the simple, thoughtless responses to crisis many considered them to be. For Nikolai Bukharin, one of the major Marxist theoreticians of the period, Bolshevik policies, however draconian, constituted elements of the necessary "first stage" in the passage from the dictatorship of the proletariat to established communism.[61]

Bukharin spoke without hesitation of social systems being sustained by the exercise of power. He alluded to the familiar work of Ludwig Gumplowicz as evidence of the fact that social science had long since recognized the reality that "war and revolution were the locomotives of history," and that all of history is the record of the exercise of power as organized violence. Having established that as a premise, Bukharin affirmed that "in the period of transition in which one structural form of production substitutes itself for another, revolutionary violence serves as a lever." Insofar as "political power as 'concentrated violence'" is employed against the class enemy (whoever that might be), it becomes a determinate historic force without which socialism becomes impossible.[62]

Bukharin contended that during the period of transition between the two social systems, capitalist and socialist, "coercion by the state is not administered exclusively against those former dominant class enemies and affiliated groups. During that period, coercion is applied—in different forms—to the workers, themselves." It was evident to Bukharin, as it was to the Bolshevik leaders, that the proletarian mass was composed of a variety of constituent elements, only very few of whom were sufficiently "class conscious" to be numbered among the "proletarian vanguard." Many, many workers had been, and remained, corrupted by the capitalist system. Many workers were indifferent to the revolution; and many were simply concerned with their own personal well-being, lacking "interior discipline." For all those social elements, state coercion was necessary until they might demonstrate their capacity for revolutionary "coercive self-discipline."[63] That was the public rationale for what has come to be known as "war communism"—the period between 1917 and 1920 during which Russia suffered spoliation on a scale experienced by few nations in modern history. Bukharin wrote off the political and economic horrors as nothing other than what was to be expected in the "period of transition" between the final crisis of capitalism and the initiation of the process that would lead to the establishment of socialism.

In the spring of 1918, Lenin had outlined the tasks of the new proletarian dictatorship. Its principal difficulty, he informed Communist party officials, lay in the "economic sphere." The semistate of the revolutionary proletariat, by then identified as nothing less than the "highest *type* of state," was compelled to rehabilitate the productive forces damaged or destroyed in the Great War, and the civil war that followed. The very future of the proletariat demanded that the economy be revived and productivity be restored and accelerated on "a national scale." That could only be accomplished by "the strictest labor discipline." The dictatorship was required to raise the productivity of labor not only by instilling in workers "devotion to principle, self-sacrifice and perseverance," but by imposing "powerful labor discipline" on the one hand and "compulsory labor service"[64] on the other.[65]

Lenin went on to speak of "intensifying labor," introducing piecework among the workers, a procedure denounced as "exploitative" not long before. He warned that those who impede the productivity of labor by corruption, or failure to obey the "strict" procedures of the Soviet government, would be summarily shot.[66] To stop threats to sustained and accelerated production, he maintained, *"requires an iron hand."*

As has been indicated, "dictatorship" meant nothing less to Lenin than "iron rule, government that is . . . ruthless in suppressing both exploiters and hooligans." Suppression was to be employed against both class enemies and those elements in the population opposed to the "proletarian dictatorship." Lenin repeated that it would be "extremely stupid and absurdly utopian to assume that the transition from capitalism to socialism is possible without coercion and without dictatorship."[67]

In 1920, in his rationale for "war communism," Bukharin was essentially giving voice to Lenin's judgments concerning the nature of "proletarian democracy." Lenin had made recourse to coercion and had spoken of the "salutary firmness [of] shooting thieves on the spot," as well as the merits of suppressing "ruthlessly the elements of disintegration." Bukharin spoke of the discipline imposed on labor as necessary both for the survival of "proletarian rule," as well as the restoration of productive enterprise.

By 1920, suffering the damage inflicted by the Great War and the civil war that followed, compounded by the exactions of "war communism," it had become evident that the economy of revolutionary Russia had all but collapsed. In that year, industrial production was but 14 percent of its prewar total. By 1921, compared to 1913, both per capita workers' productivity, and the yield of major Russian industries, remained at about 20 percent of prewar levels. Steel production was but 5 percent of its 1913 level. Real wages declined to about one-third the level of 1913. The precipitous diminution of agricultural output forced urban dwellers to depend on pillaging the countryside—where populations lived precariously at the brink of famine. It was clear that restarting the economy required even more labor discipline and self-sacrifice than had "war communism." Production, through discipline, self-sacrifice, and obedience, became a recurrent theme among the ideologues of the Bolshevik revolution. Lenin insisted that whatever talk there was of "industrial democracy" was not to be "misinterpreted." The talk of "industrial democracy" was not to be understood as a "repudiation of dictatorship" or "individual authority." Both were necessary to sustain and enhance *production*. "Formal democracy," Lenin argued, "must be subordinate to the revolutionary interest"—and the revolutionary interest turned on production.[68]

By the spring of 1921, Lenin was explicit. He told his followers that "socialism is inconceivable without large scale capitalist engineering . . . and planned organisation. . . . [It is] inconceivable without planned state organisation which keeps tens of millions of people to the strictest observance of a unified standard of production and distribution." The imposition of such "capitalist" modalities, together with centrally controlled market regularities, would give the revolutionary economy of Bolshevik Russia some of the defining properties of *"state capitalism."*[69]

Like Bukharin[70] at the same time, Lenin insisted that if the revolution was to succeed, appeal would have to be made to some form of "state capitalism." Lenin understood "state capitalism" to mean a revolutionary "development of capitalism, controlled and regulated by the proletarian state"—that would assure the rapid development of heavy industry, critically essential to the success of socialism.[71] The postrevolutionary proletarian "semistate," that, at one time, Lenin had argued would be hardly a state at all, had transformed itself into a formable state apparatus that would govern socialism's "most important and most difficult task . . . economic development."[72]

By 1921, Lenin acknowledged without reservation that Russia was an economically and culturally backward nation, unsuited to any form of socialism recognized by the founders of Marxism. Lenin recognized that what the Bolshevik revolution had discharged, in fact, were essentially "bourgeois tasks" in a "backward peasant country"—the destruction of the survivals of medievalism and barbarism—those obstinate barriers to "progress."[73]

In 1917, unaware apparently of the responsibilities of the revolution, Lenin had attempted to "erect socialism" on a primitive economic base—something both Marx and Engels consistently had counseled could not be done. By 1921, Lenin admitted that "large scale industry is the one and only real basis upon which we can . . . build a socialist society"—and went on to lament its absence in Bolshevik Russia. What had become evident by that time were the responsibilities to be assumed by the Communist party if it aspired to any form of socialism. Because the industrial base anticipated as a consequence of worldwide proletarian revolution would not be forthcoming, the dictatorship of the proletariat was obliged to create its own on a primitive, peasant economic foundation.[74]

Lenin admitted that he and his confreres had been in error when they chose to embark on the flawed attempt to "go over directly to communist production and distribution" in a "country [that] was economically, if not the most backward, at any rate one of the most backward, countries in the world."[75] It was a seriously "mistaken economic policy," violative of everything said by Marx concerning the relationship between politics and economics. The mistake cost the people of Russia incalculable hardship—and threatened the very survival of the regime.[76]

By the spring of 1921, because "it had become perfectly clear that [the revolutionary government] could not proceed with . . . direct socialist construction," Lenin announced a New Economic Policy for revolutionary Russia.[77] It was a desperate effort to "increase production first and foremost and at all costs." It abandoned all the socialist pretensions of "war communism," and fell back on "the ways, means, and methods of state capitalism"—which meant that the economic and industrial development of Russia would depend on the creation of a "capitalism that will be subordinate to the state and serve the state."[78]

There would be an effort to restore small-scale family farming, together with the sufferance of free markets, where peasants might sell produce after the payment of a state tax in kind. Alongside the revival of peasant agriculture, there was permission for the development of small, privately owned, commercial enterprises, together with the leasing of what had hitherto been state firms.[79] Commerce and trade markets were to be restarted, characterized by intense competition and individual incentives, with revolutionary

Russia prepared to grant extensive oil, coal, and iron ore concessions (at very generous terms) to foreign capitalists[80]—all in the desperate effort to stimulate the growth of the "productive forces" necessary for the construction of a socialist economy.[81]

For Lenin, the "ways, means, and methods of state capitalism" that he recommended included the payment of differential wages that reflected productivity on the part of industrial workers. It meant that "specialists," and skilled labor, would receive higher remuneration than their less skilled cohorts. It also meant a fundamental change in the traditional role of trade unions. Hitherto understood to be defense agencies of the working class, trade unions, under "proletarian state capitalism," were to serve as "transmission belts" for state policy. While expected to be "apolitical" and "nonpartisan," unions were required to "assist the working people's government, i.e., the Soviet Government," whose "principal and fundamental interest" lay in "securing an enormous increase in the productive forces of society."[82]

In effect, under the ministrations of the Leninist variant of Marxism, the trade unions were expected to be agencies of the state, sustaining and fostering the expansion of the productive base of society. The trade unions were informed that they "must collaborate closely and constantly with the government, all the political and economic activities of which are guided by the class-conscious vanguard of the working class—the Communist Party."[83] Trade unions were not expected to concern themselves directly with planning and the administration of production. That involved tasks for which a responsible manager, alone, was accountable. Trade unions were informed that "all authority in the factories should be concentrated in the hands of the management." The all-but-exclusive concerns of the labor unions involved committing labor to the productive mission of the state. To that end, trade unions in Bolshevik Russia were responsible for quickly negotiating any grievances that threatened productivity. More than that, unions were charged with reporting to the state on the "mood" of workers, and in maintaining an atmosphere of commitment and enterprise among them.[84]

As though that were not enough, trade unions were obliged to be prepared to "resort to pressure" to ensure that productivity was maintained in the workplace. Trade unions were understood to be "participants in the exercise of state power"—and given Lenin's notions about the repressive nature of the state[85]—they were advised that they could not "refuse to share in coercion."[86] If necessary, trade unions were expected to employ coercion to foster and maintain the discipline, obedience, self-sacrifice, and dedication among workers required by the system.

Lenin was very clear about the chain of responsibilities that began with the vanguard leadership of the Communist party. "Masses" were expected to "spontaneously" follow the leadership of the party. That spontaneity was not always "consciously" extended. The party apparently invoked techniques calculated to override any conscious resistance on the part of the workers. Should any of that fail, the compliance of nonparty masses was assured by the presence of the secret police, the Cheka, everywhere where dissidence might make its appearance. Lenin never invested confidence in "spontaneous" political conformity. The Cheka would remain "an effective weapon" against those who plotted against "Soviet power." Moreover, should the enemies of communism challenge that power, Lenin assured them that the challenge would be met by "terror and redoubled terror."[87]

Thus, by 1922–23, the structure, substance, and mission of the Leninist state were apparent. It displayed very little that might be traced directly to its Marxist inspiration. The Leninist state was a state that enforced ideological conformity and demanded universal obedience—while promising little more than hard work and systematic sacrifice to a primitive peasant population. What was offered to sustain the entire undertaking was the hope of a distant future in which the benefits of communism might obtain.

Lenin recognized that none of this was anticipated by the founders of Marxism. He went on to argue that none who had written tomes about Marxism before the Bolshevik revolution had written "a single book about state capitalism under communism. It did not occur even to Marx to write a word on this subject." It had been left to Lenin to put together the notion of a "Marxist" state obliged to economically and industrially develop a retrograde economy. It was left to Lenin to conceive it a "Marxist" obligation to put together a state that would mobilize masses behind a single political party, a party inspired by impeccable belief, defended by police surveillance and the threat of terror. It was left to Lenin to conceive a state in which a single political party imagined itself licensed to affirm, "We are the state."[88] It was left to Lenin to put together, for the first time in the twentieth century, the tentative outlines of the totalitarian state.

Behind that single party, with its suggestion of Great Russian nationalism, and its impeccable ideology, was a single person, a leader charged with the responsibility of maintaining the purity of doctrine, the flawless commitment of the vanguard party, and the military obedience of the masses—all in the service of an uncertain future. It was a system whose justification was sought amid the vastness of an inherited ideological tradition that would ultimately supply similar justifications for any number of revolutionary movements and political regimes in the twentieth century. Beyond the heterodox Leninism, other variants of Marxism were to thrust themselves upon our time. While Leninism was the first such heterodoxy to attain state power, the variant that brought Fascism to power was perhaps the more coherent and consistent.

CHAPTER ELEVEN

The Great War, Revolution, and Fascism

The Great War and the Bolshevik revolution provided the doctrinal impetus that gave final form to the heterodox Marxism of Benito Mussolini. It was with that variant of Marxism that Mussolini acceded to rule in postwar Italy. Other than the doctrinal developments associated with it, the war was itself significant in that it rendered hundreds of thousands of young Italians susceptible to the blandishments of Marxist, anarchist, nationalist, and Roman Catholic revolutionaries.

At the conclusion of the war, the conscripted masses of young males, filled with the energies of youth and schooled in violence, returned home. They were to be the enthusiastic foot soldiers of revolution. Every political faction on the Italian peninsula sought to recruit them to political purpose. Marxists of all varieties, Catholic intellectuals, anarchists and assorted nationalists, all contended for their attention and their allegiance.

In the beginning, the efforts of the interventionist Marxists that had collected around Mussolini fared badly.[1] Some of the interventionist leaders had died in the defense of the fatherland. Filippo Corridoni and Cesare Battisti, among many others, had fallen. Moreover, dissident socialists and syndicalists alike, because of their advocacy of Italian intervention in the Great War, had been excommunicated from the ranks of official socialism. As a consequence, they had lost their privileged access to the politically active "working masses."

Among those in the ranks of the antiwar socialists, the Bolshevik revolution exercised a peculiar fascination—and like the Bolsheviks, the official socialists disdained those who had led Italy into what they, as sometimes Leninists, deemed a "capitalist" war. The success of Bolshevism in Russia only entrenched the opinion among them that Lenin had been correct. The war had been fought exclusively for "bourgeois" interests. All of that rendered official socialism the unqualified enemy of those who had advocated Italy's intervention in the Great War. It also made official socialism the enemy of all who had served the nation. Party socialism became the adversary of the combatants returning home from the front—Mussolini among them.

From the very commencement of Italy's involvement in the Great War, the interventionist Marxists, primarily syndicalists, were cut off from their normal environment. Those who survived the bloodletting had been occupied for years as combatants. Their contacts in the ranks of labor had desiccated. Not only had they lost contact with civilian labor, their very life circumstances had been transformed. At the end of the war, they understood full well that their world had been forever changed, and many were uncertain what that meant for them as revolutionaries. United by the experience of the war, excluded by official socialism, uncertain in their iconoclasm, the first Fascists[2] collected around themselves those who had fought the war as well as those who had been scandalized by the consistent and overt wartime defeatism of official socialism.[3]

At the war's end, the Allies failed to fully deliver on the territorial promises made to Italy when the effort was being made to entice Rome to enter the lists against the Central Powers. That, together with the subsequent decline in economic activity that followed the cessation of hostilities, produced protracted crisis on the peninsula. Many argued that the victory, purchased at so high a price, had been "mutilated." Not only had the nation not been accorded those territories presumably promised by the Treaty of London, but Italy had been left to deal with its domestic economic problems without that which Italians considered suitable assistance from wartime allies. The revolutionary syndicalists, the interventionist socialists, and those offended by the reception accorded them by party socialists, all gradually came together behind Mussolini: Marxist heretic, socialist interventionist, national syndicalist, and revolutionary.

THE FIRST FASCISM

At the end of the Great War, Mussolini found himself the tribune of an indeterminate number of independent and often heretical Marxists—activists who had advocated war, many of whom had fought the war, and many who returned convinced that they had earned the right to shape the future of the nation they had served.[4] Granted the reality of all that, it was clear that Mussolini, a few days after the conclusion of the Great War, was uncertain which population elements, other than the interventionists themselves, might be attracted in order to put together an effective political and revolutionary constituency. Convinced as he was that official socialism had certified its irrelevancy in a world that had suffered the greatest catastrophe in human history, Mussolini was prepared to appeal to a broader constituency than he had ever before considered.

Before all else, Mussolini was certain that those veterans returning victorious from the war were clearly a resource. Other than veterans, he fully intended to make appeal to the working classes, in general—the recruitment base with which he was most familiar—and many of whom had fought in the trenches.[5] Equally certain was the fact that Mussolini was prepared to reach outside the "proletariat," to make an appeal to all the "productive classes"—all those who "morally and materially" sought to assure the "future of the Fatherland."[6] He announced that the movement he was to lead would be predicated on two imposing and undeniable realities: the nation and the productive base that sustained it.[7]

The first reality would draw together all those sharing a common sentiment—and that would provide the emotional sustenance for the disciplined hierarchy required for technologically proficient and expanded production.[8] Animated by shared national sentiments, soldiers and producers, workers and the entrepreneurial bourgeoisie,[9] would "fuse" in creative and constructive enterprise.[10]

All of that was to be held together by a doctrine Mussolini early identified as "national syndicalism,"[11] a doctrine the elements of which had made their appearance in the years leading up to the Great War—most prominently in the works of radical Marxists such as A. O. Olivetti, Sergio Panunzio, and Filippo Corridoni.[12] The central feature of national syndicalism was an explicit appeal to a sentiment of national belonging that its theoreticians believed would engage, in principle, the immediate commitment of all Italians of whatever economic class. Nationalism was to become the enduring imperative, the "myth," of the system of appeals.

Mussolini, in issuing his call to Italians, understood nationalism as giving expression to all those common sentiments born of long association, of shared history, and of the pride of victory. He understood nationalism to be a sentiment that might serve as the inspiration for a complex revolutionary strategy intended to assure the "grandeur" of the fatherland—a strategy that would restore, sustain, and expand upon the nation's historic "greatness," both within and beyond its borders.[13]

All the discussion surrounding national sentiment that had been commonplace among Marxists of all sorts in the years before the advent of the

Great War culminated in the enjoinments formulated by Mussolini and those who had fought the Great War. In the appeal to nationalism there was the echo of the Marxist reflections of Georges Sorel, Roberto Michels, and Otto Bauer—as well as those sentiments expressed by Mussolini himself when he served as an Italian socialist functionary in the Trentino.

The fact is that Mussolini's appeal to national sentiment—as the revolutionary myth of a doctrine that would bring him to victory—was anything other than thoughtless or opportunistic. It rested on a body of literature with which Mussolini was very familiar—literature that was essentially Marxist in origin—that argued that human beings were dispositionally social creatures identifying themselves with that community that best addressed their moral and material interests at any given time and in any given set of circumstances.[14] It was a body of literature that, at its best, contested the privative interpretation of Marxist theory that conceived economic *class*, not only the most important, but the only, agent of world history.[15]

Like many other Marxists before him, Mussolini argued that, under certain conditions, given the ingroup sentiment natural to human beings, the nation might well serve as the class of all classes.[16] Throughout history, human beings had associated, sacrificed, killed and been killed, in the service of a variety of "communities of destiny."[17] By the early twentieth century, many social theorists—Marxists and non-Marxists alike—maintained that, at that point in time, the nation served as just that community.[18]

Mussolini was to go on to argue that the properties of the modern world contributed to making the nation a symbol capable of mobilizing masses. He argued that the modern world had divided itself into "advanced" and "retrograde" nations, with the former capable of dominating the life circumstances of "those that had been left behind."[19] He went on to contend that the industrially advanced powers, those that had "arrived" and were "sated," sought to maintain their advantages against those communities still struggling to achieve modern economic proficiency.[20] Denied their "place in the sun," the economically retrograde nations, those that were "proletarian,"[21] were forced to struggle to survive.

Mussolini argued that the industrially advanced nations, possessed of the power of the purse, as well as the power projection capabilities attendant upon their ability to deploy sophisticated weaponry, could forever obstruct the passage of those less economically proficient to any higher level in the world order. The war in which Italy had advanced industrial nations as its allies had, in part, obscured that reality, but the peace negotiations at its conclusion made the inequities abundantly clear.

The Great War itself was a test of Italy's claim to be an equal among equals; and it was on the occasion of that war that Marxists in the official socialist organizations found themselves conflicted. When faced with the issue of whether or not to support their respective nations in a conflict that involved the political hierarchy of nations of an entire continent, they were, in large measure, confused, hapless, and helpless. While most organized socialists ultimately opted to support their respective governments, Italian socialists remained doggedly opposed. Few drew theoretical consequences from their individual or institutional behavior in a world of ominous possibilities. Mussolini was not one of them. Having opted to serve his nation in war, he went on to make nationalism the critical component of the revolutionary ideology that would bring him to power. It was to be the nationalism of a "proletarian people" struggling in a world dominated by "plutocratic" communities of wealth and privilege. It was the nationalism of a "proletarian people" ignored and neglected by the advanced industrial powers before the Great War. It was the nationalism of a retrograde people acknowledged only in their presence as immigrants to developed countries where they were welcomed as cheap labor and cultural primitives.[22]

Before calling the meeting that would launch the Fascist movement, Mussolini specified that if Italy would redress its grievances, *productive, economic*, and *infrastructural development* would be instrumentally critical to his revolutionary purpose.[23] Recalling the argument at the core of Corridoni's *Sindacalismo e repubblica*[24] — that Italian industry was only in its "swaddling clothes" — and Italy a proletarian nation — Mussolini focused on the economic development and modernization of the peninsula as the necessary condition for Italy's anticipated entry into the community of "great powers." If Italy was no longer to be ignored and humiliated by its neighbors, Italy must commit itself to an arduous and disciplined developmental economic and political program.

To that end, Mussolini drew attention to the political and economic postures of the "national syndicalism" of Léon Jouhoux, and the French General Confederation of Labor — to illustrate some of the developmental convictions he and his potential followers had anticipated and were prepared to support.[25] At the conclusion of the Great War, in a pamphlet entitled *Les travaileurs devant la paix*, Jouhoux, as a socialist, argued that in order to reconstruct its shattered economy, what France required was a state-sponsored collaboration of productive classes, organized around the legal recognition of bargaining agents for each, in a kind of disciplined "parliament of production." It was conceived an arrangement calculated to not only "rehabilitate and maximize production" but to stimulate and foster "national development."[26]

Mussolini conceived such a proposed "parliament" a kind of "national economic council," addressing what was clearly the "common interest" of all members of a nation emerging from the depredations of a world war and anticipating an unprecedented trajectory of growth. Composed of representatives of labor and industry, together with those of the state, such a parliament would be functional rather than political, responsible for the managerial and technical administration of production. All that, taken together, would constitute a system Mussolini identified as "integral syndicalism" or "productive socialism"—a "practical and realistic syndicalism" that "transcended the class struggle" in "the interests of production" and national economic development.[27]

Mussolini understood such a system to be particularly important in an economic environment as retrograde as that of Italy. More than simply restoring prewar production, the productive socialism he anticipated would carry Italy forward into intensive and extensive industrial and agricultural development.[28] Mussolini conceived the integral syndicalism of which he spoke as an institutional form of economic, particularly industrial, developmentalism that had grown out of the "apocalyptic and mystical syndicalism of the [prewar] school of Sorel,"[29] reformulated in the developmental nationalism of Corridoni.[30]

In the days immediately preceding the founding meeting of Fascism on the twenty-third of March, 1919, Mussolini touched on the central issues that would shape the politics of his movement in the ensuing period. On the sixteenth of March, he reaffirmed his objections to the doctrines that had come to characterize all the "official" socialisms of the time. Not only had Italian socialism failed to support Italy's war against the Central Powers, continuing to invoke class warfare as some sort of resolution of the postwar problems that then confronted Italians, but much of the leadership, and a not inconsiderable number of followers, expressed an enthusiasm for Leninism as it had unfolded in Russia.[31]

Mussolini considered their identification with Bolshevism evidence of intellectual destitution on the part of Italian socialists. His reasons for that were many, but among the most important was his Kautskyan conviction that Lenin's revolution in Russia had little, if anything at all, to do with socialism—as socialism was understood by Marxism's foremost intellectuals.[32]

During the period immediately following the Bolshevik uprising, Mussolini, like Kautsky at the same time, called the attention of all socialists to the fact that Lenin had made revolution in a Russia that lacked every precondition required of any socialism anticipated by Marx and Engels.[33]

Mussolini reminded socialists that in order to "liberate" all humankind, Marxism had traditionally and consistently anticipated proletarian revolution in circumstances of economic abundance.[34]

Marx saw socialism the product of an opulence that could only result from the full maturation of the output potential of industrial capitalism. According to accepted doctrine, Mussolini reminded his readers, only upon full maturity would capitalism achieve such a measure of productive abundance. With that maturity, according to the theory, the quantities of product reaching the market would simply overwhelm effective demand. Capitalism would produce in such quantity that it could no longer profitably empty its inventories. The absence of purchasing power among the "vast majority" of "emiserated" workers—who were forced by capitalism itself to labor for subsistence wages—would make such an outcome inevitable. Profit rates, given the logic of the theory, would eventually approximate zero. At that point, the proletariat, long schooled in the responsibilities of industrial production, simply would be compelled to assume command over a system no longer capable of sustaining itself or them. After the revolution, under the ministrations of labor, the distribution of commodities would respond to people's needs rather than provide profit for capitalists. All of that constituted the accepted doctrine of "inevitable" revolution anticipated by the founders of Marxism.[35]

No serious Marxist ever imagined that socialism might be heir to primitive economic conditions, to collective poverty, and uniform material and spiritual want. Every informed Marxist, for half-a-hundred years, had argued that "no social order ever perishes before all the productive forces for which there is room in it have developed; and new, higher relations of production never appear before the material conditions of their existence have matured in the womb of the old society itself."[36] That Lenin imagined that socialist productive relations might be imposed on a primitive economic base was not only violative of the most fundamental Marxist precepts, it was counterintuitive to right reason.

Mussolini repeated Kautsky's caution: revolution in such parlous circumstances could only produce a dictatorship of a small coterie of adventurers, to the disadvantage of the great majority of workers and peasants. The inevitable consequence could only be internecine conflict between and among "proletarian" organizations, each searching for advantage in an environment totally unsuited to socialist outcomes.[37]

In Bolshevik Russia, Mussolini went on, the result could only be that socialists proceeded to kill each other with abandon. He reported that

Mensheviks, Social Revolutionaries, and Marxist dissidents were dying at the hands of Bolsheviks in greater numbers than had ever fallen before the security forces of the Czar.[38]

More than that, Mussolini called attention to the fact that Lenin—a prisoner of circumstances, some of which he had himself created—was fully prepared to reconstruct the *state*, with all its appurtenances, after its initial destruction at the hands of his "socialists." In opposition to all that had been said by Marxism's foremost theoreticians, Lenin gave every evidence, not only of reconstructing the state, but of recreating an army, as traditional in form and function as any that supported "bourgeois" rule throughout modern history. The Red Army of Leon Trotsky was sent not only to defend the political boundaries of the new state—like every bourgeois army before it—but it forcibly, and without compensation, requisitioned goods from the people in order to sustain its deployments.[39]

All the "revolutionary" speculations that a socialist army would be composed exclusively of volunteers, without an officer corps, to be governed entirely by "democratic workers' councils," were unceremoniously abandoned. For all intents and purposes, the Leninist military served the interests of the "proletarian state"—as the state understood those interests—so that the dynamics of real and potential interstate and intrastate armed conflict were simply those of any nonsocialist state.

Beyond that, Mussolini continued, state functionaries in Bolshevik Russia took on all the unmistakable attributes of a bureaucracy, not unlike any bureaucracy in any bourgeois nation. However abundant the "antibureaucratic" pronouncements of Lenin, it was evident that the Bolshevik state could not function without office holders who performed in a fashion indistinguishable from those in traditional bureaucracies.

More than all of that, Mussolini pointed to the total failure of Leninism to protect and enhance the material foundation of his Russian homeland. In a world divided between rapacious plutocratic powers and proletarian nations, Lenin had allowed the economy of Bolshevik Russia to fall into all but total disrepair.[40] The whole of Russia, Mussolini went on, was threatened with famine and material devastation. There were reports that the schools had ceased to function; that the majority of industrial establishments were closed; that entire categories of citizens were conscripted to serve in labor armies; that opponents were confined to concentration camps; that arbitrary requisitions were imposed by armed bands; that "justice" was the capricious product of those in power; and that labor organizations were permitted to function only insofar as they served the "proletarian state."[41]

Mussolini condemned Leninism as a nightmare caricature of social-ism that poorly served its nation's needs. As an economically retrograde community competing in a Darwinian struggle for existence,[42] Italy could hardly survive rule by Leninists. What Italy required was not dysfunctional class warfare, or the dissipation of assets in pursuit of utopian goals; it re-quired the accelerated construction of an economic foundation sufficient to support the nation's entry into successful contention with the advanced industrial powers.

Mussolini argued that such paramount interests superseded "the class war." All "productive classes" among Italians shared a common interest in expanding and intensifying production in the effort to secure the nation's proper station in the world.[43] He spoke of all that as the inspiration for a responsive "new socialism"—one that would substitute itself for that "po-litical and parasitic" socialism that had survived the Great War.[44]

At the meeting that history records as the founding assembly of Fas-cism, Mussolini simply repeated what had become by then a recurrent and related set of interlocking themes.[45] He spoke of a general program for the nascent movement, predicated on two fundamental realities: the *nation*, for which so many had died and been maimed—and *production*, without which Italy, as a "proletarian nation,"[46] could not accede to "its rightful place in the world" as an equal of those communities that were, and sought perma-nently to remain, "plutocratic."[47]

It was within that context that Mussolini went on to maintain that Fas-cists did not reject official socialism because it was socialist, but because it was antinational, having opposed itself to a necessary war, and because it attempted to marshal the nation's workers behind failed policies, including flirtation with Lenin's Bolshevism. Mussolini insisted that he and his fol-lowers would have supported official socialism and Bolshevism as well—had either shown itself capable of meeting any of the nation's most urgent needs. Official socialism and Bolshevism had been found wanting. The so-cialism that found anything whatever attractive in Lenin's Bolshevism was a socialism that threatened to reduce Italy to the rank of a tertiary power in a world of intense international competition.[48]

FASCISM, DEMOCRACY, AND THE STATE

During the meeting that saw the founding of the Fascist movement, Mussolini spoke of a general commitment to "a greater political and eco-

nomic democracy" for an emergent "new Italy." Like almost all revolutionary movements of the period, socialist and nonsocialist alike, the typical invocations included a demand for "democracy." Rarely was any operational
definition of "democracy" offered, and more often than not, the democracy
that resulted had very little affinity with the representative democracy familiar in the West.

Like Lenin, Mussolini qualified the commitment to a generic democracy
by acknowledging that political movements are invariably led by "dynamic
minorities" moving "static majorities"[49]—and that Fascists would not be
averse to a leadership that matured into a "dictatorship of will and intelligence," should circumstances so require. Like Lenin, and most syndicalists and revolutionary socialists, Mussolini had little, if any, confidence in
"bourgeois democracy." He dismissed the prewar Italian parliamentary system as one that allowed self-selected minorities to impose their will upon
passive constituencies.

Clearly alluding to the arguments that had become convincing to almost
all revolutionaries by that time, Mussolini rejected parliamentarism as one
of the most objectionable institutions of the established system.[50] He spoke
instead of a functional, alternative "parliament," one composed of representatives, not of geographic regions, but of *productive* categories, related to
each other under the supervision of the political state.

Antiparliamentarian, in the sense specified, tendentially republican,
Mussolini made clear, in 1919, that such concerns were instrumental to the
achievement of the goal culture of the movement. It was clear that he held
such commitments forever contingent on surrounding circumstances. Fascists would be parliamentarian or antiparliamentarian, republicans or mon-
archists, or favor workers or entrepreneurs, or tax war profits or Church
property, as warranted by prevailing conditions. The driving imperative
of Fascist politics would not turn on the choice of specific tactics or instrumentalities, but on any arrangement that assured the "maximization of
production"—in the service of the "grandeur" of the nation. Sophisticated
and abundant industrial production was the critical and nonsubstitutable
precondition for the establishment of the nation as a power among the
great powers—the necessary condition of it attaining its appropriate "place
in the sun."[51]

What is perfectly clear, even before the official founding of Fascism as
a political movement, was Mussolini's lack of commitment to "bourgeois
parliamentarism." Like Lenin, and Engels before him,[52] Mussolini saw
"bourgeois democracy" as little other than a deception. The functional de-

mocracy of which he spoke was understood to contribute to the industrial and political development of the nation by integrating all its productive elements in agencies that were competent to address practical problems. Like revolutionary socialists and syndicalists before him, Mussolini rejected the notion that an "assembly of professional politicians" might effectively serve the "enormous complexity of contemporary Italian life." Better a council composed of functional representatives of industry, combined with their expertise, who would contribute to that marvel of "Italian industrial creativity"—to produce the heavy industries that, with their power projection products, might serve as a bulwark against the hegemonic threats of those nations industrially more advanced.[53]

With such changes, Mussolini contended, socialism would be displaced from that realm of airy abstraction to the firm ground of national reality.[54] It would be a socialism focused on "the nation and the productive classes" that composed its substance. A new and disciplined socialism[55] would appear, cognizant of urgent, concrete realities. It would seek expression in a new structure of government, displacing the old bourgeois parliamentarism that succeeded only in representing those exploitative, inert, and dysfunctional special interests that, in the past, had retarded Italy's transition into the modern world of industry, machines, and power.

What all this implied was a different kind of "democracy" than that which had become commonplace among reformist socialists. It was different from that liberal parliamentary democracy given expression in Karl Kautsky's argued objections to Lenin's dictatorship of the proletariat. And it was different, in terms of its rationale, from the dictatorship advocated by the Bolsheviks.

Italian revolutionary socialists of every stripe had long objected to "bourgeois democracy" and its embodiment in the "bourgeois state." Originally, the revolutionary syndicalists, like the revolutionary socialists, had rejected any form of political state. They spoke of voluntary associations of workers, confederated into larger, similarly voluntary, unions, administering "things," rather than ruling over workers.[56] As Europe lurched closer and closer to the Great War, after the turbulence of the events surrounding the War in Tripoli, Italian revolutionaries proceeded to more closely inspect their roster of beliefs.

As Mussolini gave evidence of his increasing intellectual restiveness prior to the war with the publication of his own journal, *Utopia*, in which revolutionaries could express their independent judgment, he published one essay that is of importance in reconstructing the ideological developments that would ultimately result in Fascism. In July 1914, on the cusp of the war that would transform the world, Mussolini published an essay by Panfilo Gentile, addressing the issue of the relationship between workers' syndicates and the state.[57]

In the preamble to that essay, Gentile admonished revolutionaries that the times required precision with respect to doctrine. "Revolutionary action," he insisted, "can no longer be based on vague premises." It was necessary to specify, with some precision, the outlines of the kind of society to which revolutionaries aspired, and for which they expected their followers to sacrifice.

Gentile argued that central to the commitments of revolutionaries was a conception of the *state*. Traditionally, Marxist revolutionaries dismissed the state as an oppressive machine serving only the interests of the bourgeoisie. Revolutionary syndicalists did not look to the state for that agency that would supervise the complex productive system of the nation after the anticipated revolution. Syndicalists cited those spontaneous associations that arise within the very body of industry as the autonomous agencies that would themselves guide the postrevolutionary economy. Antistatist and libertarian, syndicalists sought functional associations that would take the place of the political supervision, the legislative and executive controls, of the traditional state.

What Panfilo Gentile proceeded to do was to call everyone's attention to the necessity of somehow mediating any differences that might arise within and among the various syndicalist organizations that would guide and administer the larger economy after the revolution. He sought out a unity in the evident multiplicity. Syndicalist groups, Gentile argued, could not be expected to supervise themselves without some overarching rule of law, sanctioned by the authority of some agency independent of all of them.[58] Gentile identified that agency as the state. However different the postrevolutionary state might be, it would be characterized by many of the features of the state with which political history had made everyone familiar. It would be the "central authority" supervising all "the agreements, accords, pacts, mutual and reciprocal contractual obligations" sustaining production. It would be the ultimate repository of sanction and control for the entire productive system.

That Mussolini chose to publish Gentile's piece on the revolutionary conception of the state is interesting in and of itself. It is clear that Mussolini made the decision with deliberation. Critical issues were raised in the piece, and they spoke to the relationship of the individual, and associations of individuals, to the political state. Implicit in the discussion was the question of how the political reality of an anticipated, multifaceted postrevolutionary Italy was to be understood.

As will be argued, the issues involved were critical to the transformation of Mussolini's revolutionary socialism into the variant that emerged almost immediately upon Italy's involvement in the First World War. As all of this was transpiring, Mussolini gave documented evidence of his increasing interest in a conceived relationship between individuals, syndicates of individuals, revolutionary elites, and the political state.

A short time before he published Panfilo Gentile's argument in *Utopia,* Mussolini reviewed Gentile's earlier publication on political ethics for the Socialist Party's *Avanti!*[59] Clearly any review written for an official Party publication was constrained by those obligations that had led Mussolini to establish his own journal. In his "official" review, Mussolini acknowledged that Gentile was articulating criticism of some basic elements of what passed, at that time, as Marxist orthodoxy.

In fact, Gentile was a "critical idealist," rather than the "materialist" or "positivist" required by the orthodoxy of the period. Mussolini understood the implications. Panfilo Gentile, Mussolini indicated, was clearly under the influence—as Mussolini expressed it—"of the other Gentile."[60] The other Gentile was Giovanni Gentile, by that time a luminary among Italian philosophers. All of that is important. It is yet another confirmation of Mussolini's interest and knowledge of the work of Giovanni Gentile some considerable time before the Fascist revolution. It documents a stage in Mussolini's passage from a traditional antistatist, quasianarchistic syndicalist view of politics, to conceptions that were to provide much of the substance of Fascism.[61]

In his publication devoted to the "Ethicojuridical conception of socialism," Panfilo Gentile raised all the problems that had collected themselves around what passed at the time as conventional Marxism. He spoke of the absence of an adequate philosophical rationale sustaining the ethical convictions that presumably inspire socialist revolutionaries. Like many of those who called for a "return to Kant," he called for an appeal to a more substantial metaethical, cognitive foundation than any found in traditional Marxist texts. He argued that any notion that conceived the behavior of human beings determined by some form of "historic fatalism," for example, was intrinsically inadequate to deal with the moral issues surrounding that behavior.

In raising those concerns, Panfilo Gentile was echoing the criticisms leveled against classical Marxism not only by Woltmann, and Sorel, but by Giovanni Gentile as early as 1897.[62] It is not certain whether Mussolini was familiar, at that time, with Giovanni Gentile's critique of Marxism, but it is evident that he was less than dismissive of Panfilo Gentile's variations on the same themes. In the course of his review of Panfilo Gentile's book, Mussolini alluded to the different, and sometimes opposing, interpretations of Marx's conception of how human beings are moved to revolution, and how they were understood to perform as responsible political agents. He reflected on all of that—and did not choose among the various candidate interpretations of how Marxist ethics was to be understood. His reticence is easily understood. At that time, he was a spokesman for organized socialism, and could hardly depart from accepted interpretations.

In effect, immediately before the advent of the Great War, Mussolini gave increasing evidence of intellectual and political disquiet in dealing with what was considered socialist orthodoxy by the official Socialist Party. He was already familiar with Benedetto Croce's criticisms of inherited Marxist orthodoxies.[63] Croce raised many of the same issues found in the earliest work of Giovanni Gentile.[64]

The period immediately before the outbreak of the First World War was a critical juncture in Mussolini's political and intellectual life. With the advent of the Great War, Mussolini found himself more and more alienated from the official position on the conflict assumed by the Socialist Party, to pursue the course briefly outlined above. While familiar with his ideas before the Great War, what seems clear is that after the termination of that war, more and more of the ideas of Giovanni Gentile began to surface in Mussolini's political prose. That is a significant development because the political implications of *attualismo*, as Gentile's idealism came to be known, were to give overt shape to many of Mussolini's thoughts on the nature of the state and its relationship to the complexities of political life.

By the time he published *L'atto del pensare come atto puro* (*Thinking as Pure Act*)[65] in 1912, Gentile had settled on his "method of absolute immanence"—a method that was to have direct relevance to the articulation of Fascist political thought. Gentile's doctrine of immanence maintained that, if epistemology was to be philosophically consistent, all of "reality" would be unpacked into current thinking (experience, consciousness).[66] It was an argument for the ultimate, "dialectical" unity of all things in thinking—a radical form of philosophical idealism rooted in post-Kantian thought.[67]

Any effort to adequately treat the technical philosophy of Gentile would take us far afield from present concerns. What is relevant to present reflection is that Gentile took Marx's social and philosophical thought seriously, perhaps more seriously than others of his time.[68] He argued that Marx's conception of history was actually a variation of Hegelianism, and as a consequence, forever featured the *apriori* and *deductive* traits of the original. More than that, Gentile argued, Marx's conception of man as a *species being*, his rejection of the "abstract human being" of British liberal philosophy, was an obvious legacy of Hegelianism,[69] and shared important affinities with his own conception of "absolute immanence."

The notion of man as a "species being" spoke to philosophical idealism's disposition to see *unities* where others see only *multiplicities*. In terms of political life, actualists conceived the "common sense" view of others as external "things" we encounter in our personal passage through life to be one of the pervasive fictions of the modern world. For actualism, individuals cannot rationally or morally be conceived as independent of each other, as "atoms" in an accidental configuration of atoms.[70]

Actualism's argument was that to imagine that individuals stand alone, opposed to "society" or "reality," is an indefensible abstraction. Individuals cannot consistently be conceived to be independent of each other in any meaningful sense, nor can reality be "external" to them, singly or together. The "concrete" individual is one, united with others in nature, science, language, art, religion, and politics. There is an insistent unity beneath the seeming multiplicity.[71] Knowing the world and the others in it becomes comprehensible only when we realize the fundamental unity of all things. Not to understand that is to "intellectualize" life—to see the individual opposed to others and to nature as something forever "external," and alien, inassimilable and unknowable.[72]

Actualists argued that only by understanding that the individual is indissolubly one with his or her community—that his or her consciousness is always individual, but never private—might one make sense of life, science, morality, and politics. Such convictions were to provide the cognitive foundation of actualism's conception of the "ethical state" as the unity in which a people, conscious of itself as a reality, finds expression.[73] Immanent in a conscious people was the state. The state was the unitary reality of the human multiplicity that constituted its components. The state provided the indispensable grounds that allowed for personal growth in knowledge, morality, and belief. The state provided the structural form for secure continuity, and the prevalence of the rules of language and the principles of conduct, that together allowed the occasion for creative arts and machine production.[74]

By 1906–1908, the substance of those ideas were already evident in

Gentile's published pedagogical writings.[75] They were broadcast, and were known to many, both within and outside the revolutionary community—including Panfilo Gentile.[76] In effect, Mussolini could hardly escape knowing of the works of Gentile by the time of the Great War. He had early been introduced to them, as has been indicated, through the commentaries of Giuseppe Prezzolini and the authors of *La Voce*. Many of the authors with whom he debated official socialism's insistence on neutrality on the occasion of the Great War, were actualists themselves, or were influenced by actualism.[77]

Gentile, for his part, was an interventionist, arguing that it was Italy's responsibility to enter the conflict in defense of its political and ethical values. Mussolini testified, as we have seen, that he had become familiar with Gentile's work by 1908. By the time the Fascist movement was founded in 1919, it was clear that Mussolini's conception of politics, and the relationship of individuals and classes to the state, had been significantly influenced, both directly and indirectly, by the thought of Gentile.

During and after the Great War, Gentile wrote extensively on matters with which Mussolini was actively concerned. Two months before the meeting that served as the founding assembly of the first Fascism, Gentile published an essay in which the two extant concepts of political "democracy" were considered.

In that essay, Gentile spoke of the two "diametrically opposed" notions of "democracy" then in currency. He spoke of the one, predicated on the conviction that society was composed of individuals who somehow came together to create a community, and a state, that would serve as guardian of their parochial interests. And he spoke of the other democracy, which conceived society as an organic unity into which beings were born, nurtured and educated until they identified with the community in, and through which, they found their moral and intellectual substance. The first was a fictive "democracy," composed of a sum of "abstract individuals," and "classes" of such individuals, that somehow came together, each seeking his, her, or their, immediate gratification—and the other, a "true" democracy in which "concrete individuals" collaborated to foster and further the interests of that collectivity, and that state, in which they found their true selves.[78]

Coupled with such convictions was the conception that the community immanent in constituent individuals might find its effective, rational will in the leadership of a single individual, or a select group of individuals. Sensitive to prevailing collective consciousness, special individuals and/or groups could serve as the "democratic" voice of all.[79]

By the time of the founding meeting of Fascism, it was clear that the democracy to be advocated and pursued by the emergent movement was a democracy far different from anything known to Western representative government. Distinctive, it was a notion of democracy sharing some of the properties advanced by Lenin's Bolshevism. Like Bolshevism, Fascism maintained that the political state could represent a common essence, a sort of transcendent "general will." Lenin imagined that will to be the common will of the proletariat—a will that could not be captured in polls or through elections, but was known to Marxists through Marxism's "dialectical science." Fascists early imagined that will to be the common will of an historic people who realize the fundamental unity that identifies the individual and his community, its history, its mission, its moral substance, and the political state that affords effective expression to all of that.[80]

However different in philosophical substance, both Leninism and Fascism rejected the kind of representative democracy that legitimated political rule in the West. At its birth, Fascism rejected the common notion of elective democracy, not only because it was seen as allowing property to dominate labor, but because political liberalism, in and of itself, failed to understand the communitarian nature of human beings. Fascists did not pretend that the postrevolutionary state represented the dictatorship of the proletariat. For Fascists, the proletariat constituted one population element in a complex association. For Fascists, it was the state that represented all the constituents of the nation as community of destiny; and for Fascists, the state was the common will of that community. The state was the overt expression of the essence immanent in its members.

MUSSOLINI, THE STATE, AND DEVELOPMENTAL NATIONALISM

In the months following the founding assembly of the first Fascism, Mussolini spoke of Italy's inferiority in a world dominated by advanced industrial powers. He spoke of the humiliation of the nation that had just emerged victorious from the most devastating war in the history of humanity. He spoke of the nation's weaknesses, of its critical lack of natural, and specifically energy, resources—its lack of industrial minerals and chemicals, magnesium, bauxite, aluminum, sulphuric acid, and chemical fertilizers. He spoke of Italy's failure to invest in the development and articulation of its communications and transportation infrastructure; its neglect of its hydroelectric power potential; all in an environment that seemed to allow only "plutocracies" to prosper.[81] He spoke of Italy's "proletarian" status in circumstances where passage to equality of station and condition was effectively denied. He spoke of the imperative need to produce, to expand and deepen the modern economy of the peninsula, in order that Italy might "cast off the yoke of the plutocracies."[82] He called upon all the productive elements of the nation to commit themselves to the developmental enterprise so essential to the fatherland.[83]

Mussolini lamented the financial and basic developmental costs of the pandemic of labor strikes and work stoppages that overwhelmed the nation's economy in the immediate postwar years.[84]

At almost the same time that saw the inauguration of the movement that would carry him to power, Mussolini applauded the workers of Dalmine, who, while conducting protests against prevailing conditions at the regional metallurgical plants, did not employ work stoppages or slowdowns to force concessions. In his judgment, they "had not forgotten the nation . . . or its people," in their protests, seeking resolution of their grievances without impairing production.[85] The principle employed, to which he made regular recourse, was that the needs of labor would be met, but never at the cost of the nation's economic growth and stability.[86]

Long before his advent to power, Mussolini addressed a number of related problems having to do with the economy of the nation. He spoke of Italy's high population density, its dearth of arable land, and the backwardness of its agricultural methods, resulting in its inability to produce sufficient grain for its own population. The result was to drive some of its most productive citizens to seek labor and sustenance elsewhere, to ultimately serve foreign interests.[87]

Some considerable time before coming to power, Mussolini had put together a fairly comprehensive list of economic issues with which Fascism would be compelled to face. He also sought to provide some account of how they might be addressed. Fascism's first efforts in that regard were the composite result of the interaction of the thoughts of liberal economists such as Vilfredo Pareto and Maffeo Pantaleone (with whose work Mussolini was familiar, and with whom he enjoyed a certain level of intimacy)—and those of syndicalists, like Filippo Corridoni and Massimo Rocca, who were opposed to state intervention in the economy because, in their judgment, there was convincing evidence that such intervention served only negative purpose. At the same time there were Gentileans who entertained reservations concerning neoliberal economic strategies.

The first Fascism was composed of a variety of individuals representing a variety of economic and political convictions. They were dominated by Mussolini and those interventionist socialists who had left the official

Socialist Party on the occasion of the Great War. Many shared the views of those syndicalists who advocated Italy's entrance into the conflict and had collected themselves in the original interventionist "Fascio d'azione rivoluzionaria." All traced their intellectual origins to traditional Marxism modified to address the problems faced by revolutionaries in an essentially "immature" economic environment.

Traditional Marxism had very little to say about revolution in such an environment, and still less about the economy attendant on any such revolution. What the features of such an economy might be remained entirely speculative. There was absolutely nothing like consensus among committed Marxists. By the advent of the First World War, many syndicalists were prepared to argue that less developed economies would have to complete the trajectory of industrial development before one might begin to think of a "Marxist" postrevolutionary productive system. Thus, in 1915, Filippo Corridoni argued for an essentially "liberal" economic policy for retrograde Italy—a reduction in the state's intervention in the economy, an appeal to market forces, and recourse to competitive free trade—in order that the nation might attain those levels of productive maturation required by theoretical Marxism.[88]

In fact, many syndicalists, given their suspicions of the state, were dispositionally economic liberals.[89] The peculiar combination of economic liberal and syndicalist thinkers, who directly or indirectly associated themselves with Fascism, initially produced an advocacy, among many Fascists, for neoliberal economic instrumentalities in the effort to stimulate and foster the growth of the nation's laggard economy.[90] Under the circumstances, Gentileans extended a qualified approval—as long as the state was understood to remain "strong."

In the 1921 Program of the Partito nazionale fascista, neoliberal sentiments appeared as a call for a variant of the "Manchestrian state," a state "reduced to its essential juridical and political functions"—divested of any specific economic attributes—while remaining the "juridical incarnation of the nation."[91] There was a consequent recommendation that parliament be equally divested of economic functions—with the intention that "national technical councils" be charged with dealing with problems that might collect around individuals as producers.[92]

While it was clear that the first Fascists sought to limit the economic initiatives of the state, they called on the state to "foster and protect the nation's supreme interests." Those interests included economic "development" and a requirement that the state somehow "protect domestic infant industries against threatening foreign competition." Moreover, there was a call for an "organic plan of public undertakings directed toward the economic, technical, and military necessities of the nation . . . including [the construction of the nation's] rail and road infrastructure as well as its electrification of all rail lines."[93]

In the months immediately preceding the March on Rome in October 1922, Mussolini formulated the political program of the movement. He had settled on a conception of the state that he called "exquisitely Fascist," clearly Gentilean in origin that would implement tactical policies. It was a somewhat uncertain conception of the state that, nonetheless, was portentous in implication.

In a major speech in Udine,[94] one month before the March on Rome, Mussolini repeated all those assessments that provided the substance of Fascist intention. He spoke of the historic continuities that the anticipated revolution would respect. He spoke of the primacy of the nation, the respect for labor and the collaboration of all productive elements in a program of development. He spoke of the urgency of continued and expanded production, so that the nation might effectively face the impostures of those powers that sought to deny it a proper place in the world. And finally, he spoke of the state. For Fascism, Mussolini affirmed, conjoined with the primacy of the nation, there was the absolute sovereignty of the state. Mussolini stated, in language already made familiar by Gentile, "the state does not represent a party. The state represents the national community without exception, incorporating everyone, superior to everyone, protecting everyone, to oppose itself to any attempts on its imprescriptible sovereignty."

While non-Fascist supporters chose to interpret such a characterization in as bland a manner as possible, Mussolini did insist that the sovereignty of the state would require "absolute and rigid discipline" on the part of the entire nation.[95]

To communicate to the nation the sense of that sovereignty, in the context of the "historic mission" with which Italy was charged, the state was required to exercise vigilant superintendence over the entire political process.

The talk was of the articulation of a network of technical agencies that would provide guidance to the program of economic development. The economic development program, the reform of public offices, the restructuring of the financial system, the efforts at repayment of the national debt, and the introduction of inducements to increase investments in enterprise, were undertaken by Alberto De' Stefani, who enjoyed the confidence of Mussolini.[96]

Almost immediately with its accession to power, the Fascists undertook a sequence of judicial and parliamentary reforms. Agreements were entered into that provided for legal recognition of labor and enterprisory groups, compelling negotiated settlement of disputes.[97] Electoral reform was instituted that resulted in an end to proportional representation in parliament and assured political dominance of the Partito nazionale fascista. Almost immediately the state undertook the first organic reform of the nation's educational system under the administration of Gentile, who Mussolini identified as his "teacher."

Public projects were undertaken, initiating the construction of a network of roads, particularly in southern Italy. Almost immediately after the March on Rome that brought Fascism to power, the government inaugurated a competition among producers of grain to increase domestic production. It was coupled with the first efforts at rural reconstruction and comprehensive rehabilitation. The government undertook plans for rural agronomic education, together with the provision of agricultural tools, fertilizer, and enhancement of farming skills.

With the passage of time, Fascism found itself increasingly confined by the uncertain economic neoliberalism that was initially combined with the political dominance of the state. All of the imperatives surrounding the Gentilean "ethical state" drew Fascism farther and farther away from the Manchestrian state of nineteenth-century liberalism. Nationalists and Gentileans increasingly influenced policy. By 1923, even the syndicalists were calling for the creation of an omnipotent "Fascist state"—distinctive from any political form that preceded it.[98]

It seems clear that by the beginning of 1924, Fascism was restive within the confines of its initial political configuration. However true that may have been, events were precipitated by the murder in June, by Fascist thugs, of Giacomo Matteotti, a socialist deputy in parliament. Matteotti had been severely critical of Mussolini—and while it seems clear that Mussolini played no part in the decision to assault him, the Fascist government was seen by many, if not most, Italians as complicit in the murder. The crisis resulted in a demand for Mussolini's resignation, and prefigured the collapse of the regime.

In the first days of 1925, Mussolini announced that Fascism would suppress the opposition that had collected around the murder of Matteotti and rule, if necessary, with force.[99] Almost immediately after, he spoke of the emergence of a new form of democracy, characterized by the order and discipline necessary to generate the economic development of a nation devoid of natural resources and capital poor.[100] In May, he insisted that Fascism would tolerate "nothing superior to the state." He immediately drew out the practical implications. Labor and entrepreneurial syndicates, and the confederal institutions in which they were housed, were to be governed by the state and subordinated to the political interests of the "eminently proletarian nation"[101] as those interests were understood by the Grand Council of Fascism.[102]

In June, at the fourth national congress of the Partito nazionale fascista, Mussolini spoke of emergent "new Italians," characterized by "absolute intransigence," animated by a disciplined "totalitarian will," in service to the state. He admonished the new Italians to be courageous, assertive, and intrepid, but more than all else to be disciplined and responsive to authority. Their cry was to be "all power to all of Fascism!"[103]

Thus, by 1925, both Leninism and Fascism, variants of Marxism, had created political and economic systems that shared singular properties. Both sought to fuel and direct rapid economic, particularly industrial, development of backward communities, under the auspices of unitary and hegemonic political parties. They both sought to control all the forces of production through a system of comprehensive regulation. Both sought order and discipline of entire populations in the service of an exclusivistic party and an ideology that found its origins in classical Marxism, but which had been transformed by *sui generis* "creative developments." Both created a kind of "state capitalism," informed by a unitary party, and responsible to a "charismatic" leader.

Whatever became of either system after 1925 was the consequence of external circumstances and internal dynamics. The Stalinism that followed the death of Lenin, and the totalitarianism that matured in Fascism, grew out of the system already in evidence by 1925. Neither Stalinism nor Fascist totalitarianism would have been possible without the transmogrified Marxist that infilled both. That does not make Karl Marx responsible for either Stalinist or Fascist totalitarianisms—it suggests, rather, that traditional Marxism is simply a failed theory, largely irrelevant to the modern world. It became relevant to the political life of the twentieth century only after it was transformed by the needs of communities suffering the deprivations, both psychological and material, in their real, or fancied, conflict with the advanced industrial democracies. In that sense, Marxism was responsible for much of the human and property devastation that marred the tragic history of that century.

CHAPTER TWELVE

Conclusions

By the end of the 1920s, Bolshevik Russia and Fascist Italy had taken on the major political properties with which they would be known to history. The 1930s would see the full emergence of a unique state system, characterized by the institutionalization of charismatic leadership, in an arrangement that featured the dominance of a hegemonic party over a population summoned to redemptive purpose. Both systems displayed those properties. Whatever distinguished the two, there were fundamental similarities that identified them as species of the same genus. Many of the similarities turned on the nature and role of the state within that syndrome of similarities.

By the 1950s, the term "totalitarianism" was pressed into service to capture a sense of shared properties.[1] For our purposes, it is more interesting to acknowledge totalitarianism's source in the Marxism of the nineteenth century than labor over the differences between regimes. In fact, many of those putative differences have shown themselves to be less than substantial. In the twenty-first century, hardly anyone gives credence to the notion that Mussolini's Fascism was malevolent and Stalin's socialism was not. Today, hardly anyone believes that the one was "proletarian" in essence and the other not. All those pretended distinctions that made up much of the substance of bitter political disputes for half-a-hundred years no longer seem credible. We are left with institutional similarities that arrest our attention. They are shared likenesses that find their origins in a complex intellectual tradition bequeathed to the twentieth century by Karl Marx and Friedrich Engels.

Both systems with which we are here concerned grew out of the theoretical problems classical Marxism left as an intellectual legacy. Most of those problems turned on the Marxist notion of the relationship between the "economic base" of society, and its "corresponding ideological superstructure." The insistence that the economic base "determined" society's ideological superstructure created a number of critical problems for intellectuals and activists in the twentieth century. That "ideas," philosophical, moral, and legal, were a "reflection" of economic variables left many discomfited and unconvinced. The thesis seemed to deny individuals the capabilities to reflect on, as well as any freedom to choose, their behaviors—rendering the concept of moral responsibility all but meaningless. That was to feed into an entire constellation of issues that included the question of how ethics and morality related to public law and what the relationship might be between law and the revolutionary political state.

Both Leninism and Fascism were to address all these concerns. Both, having their origins in the same revolutionary tradition, were to trace different paths in the creation of their respective state systems—and yet both were to conclude their labors with singularly similar results.

REVOLUTION AND THE
REINTERPRETATION OF MARXISM

By the mid-1920s, Fascism had put together the essentials of its state. Its construction was neither fortuitous nor atheoretical. Some of the theoretical elements that would contribute to the rationale for the Fascist state had made their appearance before the commencement of the Great War. Benito Mussolini, as a Marxist revolutionary, was heir to the same tangle of doctrinal problems as was Lenin. In both cases, all the problems with which the first Marxism was heir collected around the question of how the state was to be apprised. The difference was that Lenin pretended, until his death, that his Marxism was the Marxism of the founders. Mussolini was rather prepared to acknowledge that there were a variety of alternative interpretations of Marxism, each of which had its merits.

Mussolini's early attempts at explicating his Marxist beliefs had run aground on how ethics and morality were to be understood in the context of modern revolution—and ultimately how both related to nationalism and the political state. With respect to the complex philosophical issues of how morality and ethics were to be understood, his earliest published writings provide evidence of his concern. How they influenced individual and collective behavior was a persistent topic of his reflections.

Having fallen under the influence of Sorel as early as 1904, moral issues were to occupy Mussolini throughout the remainder of his political life. It was Prezzolini and the *Vociani* who were to suggest that he would have to proceed beyond Sorel and Bergson to resolve some of the concerns that had begun to engage him. Prezzolini suggested that both analytic and substantive assistance might be found in philosophical idealism—and by the middle of the second decade of the twentieth century there were already traces, in Mussolini's thought, of Giovanni Gentile's moral doctrines.

A political, rather than a philosophical, thinker, Mussolini had few pretenses. He did remind others that he was among those socialist thinkers who had sought to redirect Italian revolutionaries away from the influence of a mechanical positivism and a thoughtless materialism. But it is clear that those efforts were not entirely the consequence of philosophical concern. Roberto Michels had early provided evidence that, because of their peculiar cultural predilections, the entire issue of moral choice and ethical vindication was particularly important to Italian revolutionaries.[2] They would hardly be content to conceive moral and ethical issues reduced to simple adjuncts of the class struggle.

Giuseppe Prezzolini and the *Vociani* not only confirmed that judgment, but they argued that philosophical materialism offered little that effectively addressed such questions. For a time, Mussolini sought resolution in the work of William James and the moral relativity of the pragmatists[3]—to ultimately commit himself to some form of epistemological (and perhaps ontological) idealism.[4] The fact was that in the period immediately preceding the Great War, Mussolini had been subject to many influences that moved him in the direction of Gentilean idealism.[5]

As has been indicated, immediately before the outbreak of the conflict, in July 1914, Mussolini chose to publish an article by Panfilo Gentile that argued the necessity to rethink the revolutionary socialist position on the "withering away" of the political state after the anticipated revolution.[6] It was a heretical suggestion, the product of a critical idealist, made to socialists who had insisted on their antistatist convictions for decades.

In the years that were to follow, it was to become evident that Mussolini would be compelled by events to revisit not only how revolutionaries were to consider revolutionary morality, law, and the state, but the nature and role of nationalism—all within that collection of theoretical issues that had caused consternation among Marxists since the turn of the century. Out of those deliberations, the lineaments of Fascism first made their appearance.

How nationalism was to be understood in the mobilization of masses was clearly an issue. Already convinced of the special efficacy of elites in the dynamic of revolution, the question of how nationalism, as myth, was to contribute to the process had to be assessed.

The then current writings of Giovanni Gentile addressed all those questions[7]—and the answers tendered were to influence the subsequent construction of a specifically Fascist political doctrine.[8] Gentile was both a statist and a nationalist, and as such, in the years immediately before the Great War, influenced a number of important Italian intellectuals. They almost all uniformly argued, as had Panfilo Gentile, that socialists would have to deal with the reality of the political state after the anticipated revolution. And they came to argue (as had Filippo Corridoni) that in an environment of retarded economic development, the *class struggle* could only be dysfunctional. A collaboration of classes recommended itself in an environment where workers, citizens of an economically retrograde *proletarian nation*, suffered more from the impostures of foreign exploitation than from the exactions of domestic capitalists. In such circumstances, one more reasonably could expect a conflict between proletarian and plutocratic nations than a domestic struggle between classes. All of that had gradually come together as the theoretical problems of nineteenth-century Marxism increasingly engaged the attention of those revolutionaries who sought to recruit foot soldiers in the face of the challenge of the Great War.

To not a few advocates of Italian intervention in the war, it had become more and more evident that a rationale for all of that was to be found in Gentilean idealism. Gentile had early assessed some of the major problems that attended the doctrines left as an intellectual heritage by Karl Marx and Friedrich Engels.[9]

Gentile was among those thinkers who took Marxism very seriously. More than that, he addressed some of its critical components with rare application. More than any other, Gentile assessed the epistemological and normative foundations of Marxism. At the very heart of his critique, Gentile contended that the philosophy of the young Marx, and "historical materialism" in its entirety, could hardly be understood to be *materialistic* in any fundamentally philosophical sense at all.[10]

For the purposes of the present discussion, perhaps the most important feature of Gentile's critique turned on his contention that materialists were invariably philosophical individualists—advocates of the primacy of the individual as opposed to any collectivity—something Marx was not. Materialists tended to focus on individuals as discrete, empirical entities—to understand *society* as nothing other than a nominal abstraction—no more than a name. For materialists, only empirical individuals were "real." Collections of individuals could be given names, but they were only real in some abstract sense.

Gentile went on to argue that Marx was neither a materialist, nor a nominalist in terms of how he understood society. Gentile held that for Marx, society was far more than an abstraction; it was very real. Marx, Gentile contended, understood society to be an *organic whole*, having continuity in time, more real than the "abstract" individuals of which materialists imagined it composed. For Marx, Gentile argued, individuals could only be understood in terms of their complex interrelationships within the organic totality that was society—and that those defining relationships persisted only as products of the "ethical ligaments" that sustained them.[11] Implicit in such an understanding is the notion that membership in any such community must ultimately depend on an understanding, a moral agreement— that society was, in some fundamental sense, an ethical reality.

Before the turn of the twentieth century, at the very commencement of his academic career, at scarcely twenty-two years of age, Gentile made very clear what he conceived to be the relationship between the individual and society. As such it not only revealed much of what Gentile's social and political philosophy was about, but a great deal as well about some of the implications buried in the conceptual density of Marxism.

Independently of its revelations about the nature and substance of what Gentile insisted was to be found at the center of Marx's thought, the notion that society was inextricably ethical in substance was to animate the social and political philosophy of some of the most important thinkers in the ranks of the first Fascism—and give character to their conception of the Fascist state.

MORALITY, LAW, AND THE STATE IN FASCISM

By the time Fascism fully revealed itself as a contender for political power on the Italian peninsula, its conception of the anticipated revolutionary state had taken form. Sergio Panunzio, an important syndicalist intellectual, who had exercised influence on Mussolini's doctrinal maturation for more than a decade, published a volume on law and the state in early 1921 that clearly prefigured future developments.[12]

Like Mussolini, Panunzio had made the transit from the kind of positivism found intellectually compatible by the first Marxists during the last quarter of the nineteenth century, to the critical idealism that had become relatively common among the socialist advocates of Italy's involvement in the Great War.[13] By that time, Panunzio no longer conceived of law—or the state that was its source and sanction—as a simple reflex of the economic base of society. He no longer found adequate the simplisms that seemed to satisfy German theoreticians. There was no longer appeal to economic determinism. Rather, he spoke of the nature and function of the state and its laws, and of their vindication. He referred to the latter effort as a *metaju-ridical* responsibility, as advancing the ethical rationale that warranted both law and state.

Panunzio saw the state as the promulgator of law, and law as intended, in the first instance, to organize, administer, and discipline all the factors of production. That was central to the state's purpose. More broadly speaking, the state's mission had immediate, mediate, and ultimate purposes. Its moral, economic, and historical responsibilities would be discharged by meeting pedagogical, maintenance, and security obligations—all embedded in a common ethical matrix. At best, specific class interests, as they were understood among the more orthodox, were a tertiary concern.

For Panunzio, at the commencement of the decade of the 1920s, the state was understood to be an ethical agency that had continuity in time, was a purveyor of culture, a creator of an environment without which individuals would only subsist and not flourish. He argued that the purposes of the state are supremely ethical—the fullest possible moral development of human beings. To that end, all the productive components of society—labor and employer syndicates, confederations of syndicates, and corporative bodies—would be integrated in law and governance through the state.

Panunzio also spoke of those special times of crisis traversed by every society, when special individuals, charged by events with historic responsibilities, express the implicit will of a revolutionary people. Not far below the surface of the account of what he identified as the "neo-Hegelian ethical state" was the unmistakable outline of Fascism, its ethos, its institutions, its vanguard elite, and its charismatic leader.[14]

In retrospect none of this can be seen as unexpected. It was not simply the opportunistic product of a time of political troubles as it is often portrayed. The progression of Panunzio's thought can be traced over more than a dozen years.[15] Over those years, like many revolutionary Marxists, he had sought to resolve some of the doctrinal puzzles left by the conventionalities of German Social Democracy. Like Woltmann and Sorel, Panunzio found the pedantic orthodoxies of Kautsky unpersuasive—and like Gentile, he found the notion that Marx was an ontological and social materialist unconvincing.[16] Over the years, both Panunzio and Gentile were to traverse much the same path.

The intellectual atmosphere of the entire period was alive with discussion of "social theory." Gentile's first work on Marxism was prompted by a recognition that such concerns occupied the time of many.[17] As early as that first work, Gentile conceived society, and by implication, the state, to be essentially *ethical* in substance. His entire philosophy was predicated on the conviction that all human experience was rooted in ethics—that all human experience was defined by choice, by the selection of truth criteria, and attendant moral judgments. Only as a consequence of those choices that established which claims might qualify as true, might "reality" be defined and scientific regularities established. All our understandings of the world rested on choice, and the choices pursued were a function of an implicit or explicit system of ethics.[18]

While the system found in Gentile's works is enormously complex, a simple and not entirely unfaithful characterization would identify self-fulfillment—as a human being—to be what Gentile considered the fundamental purpose of life.[19] He understood self-fulfillment to be an ongoing process, requiring all of life's energies.[20]

For Gentile, life is a spiritual unfolding, entirely moral in essence and impetus. It was a process that involved community. Selfhood would be impossible without all those interrelationships that create us as persons. Around the individual, conceived as a particular being,[21] the community as an historic nation, informed by the state, provides the conditions necessary for self-realization. Law, which provides for disciplined order, finds its origin in the state as moral arbiter of those circumstances surrounding a life lived in community.

Gentile early argued that the ultimate source of the state's authority to promulgate, sustain, modify, and administer law is the individual's implicit recognition that the state serves his or her ultimate purpose: moral fulfillment. It is there that the state's authority must find its source, and discipline its rationale.[22]

That individuals recognize the moral authority of the state required an education that is, at once, focused, controlled, and integrative—everything other than the agnostic and uncertain education common in liberal communities.[23] For Gentile, education was one of the prime responsibilities of the ethical state.

For Gentile, the individual achieves fulfillment only as a disciplined member of a community—a family, a religion, a language group—all set in an historic association that, in our time, is a nation. The nation, which provides the circumstances for the fulfillment of the individual, is afforded an identity, an effective will, and a personality in continuity, by the state. It is the state, through its laws, its institutions, and the security it extends, that assures its citizens a nationality, "the sacred possession bequeathed [them] by their forefathers which makes them what they are, which gives them a name, a cultural personality, and an economic, political, as well as a moral, and intellectual, future."[24]

For Gentile, it was the nation, and the state by which it was informed, that provided the moral substance of that "concrete individuality" within which "empirical" human beings found their fulfillment.[25] Only within a well-ordered community might flesh and blood entities become moral agents. Understanding that, individuals were prepared to sacrifice and labor in the service of the historic nation and its state. They understood that in the nation's service, they would find their full humanity.[26]

In all of that there was the clear echo of Otto Bauer's discussion of the commitment of workingmen each to their respective "community of destiny." The issue of nationality, and its relationship to the formation of human personality, was not unknown to the critical Marxists of the end of the nineteenth and the beginning of the twentieth century. The issues involved had been fully engaged by Austro-Marxists, Sorel, and Woltmann—Marxists all. With that background, many critical Marxists of the first years of the twentieth century responded to Gentile's reasoning—the concepts were familiar.

The intractability of the problems that turned on ethics, morality, national identity, and the revolutionary role of the state, had been appreciated among the most "orthodox" of the German Social Democrats as well as socialists of all persuasions. Michels, as a Marxist syndicalist, had written about the role of ethical judgment and revolutionary national sentiment, and had early spoken of a "proletarian nationalism" that might well inspire sacrifice and dedication among the working classes. By the time of the war in Tripoli, A. O. Olivetti had made many of the same arguments[27]—and Panunzio followed close behind.

Panunzio's thought had grown out of that tradition, and when he articulated his conception of the revolutionary function of the "neo-Hegelian ethical state," all the constituents of Fascist doctrine made themselves available. Gentile's social philosophy brought them together before the March on Rome in a coherence that was to be given recurrent expression throughout the entire Fascist period.[28]

Some considerable time before the advent of Fascism, Gentile provided the notions about the relationship between citizens and national sentiment, moral imperatives, law, and the political state, that were to serve the needs of Mussolini's developmental dictatorship. Fascists early acknowledged the economic backwardness of the Italian peninsula, to fabricate a program to address precisely that.

They understood the consequences of economic backwardness in the modern world. Italy's inferiority in the council of nations was assured by that backwardness. They argued that the nation was "poor, very poor, incapable of sustaining its own population . . . lacking raw materials, and essential capital." All of which made predictable its international inferiority and the humiliation of its citizens.

If Italy was to attain an appropriate station in the international community, Fascists advocated the nation "dismantle all that obstructs the nation's fateful development." They urged that frugality be fostered, and nonproductive consumption be curtailed, in order to assure the accumulation of capital that would allow investment in "the extension and repair of roads, irrigation, the construction of ports and rail lines, together with aggressive export marketing."[29]

Fascists conceived their tasks to include the furtherance of economic development—the "intense and progressive production" left undone by the primitive industrial capitalism that characterized the peninsula before the Great War. They proposed that the acceleration of production and extensive development be "entirely organized, and institutionalized . . . by a strong state, a virtual Leviathan, a state with overwhelming juridical power," all in "the service of the life and power of the nation."[30] It would be a state that gave personality to a nation peopled by the "warrior-producers" anticipated by the revolutionary syndicalists in the years before the First World War.[31]

The principal Fascist theoreticians argued that "every social movement delivers into history a new concept of the state and of law." That of Fascism was one of a "strong, very strong state, based on order, discipline and hierarchy,"[32] in the service of the nation's economic, military, and cultural enhancement. Discipline was the critical precondition of its success.

Together with discipline, the seamless identification of citizens with the state,[33] and with the leadership, were central to the Fascist concept of *totalitarianism*.[34] Through a series of substitutions, the ultimate interests of the individual were those of the community, and those of the community were those of the state, and those of the state were those of the party and its leader.

By 1925, doctrinal totalitarianism legitimized changes in the ruling Albertine constitution—that resulted in procedures that saw law emanating from the state, by virtue of processes largely influenced, if not ultimately determined, by the Duce of Fascism, prime minister, head of the government, and leader of the hegemonic, unitary *Partito nazionale fascista*.[35] The institutional separation of powers that had characterized the old constitution was modified to allow the leader of the single party, and the head of the government, to be largely, if not solely, responsible for the provision of public law.[36] Mussolini had become the linchpin of the system and author of the nation's laws.

By 1927, Fascist law conceived the nation "a moral, political and economic unity" that sought, through the enactments of the state, the "well-being of individuals and the development of collective power." It was an arrangement in which all voluntary associations of labor or enterprise were rendered in principle "organs of the state, subject to its control"—and uniformly "subordinated to the superior interests of production."[37]

By the early 1930s, the Fascist state was essentially complete.[38] It was a structured, hierarchically arranged edifice, at the apex of which was the unitary party and its "providential" leader—a leader gifted with "powerful, prophetic thought, superior to any in the entire history of civilization."[39]

By 1939, Fascism had completed its historic parabola. In the course of its tenure, it delivered itself of a fully formed state system unique to the twentieth century. It was unique among all similar state systems in the sense that Fascism had articulated its rationale before its construction. As will be argued, while Lenin's "dictatorship of the proletariat" shared features with Mussolini's "ethical state," it was only the latter that had been prefigured by a coherent ideological rationale. Lenin's dictatorship was jerry-built in response to totally unanticipated events—a process justified only by the most fragmentary and inconsistent rationalizations.

Sergio Panunzio, who had anticipated, and helped direct, the construction of the Fascist state, undertook to write an exposition that would provide an account of its course and substance. His *Teoria generale dello stato fascista* is perhaps the best single work available on Fascism as a state system.[40] More than that, it contains an impressive comparative analysis of what he considered a singular class of modern phenomena identified as "revolutionary dictatorships" and the totalitarianisms they produce upon maturity.[41]

Panunzio identifies a number of candidate revolutionary dictatorships, but focuses on those associated with V. I. Lenin and Benito Mussolini—

heirs of the exclusivistic belief system left as a legacy by Karl Marx and Friedrich Engels. All the properties he would identify with the distinctive revolutionary movements of the twentieth century found their origin in the neo-Hegelian thought of the founders of Marxism.

Inspired by an absolute certainty of convictions, the movements that mounted successful revolutions in the twentieth century featured leadership that conceived itself possessed of an intuitive and infallible grasp on reality—given expression in formal ideology. The "Leader" of such an enterprise would be an *epistemarch*, possessed of special truths and directive insights—"charismatic" in the Weberian sense of the term.[42] The ideology he formulated, fostered, and sustained would be binding on members during the "insurrectionary" phase, and on everyone during the period of the "revolutionary dictatorship." It would provide the substance of the totalitarian state that would unite everyone in what was understood to be a world historical enterprise.

Many, if not most, of those revolutionary movements of which Panunzio spoke found their ultimate origins in Marxism. And it was Marxism that seems to have infected them all with the conviction that political doctrine might be infallible, to inspire something like religious devotion among followers. Panunzio was to refer to those features as "ecclesiastical." In our own time, we speak of "political religions."

Panunzio identified all these properties in the state system of the Soviet Union. The informal logic that underlay the process in Lenin's Russia was the same logic found in the justificatory rationale for the Fascist state. Inspections of the thought of some of the principal thinkers of the Bolshevik revolution attest to Panunzio's insight.

He himself had ridden Marxism through its evolution from the beginning of the twentieth century until its manifestation as Fascist totalitarianism. He traced the same progression in the evolution of the state system in the Soviet Union.

MORALITY, LAW, AND THE STATE IN LENINISM

The fate of Marxism in Lenin's Russia has occupied the attention of many commentators in our time. There have been, and are, many interpretations that attempt to account for the profound doctrinal and political changes to which Marxism was made subject by Lenin and Stalin in the course of the Bolshevik revolution and the fabrication of the Soviet state.

Whatever the case, the sequence that transformed the intellectual legacy left by Marx into the rationale for Stalinism is intrinsically interesting. Considered together with the process that resulted in the creation of the Fascist state, a new perspective emerges on the history of revolution in the twentieth century.

It is generally conceded that Lenin was neither a philosopher nor a systematic social scientist. In a distracted life lived in exile, fully occupied with revolutionary activity, Lenin was ill prepared to deal with philosophical and social science issues that required intense study and undisturbed concentration. When he decided to direct his attention to such subjects, it was only because they had begun to divide members of the revolutionary community—to undermine the unity that he considered absolutely essential to his purpose. As a consequence, Lenin's writing on philosophy and social science was driven by his political, rather than specifically cognitive, concerns.[43]

The fact is that there was little in the Marxism that Lenin inherited that was serviceable to revolution in an economically backward community. The attempt to make Marxism applicable drove Lenin from one modification of received doctrine to another. From his notion of an elitist party, led by declassed bourgeois intellectuals, to a new imperialist stage in the history of revolution that saw economically, specifically industrially retrograde, nations making revolutions against the pretenses of "bourgeois" nations, Lenin had reformulated Marxism to serve entirely unanticipated purpose.

Within those successive and concurrent doctrinal modifications, Lenin had little occasion to seriously treat questions of how morals and ethics were to be understood within his Marxism.[44] His treatment of both was no more studied and academic than his general treatment of philosophy. Like all of his writings on philosophical matters, his discussion of ethics and morals was driven exclusively by *political*, rather than analytic, or essentially cognitive, considerations. One can hardly ask if Lenin's political deliberations were inspired by specifically normative assessments, because Lenin's morality, and its sustaining rationale, were not established independently, but were the derivative products of his political convictions. His own affirmations testified to that.

While Lenin was prepared to maintain that there was, in fact, "such a thing as communist ethics . . . ," and "such a thing as communist morality," his analysis of their character and scope was hardly penetrating. He told his audiences that communist ethics and morality were "entirely subordinated to the interests of the proletariat's class struggle. . . . Morality," he went on, "is what serves to destroy the old exploiting society and to unite all the working people around the proletariat."[45] Ethics and morality were thus understood to be simply instrumentalities in the service of the prior commitment to proletarian revolution. In Lenin's view, they apparently merited no more discussion than that.

Thus, toward the end of 1920, a short time before his death, Lenin spoke of ethics and morality in a manner that failed to acknowledge the time and energy devoted to the subjects by many of the foremost Marxists of the last years of the nineteenth century. Josef Dietzgen and Karl Kautsky, for example, had both struggled to provide a defensible philosophical rationale for a Marxist ethics—and Ludwig Woltmann and Georges Sorel had rehearsed all the disabilities that attended the then prevailing positivistic orthodoxies.[46]

Woltmann, as we have seen, made a point of arguing that ethical judgments and moral imperatives could not establish their warrant through an appeal to *facts*. While facts may figure in moral calculation, they cannot vindicate behaviors without recourse to specifically ethical grounds. One cannot provide empirical confirmation by providing logical demonstrations or mathematical proofs by appealing to observations, nor an ultimate vindication for ethical convictions by invoking nothing other than empirical descriptions.[47] There must be some distinctive *normative* grounds to which an ethical system appeals in order to establish credibility. To state that one's morality "stems from the interests of the class struggle of the proletariat" is to provide a description, not an ethical vindication.

What is lacking in Lenin's discussion is a coherent normative foundation for moral enjoinments. There is nothing in his voluminous writings that suggests that he entertained any more sophisticated comprehension of ethics or morality than to urge his followers to behave in the prescribed manner because such behaviors would further "proletarian revolution." Morality and ethics were simply instrumental in the service of revolutionary purpose as that purpose was understood by Lenin.

Lenin was ill disposed to entertain any complex notion of the presumptive relationship between ethical means and moral ends. Until the end of his life, Lenin sought to avoid any complications. Ethics and morality were dictated by the class struggle. The end was communism, and the means, violent revolution as he understood it.

Nor was Lenin troubled by the problem of how Marxists might convince masses to undertake revolution. Lenin had made that very clear. After he had secured rule over czarist Russia, he immediately made *law* his instrument. Lenin's view was clearly that the party spoke for the revolution, and the revolution was in the fundamental and ultimate interests of the proletariat in its entirety—whether or not the proletariat understood that to be the case.[48] After the revolution, the party and its leadership promulgated "revolutionary law" to serve its consolidation. Such laws were conceived as serving the interests of the proletariat, in its entirety, as well as the interests of its individual members[49]—whether or not they appreciated that fact. That implied, conversely, that any rule, regulation, or codified law, issued by the party, its leadership, or its courts, served the ultimate interests of the proletariat, its individual members, and the "highest ends" of socialist morality[50]—whether or not anyone other than the leadership of the party understood that to be the case. By a now familiar series of substitutions, the interests of the party, its leadership, and its state became identical with the interests of the subject individual.

Within that rationale for the system, it seemed clear, to at least some Marxist theorists in postrevolutionary Russia, that a more convincing rationale was required to justify the features of the system. Very early on, some settled on a treatment of how the state and law might be understood within the orthodoxies of classical Marxist argument.

Marxists had spoken and written extensively of the future of the state and law in a postrevolutionary world. Some Bolshevik theoreticians sought to provide a satisfying account of how both fared in the emerging Soviet Union. An interpretation of how law was to be understood was selected for analysis. It was chosen in order to satisfy the intellectual and moral sensibilities of responsible revolutionaries.

By the mid-1920s, Bolshevik legal theorists offered analyses of law that they imagined served critical thought. Among them, Evgeny Pashukanis was clearly one of the most important. His *The General Theory of Law and Marxism*, which first appeared in 1924, was among the most impressive efforts at formulating a satisfactory "Marxist theory of law"[51] in postrevolutionary Russia.

Pashukanis conceived his work a treatment of the nature and foundation of law, in which he attempted to make plausible the interpretation of modern law as a "reflection" of society's economic base, specifically a reflection of the interactive properties of commodity exchange in modern production. What that meant was that "moral law" was to be understood as nothing other than "the rule of exchange between commodity owners"—it was simply an abstract rendering of what was expected to transpire in an effective exchange of values in free market circumstances.[52]

"Moral law," in turn, provided that ground of public law. In some such fashion, the notions of morality and law were vacated to allow "class interests" to dictate both. Pashukanis's position was straightforward.

The state was an agency of class interests; morality and law no less so. Pasukanis simply drew out the implications of Marxist orthodoxy. The *content* of law was the result of class interests, and its *form* was a reflection of existing social relations, themselves the product of the economic base. Morality and law reflected the character of commodity exchange in the capitalist productive system. In that context, he went on to argue that because prevailing law could be nothing other than a reflection of prevailing relations of production, law in a postrevolutionary Russia, given the suppression of capitalism and its market, would be expected to gradually "wither away." A similar analysis, applied to the state, would confirm the traditional Marxist expectation that the political state would be an inevitable casualty of the socialist revolution.

Whatever else he accomplished, Pashukanis was to become very influential, among intellectuals, in the Russia that gradually took shape after the death of Lenin in 1924. He served as Head of the Subsection of the Institute of Soviet Construction on the General Theory of Law and State, and his influence continued until Stalin consolidated his control over all aspects of Soviet intellectual life.

With the advent of Stalin to the leadership of the Soviet Union, Pashukanis's interpretations increasingly came under criticism. Any talk of the "withering away" of law, or the state, was, at best, held to be ill considered. Stalinists argued that what was required during the "period of transition" between capitalism and communism in postrevolutionary Russia was not the withering away of law or the state, but stability, order, and absolute commitment by every member of the community—to assure the defense of the socialist community and the establishment, maintenance, and expansion of its industrial base.

Rather than a withering away of the state and law, Joseph Stalin and Andrei Vyshinsky, his Procurator General, argued that law, and the state that provides its sanction, should be formally acknowledged as essential to the creation of a communist society and the "new Soviet man" anticipated by Lenin and his revolutionary Marxists.[53] Public and private law, administrative regulations, and criminal and prosecutorial codes of conduct were all perceived, not simply as "reflections" of an economic base, but, as Lenin had insisted, as instrumental to the political purposes of the socialist state.[54]

By the time Stalin had maneuvered himself into a position of dominance after Lenin's death, Pashukanis had begun to anticipate developments. He attempted to shield himself from Stalin's wrath by admitting, in 1932, that he had been deficient in his analysis of law, its form, and function. In the effort to mollify Stalin, Pashukanis was prepared to concede that he had underestimated the "revolutionary role of the legal superstructure" in post-revolutionary circumstances. He had been mistaken. By that time, he was prepared to allow that law was not destined to wither away, but would increase its influence in the transition period between capitalism and socialism. "Its active and conscious influence upon production and other social relationships," in such circumstances, he maintained, "assumes exceptional significance."[55]

By the late 1920s, Stalin's ideologues argued that law certainly "reflected" more than bourgeois exchange of commodities in a competitive market—and it certainly was not scheduled to "wither away." By the mid-1930s, Pashukanis was prepared to surrender to Stalin's "creative development" of Marxist social theory. Stalin would have none of it. His "creative developments" of Marxism had left Pashukanis and most independent Soviet legal theoreticians defenseless. In 1937, Pashukanis disappeared into Stalin's Great Terror, and his ideas were dismissed as part of a "Trotskyist, Bukharinite, fascist plot" against the Soviet Union. Pashukanis's death signaled that by the 1930s, Stalin had not only abandoned the notion that law was a simple reflection of the equal exchange that characterized the capitalist market, but had largely rejected the "materialist" interpretation of human behavior. In 1934, Stalin affirmed that "the part played by objective conditions" in the transitional period between capitalism and communism had "been reduced to a minimum; whereas the part played by our organizations and their leaders has become decisive, exceptional."[56] The role of human beings, rather than economic factors, had become decisive in Stalin's interpretation of social and political change. Armed with that interpretation, Stalin advanced his "theory of law and the revolutionary state."

To force-draft human beings through the transitional period between capitalism and socialism, Stalin invoked all the instrumentalities of the political state. He chided Marxists for failing to "further develop" the Marxist theory of the state and law. Engels's formula, he went on to say, anticipating the withering away of both the state and its laws could not, and did not, anticipate the kinds of problems that would face an actual postrevolutionary "Marxist" state.[57] By 1930, Stalin had already insisted that he and the party stood for "the strengthening of the dictatorship of the proletariat, which is the mightiest and strongest state power that has ever existed"[58]—and it would be that state that would create law. There was no longer talk of the state and its laws being the simple "reflection" of an economic base.

Such a development can hardly be attributed exclusively to a desire on the part of Stalin to control his environment. The development appears to have been anticipated by Lenin. Even before the overthrow of czarism, Lenin spoke of "smashing" the "bourgeois state apparatus," only to insist, at the same time, that "a state of the armed workers" would be erected immediately to impose the "*strictest* control" over the behaviors of all in the new "genuinely democratic" Bolshevik state.[59]

Lenin fully appreciated what he was proposing. Whatever Marxist theory may have said about the survival or nonsurvival of the political state after socialist revolution, Lenin acknowledged that the discipline of labor, the allocation of resources, the distribution of consumer goods, clothing and comestibles, all would have to be governed by controls that took on every appearance of *law*, and law, Lenin reminded his followers, requires "an apparatus capable of *enforcing* the observance of the standards of right." The postrevolutionary Leninist state, burdened with enormous responsibilities, would be prepared to administer law with draconian rigor. That meant, he went on, that the armed workers' state, displaying all the repressive and control features of the prerevolutionary state, would not only persist, but would be the result of efforts undertaken by Bolsheviks themselves. The postrevolutionary state would be, in fact, "a bourgeois state without the bourgeoisie,"[60] constructed, enhanced, and maintained by the party of the revolutionary proletariat.

In effect, Lenin anticipated the continued existence of the "bourgeois state without the bourgeoisie" under the auspices of revolutionary Bolshevism. That prefigured the advent of the Stalinist state with its characteristic legal structure.

As has been argued, Lenin always understood the state to be nothing other than a control apparatus, employed by one class to impose its will on another. More than that, it appears that Lenin understood that the "armed workers' state" would employ "revolutionary law" to impose its will on all denizens of the socialist state—irrespective of real or fancied class membership.[61]

The only morality that counted in such circumstances was the morality of the leadership of the armed workers' state. Lenin clearly "regarded law as an arm of politics and courts as agencies of the government." Those attitudes shaped the content of Bolshevik Russia's first criminal code, produced under Lenin's direct supervision. The result was a code that, for the first time in the long history of jurisprudence, established the function of law and legal proceedings not as the dispensing of justice, but the imposition of political conformity on an inert population. However else law might be defined, it was understood to be "a disciplining principle that helps strengthen the Soviet state and develop the socialist economy."[62]

The rationale supporting such an interpretation of the nature of the state, law and morality, and their uses, was that only the self-selected elite, the Bolshevik "vanguard," knew the regnant "laws of history" that provided political institutions their "scientific" warrant. Consequently, only the party leadership knew what was morally and intellectually required to achieve "the highest aims and tasks of mankind." Only they could effectively discipline an entire society, through the agency of the state and its laws, directing revolution to its proper terminus.[63]

By the time of the passing of Joseph Vissarionovich Stalin, the Soviet conceptions of morality, law, and the state had taken on standard form. With very little variation, Soviet commentators spoke of *morality* as the totality of social behaviors, sanctioned by public approval or disapproval.[64] Usually, it was held that approval or disapproval found its impetus in "class interests," morality being in service to the "ruling class."[65] Moral behavior was variable, governed by time and circumstances, but invariably serving the interests of some given ruling class or classes.[66]

All of this is of importance in trying to understand something of the "new state" and its laws that made their first appearance in the twentieth century. As one of those states, the Stalinist state was instructive. As a "Marxist" state, it was most singular, sharing evident properties with the "Fascist state of labor." Like the Fascist state, the Stalinist state was a state governed by a unitary party, a "vanguard" of the revolution, led by an "epistemarch," especially gifted in terms of political, social, and economic insight.[67] The system was developmental, fundamentally nationalist in inspiration, and governed by a panoply of laws designed to sustain and further comprehensive control.

The Soviet system was thus not "merely a thermidorian revival of nationalist tradition, but an almost fascist like chauvinism," and featured "not merely a leader cult, but deification of a despot."[68] It was a product of Lenin's heterodox Marxism, transmogrified by Stalin under the demands of time and circumstance.

For Leninists the socialist state, and Soviet law, were products of party leadership.[69] The dictatorship would manifest itself as a "new form of state," distinctive in its features from anything to be found in classic Marxist theory, possessed of salvific "truth," and led by "the brilliant leader and teacher,

Joseph Vissarionovich Stalin"[70]—equipped to shape the development of the state, and direct the education and training of Soviet citizens through pedagogical institutions, moral schooling, and the imposition of law.

The new state would foster and defend the emergent, alternative socialist society. Subsequently, the victorious Communist Party, through the agencies of the state, would guide political and economic development, from the first period after the victory of socialism, through the extended transition to the final stage of communism. At every stage in the process, the laws of the socialist state would function in a "creative and organizational role," through the state's control, information, and pedagogical instrumentalities. The state, consistently sustained and strengthened under the ministrations of the party, would discipline, direct, and educate all the members of the evolving socialist order.[71]

By the mid-1930s, the Stalinist state was well established to proceed to decimate any remaining opposition.[72] The purges that followed swept away any possibility of domestic resistance and the regime settled into the form that would persist, with some alterations, until Stalin's death in 1953. The world has since become familiar with the criterial traits that identify the Stalinist state. Shorn of the transparent fiction that it was somehow "Marxist," or that it somehow represented the "ultimate interests of the proletariat," Stalinism was a caricature of the state system of Fascism. Panunzio, in his assessment of the class of "totalitarianisms," of which Fascism was one, acknowledged as much.

According to generic Marxist theory, humankind's liberating revolution would follow an entirely different course. The morality of the proletariat would not be the consequence of either instruction or law. It would grow spontaneously out of resistance to the oppression of the bourgeoisie in the period of capitalist rule. Social revolution would be the consequence of the growing tensions between the material productive forces and productive relations of advanced industrial capitalism, which would cause periodic economic crises—and ultimately the inevitable collapse of the system. The revolutionary program of a truly Marxist political party would represent solutions to those problems and would embody an apposite morality. Such a program would outline the strategy for the defeat of the oppressors of the working class, and provide for the creation of a "dictatorship of the proletariat"—that would supply the environment for the withering away of both the political state and the law it sustained. The state would disappear into the voluntary association of producers—which would proceed to plan production to meet the needs of all.

REVOLUTIONARY DICTATORSHIPS
AND TOTALITARIANISM

In his analysis of revolutionary dictatorships, and the totalitarianisms into which they matured, Panunzio maintained that their respective revolutionary leaderships were so convinced of the truths of their convictions, that absolute adherence to their respective ideologies becomes a measure of virtue. Any departure from that strict adherence would invite sanction. The Leader, creator and spokesman of an exclusivistic system of belief, inspires among his followers the conviction that he is a political leader and thinker superior to the greatest minds of our time.[73] He becomes the ultimate source of security, fulfillment, and meaning. The system he creates is hierarchical, authoritarian, moralizing, and relentlessly public. In such circumstances, the entire political environment is characterized by an atmosphere of high emotional salience, public liturgies, and mass display.

In his time, Panunzio identified extant members of that class of modern movements. In their number, he included Chiang Kaishek's Kuomintang,[74] as well as Hitler's National Socialism—and he speculated on others.[75] He clearly distinguished each by virtue of their respective ideological substance—they clearly differed among themselves. The doctrinal expression given to Marxism by the Bolsheviks and Stalinists distinguished it from the ideology of Fascism—and the racism of National Socialism distinguished it from both. It was their shared institutional form that rendered them members of the class of "totalitarianisms." Whether their ideological commitment was to proletarian communism, or the Nordic race, or the restoration of Italy to its proper place in the community of nations, they all chose the hierarchically structured, charismatically led, single party state to pursue their ends—a state first fixed in political doctrine by Fascism. What they did with the instrumentalities that typified that state is now indelibly recorded in history.

More than that, it was Fascism, having directly addressed the issue of revolution in an economically less developed environment, that anticipated that the twentieth century would not be a century of class struggle, but a century in which less developed nations would engage those industrially advanced for status, security, space, and resources.[76] While intimations of such a possibility are to be found in Lenin's preliminary assessments of the international implications of imperialism, Fascists argued with greater clarity, and more compelling evidence, that the struggle that would take shape in the twentieth century would be a struggle between *nations* and not classes.[77]

Fascists argued that class struggle, in any literal sense, would have precious little to do with the conflicts of the twentieth century. Those theoreticians who would provide the ideology of Fascism understood that even before the coming of the Great War. They shared with other critical Marxists the recognition that national sentiment was more pervasive and compelling than any influence arising from those material interests characteristically associated with class identification.

That, once granted, several considerations followed. If economically less developed communities sought to free themselves from exploitation at the hands of "plutocratic" powers, they would have to undertake rapid economic growth and industrial development.[78] Only the possession of power projection capabilities, afforded by industrial plants sufficient to supply modern weapons, would render less developed nations survivable in any contest with their industrially advanced protagonists.

Long before either Lenin or Stalin, it was Fascism that fully appreciated the fact that in the troubled twentieth century, a revolutionary party, that sought the rapid industrialization of a retrograde economy, would have to make recourse to an inflexible state system that could ensure the effective inculcation of an ideology of sacrifice, labor, and obedience upon a subject population.

Panunzio recognized that these obligations imposed pedagogical, and quasireligious, obligations on the revolutionary dictatorships he sought to characterize.[79] He understood that such systems, freighted with such responsibilities, could only function in an atmosphere of sustained moral tension—that would foster collective discipline, obedience, and selfless commitment. To create and maintain all that, the revolutionary dictatorship would be required to control the flow of information and shape the educational processes. There would have to be an appeal to symbols, "sacred texts," and charismatic leaders—all to create the moral equivalent of war.[80] The revolutionary dictatorships, and the totalitarianisms, that were to follow, whether of the "left" or the "right," were all marked by the same features—whatever their respective pretenses.

In the half-century following the passing of Mussolini's Fascism, the world witnessed the rise and fall of revolutionary dictatorships that shared some, if not all, the major features of its state system.[81] Like Fascism, most of those systems traced their doctrinal ancestry back to the dense, prolix, abundant, and sometimes impenetrable, literary legacy left by the founders of the first Marxism. Maoism, Kim Il Sungism, and all the satellite Marxisms of Eastern Europe and the Balkans pretended to be Marxist in inspiration. Even the political obscenity that murdered about a quarter of the entire population of gentle Cambodia imagined its ideological origins were to be found in the Marxism of Marx and Engels. Trying to find the doctrinal grounds for the single party, developmental dictatorships of the twentieth century has seen academics of all persuasion rummaging through the published works of the founders of Marxism to very little purpose. The grounds are readily found in the writings of pre-Fascist and Fascist theoreticians who published early in the last century.

Syndicalists, such as Filippo Corridoni and A. O. Olivetti had drawn out the revolutionary implications of Italy's backwardness long before Lenin and Stalin recognized that economic and industrial backwardness, and the revolutionary anticipations of classical Marxism, were entirely incompatible. Before the Great War, at a time when Lenin was expecting a worldwide "proletarian" revolution, Corridoni argued that the prospects of such a revolution, in the then international circumstances, were all but nil. That granted, the backwardness of the Italian peninsula made rapid economic and industrial development its only opinion—if any sort of revolutionary change was sought. The doctrine that followed, composed of the thought of a roster of revolutionary Marxists, was the first Fascism—harbinger of the totalitarianism that would include in its ranks, to one degree or another, most of the revolutionary regimes of the twentieth century.[82]

THE END OF TOTALITARIANISM

It is not clear that we have seen the end of totalitarianism. While it seems evident that we will not see its like again in Europe, it is not clear that we will not see some variant in those vast reaches of those underdeveloped regions of the world that still obtain. Nations and peoples afflicted by industrial backwardness, an associated feeling of inefficacy, and burdened by an abiding sense of humiliation, are disposed to the kinds of leadership and the revolutionary enterprise that produces those revolutionary regimes that grow into totalitarianism.

Some of the revolutionary currents that have most occupied our attention at the beginning of the twenty-first century show a disposition toward some kind of totalitarianism—however different from Leninism, Stalinism, or Fascism. While these contemporary movements are not Fascist in any determinate sense,[83] they do display some totalitarian features that augur ill for our time.

Radical Islamist movements, assuming some of the features of totalitarianism, do not trace their origins, however remote, to Fascism or Marxism. Their concern is not with productive systems or developing economies. Theirs is a preoccupation with the restoration of an archaic order of agrarian and nomadic religiosity—none of which precludes a role for charismatic leadership and impeccable doctrine—which, in turn, elicits conformity, obedience, discipline, and sacrifice from its followers.

At least one of these revolutions has succeeded in imposing itself on a population. The leadership of Iran has sought the kind of population controls employed by precedent totalitarianisms—but it seems that technological backwardness has rendered the efforts less than impressive. Whatever the case, the "totalitarian temptation" remains among us, perhaps in less trafficked places. It seems unlikely that new efforts would be made in those regions that have suffered a failed totalitarianism. In the past, the costs of such a system invariably have been very high.

Should there be any further totalitarianism in the new century, it probably will not find its origins in Mussolini's Fascism or in some form of heterodox Marxism. Mussolini's Fascism, generic fascism, and revolutionary Marxism, seem to have all played themselves out in the tragedies of the twentieth century. The epigones of Mussolini, Lenin, Stalin, and Marx have renounced totalitarianism. In Italy, the heirs of Mussolini abjure violence, reject the notion of political doctrines that are impeccably true, and compete in competitive elections. In the former Soviet Union, party communists advocate pension reforms, and disavow violence, as well as totalitarianism, to compete in "bourgeois" elections.

In the industrial democracies, Marxism has become the subject of classes taught to undergraduates, no longer the revolutionary creed of the working class. Fascism has become the caricature found on late-night television. Little remains, in effect, of those heterodox Marxisms that gave rise to the variegated totalitarianisms of our time.

What has been left behind is something of a cautionary tale, told in a manner that perhaps provides a better understanding of the revolutionary thought of the past century, perhaps a better comprehension of Mussolini's Fascism, and Lenin's Bolshevism—and perhaps an appreciation of the moral and intellectual complexities involved in a commitment to political and social revolution. It is a tale about the advent of revolutionary and totalitarian thought in the past century. What it is not is an accounting of the costs involved in its tenure and its passing.

NOTES AND INDEX

Notes

1. INTRODUCTION

1. One of the more recent examples of this is found in R. J. B. Bosworth, *Mussolini's Italy: Life Under the Fascist Dictatorship* (New York: Penguin Press, 2006). Capitalized, "Fascism" will refer to the Fascism of Mussolini. A lowercase "fascism" refers to a generic fascism that includes an indeterminate membership.

2. See, for example, Martin Pabst, *Staatsterrorismus: Theorie und Praxis kommunistischer Herrschaft* (Stuttgart: Leopold Stocker Verlag, 1997), chap. 2.

3. See the discussion in A. James Gregor, *Interpretations of Fascism* (New Brunswick, N.J.: Transaction Press, 2000), chaps. 2 and 3.

4. See Herbert W. Schneider, *Making the Fascist State* (New York: Oxford Press, 1928); William G. Welk, *Fascist Economic Policy* (Cambridge, Mass.: Harvard University Press, 1938), p. 243.

5. Angelo Del Boca and Mario Giovana, *Fascism Today: A World Survey* (New York: Pantheon Books, 1969), p. 145. See the discussion concerning de Gaulle on pages 170–173, 181–185, 191–207.

6. Max Horkheimer, as quoted in François Furet, *The Passing of an Illusion: The Idea of Communism in the Twentieth Century* (Chicago: University of Chicago Press, 1999), p. 368.

7. Rajani Palme Dutt, *Fascism and Social Revolution: A Study of the Economics and Politics of the Extreme Stages of Capitalism in Decay* (San Francisco: Proletarian Publishers, 1974; a reprint of the 1934 edition), pp. 16, 17.

8. See the account in F. Burlatsky, *The State and Communism* (Moscow: Progress Publishers, n.d.).

9. See the discussion in A. James Gregor, *The Faces of Janus: Marxism and Fascism in the Twentieth Century* (New Haven: Yale University Press, 2000), chap. 5.

10. Anatoly Butenko, "To Avoid Mistakes in the Future," *The Stalin Phenomenon* (Moscow: Novosti Press Agency, 1988), p. 8.

11. Gavriil Popov, "From an Economist's Point of View," and Dmitry Volkogonov, "The Stalin Phenomenon," *ibid.*, pp. 12, 41, 43.

12. Volkogonov, "The Stalin Phenomenon," *ibid.*, pp. 48, 49.

13. Boris Bolotin, "Dogma and Life," *ibid.*, pp. 30–31.

14. See the interesting discussion of the responses made by some of the intellectuals challenged by developments in the Soviet Union in Paul Hollander, *The End of Commitment: Intellectuals, Revolutionaries, and Political Morality* (Chicago: Ivan R. Dee, 2006).

15. See Mark Neocleous, *Fascism* (Minneapolis: University of Minnesota Press, 1997).

16. See the postmortem account in Peter Sperlich, *Rotten Foundations: The Conceptual Basis of the Marxist-Leninist Regimes of East Germany and Other Countries of the Soviet Bloc* (London: Praeger, 2002) and *Oppression and Scarcity: The History and Institutional Structure of the Marxist-Leninist Government of East Germany and Some Perspectives on Life in a Socialist System* (London: Praeger, 2006).

17. See the entire discussion in Furet, *The Passing of an Illusion*, chaps. 10–11.

18. See the discussion in Gregor, *Interpretations of Fascism*, chap. 5.

19. The classic statement of this notion is found in Georgi Dimitroff, *The United Front Against War and Fascism: Report to the Seventh World Congress of the Communist International, 1935* (New York: Gamma Publishing, 1974; reprint of the 1934 edition). The editor, Jack Shulman, insists that Dimitroff's analysis was relevant to the United States of the period; see *ibid.*, pp. 3–5.

20. See the more ample discussion in A. James Gregor, *A Place in the Sun: Marxism and Fascism in China's Long Revolution* (Boulder, Colo.: Westview Press, 2000), pp. 106–107.

21. Maoists in the United States and Britain put together elaborate accounts of how the Soviets had abandoned Marxism in order to restore capitalism to what had been a "socialist" society. See, for example, *How Capitalism has been Restored in the Soviet Union and What this Means for the World Struggle* (Chicago: Revolutionary Union, 1974).

22. See the discussion in Gregor, *The Faces of Janus*, chap. 4.

23. See one of the most recent efforts, Robert O. Paxton, *The Anatomy of Fascism* (New York: Alfred A. Knopf, 2004), particularly chap. 8.

24. One finds just these sorts of judgments in the 1990 "Report of the European Parliament's Committee of Inquiry into Racism and Xenophobia," in *Fascist Europe: The Rise of Racism and Xenophobia* (London: Pluto Press, 1991). See also A. James Gregor, *The Search for Neofascism: The Use and Abuse of Social Science* (New York: Cambridge University Press, 2006), chaps. 1–3.

25. This is not to say that there have not been authors who see the relationship between the various forms of Marxism and one or another form of fascism. See A. James Gregor, *The Fascist Persuasion in Radical Politics* (Princeton: Princeton University Press, 1974).

26. Dave Renton, *Fascism: Theory and Practice* (London: Pluto Press, 1999), pp. 3, 116.

27. As early as 1918, Giovanni Gentile wrote that in the best governed communities, "the will of a people is the same as the will of he who governs—and the will of he who governs is the will of those governed." Giovanni Gentile, "Il significato della vittoria," *Dopo la vittoria: Nuovi frammenti politici* (Rome: La Voce, 1920), p. 8.

28. See Gentile's discussion in *Discorsi di religione* (Florence: Sansoni, 1955; third edition of the edition of 1920), particularly pp. 20–23. "The individual has within himself, society—he forges within himself a sociality, a society immanent within him." Gentile, *Preliminari allo studio del fanciullo* (Florence: Sansoni, 1920), p. 55.

29. Benito Mussolini, "Per la vera pacificazione," *Opera omnia* (Florence: La fenice, 1955), 17, p. 295.

30. See Marco Tarchi, *Partito unico e dinamica autoritaria* (Naples: Akropolis, 1981), pp. 23–24.

31. George H. Sabine, "State," in *Encyclopaedia of the Social Sciences* (New York: Macmillan, 1934), 14, p. 330.

32. "In spite of the open hostility that exists between the U.S.S.R., on the one hand, and Fascist Italy and National Socialist Germany, on the other, there are striking similarities between them." Michael T. Florinsky, *Fascism and National Socialism: A Study of the Economic and Social Policies of the Totalitarian State* (New York: Macmillan, 1936), p. v.

33. See Martin Jaenicke, *Totalitäre Herrschaft* in *Soziologische Abhandlungen* (Berlin: Ducker und Humblot, 1971), 13, p. 62, n. 7; and the typical use among Marxists in Robert A. Brady, *The Spirit and Structure of German Fascism* (London: Gollancz, 1937), particularly pp. 39–40.

34. Herbert Marcuse is perhaps the best representative of that conviction—to apply the term "totalitarianism" to "bourgeois liberal democracy" as early as the mid-1930s. See the discussion in Douglas Kellner, *Herbert Marcuse and the Crisis of Marxism* (Berkeley: University of California Press, 1984).

35. See Carl J. Friedrich, "The Unique Character of Totalitarian Society," in Carl J. Friedrich (ed.), *Totalitarianism* (New York: Grosset and Dunlap, 1953), pp. 47–59; Juan Linz, "Totalitarianism and Authoritarian Regimes," in Fred Greenstein and Nelson Polsby (eds.), *Handbook of Political Science, Macropolitical Theory* (Reading, Mass.: Wiley, 1975).

36. One of the volumes I found most helpful was Abbott Gleason, *Totalitarianism: The Inner History of the Cold War* (New York: Oxford University Press, 1995).

37. See, for example, the volume published anonymously by "Humanus," *Fascismo rosso* (Rome: Faretra, 1946); and Thomas E. Lifka, *The Concept "Totalitarianism" and American Foreign Policy* (New York: Garland, 1988), 2, p. 495.

38. See Gleason, *Totalitarianism*, p. 70. To this day, leftist intellectuals insist that "fascism is first and foremost an ideology generated by modern industrial capital." Neocleous, *Fascism*, p. xi.

39. In fact, J. L. Talmon's *The Origins of Totalitarian Democracy* (New York: Praeger, 1960) was devoted largely to tracing the totalitarian origins of the Soviet system to the democracy of the French revolution.

40. Hannah Arendt, *The Origins of Totalitarianism* (New York: Harcourt, Brace, 1951); see Gregor, *Interpretations of Fascism*, pp. 96–107.

41. H. Stuart Hughes, "Historical Sources of Totalitarianism," *The Nation*, 24 March 1951, p. 281.

42. See Stephen F. Cohen, "Bolshevism and Stalinism," reprinted in Ernest A. Menze (ed.), *Totalitarianism Reconsidered* (London: Kennikat Press, 1981), pp. 58–80.

43. See Alberto Aquarone, *L'Organizzazione dello stato totalitario* (Turin: Einaudi, 1965), pp. 290–311.

44. With the collapse of the regime in 1943, and the occupation of Italy by National Socialist forces, Fascists became complicit in the death of about seven thousand Jews. Arendt apparently felt that was too few to qualify Fascism as a "totalitarianism." She seemed to be prepared to argue that totalitarians had to have a large population in order to carry out their mass murders. Fascist Italy's population was apparently too small. One is not certain how Arendt would characterize the Pol Pot regime in "Democratic Kampuchea," which saw the massacre of about one-third of the population of a country that had perhaps considerably less than seven million inhabitants.

45. At about that time, Herbert Marcuse argued that "the total authoritarian state," the term he employed in place of "totalitarianism," "brings with it the organization and theory of society corresponding to the monopoly stage of capitalism." Marcuse, *Kultur und Gesellschaft* (Frankfurt a.M.: Leibniz Verlag, 1967), 1, p. 37. Later he was to develop the same association between totalitarianism and industrial capitalism in *One Dimensional Man*.

46. See the objections to that tendency advanced by Karl Dietrich Bracher, "Der umstrittene Totalitarismus: Erfahrung and Aktualität," in *Zeitgeschichtliche Kontroversen: Faschismus, Totalitarismus, und Demokratie* (Munich: Pieper, 1976), pp. 33–61.

47. One of the better expositions is found in Leonard Shapiro, *Totalitarianism* (New York: Praeger, 1972).

48. See A. James Gregor, "Totalitarianism Revisited," in Menze, *Totalitarianism Reconsidered*, pp. 130–145.

49. Stanley G. Payne, *A History of Fascism 1914–1945* (Madison: University of Wisconsin Press, 1995), p. 206.

50. First suppressed by censorship, the volume by the Bulgarian Zheliu Zhelev, *Fashizmut*, recognized the totalitarian traits shared by prewar and wartime fascist, and the postwar communist, regimes.

51. See the discussion in the Epilogue to Gleason, *Totalitarianism*.

52. See, for example, David Remnick, *Lenin's Tomb: The Last Days of the Soviet Empire* (New York: Random House, 1993), pp. 37, 410. Even those most critical granted that "the totalitarian image of power dynamics in communist systems cannot be discarded entirely. The Bolsheviks and the Chinese Communists who attacked and attempted to destroy the Russian and Chinese ancien regime were Leninists. . . . Leninism was a power-concentrating ideology that systematically sought to eliminate competing centers of power and maximize the political domination of the vanguard party. . . . [The totalitarian] model did capture crucial dimensions of power dynamics under communism." Mark Lupher, *Power Restructuring in China and Russia* (Boulder, Colo.: Westview Press, 1996), p. 6. See the insightful discussion in Walter Laqueur, *The Dream That Failed: Reflections on the Soviet Union* (New York: Oxford University Press, 1994), chap. 4.

53. Neocleous, *Fascism*, pp. 7, 17.

54. See the discussion in Laqueur, *The Dream that Failed*, chap. 4; Paul Hollander (ed.), *From the Gulag to the Killing Fields* (Willmington, DE: ISI Books,

2006); and Stéphane Courtois, Nicolas Werth, Jean-Louis Panné, Andrzej Paczkowski, Karel Bartosek, and Jean-Louis Margolin, *The Black Book of Communism: Crimes Terror Repression* (Cambridge, Mass.: Harvard University Press, 1999).

55. See the discussion in A. James Gregor, *Phoenix: Fascism in our Time* (New Brunswick, N.J.: Transaction Publishers, 1999), chap. 7.

56. Richard Wolin, *The Seduction of Unreason: The Intellectual Romance with Fascism from Nietzsche to Postmodernism* (Princeton: Princeton University Press, 2004), pp. 144, 308.

2. THE ROOTS OF REVOLUTIONARY IDEOLOGY

1. Friedrich Engels, *Anti-Dühring: Herr Eugen Dühring's Revolution in Science* (Moscow: Foreign Languages Publishing House, 1962), p. 130.

2. For the purposes of the following discussion, "morality" is understood to refer to the enjoinments, prescriptions, and proscriptions governing conduct—with "ethics" referring to the systematic rationale, advanced as warrant, for just such enjoinments, prescriptions, and proscriptions.

3. Karl Marx and Friedrich Engels, *The Communist Manifesto* (New York: Penguin, 1998), pp. 73, 74.

4. Karl Marx, *The Poverty of Philosophy* (Moscow: Foreign Languages Publishing House, n.d.), pp. 122, 138. The "material productive forces" have been understood to include an assortment of factors including human and animal labor, the forces of nature, the nature of the soil, instruments of production, as well as productive experience and skill. The "relations of production" are generally spoken of as referring to how and to whom production is distributed in any given economic system. See the discussion in A. James Gregor, *A Survey of Marxism: Problems in Philosophy and the Theory of History* (New York: Random House, 1965), pp. 158–169.

5. Karl Marx, *Economic and Philosophic Manuscripts of 1844* (Amherst, N.Y.: Prometheus Books, 1988), p. 103, emphasis supplied.

6. *Ibid.*

7. Karl Marx and Friedrich Engels, *The German Ideology*, in Karl Marx and Friedrich Engels, *Collected Works* (New York: International Publishers, 1976; hereafter *MECW*), 5, pp. 31–32. The *German Ideology* was written between September 1845 and the summer of 1846.

8. *Ibid.*, pp. 36–37.

9. See the discussion in A. James Gregor, *Metascience and Politics: An Inquiry into the Conceptual Language of Political Science* (New Brunswick, N.J.: Transaction Publishers, 2003), chaps. 4, 5 and 8.

10. Marx and Engels, *The German Ideology*, pp. 50 and 53.

11. Years later, Engels spoke of "civil society" as "the realm of economic relations—the decisive element." Engels, *Ludwig Feuerbach and the End of Classical German Philosophy*, in Marx and Engels, *Selected Works* (Moscow: Foreign Languages Publishing House, 1955; hereafter *MESW*), 2, pp. 393–394.

12. *Ibid.*, pp. 53, 59.

13. *Ibid.*, p. 60.

14. "For the oppressed class to be able to emancipate itself it is necessary that

the productive powers already acquired and the existing social relations should no longer be capable of existing side by side." Marx, *The Poverty of Philosophy*, p. 196. More than three decades later, Engels described the "cause" of revolution as being "the mode of production is in rebellion against the mode of exchange, the productive forces are in rebellion against the mode of production which they have outgrown." Engels, *Anti-Dühring*, p. 378.

15. Marx and Engels, *The German Ideology*, p. 52.

16. *Ibid.*, p. 52.

17. *Ibid.*, p. 54.

18. In his full maturity, after Marx's death, Engels expressed such a notion in the following fashion, "The influences of the external world upon man express themselves in his brain, are reflected therein as feelings, thoughts, impulses, volitions—in short, as 'ideal tendencies' . . ." Engels, *Ludwig Feuerbach and the End of Classical German Philosophy*, 2, p. 376.

19. In the German text, "constraint" is given as "*Hemmnis*," often translated as "fetter" in English translation. To "overcome [*ueberwinden*]" fetters makes for an awkward mental picture. Marx and Engels, "Manifest der Kommunistischen Partei," *Werke* (Berlin: Dietz Verlag, 1959), 4, p. 468.

20. See the extensive catalog of conditions that must exist if "communism," as a revolutionary ideology, is to be *real*, as distinct from a utopian, aspiration. Communism, as a revolutionary imperative, engages the energies and commitment of revolutionaries when the productive system has supplied the "absolutely necessary practical premises." See Marx and Engels, *The German Ideology*, pp. 48–49.

21. *Ibid.*, p. 56.

22. Marx and Engels, *The Communist Manifesto*, pp. 21 and 31.

23. See the discussion in Gregor, *A Survey of Marxism*, chap. 5.

24. Marx, *The Poverty of Philosophy*, p. 122.

25. Marx, *Capital: A Critical Analysis of Capitalist Production* (Moscow: Foreign Languages Publishing House, 1954), 1, p. 372, n. 3.

26. *Ibid.*

27. In his letter to P. V. Annenkov, on 28th December 1846, Marx wrote that "men are not free arbiters of their productive forces," and that "as they develop their productive faculties, they develop certain relations with one another. . . . What has not [been] grasped is that these men . . . who produce their social relations in accordance with their material productivity, also produce *ideas, categories*, that is to say the abstract ideal expression of these same social relations." *MESW*, 2, pp. 442, 446–447.

28. In March 1850, in their "Address of the Central Authority to the League," they wrote that "a new revolution is impending." *MECW*, 10, p. 278. They continued to expect imminent revolution throughout their lives.

29. Engels to Marx, letter of 27 November 1851, in *MESW*, 2, pp. 446–447.

30. See the discussion in Eduard Bernstein, *Ferdinand Lassalle: Eine Würdigung des Lehrers und Kämpfers* (Berlin: Paul Cassirer, 1919).

31. Dietzgen (1828–1888) enjoyed Marx's support. Marx spoke of him as "stronger" than his "bourgeois" critics. Marx, *Capital*, 1, p. 16. Engels reported that Dietzgen, independently of Hegel and Marx, had discovered "materialist dialectics." Engels, *Ludwig Feuerbach and the End of Classical German Philosophy*, p. 386. For years

after his death, Dietzgen was cited not only as an authority in these matters but as one of the founders of "Marxist materialist ethics" by Karl Kautsky, one of the twentieth century's most prominent Marxist scholars. See Kautsky, *Ethik und materialistische Geschichtsauffassung* (Stuttgart: Verlag von J. H. W. Dietz, 1919), pp. v, 51.

32. Anton Pannekoek, "Introduction" to Josef Dietzgen, *The Positive Outcome of Philosopy* (Chicago: Charles H. Kerr & Company, 1906), p. 21.

33. Dietzgen, *ibid.*, p. 138.

34. *Ibid.*, p. 171.

35. "From the foregoing follows the postulate that morality must be studied inductively or scientifically." *Ibid.*, p. 151; see pp. 133, 134, 143–144.

36. *Ibid.*, pp. 136, 147.

37. Henriette Roland-Holst, *Josef Dietzgens Philosophie in ihrer Bedeutung für das Proletariat* (Munich: Verlag der Dietzgensche Philosophie, 1910), pp. 29–35.

38. Dietzgen, *The Positive Outcome of Philosophy*, p. 158. Dietzgen insisted that "human welfare" was "the common end of all ends." *Ibid.*, p. 159.

39. *Ibid.*, pp. 169, 171, 172.

40. Roland-Holst, *Josef Dietzgens Philosophie*, p. 38.

41. Dietzgen, *The Positive Outcome of Philosophy*, pp. 159, 163.

42. *Ibid.*, p. 170.

43. See Josef Dietzgen, "Der wissenschaftliche Sozialismus," *Kleinere philosophische Schriften: Eine Auswahl* (Stuttgart: Verlag von J. H. W. Dietz, 1903), pp. 1–11. Dietzgen regularly called upon the methods of "exact science," what he called the "monistic worldview, the unity of nature: the unity of 'spirit' and 'matter'," to justify Party policies. See *ibid.*, pp. 112, 117, 137–138, 139, 213–214, 217, 226, 230.

44. Dietzgen, "Die Moral der Sozialdemokratie," in *ibid.*, pp. 77–78, 81–83, 85, 87.

45. Dietzgen devoted some considerable space to a discussion of the relationship between "Darwin and Hegel." See *ibid.*, pp. 226–252; and Bertram D. Wolfe, *Marxism: One Hundred Years in the Life of a Doctrine* (Boulder, Colo.: Westview Press, 1985), pp. 236–237.

46. Dietzgen, "Die Moral . . . ," p. 90.

47. In the *Manifesto*, Marx had argued that the very nature of industrial capitalism had produced conditions which forced the working poor to "sink deeper and deeper below the conditions of existence." He went on to argue that the industrial bourgeoisie was no longer fit to rule "because it is incompetent to assure an existence to its slave within his slavery." The immediate and *inevitable* consequence would be a cataclysmic revolution in response to the will to survive of the entire proletariat. Marx and Engels, *The Communist Manifesto*, p. 65.

48. Dietzgen, "Die Moral . . . ," pp. 84, 89, 92.

49. See the entirety of Dietzgen's, "Die Moral . . . ," pp. 77–93, particularly pp. 85, 87, 89–93.

50. It seems clear that both Marx and Engels held Darwin in considerable regard, but they nowhere seem to be prepared to incorporate specifically Darwinian elements into their distinctive worldview. See Engels's discussion in *Anti-Dühring*, pp. 97–107. Engels's discussion of human evolution in "The Part Played by Labour in the Transition from Ape to Man," in 1876, says very little about Darwinism, per se. He identified the major mechanism of human change as the Lamarckian inheri-

tance of acquired characteristics. See, *MESW*, 2, pp. 80–92, particularly pp. 81–82.

51. "Only infinite progress is eternally or absolutely moral." Dietzgen, "Die Moral . . . ," p. 92.

52. *Ibid.*, pp. 91, 92.

53. *Ibid.*, pp. 78–81.

54. Engels spoke of a "really human morality," in *Anti-Dühring*, p. 132.

55. Dietzgen, "Die Moral . . . ," pp. 78, 83.

56. See Marx's positive reference to the work of Dietzgen in the Afterword to the Second German Edition of *Capital*, p. 16, and that of Engels, *Ludwig Feuerbach and the End of Classical German Philosophy*, p. 386.

57. Engels, *Anti-Dühring*, p. 36; see *ibid.*, pp. 97–107; and *Ludwig Feuerbach and the End of Classical German Philosophy*, p. 388.

58. See the entire discussion in "Die sozialen Triebe," in Dietzgen, *Kleiner philosophische Schriften*, pp. 57–68.

59. See Engels, "The Part Played by Labor in the Transition from Ape to Man," *MESW*, 2, pp. 80, 81, 85.

60. See the entire discussion entitled "Der Organismus der menschlichen Gesellschaft: Die technische Entwicklung," in Kautsky, *Ethik und materialistische Geschichtsauffassung*, pp. 79–91.

61. Engels, *Anti-Dühring*, pp. 378, 379.

62. Marx, *Capital*, 1, p. 386.

63. Kautsky, *Ethik und materialistische Geschichtsauffassung*, p. 84.

64. *Ibid.*, pp. 98–106.

65. *Ibid.*, pp. 106–107.

66. *Ibid.*, p. 120.

67. *Ibid.*, pp. 86–91, particularly p. 90.

68. See "Vorrede" in *ibid.*, p. v.

69. Marx and Engels, *The German Ideology*, pp. 31–32.

70. Around the same time, Engels wrote that the radical leaders of the Great Peasant War of the sixteenth century had failed to understand that revolutionary demands could not exceed the material capabilities of the primitive productive base of the time. The will of such leaders was infilled with "chiliastic dream-visions," unreal expectations given the material conditions of the time. Such revolutionary demands were "premature." See Engels, *The Peasant War in Germany*, in *MECW*, 10, pp. 415, 422, 469–471.

71. See the discussion in Marx and Engels, *The German Ideology*, pp. 193–195, 447.

72. *Ibid.*, pp. 196–197.

73. *Ibid.*, p. 43.

74. We are informed that "will [is] conditioned and determined by the material relations of production." *Ibid.*, p. 195.

75. *Ibid.*, pp. 43, 89, 419.

76. *Ibid.*, pp. 88, 90.

77. Preface to *ibid.*, p. xvii.

78. See the account in *ibid.*, pp. 45, 48–49, 51–52.

79. In 1847, in his preambulatory essay in preparation for the writing of *The*

Communist Manifesto, Engels wrote, "Communists . . . know all too well that revolutions are not made intentionally and arbitrarily, but that everywhere and always they have been the necessary consequence of conditions which are wholly independent of the will and direction of individual parties and entire classes." Engels, *The Principles of Communism*, Appendix to the Monthly Review edition of *The Communist Manifesto* (New York: Monthly Review Press, 1998), p. 76.

80. *Ibid.*, pp. 54, 74. In his preparatory essay to *The Communist Manifesto*, Engels wrote, "Every change in the social order, every revolution in property relations, is the necessary consequence of the creation of new forces of production which no longer fit into the old property relations." Engels, *The Principles of Communism*, p. 75.

81. Friedrich Engels produced what are now identified as volumes two and three of *Das Kapital* by quarrying the mountains of excerpted and annotated material left by Marx after his death. The "fourth volume" of *Das Kapital* was produced by Karl Kautsky—at Engels's behest—out of those extracts and critical commentaries that still remained after the winnowing by Engels.

82. See the comments by Karl Kautsky, *Die materialistische Geschichtsauffassung* (Berlin: Dietz Verlag, 1929), I, pp. 15–16.

3. THE HETERODOX MARXISM OF LUDWIG WOLTMANN

1. First given public expression in 1898, it is clear that Bernstein already entertained reservations concerning Marxism as it found form as early as the years before Engels's death. By 1898, his thoughts were subjected to review by the Social Democratic party as being "unorthodox," and with the Hanover Conference of the party in 1899, were rejected as threatening not only the ideological integrity of the movement, but its political integrity as well. See the "Preface to the English Edition," Eduard Bernstein, *Evolutionary Socialism: A Criticism and Affirmation* (New York: Schocken Books, 1961; an abbreviated version of *Die Voraussetzungen der Sozialismus und die Aufgaben der Sozialdemokratie*, originally published in 1898).

2. See the account in Bernstein, *Der Sozialismus einst und jetzt: Streitfragen des Sozialismus in Vergangenheit und Gegenwart* (Berlin: J. H. W. Dietz, 1923), chaps. I and II.

3. See Bernstein, *Evolutionary Socialism*, pp. 2–3.

4. See Bernstein, *Der Sozialismus einst und jetzt*, chap. 8.

5. V. I. Lenin thought enough of Ludwig Woltmann's book, *Der historische Materialismus: Darstellung und Kritik der marxistischen Weltanschauung* (Düsseldorf: Hermann Michels Verlag, 1900), to recommend it to his readers. See V. I. Lenin, "Karl Marx," *Collected Works* (Moscow: Foreign Languages Publishing House), 21, p. 87.

6. Ludwig Woltmann, *System des moralischen Bewusstseins mit besonderer Darlegung des Verhältnisses der kritischen Philosophie zu Darwinismus und Socialismus* (Düsseldorf: Hermann Michels Verlag, 1898) and *Die Darwinsche Theorie und der Sozialismus: Ein Beitrag zur Naturgeschichte der menschlichen Gesellschaft* (Düsseldorf: Hermann Michels Verlag, 1899).

7. See the discussion in Karl Kautsky's *Ethik und materialistische Geschichtsauffassung* (Stuttgart: J. H. W. Dietz, 1919, but written in 1906), chaps. 1–3.

8.   See Woltmann, *Der historische Materialismus*, pp. 217–225, 238–251.

9.   See the specific discussion in *ibid.*, p. 404 as well as *ibid.*, pp. 5, 234–235, 250–251, 255–256, 303–305; consult Woltmann, *Die Darwinsche Theorie*, pp. 27–28.

10.   Woltmann, *System des moralischen Bewusstseins*, pp. 194–198.

11.   See his critical discussion of the notion of the external world being "reflected" or "pictured" in thought as it refers to both moral and epistemological issues in Woltmann, *Der historische Materialismus*, pp. 285–291.

12.   See the discussion in Woltmann, *Die Darwinsche Theorie*, pp. 259–270.

13.   See the account in *ibid.*, pp. 79–134.

14.   See the comments in Woltmann, *System des moralischen Bewusstseins*, pp. 284–285 and *Die Darwinsche Theorie*, pp. 270–275.

15.   See the discussion in Woltmann, *System des moralischen Bewusstseins*, book two, chaps. 6–9.

16.   Friedrich Engels, *The Peasant War in Germany* in Marx and Engels, *Collected Works* (New York: International Publishers, 1978; hereafter *MECW*), 10, pp. 415, 422, 469–470.

17.   Woltmann, *Die Darwinsche Theorie*, p. 3. "We can only accept the historical theory of economic materialism with qualification. We must resist the claim that the spiritual life of humanity in society is the passive reflex of economic relations. . . . What the ethicist demands is the recognition that the historical evolution to socialism is not a deterministic process like that of natural law, but rather one that follows cultural patterns that are the result of intellectual and moral forces." Woltmann, *System des moralischen Bewusstseins*, pp. 333, 338, passim pp. 333–340. "In order to fully appreciate the history of human life processes one must understand the production and reproduction of intellectual (*geistigen*) life in its highest ideological form as a self-initiating activity with its own needs, laws and goals." Woltmann, *Der historische Materialismus*, pp. 410. It was in that sense that Kant's philosophy of practical and pure reason was understood to serve Marxism as a necessary supplement. *Ibid.*, pp. 402–403 and *System des moralischen Bewusstseins*, pp. 157–167.

18.   See Kautsky's argument in his *Ethik und materialistische Geschichtsauffassung*, chap. 5, and pp. 44, 61, 63, and 67.

19.   "At the very heart of Marxist philosophy glows the pure flame of a higher human morality that seeks, with the strength of enlightenment and freedom, to find expression." Woltmann, *Der historische Materialismus*, p. 367. See Woltmann's comments, *Die Darwinsche Theorie*, pp. 52–53, 389.

20.   "Ethics cannot be physics. Physics concerns itself with [empirical] causalities. The moral world is teleological—occupied with means and ends." Woltmann, *Der historische Materialismus*, p. 398.

21.   See the sophisticated discussion in *System des moralischen Bewusstseins*, chap. 1.

22.   Another major Marxist intellectual, Max Adler, made much the same distinction in his discussion *Kant und der Marxismus* (Berlin: E. Laub'sche Verlag, 1925), particularly pp. 90–92.

23.   See the discussion in Woltmann, *System des moralischen Bewusstseins*, pp. 72–73. It is difficult to make a persuasive case for Woltmann's position without making this segment of the exposition a work on moral philosophy. It is sufficient to suggest that while feelings play a role in all judgments of truth—only in moral

judgments and ethics are feelings an intrinsic component of their truth conditions.

The distinction between "normal" and "idiosyncratic" sensory experience becomes significant at this point. By analogy, such a distinction would speak to the differences in "moral sentiment" that distinguishes individuals and groups of individuals.

24. Woltmann held that Engels, who produced the bulk of all Marxist philosophical speculation, argued fruitlessly against both Hume and Kant. See Woltmann's comments in *Der historische Materialismus*, p. v.

25. See the discussion in *ibid.*, pp. 295–297.

26. See Bernstein, *Evolutionary Socialism*, pp. 222–224 and Franz Mehring in *Die Neue Zeit*, 27 (1908–1909), 1, p. 310. In this context see the account given by Karl Vorländer, *Kant und Marx: Ein Beitrag zur Philosophie des Sozialismus* (Tübingen: Dietz Verlag, 1911).

27. Woltmann made epistemology one of the major concerns of classical Marxism. See, for example, Woltmann, *Der historische Materialismus*, p. 6. "Epistemology" is generally spoken of as an inquiry into "the nature and grounds of knowledge." For my characterization of some of its critical issues, see A. James Gregor, *Metascience and Politics: An Inquiry into the Conceptual Language of Political Science* (New Brunswick, N.J.: Transaction Publishers, 2003), particularly chap. 3.

28. Before becoming inextricably involved in economic studies, Marx had been trained as a philosopher and it seems clear that his philosophical system, had he the opportunity to publicly articulate one, would have been significantly more sophisticated than that of Engels. See A. James Gregor, *A Survey of Marxism: Problems in Philosophy and the Theory of History* (New York: Random House, 1965), chap. 2. See Woltmann, *Der historische Materialismus*, p. 2.

29. See the entire discussion in Woltmann, *Der historische Materialismus*, pp. 404–415.

30. Engels, *Ludwig Feuerbach and the End of Classical German Philosophy*, in Marx and Engels, *Selected Works* (Moscow: Foreign Languages Press, 1955; hereafter *MESW*), 2, p. 385, n. 1.

31. Engels, Letter to H. Starkenburg, 25 January 1894, in *MESW*, 2, p. 505.

32. Engels, "Principles of Communism," the reply to Question 16, in Appendix to Marx and Engels, *The Communist Manifesto* (New York: Monthly Review Press, 1998), p. 76.

33. Engels, Letter to J. Bloch, 21–22 September 1890, in *MESW*, 2, p. 489.

34. *Ibid.*

35. Marx, *Capital* (Moscow: Foreign Languages Press, 1954), 1, p. 19.

36. See the discussion in Gregor, *A Survey of Marxism*, pp. 165–169, 250–251.

37. Although the title of the study reads *Die Darwinsche Theorie und der Sozialismus*, it was clear that the "socialism" used in the title referred to Marxian socialism.

38. See his discussion in Woltmann, *ibid.*, pp. 5–8.

39. Marx, *Capital*, 1, p. 372, n. 3. Compare Woltmann, *Die Darwinsche Theorie*, p. 25 and *Der historische Materialismus*, pp. 197, 199.

40. See the account in Karl Kautsky, "Darwinismus und Marxismus," *Die Neue Zeit*, 13 (1894–1895), nr. 23, p. 709.

41. In another place in *Capital*, Marx alludes to such a symmetry when he speaks

of the "natural organs of plants and animals" and compares them to the tools used by workmen in Birmingham factories. See *ibid.*, p. 341, n. 1.

42. See Woltmann's catalog of the socialist intellectuals who found in Darwinism a support of Marxian socialism. Woltmann, *Die Darwinsche Theorie*, pp. 32–80.

43. At the time, Kautsky spoke without qualification of the primacy of tools and technology, in general, with respect to the "superstructural" activity of associated humankind. See Kautsky, *Ethik und Historische Materialismus*, pp. 127–132, particularly p. 128. See Woltmann's affirmation of the same technological interpretation of historical materialism. Woltmann, *Der historische Materialismus*, pp. 324, 340–341 and *Die Darwinsche Theorie*, pp. 247–259.

44. In his *Die Darwinsche Theorie*, Woltmann reviewed the ample literature generated by those who saw the two theories as mutually supportive and those who saw Darwinism as a refutation of Marxism. At the time, in his *Ethik und materialistische Geschichtsauffassung*, Kautsky attempted to illustrate the compatibility of the two—without much enthusiasm or success.

45. See the discussion in Woltmann, *Der historische Materialismus*, pp. 321–330.

46. See Engels, *Anti-Dühring: Herr Eugen Dühring's Revolution in Science* (Moscow: Foreign Languages Publishing House, 1962), p. 374; see *ibid.*, pp. 97–107.

47. Marx did express some qualifying reservations, but it is evident that he considered Darwin a paradigmatic scientist. Had that not been the case, Engels would not have compared the two over Marx's grave.

48. See Woltmann, *Die Darwinsche Theorie*, pp. iii, iv, 29–31, *Der historische Materialismus*, pp. 210–216.

49. Engels, "The Part Played by Labour in the Transition from Ape to Man," *MESW*, 2, pp. 80–81, 84, 85.

50. By the time Woltmann reported on Engels's thesis, he was writing, without qualification, of biological heredity in terms of Mendelian and Weismannian laws. He clearly dismissed the Lamarckian notions of the inheritance of acquired characteristics. See Woltmann, *Die Darwinsche Theorie*, pp. 208–234, 504; see his comments on Lamarckianism, *Der historische Materialismus*, p. 322.

51. Woltmann, *Die Germanen und die Renaissance in Italien* (Leipzig: Justus Dörner Verlag, 1936; a reprint of the 1905 edition), p. 31.

52. Woltmann, *Politische Anthropologie: Eine Untersuchung über den Einfluss der Descendenztheorie auf die Lehre von der politischen Entwicklung der Völker* (Jena: Verlegt bei Eugen Diederichs, n.d. but probably 1904), pp. 23–35.

53. See Engels, "Speech at the Graveside of Karl Marx," *MESW*, 2, p. 167.

54. Engels, *The Origin of the Family, Private Property and the State*, *MESW*, 2, pp. 170–171; see Woltmann's comments, *Die Darwinsche Theorie*, p. 26 and *Der historische Materialismus*, pp. 218–219.

55. Woltmann, *Der historische Materialismus*, p. 166.

56. See the discussion in *ibid.*, pp. 328–330.

57. "Apart from the degree of development, greater or less, in the form of social production, the productiveness of labor is fettered by physical conditions. These are all referable to the constitution of man himself (race, etc.) . . ." Marx, *Capital*, p. 512.

58. Engels, letter to H. Starkenburg, 25 January 1894, *MESW*, 2, p. 504.

59. "Castes and guilds arise from the action of the same natural law that regu-

lates the differentiation of plants and animals into species and varieties . . ." Marx went on to speak of the laws of heredity, and the "natural selection" that "preserves or suppresses each small variation . . ." *Capital*, p. 340 and n. 1 together with p. 341, n. 1. See Woltmann's comments in *Der historische Materialismus*, pp. 199, 329.

60. See Woltmann, *Politische Anthropologie*, chaps. 5, 7–9.

61. Marx regularly formulated his views in the following synoptic fashion: "Technology discloses man's mode of dealing with Nature, the process of production by which he sustains his life, and thereby also lays bare the mode of formation of his social relations, and the mental conceptions that flow from them." *Capital*, 1, p. 372, n. 3.

62. See the discussion in Woltmann, *Die Darwinsche Theorie*, pp. 313–314, 329, 331, 338–341.

63. *Politische Anthroplogie*, pp. 1–2; confer pp. 4–7, 10–12, 91–93.

64. *Ibid.*, pp. 149–153.

65. Friedrich Engels, "Democratic Panslavism," in P. W. Blackstock and B. F. Hoselitz (eds.), *The Russian Menace to Europe* (Glencoe, Ill.: The Free Press, 1952), pp. 71, 72, 75, 76.

66. *Ibid.*, p. 72.

67. Karl Marx, "Revolution in China and in Europe" (*New York Daily Tribune*, 14 June 1853), in *Marx on China* (London: Lawrence & Wishart, 1968), p. 3; Friedrich Engels, "Hungary and Panslavism," in *The Russian Menace to Europe*, p. 63.

68. Karl Marx, "Panslavism—The Schleswig Holstein War," in Eleanor Marx Aveling (ed.), *Revolution and Counter Revolution* (London: Unwin, 1971), p. 48.

69. Friedrich Engels, "Po und Rhein," in Marx and Engels, *Werke* (Berlin: Dietz Verlag, 1959), 13, p. 267.

70. Engels, "Hungary and Panslavism," *The Russian Menace to Europe*, p. 61.

71. "For entirely morphological and physiological reasons one must come to the conclusion that the race of robust and large skulled humans with facial dolichocephaly and light pigmentation—the north European race—is the most perfect representive of the human race and the most advanced product of organic evolution . . . [as well as] the most culture-capable. The world's foremost culture creators are representatives of that race or individuals that show a strong intermixture of Germanic blood in their veins." Woltmann, *Politische Anthropologie*, pp. 254, 255.

72. Woltmann, *Die Germanen und die Renaissance in Italien* (Leipzig: Justus Dörner Verlag, 1936; reprint of the 1905 edition) and *Die Germanen in Frankreich* (Leipzig: Justus Dörner Verlag, 1936; reprint of the 1907 edition).

73. Even those most enthusiastic about Woltmann's racism admitted that some considerable part of his research was seriously flawed. See the candid comments of O. Reche, "Vorwort des Herausgebers," *Die Germanen und die Renaissance in Italien*, pp. 7–21.

74. *Ibid.*, p. 39.

75. Moses Hess, *Rom und Jerusalem*, in Horst Lademacher (ed.), *Ausgewählte Schriften* (Cologne: Akademische Verlag, 1962). An English translation is available as *Rome and Jerusalem* (New York: Philosophical Library, 1958). I have offered a brief discussion of Hess's work in A. James Gregor, *The Faces of Janus: Marxism and Fascism in the Twentieth Century* (New Haven: Yale University Press, 2000), pp. 159–161.

76. See the discussion in Woltmann, *Politische Anthropologie*, pp. 317–326.

77. *Ibid.*, pp. 307–309.

78. There was a substantial body of racist literature that preceded the war. Among the most important works were Arthur Gobineau's *Essai sur l'inégalité des races humaines* (an abridged English version is available as *The Inequality of Human Races* [New York: G. P. Putnam's Sons, 1915]) that appeared in the mid-1850s, about the time of the publication of Gustav Friedrich Klemm's *Die Verbreitung der aktiven Menschenrasse über den Erdball*. In 1879, Gobineau prepared a manuscript published years later as *Die Bedeutung der Rasse im Leben der Völker* (Munich: J. F. Lehmanns Verlag, 1926). By the 1880s, Karl Penka published his works on the origin of the Aryans and G. Vacher de Lapouge's lectures on the same subject appeared. Between the 1870s and the 1880s the works of Paul de Lagarde on race and history were published. At the turn of the century, Woltmann's works appeared at about the same time as those of Houston Steward Chamberlain, the author of *Die Grundlagen des 19. Jahrhunderts* (*The Foundations of the Nineteenth Century* [London: John Lane, 1911]). Immediately before his accidental death, Woltmann served as editor of *Politisch-Anthropologische Revue*. After the war there was a proliferation of such material. For an account of the history of *Rassenkunde* ("race science") in Germany, see Hans F. K. Günther, *Rassenkunde des deutschen Volkes* (Munich: J. F. Lehmanns Verlag, 1922), chap. 2. See the discussion in Theophile Simar, *Etude critique sur la formation de la doctrine des races au XVIIIe Siécle* (Brusselles: Marcel Hayez, 1922), chaps. 5–8.

79. See the references to Woltmann in the works of Günther, who was to receive the first National Socialist Gold Medal for science. See, for example, his *Rassenkunde des deutschen Volkes*, and his *Der nordische Gedanke unter den Deutschen* (Munich: J. F. Lehmanns Verlag, 1925).

80. See the discussion in A. James Gregor, *Contemporary Radical Ideologies: Totalitarian Thought in the Twentieth Century* (New York: Random House, 1968), chap. 5.

81. V. I. Lenin, "Karl Marx," *Collected Works*, 21, pp. 85, 87, 88.

4. THE HETERODOX MARXISM OF GEORGES SOREL

1. Only in 1888, after the death of Marx, did Engels make a modest attempt to define the critical terms "bourgeoisie" and "proletariat." See footnote number 1 to *The Communist Manifesto*. See Sorel's comment, Georges Sorel, *Saggi di critica del Marxismo* (Milan: Sandron, 1903), p. 276, n. 3; and the discussion in A. James Gregor, *The Fascist Persuasion in Radical Politics* (Princeton: Princeton University Press, 1974), pp. 26–31.

2. At the end of the nineteenth century, Benedetto Croce could lament that the work of Karl Marx was far from easy to understand, not only because of the intrinsic difficulty of the subject matter, but because "anyone who desired to reconcile all the forms with which Marx and Engels have endowed it would stumble upon contradictory expressions, which would make it impossible for the careful and methodical interpreter to decide what, on the whole, historical materialism meant for them"—and further, with respect to the account provided in *Das Kapital*, "throughout, [Marx] despised and neglected all such preliminary and exact explanations as might have made his task plain." He states, in conclusion, that he is un-

certain how many of the "concepts and opinions expressed by Marx . . . deserve to undergo revision," but insists that "Marx, as a sociologist, has in truth not given us carefully worked out definitions." Croce, *Historical Materialism and the Economics of Karl Marx* (New York: The Macmillan Company, 1914), pp. 49, 78–79, 115, 118; see further comments on pp. 55, 70–71.

3. Karl Kautsky, *Die materialistische Geschichtsauffassung* (Berlin: Verlag J. H. W. Dietz, 1929), pp. 196–197.

4. Roberto Michels, *Storia del Marxismo in Italia* (Rome: Luigi Mongini, Editore, 1909), pp. 8–9.

5. See the contemporary discussion in the preface to *ibid.* Years later Michels referred to the work of Antonio Graziadei as a major representative of revisionism in Italy. See the discussion in Michels, *La teoria di C. Marx sulla miseria crescente e le sue origini* (Turin: Fratelli Bocca, 1922), pp. 184–185. In 1897, Saverio Merlino published *Pro e contro il socialismo: Esposizione critica dei principii e dei sistemi socialisti* (Milano: Fratelli Treves, 1897), which both reflected many of the analyses of Bernstein and anticipated others that were to subsequently transform Marxism as a twentieth-century revolutionary creed.

6. Jules Guesde, *Le Socialisme au jour le jour* (Paris: Revell, 1899), p. 268.

7. See the account in Hubert Lagardelle, "Le Syndicalisme et le Socialisme en France," *Syndicalisme & Socialisme* (Paris: Librairie des Sciences Politiques & Sociales, 1908), pp. 35–54.

8. See the contemporary discussion in Werner Sombart, *Socialism and the Social Movement* (New York: Augustus M. Kelley, 1968; reprint of 1908 edition), chap. 5.

9. Georges Sorel, "L'Avenir socialiste des syndicats," *L'Humanité nouvelle*, I, no. 9 (March 1898), particularly pp. 304–306. "L'Avenir" was reprinted in its entirety in *Matériaux d'une théorie du prolétariat* (Paris: Marcel Riviere, 1921).

10. See Benedetto Croce, *Materialismo storico ed economia Marxista* (Bari: Gius. Laterza & Figli, 1951; revised ninth edition, originally published in 1897), p. 62. Croce's judgment was made in 1897 and was never revised.

11. There is an abundance of competent scholarly work on the thought of Sorel. Among the best, in the context of the central discussion of the present work, is that by Zeev Sternhell (with Mario Sznajder and Maia Asheri), *The Birth of Fascist Ideology: From Cultural Rebellion to Political Revolution* (Princeton: Princeton University Press, 1994), chap. 1. The work by James H. Meisel, *The Genesis of Georges Sorel* (Ann Arbor, Michigan: George Wahr, 1951) offers rich resources. Pierre Andreu, *Notre maitre, M. Sorel* (Paris: Bernard Grasset, 1953) is an insightful account by one of Sorel's more intimate followers.

12. Georges Sorel, *Contribution à l'étude profane de la Bible* (Paris: Marcel Riviere, 1889) and *Le Proces de Socrate* (Paris: Marcel Riviere, 1889).

13. See the comments in Meisel, *The Genesis of Georges Sorel*, pp. 15–19; Giuseppe La Ferla. *Ritratto di Georges Sorel* (Milan: "La Cultura," 1933), chaps. 2–3.

14. See Edouard Berth's Preface to Georges Sorel, *D'Aristote à Marx (L'Ancienne et la Nouvelle Métaphysique)* (Paris: Marcel Riviere, 1935; a reprint of the article of 1894), p. 3, and his Introduction, *ibid.*, pp. 7–10.

15. *Ibid.*, p. 94. See the discussion in Paolo Pastori, *Rivoluzione e continuità in Proudhon e Sorel* (Varese: Giufre, 1980), chap. 2, particularly pp. 49–50.

16. The Italian edition appeared in 1895, published in Bari by Laterza. The

French edition which contained Sorel's preface appeared as *Essais sur la conception matérialiste de l'histoire* (Paris: Giard et Briere, 1897). Labriola's book is available in English translation as *Essays on the Materialistic Conception of History* (Chicago: Charles H. Kerr, 1904).

17. "The publication of this work marks a date in the history of socialism." Sorel went on to affirm that Labriola's work was comparable to "the classics of Marx and Engels." Sorel, Preface to Labriola, *Essais*, p. 19.

18. Labriola, *Essays*, pp. 35, 152. Elsewhere he says that while society is so complicated "that it conceals the economic substructure which supports all the rest," it is evident that "the laws of economics . . . have shown themselves to be the directing power of social life." *Ibid.*, pp. 143, 167.

19. *Ibid.*, pp. 9, 15; on p. 48, Labriola provides a standard Marxist definition of the "material means" and "relations of production." Labriola spoke without qualification of the "intrinsic and imminent necessity of the revolution," and of the "objective necessity" of the processes of history. See *ibid.*, pp. 26, 29, 30, 34, 73, 81.

20. *Ibid.*, pp. 17–19.

21. *Ibid.*, pp. 72, 74–75, 101, 110. Labriola spoke of persons acting "not by free choice, but because they could not act otherwise." *Ibid.*, p. 99.

22. One need only consult Friedrich Engels, *Anti-Dühring: Herr Eugen Dühring's Revolution in Science* (Moscow: Foreign Languages Publishing House, 1962), part one, chapters 9 through 11, in which we are told that "all moral theories have been hitherto the product, in the last analysis, of the economic conditions of society," and are to be studied as any science is studied, by seeking material causes "reflected" in human consciousness. *Ibid.*, pp. 131, 134. In *The Communist Manifesto*, Marx asserted that "your very ideas are but the outgrowth of the conditions of . . . bourgeois production." Karl Marx and Friedrich Engels, "Manifesto of the Communist Party," in Marx and Engels, *Selected Works in Two Volumes* (Moscow: Foreign Languages Publishing House, 1955), 1, p. 49. In the Preface to Marx's *The Critique of Political Economy*, we are told that "It is not the consciousness of men that determines their being, but, on the contrary, their social being that determines their consciousness." *Ibid.*, p. 363. If one wishes to understand moral, legal, religious, and philosophical ideas, one is required to study "material conditions of production." In principle, that would seem to reduce all those disciplines to the status of empirical sciences.

23. Edouard Berth, in writing the preface to Sorel, *D'Aristote à Marx*, p. 3, so identified him.

24. Labriola, *Essays on the Materialistic Conception of History*, pp. 124, 152–154.

25. *Ibid.*, p. 64. Elsewhere, Labriola states that "man has made his history not by a metaphorical evolution nor with a view of walking on a line of preconceived progress. He has made it by creating his own conditions, that is to say, by creating through his labor an artificial environment, by developing successively his technical aptitudes. . . . Where shall we find the laws of this formation and of this development? The very ancient formations are not evident at first sight. . . . [We find] embryonic traces of its origin and its processus. . . . In fact in different countries it has different modes of development." *Ibid.*, pp. 77–78. There clearly is enough room in this kind of speculation for human will and volition to operate to considerable effect.

26. Georges Sorel, Preface to Labriola, *Essais sur la conception matérialiste de l'histoire*, p. 7.

27. See Sorel, *Saggi di critica del Marxismo*, pp. 48, 70, 88–89, 123–125, 241, 248 n. 2, 277–278, 302.

28. *Ibid.*, pp. 12–15.

29. Georges Sorel, *Le procès de Socrate* (Paris: F. Alcan, 1889), p. 329, and "De la cause en physique," *Revue philosophique de la France et de l'etranger*, 13, part 26 (1888), p. 471 and *Saggi di critica del Marxismo*, p. 181. Years later, Sorel made essentially the same point in Sorel, *De l'utilité du Pragmatisme* (Paris: Marcel Riviere, 1928; second edition), pp. 194–210.

30. Sorel, *Le procès de Socrate*, p. 316.

31. See the discussion in Georges Sorel, "Essai sur la philosophie de Proudhon," *Revue philosophique de la France et de l'etranger*, 13, part 33 (1892), p. 635.

32. See the entire discussion in Paolo Pastori, "Natura e umanità in Sorel," *Storia e politica*, 9, 3 (July–September 1970), pp. 445–461.

33. See Sorel, *La procès de Socrate*, particularly pp. 239, 316, and 330–332.

34. See the discussion in Georges Sorel, "Essai sur la philosophie de Proudhon," *Revue philosophique e la France et de l'étranger*, 17, 33 (1892), pp. 634–655. Proudhon had made a distinction between the material and/or biological influences on human conduct, but emphasized the role of ethical judgment in its vindication. See the discussion in Pierre-Joseph Proudhon, *Qu'est-ce que la propriété?* chap. 4, part 1.

35. See the discussion in Sorel, "Essai sur la philsophie de Proudhon," 17, 34, pp. 44–65 and *La procès du Socrate* and *Contribution à l'étude de la Bible* (Paris: A. Ghio, 1889), passim.

36. See the intimations in Georges Sorel, "Science et socialisme," *Revue philosophique de la France et de l'étranger*, 18, 35 (1893), pp. 510–512 and the account to be found in "Essai sur la philosophie de Proudhon," 34, pp. 43–47.

37. Sorel, *D'Aristote à Marx*, pp. 253, 260–261.

38. *Ibid.*, p. 263.

39. In one place, where he addresses the apparent "incompatibility of rational science and idealistic morals," he speaks of resolution being impossible as long as "there remains the insistence that individuals continue to be conceived entirely separate from each other, as though each one constituted a species unto itself, like the angels in Thomistic doctrine." Sorel, *D'Aristote à Marx*, pp. 177–178; see *ibid.*, p. 260.

40. It is clear that Sorel perceived the ethical potential of the emerging industrial world. He maintained that Marx "could not help but seek the fundamental principles of ethics in the human phenomena that develop around machinery." *Ibid.*, p. 260. Sorel said, "I am persuaded that work can serve as a basis for a culture that would give no cause to regret the passing of bourgeois civilization." Sorel, *The Illusion of Progress* (Berkeley: University of California Press, 1969), p. 157.

41. Karl Marx, *Capital* (Moscow: Foreign Languages Publishing House, 1954), I, p. 372, n. 3.

42. Woltmann referred to the same passage in *Capital* in order to make his point that the materialist conception of history ultimately turned on the creativity of individuals and groups. See Ludwig Woltmann, *Die Darwinsche Theorie und der*

Sozialismus (Düsseldorf: Hermann Michels Verlag, 1899), p. 25 and *Der historische Materialismus* (Düsseldorf: Hermann Michels Verlag, 1900), pp. 197–199.

43. See Georges Sorel, "Etude sur Vico," *Le devenir social*, 2, no. 9 (October 1896), pp. 809–813 and his discussion concerning the role of race in the process, *Saggi di critica del Marxismo*, pp. 95–108, 186.

44. The biological variant now identified with Woltmann did not fully manifest itself until the appearance of Ludwig Woltmann, *Politische Anthropologie*, which appeared after the turn of the twentieth century.

45. Croce was never an orthodox Marxist, but out of his initial enthusiasm, the consequence of his mentoring of Antonio Labriola, he published his first analysis of Marxism as an interpretation of history in 1896. See Benedetto Croce, "Sulla concezione materialistica della storia," *Atti dell'Accademia Pontaniana di Napoli*, 26 (3 May 1896), reprinted in *Materialismo storico ed economia Marxistica* (Bari: Giuseppe Laterza, 1951; ninth edition), pp. 1–20. In the same context, the work of Saverio Merlino, *Pro e contro il socialismo* (Milan: Treves, 1897), deserves mention.

46. Sorel, "Etude sur Vico," *Le devenir social*, 2, no. 9 (October 1896), particularly pp. 800–813, and 2, no. 11 (November 1896), particularly pp. 938–940. See the comments of Giovanni Santonastaso, *Studi di pensiero politico* (Naples: Giannini, 1973), pp. 137–139.

47. See Sorel, *Matériaux d'une théorie du prolétariat* (Paris: M. Riviere, 1921), pp. 252–253.

48. Marx, *Capital*, 1, p. 372, n. 3.

49. Sorel, "Pro e contro il socialismo," *Le devenir social*, 3, no. 10 (October 1897), pp. 854–888 and Benedetto Croce, "Come nacque e come mori il Marxismo teorico in Italia (1896–1900)," in *Materialismo storico ed economia marxistica*, pp. 271–316. In a letter to Croce, Labriola identified Bernstein, Merlino, and Sorel as those intellectuals responsible for the unraveling of classical Marxism. Labriola, *ibid.*, p. 314.

50. See Sorel, *Saggi di critica del Marxismo*, pp. 139–142, 272–274, 302, 306, 334–336.

51. See Sorel, "La necessità e il fatalismo nel marxismo," *La riforma sociale* 5, no. 8 (15 August 1898), pp. 708–732; "La crisi del socialismo scientifico," *Critica sociale*, 8 (1898), pp. 134–138; "L'éthique du socialisme," *Revue de Metaphysique et de Moral*, 7 (1899), particularly pp. 296–297.

52. Sorel, "L'avenir socialiste des syndicats," *L'Humanité nouvelle*, 1, no. 9 (March, April, and May 1898), particularly pp. 304–306 and 435–440.

53. Labriola, *Essays on the Materialist Conception of History*, p. 65.

54. Sorel, *Introduction à l'économie moderne* (Paris: M. Riviere, 1922; twelfth enlarged edition), pp. 36–38, 55, 153–156.

55. Sorel's relationship to Proudhon is both well known and equally well documented. For some of Sorel's views see, for example, G. Sorel, "Essai sur la philosophie de Proudhon, *Revue philosophique*, 23–24 (June–July 1892), pp. 622–638, 41–68. One of the best accounts of the relationship is Pastori, *Rivoluzione e continuità in Proudhon e Sorel*.

56. See Karl Marx, "On Proudhon," in Karl Marx and Friedrich Engels, *Selected Works in Two Volumes* (Moscow: Foreign Languages Publishing House, 1955), 1, p. 391.

57. The subsequent discussion will follow the argument in Georges Sorel, *Introducion à l'économie moderne*, originally published in 1903.

58. See the discussion in G. Sorel, "L'Éthique du socialisme," *Revue de la métaphysique et de la morale* (May 1899), particularly pp. 12–14.

59. "*Ricorso*" is sometimes translated as "reflux," an awkward, but perhaps accurate rendering. Vico's *ricorso* was a restorative reaction, a rebirth of an ancient glory.

60. See *ibid.*, particularly pp. 127 and 357.

61. See the discussion in Richard Humphrey, *Georges Sorel: Prophet Without Honor* (Cambridge: Harvard University Press, 1951), pp. 70–71.

62. As has been indicated, Karl Kautsky, as late as the final years of the 1920s, was prepared to acknowledge that Woltmann's heterodoxy was reasonable. See Karl Kautsky, *Die materialistische Geschichtsauffassung* (Berlin: J. H. W. Dietz, 1929), I, p. 197.

63. Georges Sorel, *Réflexions sur la violence* (Paris: M. Rivere, 1908); in English as *Reflections on Violence* (London: Collier-Macmillan, 1950).

64. Edward Shils's introduction to the English language edition, Sorel, *Reflections on Violence*, p. 15.

65. The introduction by Edward Shils to the American edition of *Relections on Violence*, pp. 13–29, provides an instructive summary of Sorel's work.

66. Unhappily, Sorel's exposition in *Réflexions* is no more coherently structured or transparent than any of his earlier works. Any number of different interpretations have been drawn from his texts. There is no pretense that the present interpretation is the only correct, or the only possible, rendering.

67. Sorel, *Reflections on Violence*, p. 40.

68. See *ibid.*, pp. 40–41, 43, 50–51, 104–105, 112–113, 117, 136–137, 234–242, 249–252, 254, 267–269, 274–278. The appendix, "Unity and Multiplicity," added to the text by Sorel in 1910 is instructive in all these regards.

69. See Sorel's comments to Daniel Halevy in the Introduction to *ibid.*, pp. 36–40.

70. See the discussion in *ibid.*, pp. 286–287.

71. *Ibid.*, p. 247.

72. See *ibid.*, pp. 35, 59, 67–68, 107, 159 n. 37, 200 and n. 43.

73. See *ibid.*, pp. 250, 252, 254.

74. See *ibid.*, pp. 213, 298.

75. In several places Sorel speaks of the "masses" and the "workers" as "not accustomed to thinking." They require some sort of intervention, either by life or by mentors of some sort. He speaks of the "moral progress of the proletariat" as necessary to the regenerative revolution. It is clear from his exposition that Sorel is convinced that populations can be taught servility—or heroism and moral rectitude. See *ibid.*, pp. 213, 250, 292, 296.

76. *Ibid.*, pp. 298, 300.

77. *Ibid.*, pp. 58–59, 140, 142–143.

78. *Ibid.*, pp. 57, 144; see p. 147.

79. *Ibid.*, pp. 48–49, 234.

80. *Ibid.*, p. 301; see p. 234.

81. Sorel to Daniel Halevy, "Introduction," *Reflections*, p. 53.

82. Henri Bergson, *Essai sur les données immédiates de la conscience* (Paris: Alcan, 1889)—an English translation is available as *Time and Free Will: An Essay on the Immediate Data of Consciousness* (New York: Macmillan, 1913); *L'Evolution créatrice* (Paris: Alcan, 1907)—with an English translation, *Creative Evolution* (New York: Henry Holt, 1911).

83. See the discussion in Bergson, *Creative Evolution*, pp. 98, 153–165; and Bergson, "Introduction à la Métaphysique," *Revue de Métaphysique et de Morale*, January 1905, pp. 9–15, 27–31.

84. See the discussion in Bergson, *Creative Evolution*, pp. 208, 218–219, 238.

85. See *ibid.*, pp. 237, 267–268.

86. Sorel, "Letter to Daniel Halevy," *Reflections on Violence*, p. 53.

87. See Sorel, "Etude sur Vico," pp. 796–797.

88. See the notable discussion in Sorel, *De l'utilité du Pragmatisme*, chap. 4; and "Le systeme des mathématiques," *Revue de Métaphysique et de Morale*, 8 (1900), pp. 407–428; "Sur divers aspects de la mécanique," *ibid.*, 11 (1903), pp. 716–748.

89. See the discussion in Sorel, *Saggi di critica del Marxismo*, pp. 33, 170–171, 177, 234, 266, 290, and Meisel, *The Genesis of Georges Sorel*, pp. 114–115.

90. See the discussion in "Letter to Daniel Halevy," *Reflections on Violence*, pp. 50–53.

91. See Sorel, "Les polemiques pour l'interprétation du marxisme," *La Revue Internationale de Sociologie* (April–May 1900), reprinted as a separate by Giard & Briere in Paris in 1900; and Sorel's comments in the Introduction to *The Decomposition of Marxism*, in Irving L. Horowitz, *Radicalism and the Revolt Against Reason: The Social Theories of Georges Sorel* (New York: The Humanities Press, 1961), pp. 211–218.

92. Bergson, *Creative Evolution*, p. 139.

93. See the discussion in Sorel, "La necessità e il fatalismo nel Marxismo," *Saggi di critica del Marxismo*, pp. 59–94; and *Reflections on Violence*, p. 142.

94. Sorel quoting the *Journal de Geneve*, 4 February 1918, in *Reflections on Violence*, pp. 303–304.

5. THE HETERODOX MARXISM OF V. I. LENIN

1. Max Hirschberg, "Bolschewismus: Versuch einer prinzipiellen Kritik des revolutionären Sozialismus," *Archiv für Sozialwissenschaft und Sozialpolitik*, 48 (1920/1921), pp. 4–5.

2. Whatever French or Italian revolutionary thought penetrated into the confines of Marxist orthodoxy among Russians was rejected with dispatch. Before the end of the first decade of the twentieth century, Plekhanov summarily dismissed syndicalist thought as it found expression in Arturo Labriola's *Riforme e rivoluzione sociale* (Naples: Partenopea, 1904). See Georgi Plekhanov, *Sindicalismo y marxismo* (Mexico, D. F.: Grijalbo, 1968).

3. Georgi Plekhanov, *The Development of the Monist View of History*, in *Selected Philosophical Works* (Moscow: Foreign Languages Publishing House, n.d.), 1, pp. 653–654. In the section cited, Plekhanov quotes from Karl Marx, "Wage Labour

and Capital," in Karl Marx and Friedrich Engels, *Selected Works* (Moscow: Foreign Languages Publishing House, 1955), I, pp. 89–90.

4. Plekhanov, *The Development of the Monist View of History*, pp. 673, 676, 682, 690, 691, 704, 705, 712, 724.

5. "Marxism is Darwinism in its application to social science." *Ibid.*, p. 740, n.

6. "The historical progress of humanity is determined by the development of the productive forces," which, in turn, determine the appearance of "human ideas, feelings, aspirations and ideas." *Ibid.*, p. 727. See *ibid.*, pp. 719, 724, 727.

7. *Ibid.*, pp. 742, 751, 754, 761–762, 779–780.

8. *Ibid.*, pp. 648–649, 658, and 783–784; see also V. Fomina, "Introductory Essay," to *ibid.*, pp. 17, 28–29.

9. V. I. Lenin, *What is to be Done?* in *Collected Works* (Moscow: Foreign Languages Publishing House, 1961; hereafter *LCW*), 5, pp. 347–529.

10. Ludwig Woltmann, *Der historische Materialismus: Darstellung und Kritik der Marxistischen Weltanschauung* (Düsseldorf: Michels' Verlag, 1900), chap. 4. See A. James Gregor, *A Survey of Marxism: Problems of Philosophy and the Theory of History* (New York: Random House, 1965), pp. 38–39.

11. Sorel found the same evidences that Marx considered race a factor in historical development, but assigned it a far more restricted role than did Woltmann. Sorel cites the same reference to race referred to by Woltmann; see Georges Sorel, *Saggi di critica del Marxismo* (Milan: Sandron, 1903), p. 186, and the entire discussion of the role of race as a factor on pp. 95–108.

12. See the contemporary discussion by Rosa Luxemburg, *Social Reform or Revolution* (Colombo, Ceylon: A Young Socialist Publication, 1966; reprint of the 1900 edition) and Werner Sombart, *Socialism and the Social Movement* (New York: Augustus M. Kelley Publishers, 1968; reprint of the 1908 edition), chap. 4.

13. Karl Kautsky, *Der Weg zur Macht: Politische Betrachtungen über des Hineinwachsen in die Revolution* (Berlin: Buchhandlung Vorwärts, 1909), chap. 4.

14. See the entire discussion in Labriola, *Riforme e rivoluzione sociale*, chap. 6.

15. See the standard account in Kautsky, *Die Soziale Revolution: Am Tage nach der sozialen Revolution* (Berlin: Buchhandlung Vorwärts, 1904), pp. 14–21, 25–27; Kautsky and Bruno Schoenlank, *Grundsätze und Forderungen der Sozialdemokratie: Erläuterungen zum Erfurter Programm* (Berlin: Buchhandlung Vorwärts, 1905), pp. 5–6, 9–14, 23–27. The ultimate reference is, of course, the economic works of Marx and the commentaries by Engels.

16. Kautsky, *The Class Struggle (Erfurt Program)* (New York: W. W. Norton and Company, 1971; originally published in German in 1892), p. 90.

17. Kautsky, *Der Weg zur Macht*, pp. 47–48.

18. See the standard account in Kautsky, *The Class Struggle*, chaps. 2, 3 and 5, particularly pp. 32–33, 89, 90, 94, 116–119, 161, 191.

19. "The conditions of life determine the manner in which the will manfests itself." Kautsky, *Der Weg zur Macht*, p. 49.

20. See Kautsky, *Die Soziale Revolution*, pp. 45–46.

21. Kautsky, *The Class Struggle*, p. 90.

22. *Ibid.*, p. 115.

23. Kautsky, *Der Weg zur Macht*, pp. 58–59, 117.

24. Plekhanov argued that, in the last analysis, economic conditions would create enough leaders of suitable conviction that the anticipated inevitabilities would result. See the discussion in Plekhanov, *The Role of the Individual in History* (New York: International Publishers, 1955).

25. Kautsky, *The Class Struggle*, p. 199.

26. V. I. Lenin, "What the 'Friends of the People' Are and How They Fight the Social Democrats," *LCW*, 1, pp. 136, 138.

27. *Ibid.*, pp. 140–141, 142.

28. See the account in Rolf H. W. Theen, *Lenin: Genesis and Development of a Revolutionary* (Princeton: Princeton University Press, 1973), chap. 4, particularly pp. 103–114; Adam Ulam, *The Bolsheviks* (New York: The Macmillan Company, 1965), particularly p. 178.

29. See the account in Louis Fischer, *The Life of Lenin* (New York: Harper & Row, Publishers, 1964), chap. 4, particularly p. 59.

30. See his discussion in Lenin, "The Tasks of the Russian Social-Democrats," *LCW*, 2, pp. 330–334.

31. Lenin, "What the 'Friends of the People' Are," *LCW*, 2, pp. 165, 166.

32. See the account in Kautsky and Schönlank, *Grundsätze und Forderungen der Sozialdemokratie: Erläuteungen zum Erfurter Programm*, and Kautsky, *The Class Struggle (Erfurt Program)* (New York: W. W. Norton & Company, 1971; a translation of the 1892 edition).

33. See the discussion in Peter Gay, *The Dilemma of Democratic Socialism: Eduard Bernstein's Challenge to Marx* (New York: Collier Books, 1962), chap. 2, particularly pp. 62–64.

34. Engels, "Principles of Communism," in Marx and Engels, *Collected Works* (New York: International Publishders, 1976), 4, pp. 349.

35. As has been suggested, Woltmann had grave reservations about the automatic quality of imagined human response to the revolutionary demands of the "economic base." Arturo Labriola complained that the "system of Marx" had given rise to the persistent "legend" that "the evolution of human society is accomplished in a mechanical and automatic manner . . . in a direction that is mathematically determinate." Labriola, *Riforme e rivoluzione sociale*, p. 135.

36. See Kautsky's commentary on the draft program of the Austrian Social Democratic party in *Neue Zeit*, 20 (1901–1902), part 1, no. 3, p. 79.

37. Marx and Engels, *The Communist Manifesto* (New York: Monthly Review Press, 1998), p. 20.

38. See a discussion of the fundamental doctrinal change involved in A. James Gregor, *The Fascist Persuasion in Radical Politics* (Princeton: Princeton University Press, 1974), pp. 189–191.

39. Lenin, "Where to Begin," "On the Twenty-Fifth Anniversary of the Revolutionary Activity of G. V. Plekhanov," *LCW*, 5, pp. 17, 321.

40. Lenin, "A Talk with Defenders of Economism," *LCW*, 5, p. 316.

41. *Ibid.*

42. *Ibid.*, p. 320.

43. See the discussion in Lenin, "One Step Forward, Two Steps Back (The Crisis in our Party)," *LCW*, 7, p. 206.

44. Lenin, "What is to be Done? *LCW*, 5, pp. 365, 369.

45. *Ibid.*, pp. 353, 355, 371, 372.

46. *Ibid.*, pp. 421–424.

47. *Ibid.*, p. 347.

48. See the discussions in *One Step Forward, Two Steps Back (The Crisis in our Party)*, *LCW*, 7, pp. 242, 245, 251, 293, 387–389, 394, 396, 399, 400, 404–406.

49. *Ibid.*, pp. 392–393; see the regular references to "anarchists" and "opportunists" to identify those, who in his judgment, do not understand the merits of ideological consistency, party discipline, and hierarchical controls. *Ibid.*, pp. 256–259, 262, 274, 277, 284–286, 327, 345, 347, 348, 357, 359, 360, 364, 366–367, 371–375, 382–388, 391–395, 403, 410.

50. *Ibid.*, pp. 403–404.

51. "The theory of socialism . . . grew out of the philosophic, historical, and economic theories elaborated by educated representatives of the propertied classes, by intellectuals." Lenin, "What is to be Done?" *LCW*, 5, p. 375.

52. See the assessment in Rosa Luxemburg, *The Russian Revolution and Leninism or Marxism?* (Ann Arbor: University of Michigan Press, 1961), pp. 96–97.

53. Lenin, "What is to be Done?" *LCW*, 5, p. 452. Lenin tells us that those sufficiently talented to discharge such functions "are not born by the hundreds." *Ibid.*, p. 461.

54. "We are the party of a class, and therefore almost the entire class . . . should act under the leadership of our Party, should adhere to our Party as closely as possible. . . . To forget the distinction between the vanguard and the whole of the masses gravitating towards it, to forget the vanguard's constant duty of raising ever wider sections to its own advanced level, means simply to deceive oneself . . ." Lenin, "One Step Forward, Two Steps Back," *LCW*, 7, pp. 260, 261.

55. See the discussion in Theen, *Lenin: Genesis and Development of a Revolutionary*, chap. 4, particularly p. 115.

56. Engels, *The Peasant War in Germany*, *MECW*, 10, pp. 470–471.

57. Luxemburg, *The Russian Revolution and Leninism and Marxism?*, p. 88.

58. *Ibid.*, pp. 86–91.

59. Engels, "Principles of Communism," in Marx and Engels, *The Communist Manifesto*, Question 19, p. 80. As has been suggested both authors used such locutions throughout their work.

60. See the account in Daniel Guerin, *Rosa Luxemburg et la spontanéité révolutionnaire* (Paris: Flammarion, 1971), chap. 1.

61. See, for example, Lenin, "One Step Forward, Two Steps Back," *LCW*, 7, pp. 314, 366.

62. Lenin, "The Economic Content of Narodism and the Criticism of it in Mr. Struve's Book," *LCW*, 1, p. 421.

63. Karl Marx, *Capital* (Moscow: Foreign Languages Publishing House, 1954), 1, p. 18.

64. See Lenin's reference in "What the 'Friends of the People' are," *LCW*, 1, pp. 169.

65. Lenin, "The Economic Content of Narodism," *LCW*, 1, pp. 399, 403, 405, 406, 410–411.

66. *Ibid.*, p. 410.

67. *Ibid.*, p. 411.

68. "The Marxist proceeds from the same ideal" as the *petite bourgeois* Narodnik. *Ibid.*, p. 416.

69. *Ibid.*, pp. 413–415.

70. *Ibid.*, p. 422.

71. *Ibid.*, p. 421.

6. THE HETERODOX MARXISM OF BENITO MUSSOLINI

1. Lenin never cited any of Sorel's works in his published writings, and we know that Plekhanov, his mentor, advanced major objections to revolutionary syndicalism as a system.

2. Mussolini, as early as 1904, specifically referred to Sorel's works. See Benito Mussolini, "La teppa," *Opera omnia* (Milan: La fenice, 1951; hereafter *Oo*), 1, pp. 91–93. In 1909, he mentioned that he had read Sorel's *La ruine du monde antique* when it appeared. See Mussolini, "Lo sciopero generale e la violenza," *Oo*, 2, p. 163. Throughout this period, as will be indicated, Mussolini made regular reference to Sorel's views.

3. Mussolini, "Il romanzo russo," *Oo*, 1, pp. 3–4 and "La mia vita dal 29 luglio 1883 al 23 novembre 1911," *Oo*, 33, p. 243.

4. Mussolini, "Uomini e idee: 'L'Individuel et le social,'" *Oo*, 1, pp. 73–74.

5. In a letter to Giuseppe Prezzolini in 1909, Mussolini indicated that he had been a syndicalist since 1904. Letter dated 4 April 1909 in Emilio Gentile (ed.), *Mussolini e "La Voce"* (Florence: G. C. Sansoni, 1976), p. 37.

6. Mussolini, for a variety of reasons that need not detain us, has rarely been considered an "intellectual." Renzo De Felice, his principal biographer, does not hesitate to so characterize Mussolini. See De Felice, *Mussolini il rivoluzionario 1883–1920* (Turin: Giulio Einaudi editore, 1965), chaps. 2–6. During the period between 1901 and approximately 1905, Mussolini was known to be a voracious reader. He began to put together a history of philosophy and began a systematic reading of the works of Roberto Ardigò, the foremost exponent of philosophical positivism in Italy. He read and reviewed many of the authors of the period, including Rosa Luxemburg, Werner Sombart, and Vilfredo Pareto for the various publications to which he regularly contributed. He attended Pareto's lectures—all while working as a day laborer to support himself. It was during this period, Mussolini translated, from the French, Petr Kropotkin's *Les Paroles d'un Révolté*, together with a pamphlet by A. H. Malot on the exploitation of workers by the Roman Catholic clergy. At about the same time, he translated, from German, Karl Kautsky's *Am tage nach der sozialen Revolution* and Wilhelm Liebknecht's *Karl Marx und der historische Materialismus*. He received certification to teach French; undertook instruction in Latin; read and began a systematic study of German. He contributed newspaper articles to many, if not all, of the more radical socialist publications of the period. He was regularly selected to represent the political and ideological interests of the most radical segments of the socialist movement in Italy.

7. In full intellectual maturity, Marx continued to insist that given the "contradictions inherent" in industrial capitalism, its "crowning point" must be "the uni-

versal crisis." Marx, "Afterword to the Second German Edition," *Capital* (Moscow: Foreign Languages Publishing House, 1954), p. 20.

8. Mussolini, "Karl Marx (nel 25° anniversario della sua morte)," *Oo*, 1, p. 103. See "Una caduta," "Delinquenza moderna," *Oo*, 1, pp. 10, 14.

9. Mussolini, "Pagine rivoluzionarie," "Il congresso dei socialisti italiani in Svizzera," "Opinioni e documenti: La crisi risolutiva," "Uomini e idee," "La teppa," *Oo*, 1, pp. 51–53, 54–55, 70–71, 74–75, 91–93.

10. Mussolini, *L'uomo e la divinità*, *Oo*, 33, p. 22.

11. Engels, "Speech at the Graveside of Karl Marx," *MESW*, 2, p. 167. Mussolini repeated precisely that argument in his discussion of the "ideological reflexes" that characterize human reflection. See Mussolini, "Karl Marx," *Oo*, 1, p. 103.

12. "Examine all the movements of human thought and you will find that they were 'determined' by economic and profane motives." Mussolini, "Karl Marx (nel 25° anniversario della sua morte," *Oo*, 1, p. 103.

13. Mussolini, *L'uomo e la divinità*, *Oo*, 33, pp. 22–23.

14. *Ibid.*, p. 27.

15. Engels, *Anti-Dühring: Herr Eugen Duehring's Revolution in Science* (Moscow: Foreign Languages Publishing House, 1962), p. 132. Engels added that such a morality might be "possible only at a stage of society which has not only overcome class antagonisms but has even forgotten them in practical life." *Ibid.*

16. Woltmann argued that ethics and morality could not be conceived products of any set of specific economic conditions. He spoke of moral principles, universal in character, that bore no relationship to any economic base. He also referred to the morality above class interests that Engels made part of the revolutionary program of the proletariat. See Ludwig Woltmann, *Historische Materialismus: Darstellung und Kritik der Marxisischen Weltanschauung* (Düsseldorf: Hermann Michels Verlag, 1900), p. 229 and pp. 389–403.

17. Mussolini, *L'uomo e la divinità*, *Oo*, 33, pp. 35–36.

18. *Ibid.*, p. 20.

19. See Mussolini, "Socialismo e movimento sociale nel secolo XIX," *Oo*, 1, pp. 43–45.

20. See Sorel's discussion in "Morale et socialisme," *Le Mouvement socialiste*, March 1899, p. 209 and "L'éthique de socialisme," *Revue de Metaphysique et de Morale*, May 1899, p. 298.

21. Mussolini, "Socialismo e socialisti," *Oo*, 1, p. 139.

22. See the discussion in Roberto Michels, "'Endziel,' Intransigenz, Ethik," *Ethische Kultur*, 11, no. 50 (12 December 1903), pp. 393–395. Michels was a syndicalist author favored by Mussolini.

23. See the account in A. James Gregor, *Young Mussolini and the Intellectual Origins of Fascism* (Berkeley: University of California Press, 1979), pp. 35–50.

24. Mussolini, "Pagine rivoluzionarie," *Oo*, 1, p. 51.

25. See Mussolini's comments in writing of the night of the fourth of August 1789, immediately preceding the French revolution. Mussolini, "Intorno alla notte del 4 agosto," *Oo*, 1, p. 61. together with "L'attuale momento politico," *Oo*, 1, p. 120.

26. Mussolini, "Pagine rivoluzionarie," and "Opinioni e documenti: La crisi risolutiva," *Oo*, 1, pp. 52, 70.

27. Mussolini, *L'uomo e la divinità*, *Oo*, 33, p. 17.

28. Naples: Francesco Perrella, 1909.

29. Mussolini, "La teoria sindacalista," *Oo*, 2, p. 124.

30. Renzo De Felice, *Mussolini il rivoluzionaria 1883–1915* (Turin: Einaudi, 1965), p. 40.

31. What follows is a summary of Mussolini's review of Prezzolini's account. Mussolini, *La teoria sindacalista*, *Oo*, 2, pp. 123–128.

32. Prezzolini characterized the elitism of revolutionary syndicalism as "an aristocracy . . . an organized minority . . . possessed of unique rights . . . that leads masses." *Ibid.*, pp. 95, 180–181, 191.

33. Prezzolini identified the moral and functional education of the proletariat one of the "most fundamental" of the responsibilities of the syndicates. *Ibid.*, pp. 191–197.

34. Prezzolini states "syndicalism . . . places ethical consciousness above economic necessity." *Ibid.*, p. 46.

35. *Ibid.*, pp. 285–297, particularly pp. 294–295.

36. *Ibid.*, pp. 304–306, 315–316, 323, 330–335. Prezzolini recommended the idealist epistemology of Benedetto Croce and Giovanni Gentile (see Prezzolini, "Io devo . . . ," *La Voce*, pp. 386–391; and the discussion in Emilio Gentile, *Mussolini e La Voce* [Florence: Sansoni, 1976], pp. 13–15).

37. In the announcement of the forthcoming periodical, *La Voce*, both Croce and Gentile are listed as "collaborators." See Giuseppe Prezzolini, *Il tempo della Voce* (Milan: Longanesi and Vallecchi, 1960), illustration facing p. 16. Prezzolini consciously moved from a form of pragmatism that Papini had featured in *Leonardo* (see Giovanni Papini, *Pragmatismo* [Florence: Vallecchi, 1943; reprint of the 1913 edition]) to embrace idealism in Crocean, and subsequently Gentilean, form.

38. See the discussion in *ibid.*, pp. 204–205.

39. *Ibid.*, pp. 77–78.

40. Mussolini, "Lo sciopero generale e la violenza," *Oo*, 2, p. 165.

41. *Ibid.*, p. 167.

42. Mussolini, "Il proletariato ha un interesse alle conservazioni delle patrie attuali?" *Oo*, 2, p. 169. In his discussion, Mussolini followed the assessments to be found among syndicalists in general. The recognition that "patriotism," however construed, was a natural expression of group sentiment, was acknowledged not only by Sorel himself, but by some of the more interesting syndicalist theoreticians as well. In 1904, Michels spoke of patriotism as a universal sentiment that found expression in a variety of forms. What he advocated was a kind of patriotism that spoke to the "moral, intellectual and economic uplift of one's compatriots." He did not reject patriotism as a natural sentiment among humans. He dismissed the identification with one's leaders or the specific institutions of one's nation as "true" patriotism. He spoke of the ethical and moral foundation of true patriotism to rest on "a life lived together, with shared speech, culture and a common history" calculated to achieve collective moral purpose. Roberto Michels, "Renaissance des Patriotismus," *Das Magazin für Litteratur*, 73, nos. 5–6 (1907), pp. 153–156.

43. Mussolini, "Il proletariato ha un interesse alle conservazioni delle patrie attuali?" *Oo*, 2, p. 170.

44. Mussolini, "Un grande amico dell'Italia Augusto von Platen," *Oo*, 2, pp. 171–172, 175.

45. *Ibid.*, 2, pp. 172, 175.

46. At that point, Mussolini spoke without hesitation of the relationship of Croce and Sorel as though he, as a revolutionary Marxist, had no intrinsic objection to philosophical idealism. See Mussolini, "Lo sciopero generale e la violenza," *Oo*, 1, pp. 163–164.

47. In this context, Marx had argued that socialist revolutionaries would have to deal with national political issues both in the runup to revolution and the transition to internationalism. Contemporary Marxists have attempted to reconstruct some of Marx's thought in order to accommodate that. They have found it necessary to attempt to address the realities of the twentieth century—and many themes dealt with in the prose of Sorel and Mussolini have resurfaced in the literature. See, for example, Ephraim Nimni, *Marxism and Nationalism: Theoretical Origins of a Political Crisis* (London: Pluto Press, 1991).

48. Mussolini insisted that the internationalist sentiments of socialism "did not cancel the reality of nations." Mussolini, "Lo sciopero dei cantonieri: Zivio!" *Oo*, 2, p. 196.

49. No pretense will be made here that either the history of the journal or an adequate account of the thought of its major collaborators will be undertaken. The selection of material and an account of the content of the journal is governed by the interests of the present rendering. There are many works devoted to *La Voce* and its collaborators. Those that I have found most helpful include Giuseppe Prezzolini, *Il tempo della Voce* (Milan: Longanesi & C. Vallechi, 1960) and Prezzolini, *La Voce 1908–1913: Cronaca, antologia e fortuna di una rivista* (Milan: Rusconi, 1974). For a discussion of the relationship between Mussolini and *La Voce*, the account by Emilio Gentile, "Storia di un politico fra gli intellettuali de 'La Voce,'" in Gentile, *Mussolini e La Voce*, pp. 1–32, is highly recommended.

50. In April 1909, Mussolini wrote a laudatory article for the journal *Vita Trentino*, entitled "La Voce," in which he identified himself with the enterprise of the two intellectuals, Prezzolini and Papini. He spoke of the necessity of creating a "Third Italy," a successor to the Italy of ancient Rome, and the Italy of the Universal Church. It would be a modern Italy, one in which time pieces and railroads ran on time—an Italy in which there was more action and less talk. "La Voce," *Oo*, 2, pp. 53–56.

51. Years later, Mussolini told Prezzolini that his reading of the essays in *Leonardo* had helped transform him intellectually. See the letter of 20 October (perhaps 1914), Prezzolini, "Da Benito Mussolini," *Il tempo della Voce*, p. 631.

52. Mussolini acknowledged the role of Papini in the philosophical rejection of the then prevailing positivism. Mussolini, "La Voce," *Oo*, 2, p. 53. See the collection of articles dated from as early as 1903; Giovanni Papini, *Pragmatismo* (Florence: Vallecchi, 1943; reprint of the 1913 edition).

53. Giovanni Papini, "Un programma nazionalista," in Giovanni Papini and Giuseppe Prezzolini, *Vecchio e nuovo nazionalismo* (Rome: Volpe, 1967; reprint of the 1914 edition), pp. 1–36.

54. Prezzolini pointed out that the leadership of the revolutionary socialists was

almost invariably of bourgeois provenance. Prezzolini, in his response to the comments of Vilfredo Pareto, in "La borgesia può resorgere?" *ibid.*, p. 54.

55. See Prezzolini's comments in "Le due Italie," *ibid.*, pp. 71–73.

56. See the discussion in Prezzolini, "L'Italia rinasce," *ibid.*, pp. 128–131.

57. They remain constant in Prezzolini's comments of 1914. See the Preface to *ibid.*, pp. i–xiii.

58. In October 1909, Mussolini wrote to Prezzolini that the effort to "create an 'Italian' spirit is a superb mission." It would be necessary for Italians to "know themselves—from the North to the South—to temporize and harmonize differences and love ourselves." Mussolini, Letter of 1 October 1909, in Gentile (ed.), *Mussolini e 'La Voce,'* p. 43.

59. See the discussion in the articles made available in Prezzolini and Papini, *Vecchio e nuovo nazionalismo*. See also the discussion in A. James Gregor, *Young Mussolini and the Intellectual Origins of Fascism* (Berkeley: University of California Press, 1979), pp. 87–100.

60. See Mussolini's comments in Yvon De Begnac, *Palazzo Venezia: Storia di un regime* (Rome: La Rocca, 1950), p. 131.

61. Mussolini, "Il Trentino veduta da un socialista," *Oo*, 33, p. 187.

62. As cited, Ettore Fabietti, *Cesare Battisti: L'anima-la vita* (Florence: Vallecchi, 1928), p. 131.

63. See the account in *L'Avvenire del lavoratore*, 13 October 1898, cited in *ibid.*, p. 137.

64. See the discussion in Ephraim Nimni, *Marxism and Nationalism*, pp. 124–127.

65. Mussolini, "Ciccaiulo!" "Lo sciopero dei cantonieri," *Oo*, 2, pp. 196, 203.

66. Mussolini, "Vecchia Vaticana lupa cruenta," "Gli uomini del giorno: Bleriot," "Di quà e di là, Emigranti Italiani," and "L'attualità," *Oo*, 2, pp. 194, 208, 238, 240.

67. Mussolini, "Artificio avvocatesco," "Primo Maggio 1909," "Medaglioni borghesi," "Bolzano," "Il proletariato ha un interesse alle conservazioni delle patrie attuali?" *Oo*, 2, pp. 64, 101, 102, 119, 170.

68. Mussolini was familiar with the syndicalist thought of Roberto Michels who argued for the importance of national sentiment in terms of language and culture. Michels argued that socialist internationalism would not extinguish the differences between peoples. See Roberto Michels, "Der Internationalismus der Arbeiterschaft," *Ethische Kultur*, 12, no. 15 (1 August 1904), p. 113. Like Mussolini, Michels held national sentiment to be "heartfelt," the result of the historical and cultural ties that unite an identifiable body of persons in common will and a common destiny. Michels, "Renaissance des Patriotismus," *Das Magazin für Litteratur*, 73, nos. 5–6 (1907), p. 155. He voiced some of the same sentiments one finds in Mussolini's writings of the period—the fact, for example, that the proletariat, irrespective of any sentiments, could hardly be political nationalists because of their abuse by the possessing classes. See Roberto Michels, *Patriotismus und Ethik* (Leipzig: Felix Dietrich, 1906), particularly pp. 28–32.

69. Mussolini, *Il Trentino veduto da un socialista*, *Oo*, 33, pp. 151–213.

70. *Ibid.*, pp. 153–161.

71. Mussolini's comments on the eugenic strategies of the racial socialism of

German social democracy directly or obliquely refer to Woltmann's account in his "Anthropological Foundations of Political Development," in his *Politische Anthropologie* (Jena: Eugen Dietrich, n.d., but probably 1902), pp. 317–326.

72. Mussolini, *Il Trentino veduto da un socialista*, *Oo*, 33, p. 173.

73. *Ibid.*, pp. 175–183.

74. *Ibid.*, p. 186.

75. *Ibid.*, p. 200.

76. In October 1909, Mussolini could speak of the "creation of a new world," the fulfillment of a Sorelian "mission terrible, grave and sublime." "Ai compagni!" *Oo*, 2, p. 255. In November 1910, he insisted that Sorel's "syndicalism was nothing other than a movement of reaction." He went on to insist that he "had never believed in [Sorel's] revolutionism"—something patently untrue. "L'ultima capriola," *Oo*, 3, p. 272. See the treatment of Sorel in "Fine stagione," *Oo*, 3, pp. 289–292.

7. THE NATIONAL QUESTION AND MARXIST ORTHODOXY

1. Sorel was particularly critical of any such interpretation of Marxism. "It is said," he wrote, "that according to Marx all political, moral, and aesthetic phenomena are determined (in the precise sense of the word) by economic phenomena. What might such a formula mean? To maintain that one thing is determined by another, without providing, at the same time, a precise idea of their relationship is to utter foolishness." Georges Sorel, Preface to Antonio Labriola, *Essais sur la conception matérialiste de l'histoire* (Paris: Giard et Briere, 1901), p. 7. To which Labriola added, "It is said [about the materialist conception of history] that it demands that one explain all human behavior through calculation of material interests, with no value accorded ideal concerns. The inexperience, incapacity and propagandistic haste of some of the doctrine's advocates has contributed to these confusions." *Ibid.*, p. 119.

2. Max Adler, *Kausalität und Teleologie im Streite um die Wissenschaft* (Vienna: Marx-Studien, 1904), pp. 430–431.

3. See the entire discussion in Sorel, "Letter to Daniel Halevy," in *Reflections on Violence* (London: Collier-Macmillan, 1950), pp. 31–65.

4. See the entire discussion in Engels, *The Origin of the Family, Private Property and the State*, in Marx and Engels, *Selected Works* (Moscow: Foreign Languages Publishing, 1955).

5. See Engels emendation, in the Preface to the English edition of 1888, and footnote 2 of the text of *The Communist Manifesto* (New York: Penguin Group, 1998), pp. 46–47, 50.

6. Ludwig Woltmann cites Engels's text and then proceeds to discuss the struggle for existence among human *groups* before there were classes. See Ludwig Woltmann, *Die Darwinsche Theorie und der Sozialismus* (Düsseldof: Hermann Michels Verlag, 1899), particularly pp. 26, 302; and *Der historische Materialismus* (Düsseldorf: Hermann Michels Verlag, 1900), pp. 217–225.

7. The modification of doctrine was so egregious that Soviet commentators, seven decades later, were obliged to object. See Engels, *The Origin of the Family, Private Property and the State*, p. 171, n. 1.

8. Tom Nairn, *The Break Up of Britain* (London: New Left Books, 1981), p. 329.

9. Ephraim Nimni, *Marxism and Nationalism: Theoretical Origins of a Political Crisis* (London: Pluto Press, 1991), pp. 4–5, 194–195.

10. Karl Marx and Friedrich Engels, *The Communist Manifesto*, pp. 55, 63, 72, 73.

11. See the discussion in A. James Gregor, *A Survey of Marxism: Problems in Philosophy and the Theory of History* (New York: Random House, 1965), chap. 5.

12. Karl Marx, *Poverty of Philosophy* (Moscow: Progress Publishers, n.d.), p. 122.

13. *The Communist Manifesto*, p. 73.

14. This is not to say that the founders of Marxism failed to make any attempt to explain how historical actors came to their beliefs. None of the efforts produced convincing results. The explanations became increasingly complex and confusing. See the discussion in Gregor, *A Survey of Marxism*, chap. 5.

15. See Marx's Preface to the 1882 Russian edition of *The Communist Manifesto*, p. 34.

16. Engels was very explicit. He maintained that "the worst thing that can befall the leader of an extreme party is to be compelled to assume power at a time when the movement is not ripe for the domination of the class he represents. . . . What he *can* do depends not on his will but on . . . the level of development of the material means of existence, on the conditions of production and commerce. . . . The social changes of his fancy [have] little root in the then existing economic conditions." Engels, *The Peasant War in Germany* in Karl Marx and Friedrich Engels, *Collected Works* (New York: International Publishers, 1978), 10, pp. 469–470.

17. Lenin, "Critical Remarks on the National Question," *Collected Works* (Moscow: Foreign Languages Press, 1960; hereafter *LCW*), 20, p. 41. Lenin insisted that Russia was "a country most backward economically." Lenin, *Imperialism, the Highest Stage of Capitalism: A Popular Outline*, *LCW*, 22, p. 250.

18. It is evident that Lenin did not expect socialism immediately. He variously conceived the process that would ultimately end in socialism—but it seems clear that he did not expect to immediately bring socialism to Russia in 1917.

19. See the discussion in Lenin, "Contemporary Russia and the Working-Class Movement," *LCW*, 19, p. 50.

20. Lenin, "Critical Remarks on the National Question," *LCW*, 20, p. 45.

21. *Ibid.*, p. 34.

22. *Ibid.*, p. 28. "The proletariat cannot support any consecration of nationalism; on the contrary, it supports everything that helps to obliterate national distinctions and remove national barriers." *Ibid.*, p. 35.

23. *Ibid.*, p. 26.

24. *Ibid.*, p. 34.

25. *Ibid.*, pp. 26–27.

26. J. V. Stalin, "The Social-Democratic View of the National Question," *Works* (Moscow: Foreign Languages Publishing, 1952; hereafter *SW*), 1, pp. 31, 34, 50–51.

27. Stalin, "Marxism and the National Question," *SW*, 2, p. 301.

28. Stalin, "The Social-Democratic View of the National Question," p. 35.

29. Stalin, "Marxism and the National Question," p. 307.

30. *Ibid.*, pp. 316, 317, 319.

31. "Marxism cannot be reconciled with nationalism. . . . In place of all forms of nationalism Marxism advances internationalism, the amalgamation of all nations in the higher unity." Lenin, "Critical Remarks on the National Question," *LCW*, 20, p. 34.

32. See the discussion of Sun Yat-sen's successful antidynastic revolution in China in Lenin, "Democracy and Narodism in China," *LCW*, 18, pp. 163–169.

33. "In its essence [the national struggle] is always a bourgeois struggle, one that is to the advantage and profit mainly of the bourgeoisie." Stalin, "Marxism and the National Question," *SW*, 2, p. 319.

34. *Ibid.*, p. 319.

35. Nimni, *Marxism and Nationalism*, p. 119.

36. "Among all the nations and petty ethnic groups of Austria there are only three which have been the carriers of progress . . . —the Germans, the Poles and the Magyars. . . . The chief mission of all the other races and peoples—large and small—is to perish. . . . They are counterrevolutionary." Elsewhere, "Tiny nationalities which for centuries have been dragged along by history against their will must necessarily be counterrevolutionary." Friedrich Engels, "Hungary and Panslavism," and "Democratic Panslavism," in Karl Marx and Friedrich Engels, *The Russian Menace to Europe* (Glencoe, Ill.: The Free Press, 1952. Edited by Paul W. Blackstock and Bert F. Hoselitz), pp. 59, 71. There clearly was no concern for national sensibilities.

37. Otto Bauer, *Die Nationalitätenfrage und die Sozialdemokratie* (Vienna: Marx-Studien, 1907).

38. See the discussion in Karl Kautsky, "Die moderne Nationalität," *Neue Zeit* (1887), 5, pp. 355–360

39. See Rosa Luxemburg's "Theses on the Tasks of International Social Democracy," in *The Junius Pamphlet* (Colombo, Ceylon: Young Socialist Publications, 1967; a reprint of the 1915 essay), pp. 85, 86. Most of the Marxists who assumed this position were prepared to argue that during an interim period, in dealing with nationalistically oriented associations, that the lure of "national self-determination" would be offered. It was eminently clear that only that much "self-determination" would be allowed that was compatible with the "interests" of the "international proletariat." Stalin insisted that national self-determination was to be understood entirely in terms of "the correctly understood interests of the proletariat." Whatever self-determination Bolshevism anticipated for nations would have to find expression "in the way that will best correspond to the interests of the proletariat." Stalin, "Marxism and the National Question," *SW*, 2, pp. 368, 369.

40. See Tom Bottomore, "Introduction," in Tom Bottomore and Patrick Goode (eds.), *Austro-Marxism* (Oxford: Clarendon Press, 1978), pp. 1–44.

41. The subsequent discussion will refer to Bauer's principal work on national sentiment and nationalism, *Die Nationalitätenfrage und die Sozialdemokratie*. Page references will be provided for major quotes. A fragment of Bauer's work is available in the translations made available in the collection edited by Bottomore and Goode, *Austro-Marxism*.

42. Bauer, *Die Nationalitätenfrage*, pp. 84–94, 137, 177, 185.

43. See *ibid.*, pp. 15–26, particularly n. 1, p. 19. On *ibid.*, p. 23, Bauer speaks specifically of breeding circles.

44. Compare *ibid*., pp. 29, 131, with Adolf Bastian, *Die Rechtverhältnisse bei verschiedenen Völkern der Erde* (Berlin: G. Reimer Verlag, 1872) I, p. viii and the account in Ludwig Gumplowicz, *Outlines of Sociology* (New York: Paine-Whitman Publishers, 1963; translation of the 1885 edition), pp. 110–112.

45. Bauer, *Die Nationalitätenfrage und die Sozialdemokratie*, pp. 144–145, 186.

46. See the account in *ibid*., pp. 138–145. The definition of "nation" is found in *ibid*., p. 135.

47. See the rendering in *ibid*., pp. 77–94.

48. "National distinctiveness does not diminish with the transfer of material culture. The consciousness of national differences has never been so emphatic as in our own time, irrespective of the fact that nations learn more and more rapidly from other nations than ever before." *Ibid*., p. 158.

49. See *ibid*., pp. 172–174.

50. See the entire discussion in *ibid*., pp. 10–26.

51. See the discussion in *ibid*., particularly, pp. 50, 84–109, 302–304, 533.

52. Bauer's allusion was to the writings of both Marx and Engels that included frequent references to the less industrialized communities of Europe as being "historyless." Bauer argued against any such characterization. He advocated, instead, a "conscious internationalism," as opposed to a "naive cosmopolitanism," one that respected the historic and cultural integrity of the national sentiment of all workers. The goal would remain international revolution, directed against the exploitation of the possessing classes, but an international revolution that advanced a political program that would respect the national sensibilities of the revolutionary proletariat. See the discussion in *ibid*., pp. 302–325, 522, 526–533.

53. Bauer refers to *Willensrichtungen*. *Ibid*., pp. 110–111.

54. See Bauer's affirmation of the Brünn (Brno) program which called for the "right of each nationality to national existence and national development." *Ibid*., p. 528. It was this commitment that drew the scorn of both Stalin and Lenin. See Stalin, "Marxism and the National Question," *SW*, 2, pp. 326–327; Lenin, "Critical Remarks on the National Question," *LCW*, 20, pp. 38–39. Both refused to consider the possibility of a "national" as distinct from a "class" culture.

55. See the account in Karl Kautsky, *Die materialistische Geschichtsauffassung* (Berlin: Verlag J. H. W. Dietz, 1929), I, pp. 196–219.

56. "Just as Darwin discovered the law of development of organic nature, so Marx discovered the law of development of human history." Friedrich Engels, "Speech at the Graveside of Karl Marx," in Marx and Engels, *Selected Works* (Moscow: Foreign Languages Publishing, 1955), 2, p. 167; See Engels, *Dialectics of Nature* (Moscow: Foreign Languages Publishing, 1954), pp. 29, 265, 337–338, 402–404.

57. Karl Kautsky, *Die materialistiche Geschichtsauffassung* (Berlin: Verlag J. H. W. Dietz, 1929), I, pp. 196–200.

58. Bauer, *Die Nationalitäten Frage und die Sozialdemokratie*, p. 130.

59. In his introduction to the concept of the "nation," Bauer makes reference to the elements that together constitute the nation: common territory, descent, language, customs and usage, history, law, and religious beliefs. He speaks of the "Italian sociologists" who provide such a catalog. *Ibid*., p. 130.

60. Gaetano Mosca, *Elementi di scienza politica* (Bari: Laterza, 1953; first published in 1896), I, chap. 3, section 2, pp. 111, 112; section 5, p. 122.

61. *Ibid.*, pp. 31, 97, 100, 111, 112, 148.

62. Irving L. Horowitz, "Editor's Preface," to Gumplowicz, *Outlines of Sociology* (New York: Payne-Whitman, 1963), p. 7.

63. Years later, Karl Kautsky referred to Woltmann's effort to unite the two. Karl Kautsky, *Die materialistische Geschichtsauffassung* (Berlin: Verlag J. H. W. Dietz, 1929), 1, pp. 196–197.

64. See Ludwig Woltmann, *Die Darwinsche Theorie und der Sozialismus* (Düsseldorf: Michels, 1899), pp. 330–331.

65. It is unfortunate that Gumplowicz titled his book *Der Rassenkampf* which translates into "Race War." The entities that conducted the "war" to which he alludes were almost always non-racial. They were consistently identified as "heterogeneous social elements," any population element that distinguishes itself from others on the grounds of high social visibility, or cultural differences. They hardly ever were racial in any specific sense. Gumplowicz took pains to indicate that the term "race" had no specific scientific meaning. See his discussion, Gumplowicz, *Der Rassenkampf: Sociologische Untersuchungen* (Innsbruck: Verlag der Wagner'schen Universität-Buchhandlung, 1883), particularly pp. 193–194. The reason he referred to "race" was to provide some indication of how group differences arise—through endogamy and genetic isolation—the results of ingroup amity and outgroup enmity—the same mechanisms that produced biological races.

66. See, for example, the discussion in Gumplowicz, *Outlines of Sociology*, part 4.

67. See the discussion in Ludwig Woltmann, *Der historische Materialismus* (Düsseldorf: Michels, 1900), pp. 372, 396–397. Gumplowicz spoke of the conflict between his elemental social groups as a "racial conflict (*Rassenkampf*)." He made very clear that when he spoke of "social aggregates," he did not mean "racial" in any biological or anthropological sense. He consistently reminded his audience that social scientists employed the term "race" in what was, at best, vague and ambiguous fashion. He was content to speak of "heterogeneous social groups." Most of the references that Gumplowicz occasionally called racial, would more accurately be considered ethnic groups, social aggregates, "folkish" communities, tribes, swarms, or hordes. See Gumplowicz, *Der Rassenkampf*, pp. 186–187.

68. Ultimately, Woltmann saw the conflict between races as the major historical determinant—something completely alien to the thought of Gumplowicz.

69. See the account in Gumplowicz, *Der Rassenkampf*, pp. 158–166, 169–172, 176–194; Gumplowicz, *Outlines of Sociology*, pp. 153–156, 158–160, 168, 178–179, 223.

70. War was understood to be "the result of a natural law of strife," so much so that even peace was "only a latent struggle." Gumplowicz, *Outlines of Sociology*, p. 208.

71. Gumplowicz, *Die sociologische Staatsidee* (Innsbruck: Verlag der Wagner'sche Universitäts-Buchhandlung, 1902), p. 115.

72. Gumplowicz, *Outlines of Sociology*, pp. 206, 214–216.

73. See the discussion in Gumplowicz, *Die sociologische Staatsidee*, pp. 183–189.

74. Mussolini, "Di quà e di là: Emigranti Italiani," and "L'Attualità," *Opera omnia* (Milan: La fenice, 1965), 2, pp. 208, 238, 240.

75. Mussolini considered Bauer "certainly one of the most formidable and genial intelligences among the Austro-Hungarian socialists." Mussolini, "I pericoli del riformismo," *ibid.*, 6, p. 16.

8. REVOLUTIONARY SYNDICALISM AND NATIONALISM

1. In Germany, Michels early suffered for his revolutionary socialist convictions. Max Weber, who identified Michels as a gifted scholar, lamented the fact that a cultured nation could still exact costs from those whose ideas differed from those of the politically correct mainstream. See Wilfred Röhrich, *Robert Michels: Von sozialistich-syndicalistischen zum fascistischen Credo* (Berlin: Duncker & Humblot, 1972), pp. 7–8.

2. See the account in Paolo Orano, "Roberto Michels: L'amico, il maestro, il camerata," in *Studi in memoria di Roberto Michels* (Padua: CEDAM, 1937), p. 9.

3. Roberto Michels, *Storia del Marxismo in Italia: Compendio critico* (Rome: Mongini, 1909). The substance of the volume appeared in German in 1907 in the *Archiv für Sozialwissenschaft und Sozialpolitik* when Michels was barely thirty years of age.

4. Quite independently of Bakunin's influence, many Marxists understood Marxism to be fundamentally anarchistic in inspiration. Some of the first popularizers of Marxism in Europe were anarchists. Johann Most, who was instrumental in making Marx's ideas known in Germany; Ariol Editeur, who translated a summary of *Das Kapital* for francophone readers; and F. D. Nieuwenhuis, who provided a compendium of Marx's works for Dutch speakers, were all anarchists. See Michels's comments, *Storia del Marxismo in Italia*, pp. 55–61, and particularly p. 65, n. 1.

5. See the discussion in Napoleone Colajanni, *Il socialismo* (Catania: Filippo Tropea, 1884).

6. See Enrico Ferri, *Socialismo e scienza positiva (Darwin-Spencer-Marx)* (Rome: Casa editrice italiana, 1894) and Michelangelo Vaccaro, *La lotta per l'esistenza* (Turin: Bocca, 1902).

7. Michels, *Storia del Marxismo in Italia*, pp. 80, 98, "Ancora una parola sul marxismo in Italia," *Rivista popolare*, 17, 8 (30 April 1911), p. 207.

8. Michels, *Storia del Marxismo in Italia*, p. 80.

9. *Ibid.*, pp. 7, 9, 10, 121–122; see pp. 92, 103.

10. Michels, "Der ethische Faktor in der Parteipolitik Italien," *Zeitschrift für Politik*, 3 (1909), 1, pp. 56–91; see particularly pp. 67–68, 69–72.

11. Michels, "'Endziel,' Intransigenz, Ethik," *Ethische Kultur*, 11, 50 (12 December 1903), p. 393.

12. See Michels, *Il proletariato e la borghesia nel movimento socialista italiano* (Turin: Bocca, 1908), pp. 333–396; particularly pp. 352, n. 11, 372, 377–396.

13. The clear exception is the excellent exposition of syndicalist ideas found in the English translation of Zeev Sternhell (with Mario Sznajder and Maia Asheri), *The Birth of Fascist Ideology: From Cultural Rebellion to Political Revolution* (Princeton: Princeton University Press, 1994), chaps. 3, 4.

14. *Ibid.*, p. 191. A brief account of the process is offered in A. James Gregor, *Young Mussolini and the Intellectual Origins of Fascism* (Berkeley: University of California Press, 1979), chaps. 5 and 7.

15. Michels, *Patriotismus und Ethik* (Leipzig: Felix Dietrich, 1906), see particularly pp. 28–32.

16. See the discussion in Michels, "Nationalismus, Nationalgefühl, Internationalismus," *Das freie Wort*, 2 (1903), pp. 107–111.

17. "Internationalismus bedeutet nicht Vaterlandslosigkeit." Michels, "Der Internationalismus der Arbeiterschaft," *Ethische Kultur*, 12, 15 (1 August 1904), p. 113.

18. See the discussion in Michels, "Renaissance des Patriotismus," *Das Magazin für Litteratur*, 73, 5–6 (1907), pp. 153–156.

19. See Rörich, *Robert Michels*, p. 9.

20. Michels regularly cited Gumplowicz's work in his publications; see Michels, "Neomalthusianismus," *Frauen-Zukunft*, 1, 1 (1910), pp. 42, 52.

21. The unanimity of some of the central ideas of Mosca with those of Gumplowicz is obvious. Mosca articulates an objection to the ideas of Gumplowicz insofar as he imagines that the ideas in *Der Rassenkampf* are "racist," and that, moreover, the concept "race" is far too ambiguous and vague to serve as an independent variable in accounting for social evolution. See Mosca, *Elementi di scienza politica* (Bari: Laterza, 1953; fifth edition), 1, pp. 31, 76–77, note to chapter 1. We have seen that Gumplowicz's notions were not "racist" in the sense with which we have become familiar. Gumplowicz fully acknowledged that the concept "race," in and of itself, was too imprecise and uncertain to serve scientific purpose. He clearly preferred "heterogeneous social element" to designate his "agents of history." He speaks of those "elements" as being formed by "culture," language, custom, art, religion, law, history, collective aspirations, and community experience—and appearing in history as hordes, tribes, moities, clans, nations, and/or classes. See Gumplowicz, *Der Rassenkampf: Sociologische Untersuchungen* (Innsbruck: Verlag der Wagner'schen Universitäts-Buchhandlung, 1883), pp. 186–187, 193, 231–233, 248–253; consult Irving L. Horowitz, "Introduction: The Sociology of Ludwig Gumplowicz," in Gumplowicz, *Outlines of Sociology* (New York: Paine-Whitman, 1963), pp. 39–49. Gumplowicz's preoccupation was to describe the collective and individual behavior of the members of such "*Gemeinschaften*."

22. See Mosca, *Elementi di scienza politica*, chap. 3, section 2, pp. 111–113. Mosca regularly speaks of "national sentiment" and "class solidarity" as predicated on the sense of community born of imitation and the sentiment of fellow feeling. See *ibid.*, chap. 4, section 5, pp. 148–151.

23. See the discussion in *ibid.*, chap. 7, section 1, pp. 240–242.

24. See, for example, the discussion in Michels, *Patriotismus und Ethik*, p. 17.

25. Michels, *Cooperazione* (Turin: Bocca, 1908), and reprinted in *Saggi economico-statistici sulle classi popolari* (Milan: Remo Sandron, 1913). See Mussolini's review in "Fra libri e riviste," *Opera omnia* (Florence: La fenice, 1951 [*Oo*]), 2, pp. 248–249.

26. Michels, *Saggi economico-statistici*, pp. 75–87.

27. Like Gumplowicz, Mosca, Bauer, and a number of others, Mussolini acknowledges the phenomena. "Cooperation," Mussolini notes, is characterized by two "contradictory" features: the first finds expression in the "practical solidarity" of the primary group and the other in its "struggle" against outgroups. See Mussolini, "Fra libri e riviste," *Oo*, 2, pp. 248–249.

28. See the discussion in Michels, "Wirtschafts- und sozialphilosophische Randbemerkungen," and "Zur historischen Analyse des Patriotismus," *Archiv für Sozialwissenschaft und Sozialpolitik*, 4, no. 3 (1911), pp. 441–442, and *ibid.*, 36, nos. 1 and 2 (1913), pp. 14–43.

29. *Ibid.*, p. 446.

30. Michels, "Renaissance des Patriotismus," *Der Magazin für Litteratur*, 73, nos. 5–6 (1907), p. 155.

31. A. O. Olivetti, "Sindacalismo e nazionalismo," *Pagine libere*, 5, 4 (15 February 1911), reprinted in Giulio Barni, Alceste De Ambris, Arturo Labriola, Paolo Mantica, A. O. Olivetti, Alfredo Polledro, Libero Tancredi, *La guerra di Tripoli: Discussioni nel campo rivoluzionario* (Naples: Società editrice Partenopea, 1912), pp. 11–27. The discussion that follows is drawn from Olivetti's account.

32. Engels had traced that long history in his *The Origin of the Family, Private Property and the State*, and his account figured in that advanced by most of the major Marxist theoreticians at the turn of the twentieth century.

33. See Olivetti's comments in "L'altra campana," in *La guerra di Tripoli*, p. 110.

34. See Olivetti's discussion in "Sindacalismo e nazionalismo," *ibid.*, pp. 22–23.

35. The original argument is contained in Olivetti, "L'altra campana," published originally in *Pagine libere*, 5, 22 (15 November 1911) shortly after the commencement of the war, and reprinted in *La guerra di Tripoli*, pp. 107–122.

36. *Ibid.*, pp. 116–117, 122.

37. Olivetti, "Ribattendo il chiodo," *ibid.*, pp. 241–242.

38. It was about this time that Michels was completing his major work on the sociology of political parties, *Sociologia del partito politico nella democrazia moderna* (Turin: UTET, 1912). The work has since become a classic in political sociology.

39. See the discussion of nationalist doctrine as it had begun to find expression before the Great War in A. James Gregor, *Mussolini's Intellectuals: Fascist Social and Political Thought* (Princeton: Princeton University Press, 2005), chaps. 2 and 3.

40. See the same intellectual development in the work of Sergio Panunzio, who was to go on to be among the most distinguished social thinkers of Mussolini's Fascism. See the account in *ibid.*, chap. 4.

41. Michels, *L'imperialismo italiano: Studi politico-demographici* (Milan: Società editrice libreria, 1914).

42. *Ibid.*, pp. xii, 4.

43. *Ibid.*, pp. 120–121.

44. "The thesis that Italy embarked on the war in Tripoli for commercial reasons cannot be sustained." *Ibid.*, p. 138.

45. *Ibid.*, p. 180.

46. *Ibid.*, pp. 83–84.

47. *Ibid.*, pp. 56–57.

48. Michels reminded his readers that while those migrants did make regular financial contributions to the support of relatives that remained behind—Italian workers benefited their host country by providing it a concrete legacy far more valuable than any transfers to their dependents in the homeland. Their labor intensive employments in agriculture and industry, the construction of the transportation, educational, and communications infrastructure of the economies of North Europe, North and South America, were material values lost to Italy.

49. Michels reports that the Italian newspapers of the period invoked the memories of the ancient glories of Rome: "People of Tripoli! Italy disembarks on this shore united in geography and the ancient ties of a common fatherland." Elsewhere it was said that "We bring to these lands, lapsed into decadence, where once Rome

brought redemptive civilization, the civilizing standard of the new Italy." See *ibid.*, pp. 115–116.

50. Michels speaks of the appeals to the memory of Rome as a "tactical method," used to "ignite a passionate enthusiasm" that would provide the energies for social revolution. See *ibid.*, p. 118.

51. He spoke of the myth of ancient glories invoked by the nationalists of Greece, Germany, France, and Serbia. The Greeks alluded to the Empire of Alexander the Great, or less grandiose, the Byzantine Empire. The Germans return to the memories of the Holy Roman Empire. The French made recourse to the Napoleonic conquests. The Serbs rummaged in their history for their own own mobilizing national myth. See *ibid.*, pp. 116–117.

52. See the comments of Vito Rastelli, *Filippo Corridoni: La figura storica e la dottrina politica* (Rome: "Conquiste d'Impero," 1940), p. 19.

53. There is a collection of Corridoni's writings in Ivon De Begnac, *L'Arcangelo sindacalista (Filippo Corridoni)* (Verona: Mondadori, 1943) in an extended appendix. Extensive quotations are found in the text as well.

54. In fact, Olivetti appeared in Corridoni's defense in his trial for "subversion"—as a consequence of the publication of Corridoni's long essay on sabotage.

55. One finds almost all the elements of Corradini's thought in the published works of A. O. Olivetti. Corradini's exposition differs in the order of presentation and in terms of the passion with which they are delivered. It is evident that Corradini's convictions are those of what came to be identified as "national syndicalism" in the years after the Great War. The references to Olivetti's writings will be taken from the unpublished collection provided by Olivetti's family, *Battaglie sindacaliste: Dal sindacalismo al fascismo*. As will be indicated, most of the material is to be found in the pages of *Pagine libere* of the period.

56. Although there is no direct evidence that Corridoni had read any of the works of Michels, there was a commonality of content that was sure evidence of a shared perspective. See the comments of De Begnac, *L'Arcangelo sindacalista*, p. 139. The influence of the thought of Olivetti is evident throughout much of Corridoni's essays. See the citations in *ibid.*, passim.

57. The clearest expression is found in Rastelli, *Filippo Corridoni*, pp. 23, 28, 71, with a Preface written by Corridoni's friend and compatriot during his history as a syndicalist leader: Amilcare De Ambris, who clearly identified Corridoni as a precursor of Fascism. Immediately before the final days of the Fascist Social Republic in the North of Italy during the agony of the regime at the end of the Second World War, young Fascists took the initiative to publish a "second edition" of Corridoni's *Sindacalismo e repubblica* as a final doctrinal testament of the Fascist revolution. The text was published in February 1945 by the Bibliotechina sociale in Milan. Citations will be made from that edition.

58. In the Author's preface, Corridoni's tells us that "syndicalism," in his judgment, is nothing other than the promise of Marxism. It is its "fulfillment." *Sindacalismo e repubblica*, p. 12. See Corridoni's references to Marx, *ibid.*, pp. 17–18, 25–26, 46, 77.

59. See the entire discussion in *ibid.*, pp. 17–23. This was clearly a variant on Lenin's notion that the working class in the advanced industrial nations was sub-

orned by capitalism's "superprofits"—extorted from the less developed periphery of the international system.

60. *Ibid.*, pp. 23, 25.

61. See the discussion, *ibid.*, pp. 38, 48–49, 55–56.

62. Corridoni argued that "three quarters of Italy remained at a precapitalist level and there was little that suggested any improvement." *Ibid.*, p. 23.

63. Hobson's book, *Imperialism: A Study*, was first published in 1902, and has since run into many editions. It is clear that much of Lenin's substance on his notions of capitalist imperialism was drawn from Hobson's book. See the discussion in Tom Kemp, *Theories of Imperialism* (London: Dennis Dobson, 1967), chap. 3.

64. See Corridoni's discussion in *Sindacalismo e repubblica*, pp. 30–34, 41–42.

65. *Ibid.*, pp. 55–56.

66. "The proletarian movement is the self-conscious, independent movement of the immense majority . . ." Marx and Engels, *The Communist Manifesto* (New York: Monthly Review Press, 1998), p. 22.

67. Corridoni, *Sindacalismo e repubblica*, p. 70.

68. *Ibid.*, pp. 34, 37–38. Two months before Italy's declaration of war against Germany and Austria-Hungary, Olivetti wrote that, under some set of contingent conditions, "national interests" might unite proletarians and the bourgeoisie. See Olivetti, "Postilla a 'Socialismo e guerra sono termini antitetici?'" *Pagine libere*, 20 October 1915.

69. See Corridoni, "Lettera testamento," Appendix to Rastelli, *Filippo Corridoni*, pp. 100–101, and "Il testamento politico," in Corridoni, *Sindacalismo e repubblica*, pp. 109–111 and *ibid.*, pp. 71–72.

70. Olivetti had made the same case in "Risposta alla inchiesta sulla guerra europea," *Pagine libere*, 30 October 1914.

71. See the entire discussion in Corridoni's "Il testamento politico," in *Sindacalismo e repubblica*, pp. 109–111.

72. *Ibid.*, p. 90.

73. Corridoni spoke of that transitional revolution as a "rivoluzione di assestamento." *Ibid.*, pp. 71–73. See the discussion in Rastelli, *Filippo Corridoni*, pp. 65–66, 74–75.

74. See Corridoni, *Sindacalismo e repubblica*, pp. 48–49, 97–99.

75. Olivetti had made precisely the same case; see Olivetti, "Noi e lo stato," *Pagine libere*, 15 November 1914.

76. Corridoni, shortly before his death in combat, spoke of his "desperate love" for the fatherland. Corridoni, "Lettera testamento," in Rastelli, *Filippo Corridoni*, p. 101.

77. See, for example, A. O. Olivetti, "Il problema della folla," *Nuova antologia*, 38, no. 761 (1 September 1903), pp. 281–291; Paolo Orano, *La psicologia sociale* (Bari: Laterza, 1902). As has been suggested, similar ideas are found among many of the early Marxists, and became the critical center of the thought of Otto Bauer. See the discussion in A. James Gregor, *The Ideology of Fascism: The Rationale of Totalitarianism* (New York: Free Press, 1969), pp. 72–92.

78. Arturo Labriola, *La guerra di Tripoli e l'opinione socialista* (Naples: Scintilla, 1912), pp. 19 and 114. In the *Tribuna* of Turin, on 27 November 1912, Giovanni Pascoli

spoke of Italy as "The Great Proletariat." See the citations in Michels, *L'imperialismo italiano*, p. 92, n. 4.

9. THE GREAT WAR AND THE RESPONSE OF REVOLUTIONARY MARXISTS

1. By the time of his death, Woltmann argued for a "racial socialism" in which all the values of socialism would be achieved through a racially sensitive program—protecting the "culture creators" so that a higher order of civilization could both be provided and sustained against those incapable of its creation or maintenance. See the discussion in Ludwig Woltmann, *Politische Anthropologie: Eine Untersuchung über den Einfluss der Descendenztheorie auf die Lehre von der politischen Entwicklung der Völker* (Jena: Verlegt bei Eugen Diederichs, n.d.), pp. 317–326. Arturo Labriola identified Woltmann among those German theorists, both socialists and nonsocialists who supplied the theoretical rationale for the pan-Germanism that contributed to the coming of the First World War. See Arturo Labriola, *La conflagrazione europea e il socialismo* (Rome: Athenaeum, 1915), pp. 100–105. As has been indicated, Mussolini had identified the Marxist Woltmann with the pan-Germanism of Austrian socialism. See Benito Mussolini, *Il trentino veduto da un socialista*, *Opera omnia* (Milan: La fenice, 1955; hereafter *Oo*), 33, pp. 158–161.

2. All of this had been part of the theoretical legacy of Karl Marx. All those predictions are to be found in *The Communist Manifesto*, written in Marx's youth, as well as in the last chapters of the first volume of *Das Kapital*, written in his maturity.

3. See the insightful discussion in Bertram D. Wolfe, *Marxism: One Hundred Years in the Life of a Doctrine* (London: Westview Press, 1985), chap. 18.

4. Karl Kautsky, *Die materialistische Geschichtsauffassung* (Berlin: J. H. W. Dietz, 1929), in two volumes, remains among the best of the accounts of classical Marxism.

5. Karl Marx, *Capital* (Moscow: Foreign Languages Publishing House, 1954), p. 9.

6. Syndicalists saw in that logic the rationale for pan-Germanism. See Labriola's discussion in *La conflagrazione europea e il socialismo*, chaps. 6 and 7.

7. See the discussion in Ephraim Nimni, *Marxism and Nationalism: Theoretical Origins of a Political Crisis* (London: Pluto, 1991), pp. 26, 30–31.

8. As has been indicated, Woltmann had made much of the distinction—one he found both explicit and implicit in Marx's historical materialism. He spoke of civilized and primitive races, and suggested that Marx had made those properties a function of genetic endowment.

9. See Letter of 2 December 1847, and Marx and Engels, *Collected Works* (New York: International Publishers, 1978; hereafter *MECW*), 7, p. 422.

10. These kinds of characterizations were employed by Ludwig Woltmann and the pan-Germanic theoreticians among the turn-of-the century socialists to justify German dominance in the European east and southeast. In the case of Woltmann, these judgments were employed to support his particular form of biological racism that was to resurface in the thought of Adolf Hitler. See A. James Gregor, *Contem-*

porary Radical Ideologies: Totalitarian Thought in the Twentieth Century (New York: Random House, 1968), pp. 181–212.

11.   Engels, "French Rule in Algeria," in Schlomo Avineri, *Karl Marx on Colonialism and Modernization* (Garden City: Doubleday, 1968), p. 44.

12.   Engels, "Democratic Panslavism," in P. W. Blackstock and B. F. Hoselitz (eds.), *The Russian Menace to Europe* (Glencoe, Ill.: The Free Press, 1952), pp. 71, 74–76.

13.   Engels, "Letter from Germany: The War in Schleswig-Holstein," Marx and Engels, *MECW*, 10, pp. 392–394.

14.   Marx, as quoted in Leopold Schwarzchild, *The Red Prussian: The Life and Legend of Karl Marx* (London: Hamish Hamilton, 1948), pp. 189–190.

15.   See the discussion in *ibid.*, pp. 334–335.

16.   See the convenient collection of the writings of Marx and Engels on the role of Russia in the projected proletarian revolution in Blackstock and Hoselitz (eds.), *The Russian Menace to Europe* and J. A. Doerig (ed.), *Marx vs. Russia* (New York: Frederick Ungar Publishing, 1962).

17.   Wolfe, *Marxism*, p. 25.

18.   See the discussion in Wolfe, *Marxism*, chap. 3, particularly pp. 56–57. Again, the suggestion that such a war would involve "race," suggested the racial interpretation of history that became identified with the "racial socialism" of Ludwig Woltmann.

19.   Engels to A. Bebel, in Karl Marx and Friedrich Engels, *Briefe an A. Bebel und Andere* (Berlin: Dietz, 1933), p. 412.

20.   As cited in Wolfe, *Marxism*, pp. 67, 68 and notes 29, 30, 31.

21.   Letter dated 13 October 1891, as cited in Gustav Mayer, *Friedrich Engels: A Biography* (New York: Knopf, 1936), pp. 514–555.

22.   As cited in Wolfe, *Marxism*, p. 76.

23.   To this day, there is no single, universally accepted interpretation of Marx's epistemological convictions. Throughout its history, Marxism has been characterized in fundamentally different fashion by some of its adherents. See the discussion in A. James Gregor, *A Survey of Marxism: Problems in Philosophy and the Theory of History* (New York: Random House, 1965), chap. 3.

24.   Lenin fabricated his interpretation of the epistemology of Marxism in his *Materialism and Empiriocriticism* in *Collected Works* (Moscow: Foreign Languages Press, 1962; hereafter *LCW*), 16. It was fashioned out of the writings of the mature Engels, innocent of the now familiar writings of the young Marx. It is not at all clear that Engels's interpretation of Marxist epistemology was fully compatible with that of Karl Marx. The materials that originate from the pen of the young Marx seem radically incompatible with the positivism of the mature Engels—and that of Lenin. See the account in Gregor, *A Survey of Marxism*, chap. 3.

25.   See the comments of V. Fomina's introductory essay to Georgi Plekhanov, *Selected Philosophical Works* (Moscow: Foreign Languages Publishing House, n.d.), 1, p. 9.

26.   Engels in a letter to Bebel dated 17 November 1885 in Marx and Engels, *Briefe an A. Bebel*, p. 412.

27.   See the discussion in Lenin, "Speech Delivered at an International Meeting in Berne, February 8, 1916," *LCW*, 22, p. 123.

28.   V. I. Lenin, "The Tasks of Revolutionary Social-Democracy in the European War," *LCW*, 21, pp. 15–16.

29. "The Position and Tasks of the Socialist International," *LCW*, 21, pp. 35, 36.

30. *Ibid.*, p. 40.

31. "What Next?" *LCW*, 21, p. 109.

32. "The Russian Brand of Suedekum," and "Under a False Flag," *LCW*, 21, pp. 118–124, 141, 142.

33. "To the Editors of *Nashe Slovo*," *LCW*, 21, p. 126.

34. Marx and Engels, *The Communist Manifesto* (New York: Penguin Group, 1998), p. 56.

35. See the discussion in Lenin, *Imperialism, the Highest Stage of Capitalism: A Popular Outline* in *LCW*, 22, pp. 241–242, 276–278; see *ibid.*, pp. 143, 192.

36. Robert Conquest, *V. I. Lenin* (New York: Viking, 1972), p. 71.

37. "Under a False Flag," *LCW*, 21, pp. 148–151.

38. "Under a False Flag," and "The Conference of the R.S.D.L.P. Groups Abroad," *LCW*, 21, pp. 151–153, 161.

39. Lenin defined "opportunism" in terms of the repudiation of both the class struggle and proletarian revolution, together with the recognition of the merits of patriotism. "Social chauvinism" or "social patriotism" was seen as derivative of "opportunism," in which workers were deceived by the petty bourgeoisie and the exiguous labor aristocracy battening on the super profits of imperialist exploitation of less developed countries. "The Conference of the R.S.D.L.F. Groups Abroad," "The Collapse of the Second International," *LCW*, 21 pp. 161, 212, 249.

40. "The Social-Chauvinists' Sophisms," *LCW*, 21, pp. 185–186.

41. "The Collapse of the Second International," *LCW*, 21, pp. 211, 213–216, 221–224, 228, 235.

42. Lenin, *Imperialism*, pp. 195, 205, 210, 218, 220–223, 234, 254, 298–300.

43. *Ibid.*, pp. 271–272.

44. *Ibid.*, p. 265.

45. *Ibid.*, pp. 241, 261.

46. *Ibid.*, p. 192.

47. See *ibid.*, pp. 192, 194, 278–279, 281, 283–284, 301.

48. *Ibid.*, pp. 262, 274. Thus while finance capitalists neglect agriculture in their own domestic environments, they seek to foster agrarian productivity in their colonies. See *ibid.*, p. 261. Lenin goes on to argue that some of the less developed peripheral countries, like Japan, are rapidly maturing into competitive systems, thereby making the "struggle among the world imperialisms . . . more acute." *Ibid.*, pp. 274–275.

49. *Ibid.*, pp. 241–242, 243, 274–275. See the implications of Lenin's comments on the possible transfer of agricultural, mining, and industrial labor from the advanced capitalist nations to "the colored races" in Asia and Africa. He admits that Japan had gradually emerged as an industrializing power, as Germany had a few decades earlier, suggesting that there remained considerable room for industrialization among less developed nations. *Ibid.*, pp. 281, 295. In making those assertions, Lenin was repeating those of J. A. Hobson's *Imperialism: A Study* (Ann Arbor: University of Michigan Press, 1965), a book that we know Lenin used in the preparation of his own *Imperialism*.

50. Lenin objected to any suggestion that imperialism might be "progressive." He was particularly dismissive if the suggestion came from Marxist intellectuals. See

his *Imperialism*, p. 270. The fact is that Marx and Engels both considered "colonialism" part of the "cunning of history" and integral to the anticipated "progressive" world revolution.

51. *Ibid.*, p. 277.

52. *Ibid.*, p. 297.

53. *Ibid.*, p. 300.

54. *Ibid.*, p. 259.

55. In his *Peasant War in Germany*, Engels reviewed the history of the revolutionary religious communists of the sixteenth century. Of those he held that "The worst thing that can befall the leader of an extreme party is to be compelled to assume power at a time when the movement is not yet ripe for the domination of the class he represents. . . . What he *can* do depends not on his will but . . . on the level of development of the material means of existence, on the conditions of production and commerce . . ." Engels was particularly emphatic about communist revolutionaries undertaking revolution when "the social changes of [their] fancy had little root in the then existing economic conditions." Under such conditions, they must inevitably fail; their revolutions lapsing back into the oppressive features of a political system resting on an immature economic base. Engels, "The Peasant War in Germany," in *MECW*, 10, pp. 469–470, 471.

56. See the discussion in Gregor, *A Survey of Marxism*, chap. 5.

57. Mussolini, "Nazionalismo," *Oo*, 3, p. 281.

58. Mussolini, "L'anno ch'è morto . . ." *Oo*, 6, p. 33.

59. On the eve of the First World War, Lenin maintained that "the growth of armaments, the extreme intensification of the struggle for markets . . . were inevitably bound to bring about this war." "The War and Russian Social-Democracy," *LCW*, 21, p. 27.

60. See the interesting discussion making the comparison in Domenico Settembrini, *Fascismo controrivoluzione imperfetta* (Florence: Sansoni, 1978), chap. 1.

61. Mussolini, "Per l'intransigenza del socialism: Le ragioni del cosidetto 'pacifismo'," *Oo*, 5, p. 134.

62. See Mussolini's comments in "L'impresa disperata," *Utopia*, 2, no. 1 (15 January 1914), p. 1.

63. The folk wisdom of contemporary history and social science often pretends that Mussolini was fundamentally ignorant of Marxist thought. Everything he wrote and published during this period gives the lie to that canard. He speaks knowledgably of Rosa Luxemburg, Otto Bauer, Karl Kautsky, Rudolf Hilferding, and Victor Adler in the first pages of *Utopia*. See, for example, Mussolini, "Il pericolo del riformismo," *Utopia*, 1, no. 2 (10 December 1913), pp. 1–4. From the time of his early manhood, Mussolini provided evidence of his familiarity with Marxist thought.

64. Mussolini, "Al largo," *Utopia*, 1, no. 1 (22 November 1913), pp. 1–4.

65. Mussolini spoke of such "ideological" or "doctrinal" formulations as "derivations" in the Paretan sense—an effort to capture in language some collection of empirical realities and the relationships among them. See Vilfredo Pareto, *The Mind and Society: A Treatise on General Sociology* (New York: Dover Publications, 1935), 1, para. 162.

66. See Mussolini on the "fatalism" implied in the positivistic interpretation of classical Marxism in "Il valore attuale del socialismo," *Oo*, 6, pp. 181–182.

67. See Mussolini's discussion in "L'impresa disperata," *Utopia*, 2, no. 2 (15 January 1914), pp. 1–5.

68. *Ibid.*, p. 5.

69. Mussolini published Valentino Piccoli's positive article on "Sorel and Bergson," in the February 1914 issue of *Utopia*. Mussolini had literally absolute control of whatever material entered the pages of his journal.

70. Mussolini, "Abbasso la guerra!" *Oo*, 6, pp. 287–288.

71. Mussolini, "Mezzo milione di organizzati sono col Partito Socialista per la neuralità assolute dell'Italia," and "La triplice non è ancora liquidata," *Oo*, 6, pp. 311, 364.

72. Mussolini, "Un accordo Anglo-Franco-Russo per la discussione delle condizioni di pace," *Oo*, 6, p. 359.

73. Mussolini, "La situazione internazionale," and "Un accordo Anglo-Franco-Russo per la discussione delle condizioni di pace," "Contro la guerra," *Oo*, 6, pp. 359, 361, 366.

74. See Mussolini's interview with *Giornale d'Italia* in October 1914, "Neutralità e socialismo," *Oo*, 6, particularly p. 377. Mussolini's position "evolved" in the weeks between the declaration of war by the major powers and October. See "'La subordinata' . . . ," *Oo*, 6, p. 350. In September, Mussolini made very clear that in the rapidly changing situation, "only lunatics and the dead have the luxury of not altering their ideas." "La situazione internationale," *Oo*, 6, p. 363. He speaks of uncertainty and vacillation in an environment undergoing such taxing complexity and catastrophic implications. His francophila varied with time, and he acknowledged that a war against Austria would not be strenuously opposed by Italian socialists. See "Intermezzo polemico," *Oo*, 6, pp. 382–383.

75. "Should the Austrians . . . mount a punitive expedition against Italy [for failing to meet its treaty obligations] . . . many of those who today are considered antipatriotic will discharge their duty." Mussolini, "De profundis," *Oo*, 6, p. 295. Mussolini reminded his readers that socialists, communists and communards, rather than the bourgeoisie, had resisted the German invasion of 1870. Mussolini, "Hervé: La guerra e immonda," *Oo*, 6, p. 307.

76. Mussolini, "Note di guerra," *Oo*, 6, pp. 322–323.

77. Mussolini, "Contro confusioni, lusinghe, sofismi per la via diritta del socialismo: Il 'delirium tremens' nazionalista," *Oo*, 6, p. 343.

78. Mussolini, "I communisti e la guerra," *Oo*, 6, p. 334.

79. Mussolini, "Note di guerra," *Oo*, 6, p. 321.

80. Mussolini, "La polemica Mussolini-Tancredi: Fra la paglia e il bronzo," *Oo*, 6, p. 392.

81. This was precisely the position assumed by Georgi Plekhanov, Russia's foremost Marxist, in advocating socialist support for czarist Russia's war against Germany. See the account given by Arturo Labriola, *La conflagrazione europea e il socialismo*, pp. 97–98. He was vehemently denounced by Lenin as a consequence.

82. Mussolini, "Dalla neutralità assoluta alla neutralità attiva ed operante," *Oo*, 6, pp. 393–403.

83. Mussolini, "La neutralità socialista: Una lettera del Prof. Mussolini," *Oo*, 6, p. 421.

84. Mussolini, "La situazione internazionale e l'atteggiamento del partito," *Oo*, 6, pp. 427–429.

85. Mussolini, "Mussolini riconferma la sua avversione alla neutralità: Il nuovo giornale sta per uscire," *Oo*, 6, pp. 430–452.

10. THE GREAT WAR, REVOLUTION, AND LENINISM

1. One of the most recent statements of this position is found in Mark Neocleous, *Fascism* (Minneapolis: University of Minnesota Press, 1997), chap. 1. Very similar notions are to be found in Dave Renton, *Fascism: Theory and Practice* (London: Pluto Press, 1999).

2. See the introductory discussion to Steven Kull, *Burying Lenin: The Revolution in Soviet Ideology and Foreign Policy* (Boulder, Colo.: Westview Press, 1992), pp. 1, 6; and that in Richard Pipes, *Russia under the Bolshevik Regime* (New York: Random House, 1995).

3. See the discussion in Walter Laqueur, *The Dream that Failed: Reflections on the Soviet Union* (New York: Oxford University Press, 1994), pp. 147, 149.

4. See Mikail Agursky, *The Third Rome: National Bolshevism in the USSR* (Boulder, Colo.: Westview Press, 1987).

5. Lenin, "Critical Remarks on the National Question," and "On the National Pride of the Great Russians," in *Collected Works* (Moscow: Progress Publishers, 1964; hereafter *LCW*), 20, p. 34; 21, p. 103.

6. Lenin, "On the National Pride of the Great Russians," pp. 104, 106.

7. *Ibid.*, p. 103.

8. Friedrich Engels, Letter to Marx, 15 August 1870.

9. See the discussion in chapter nine of the present text. The writings of Marx and Engels that cover this entire strategy in extensive exposition are conveniently collected in *Marx on China* (with an Introduction by Dona Torr; London: Lawrence & Wishart, 1968); J. A. Doerig (ed.), *Marx vs. Russia* (New York: Frederick Ungar Publishing Co., 1962); and Paul W. Blackstock and Bert F. Hoselitz (eds.), *The Russian Menace to Europe* (Glencoe, Ill.: The Free Press, 1952).

10. These were the grounds for the claim that Marx was, in some comprehensible sense, a German nationalist. See the discussion in Leopold Schwarzschild, *The Red Prussian: The Life and Legend of Karl Marx* (London: Hamish Hamilton, 1948).

11. "History has now confronted [the Russian proletariat] with an immediate task which is the *most revolutionary* of all the *immediate* tasks confronting the proletariat of any country. . . . [That] will make the Russian proletariat the vanguard of the international revolutionary proletariat." Lenin, "What is to be Done?" *LCW*, 5, p. 373.

12. Lenin, "On the National Pride of the Great Russians," *LCW*, 21, p. 105.

13. Lenin, "Revision of the Party Programme," *LCW*, 26, pp. 168–169.

14. Karl Marx, "Persia-China," *New York Daily Tribune*, 5 June 1857, in *Marx on China*, pp. 48–49.

15. *Ibid.*, p. 50 and Dona Torr, "Introduction" to *Marx on China*, p. xvii.

16. For example: "The world proletarian revolution is clearly maturing," and "The time is near when the first day of the world revolution will be celebrated everywhere." *The State and Revolution: The Marxist Theory of the State and the Tasks of the Proletriat in the Revolution* and "Speech at a Rally in Honour of the Austro-Hungarian Revolution November 3 1918," in *LCW*, 25, p. 383; 28, p. 131. Lenin regularly insisted that "imperialism" had "created all the objective conditions for the achievement of socialism. In Western Europe and in the United States, therefore, the revolutionary struggle of the proletariat for the overthrow of capitalist governments and the expropriation of the bourgeoisie is on the order of the day." Lenin regularly spoke of "the impending proletarian revolution in Europe—in Austria, Italy, Germany, France and even Britain." Lenin, "The Socialist Revolution and the Right of Nations to Self-Determination," and "The Proletarian Revolution and the Renegade Kautsky," *LCW*, 22, p. 143; 28, p. 105.

17. Lenin, *Imperialism*, p. 194.

18. Rosa Luxemburg, *The Russian Revolution and Leninism or Marxism?* (Ann Arbor: University of Michigan Press, 1961).

19. Karl Kautsky, *The Dictatorship of the Proletariat* (Ann Arbor: University of Michigan Press, 1964; first published in 1919).

20. See the discussion in John Kautsky, "Introduction" to *ibid.*, p. viii.

21. *Ibid.*, p. 2.

22. *Ibid.*, p. 6.

23. *Ibid.*, pp. 13–15.

24. *Ibid.*, p. 16.

25. Marx and Engels, *The Communist Manifesto*, section I.

26. Kautsky, *The Dictatorship of the Proletariat*, p. 17.

27. Kautsky had made the argument long before his controversy with the Bolsheviks. See his *Die soziale Revolution. II Am Tage nach der Sozialen Revolution* (Berlin: Vorwärts, 1904), pp. 45–48; *The Road to Power* (Chicago: Samuel A. Bloch, 1900); and *Parlamentarismus und Demokratie* (Stuttgart: Verlag von J. H. W. Dietz, 1911; first edition 1893).

28. See the discussion in Kautsky, *The Class Struggle (Erfurt Program)* (New York: W. W. Norton and Co., 1971), pp. 90–91.

29. Kautsky, *Der Weg zur Macht: Politische Betrachtungen über das Hineinwachsen in die Revolution* (Berlin: Buchhandlung Vorwärts, 1909), pp. 71–72.

30. "The most effective weapon of the proletariat is its numerical strength. It cannot emancipate itself until it has become the largest class of the population, and until capitalist society is so far developed that the small peasants and the lower middle classes no longer overweight the proletariat." Kautsky, *The Dictatorship of the Proletariat*, p. 29; see the discussion on p. 19.

31. "The Bolshevist Revolution was based on the supposition that it would be the starting point of a general European revolution, and that the bold initiative of Russia would summon the proletariat of all Europe to rise." *Ibid.*, p. 62.

32. Marx, "Preface to the Russian Edition of 1882" of *The Communist Manifesto*. A great deal has been written concerning Marx's comments in the Preface of 1882 to the *Manifesto*. See Teodor Shanin, *Late Marx and the Russian Road: Marx and 'The*

Peripheries of Capitalism'. In the final analysis, Marx's comments in the Preface constituted his closing thoughts on revolution in a backward industrial environment. At almost the same time as he wrote the 1882 preface to the *Manifesto*, Marx wrote a draft reply to Vera Zasulich, who had posed the question of whether a Russian revolution might or might not escape the stages of capitalist development in attaining socialism. In his drafts, Marx wrote that common land ownership in Russia might provide the basis for an indigenous socialist system since the "contemporaneity of capitalist production" in Europe and North America would "provide it with ready-made material conditions for huge-scale common labor" (*ibid.*, p. 111). Marx and Engels had both written too much to imagine that they could argue that a backward economy might "skip stages" and "leap" from an agrarian to a "socialist" economy. In 1867, Marx had written that "even when a society has got upon the right track . . . it can neither clear by bold leaps, nor remove by legal enactments, the obstacles offered by the successive phases of normal developement." Marx, *Capital* (Moscow: Foreign Languages Publishing House, 1954), p. 10. See the comments by Derek Sayer and Philip Corrigan, "Late Marx: Continuity, Contradiction and Learning," in Shanin, *Late Marx and the Russian Road*, p. 80.

33. See Kautsky's discussion in *Grundsätze und Forderungen des Socialdemokratie: Erleutergungen zum Erfurter Programm* (Berlin: Buchandlung Vorwärts, 1905).

34. Kautsky, *The Dictatorship of the Proletariat*, p. 26.

35. See Kautsky's detailed discussion in "Monarchischer und parlamentarischer Absolutismus," and "Die moderne Demokratie," in Kautsky, *Parlamentarismus und Demokratie*, pp. 42–63.

36. See the discussion in Kautsky's two forwards to the two editions of *Parlamentarismus und Demokratie*, the first written during Engels's lifetime.

37. Kautsky, *The Dictatorship of the Proletariat*, p. 28.

38. *Ibid.*

39. *Ibid.*, p. 46.

40. See the comments by John Kautsky in *ibid.*, pp. xx–xxi.

41. Lenin, "The Proletarian Revolution and the Renegade Kautsky," *LCW*, 28, pp. 229, 230.

42. *Ibid.*, pp. 235, 236.

43. *Ibid.*, pp. 237, 238–239.

44. See Lenin's account in *The State and Revolution*, *LCW*, 25, pp. 390–391, 415–416.

45. Lenin, "The Proletarian Revolution and the Renegade Kautsky," pp. 240, 241.

46. Engels, "Introduction," Marx, *The Civil War in France* in *MESW*, 1, p. 485.

47. Lenin, "Proletarian Revolution and the Renegade Kautsky," pp. 244, 245.

48. *Ibid.*, pp. 247, 248, 249.

49. *Ibid.*, pp. 250, 251, 255, 260, 268.

50. See Lenin's comments in *The State and Revolution*, *LCW*, 25, p. 408 and passim.

51. See particularly, Kautsky, *The Dictatorship of the Proletariat*, p. 85.

52. Lenin added a section, "The Presentation of the Question by Marx in 1852," to *The State and Revolution*, in 1919, making reference to Kautsky's pamphlet; see pp. 411–413.

53. *Ibid.*, p. 484.

54. *Ibid.*, pp. 386, 387, 392, 393.

55. *Ibid.*, pp. 463, 468, 470.

56. *Ibid.*, pp. 393, 400, 404, 425, 426, 436. Lenin insisted that "Marx was a centralist." *Ibid.*, p. 429.

57. In *The Communist Manifesto*, Marx acknowledges that the peasantry does find itself allied with the bourgeoisie in order to "to save from extinction their existence as fractions of the middle class. They are therefore not revolutionary, but conservative. Nay, more, they are reactionary." Engels, in his "prefatory note" to *The Peasant War in Germany* does speak of "agricultural laborers" as "natural allies" of the proletariat, but it is clear that the relationship is not expected to be enduring. Engels, "Prefatory Note to *The Peasant War in Germany*, *MESW*, 1, pp. 644–647.

58. Lenin, *The State and Revolution*, p. 406.

59. *Ibid.*, pp. 411–412. See Lenin quoting Engels on the role of the postrevolutionary state, *ibid.*, p. 440. Lenin spoke of an arrangement in which the "political power" did not suppress the majority—only the minority, the "exploiters"—hence did not require a "state." See *ibid.*, p. 441.

60. Louise Bryant, the widow of John Reed, the author of *Ten Days that Shook the World*, was prepared to argue that "the Red Terror" that devastated Russia in the early years of the Soviet Union was only to be expected given the dreadful realities of war and revolution. Louise Bryant, *Mirrors of Moscow* (New York: Host, 1937), pp. 48–49.

61. See the entire discussion in Nikolai Bukharin, *Economia del periodo di trasformazione* (Milan: Jaca, 1971), chap. 8.

62. *Ibid.*, pp. 150–152.

63. See the entire discussion in *ibid.*, pp. 154–157.

64. Lenin speaks of introducing compulsory labor *first*, before instituting it as a feature of the economy.

65. Lenin, "The Immediate Tasks of the Soviet Government," *LCW*, 27, pp. 241, 245, 251, 252, 253.

66. See the account in Geoffrey Hosking, *The First Socialist Society: A History of the Soviet Union from Within* (Cambridge, Mass.: Harvard University Press, 1985), pp. 68–84.

67. *Ibid.*, pp. 263, 264.

68. Lenin, "Once Again on the Trade Unions, the Current Situation, and the Mistakes of Trotsky and Bukharin," *LCW*, 32, pp. 74, 82, 84, 85, 86.

69. Lenin, "The Tax in Kind," *LCW*, 32, pp. 334, 335, 336.

70. "The system of socialist dictatorship could be called state socialism if the phrase had not been so misused in common usage." The phrase would be serviceable if one kept in mind that "the working class collectively organized as the *proletarian* state administered the economy." Bukharin, *Economia del periodo di trasformazione*, pp. 117–120.

71. Lenin, "Third Congress of the Communist International," *LCW*, 32, p. 458. Elsewhere, Lenin characterized "state capitalism" as a system that involved "a free market and capitalism, both subject to state control," in "The Role and Functions of the Trade Unions under the New Economic Policy," *LCW*, 33, p. 184.

72. Lenin, "Fourth Anniversary of the October Revolution," *LCW*, 33, p. 57.

73. *Ibid.*, pp. 51, 57, 58.

74. Lenin, "Tenth All-Russia Conference of RCP (B)," *LCW*, 33, p. 408. The acknowledgment of the primitive economy of Russia is found throughout Lenin's writings and speeches. See, for example, Lenin, "Better Fewer, but Better," *LCW*, 33, pp. 500–501.

75. Lenin, "The New Economic Policy and the Tasks of the Political Education Departments," *LCW*, 33, p. 62.

76. Lenin, "Seventh Moscow Gubernia Conference of the Russian Communist Party," *LCW*, 33, p. 85.

77. In speaking of the decision to implement the New Economic Policy, Lenin said that "sheer necessity has driven us to this path." "Ninth All-Russia Congress of Soviets," *LCW*, 33, p. 158.

78. Lenin, "The New Economic Policy and the Tasks of the Political Education Departments," *LCW*, 33, p. 66.

79. Lenin, "Seventh Moscow Gubernia Conference . . . ," *LCW*, 33, pp. 94, 99. "The transfer of state enterprises to the so-called profit basis is inevitably and inseparably connected with the New Economic Policy; in the near future this is bound to become the predominant, if not the sole, form of state enterprise." Lenin, "The Role and Functions of the Trade Unions under the New Economic Policy," *LCW*, 33, 185.

80. See Lenin, "Tenth Congress of the RCP (B)," *LCW*, 33, p. 266, "The International and Domestic Situation of the Soviet Republic," *ibid.*, p. 222, and "Eleventh Congress of the RCP (B)," *ibid.*, p. 285.

81. Lenin, "Fourth Anniversary of the October Revolution," *LCW*, 33, p. 59, "Ninth All-Russia Congress of Soviets," *LCW*, 33, p. 161. In the same context, Lenin spoke of undertaking the arduous task of "economic development" for backward Russia. *Ibid.*, p. 172. See Lenin's comments on the increasing trade with foreign capitalists in his report to the "Eleventh Congress of the RCP (B)," *ibid.*, p. 283, and his comments on the necessity of a requisite "material base" for socialism in "On Cooperation," *ibid.*, pp. 474–475.

82. Lenin, "The Role and Functions of the Trade Unions," *LCW*, 33, pp. 188, 189.

83. *Ibid.*, p. 190. "The Party is the leader, the vanguard of the proletariat, which rules directly." Lenin, "Once Again on the Trade Unions," *LCW*, 32, p. 98.

84. Lenin, "The Role and Functions of the Trade Unions," *LCW*, 33, pp. 190, 191, 192. The trade unions were told that the "right of decision lies solely with the business organisations." *Ibid.*, p. 190.

85. "The state is the sphere of coercion." Lenin, "Once Again on the Trade Unions," *LCW*, 32, p. 97.

86. Lenin, "The Role and Functions of the Trade Unions," *LCW*, 33, p. 193.

87. Lenin, "Ninth All-Russia Congress of Soviets," *LCW*, 33, p. 174, and "International and Domestic Situation," *ibid.*, p. 219.

88. Lenin, "Eleventh Congress of the RCP(B)," *LCW*, 33, p. 278.

11. THE GREAT WAR, REVOLUTION, AND FASCISM

1. Years later, in conversations with Yvon De Begnac, Mussolini testified that in March 1919, when the Fascist movement was founded, there were few prepared to follow. See Yvon De Begnac, *Palazzo Venezia: Storia di un regime* (Rome: Editrice la Rocca, 1950), p. 161.

2. The term *"fascio"* is a generic term that refers, in general, to "association." It was used quite indiscriminately in Italy prior to the Great War. There were Sicilian *fasci* that in the 1890s organized agricultural workers in combinations for the protection of their interests. In the early 1900s, there had been a *Fascio medicale parlamentare*, a parliamentary interest group devoted to the interests of medical doctors—and during the war, the Marxist interventionists organized themselves into a *Fascio d'azione rivoluzionaria*. At the end of 1918, A. O. Olivetti proposed the term *"fascismo,"* and *Fasci Italiani di combattimento*, to identify the various groups of Marxist interventionists, and ultimately all veterans that had served in the war, who opposed "antinational socialism." See Mussolini's discussion in "A raccolta!" *Opera omnia* (Florence: La fenice, 1953; hereafter *Oo*), 12, pp. 27–28.

3. See, for example, Mussolini's complaint against official socialism's defeatism during the war. Mussolini, "Fiasco," *Oo*, 13, p. 44. There were any number of similar complaints in his speeches and writings during this period.

4. Mussolini spoke of a government of those who had fought in the trenches—a "trenchocracy"—as well as an "aristocracy of the trenches." Mussolini, "'Il popolo d'Italia' nel 1919," *Oo*, 12, p. 70, and "Agli Arditi di Trieste," and "Guglielmo Oberdan," *Oo*, 12, pp. 80, 90, "Convergere gli sforzi!" *Oo*, 13, pp. 37–38.

5. Mussolini, "Le otto ore di lavoro: Una lettera di Prezzolini," *Oo*, 12, pp. 9–10.

6. Mussolini, "Il nostra costituente," *Oo*, 12, pp. 3–5.

7. Mussolini, "Atto di nascita," *Oo*, 12, p. 325. In May, that same year, Mussolini maintained that a realistic and active socialism would be predicated on "the nation and the productive classes" of which it was composed. "The rest," he maintained, "would follow." Mussolini, "Dopo quattro anni," *Oo*, 11, p. 55. In a major speech that same month, Mussolini insisted that Italians must demonstrate their potential as a "nation of producers," in order to assure themselves a place among the "leaders of modern civilization." Mussolini, "La vittoria fatale," *Oo*, 11, pp. 86–87. "Italians," Mussolini insisted, were to manifest themselves as a "new race of producers, of constructors, of creators." Mussolini, "Intermezzo velivolare: Il mio collaudo sullo 'SVA,'" *Oo*, 11, p. 171. See Mussolini, "Dopoguerra: Andate incontro al lavoro che tornerà dalle trincee," *Oo*, 11, pp. 469–470.

8. In April, Mussolini had made the position of his "national syndicalism" explicit. See Mussolini, "Variazioni su vecchio motivo: Il fucile e la vanga," *Oo*, 11, p. 35.

9. In May 1920, in the "postulates" of its program, Fascism "acknowledged the immense value of that 'working middle class [borghesia di lavoro]' which constitutes, in all fields of human activity (that of industry and agriculture, from science to the liberal professions), that precious and indispensable element for the progress and the triumph of our national fortunes." "Postulati del programma fascista (Mag-

gio 1920)," in Renzo De Felice, *Mussolini il rivoluzionario (1883–1920)* (Turin: Giulio Einaudi editore, 1965), p. 746.

10. Mussolini, "Novità . . . ," *Oo*, 11, pp. 242–243; see Mussolini, "Orientamenti e problemi," *Oo*, 11, pp. 282–284.

11. Mussolini, "Il sindacalismo nazionale: Per rinascere!" *Oo*, 12, pp. 12–14. See Mussolini's comments in "Idee e propositi durante e dopo la guerra dell'Unione italiana del laboro," *Oo*, 11, pp. 262–263.

12. A detailed account of the influence of others would exceed the space available. Mussolini, for example, identified Roberto Forges-Davanzati, and Paolo Orano as important. Both were early revolutionary syndicalists, who, before the Great War, sought to bridge the distance between syndicalism and nationalism. Sergio Panunzio, of course, was far more influential than either. For a more comprehensive account of the work of Panunzio, see A. James Gregor, *Mussolini's Intellectuals: Fascist Social and Political Thought* (Princeton: Princeton University Press, 2005), chap. 4, and *Sergio Panunzio: Il sindacalismo ed il fondamento razionale del fascismo* (Rome: Volpe, 1978).

13. Mussolini, "Blocco Latino: Italia e Francia," *Oo*, 12, p. 43; see "La nostra risposta al consiglio comunale di Fiume," *ibid.*, p. 60.

14. For a more extensive discussion, see the account in A. James Gregor, *Young Mussolini and the Intellectual Origins of Fascism* (Berkeley: University of California Press, 1979), chap. 4.

15. See Mussolini's comments on the lack of definition in dealing with the various classes in "Guglielmo Oberdan," *Oo*, 12, p. 91.

16. Mussolini, "Per intenderci: In tema di 'costituente'," *Oo*, 12, p. 53.

17. As has been indicated, Mussolini was fully aware of this body of literature, and found its essentials unobjectionable. In 1909, when he was in his mid-twenties, he favorably reviewed Roberto Michels's tract, *Cooperazione*, which dealt with generic group sentiment, ingroup amity, and outgroup enmity. Mussolini, "Fra libri e riviste," *Oo*, 2, pp. 248–249.

18. For a more extended account, see A. James Gregor, *The Ideology of Fascism: The Rationale of Totalitarianism* (New York: Free Press, 1969), pp. 72–92. In one place, Mussolini clearly argued for the rise of European nationalism as a consequence of political, material, and military circumstances. See Mussolini, "Francia e Italia," *Oo*, 11, pp. 198–199.

19. See the treatment in Mussolini, "Un altro passo," *Oo*, 12, pp. 228–230.

20. See Mussolini's discussion of the various "imperialisms" of the period in "Primo dell'anno prima divagazione," *Oo*, 12, pp. 100–103.

21. Mussolini regularly referred to Italy as a "proletarian nation." It had become commonplace among nationalists and syndicalists to so characterize their nation. See, for example, Mussolini, "Ideali e affari," *Oo*, 13, p. 72.

22. See Mussolini, "Scoperte . . . ," *Oo*, 11, pp. 288–289.

23. Mussolini, "Il sindacalismo nazionale: Per rinascere," *Oo*, 12, pp. 11–14, "Precisiamo!" *ibid.*, pp. 20–21, "Doveri comuni," *ibid.*, pp. 35–36, "La politica nazionale: Primo squillo," *ibid.*, p. 223.

24. See Filippo Corridoni, *Sindacalismo e repubblica* (Milan: S.A.R.E.P., 1945; reprint of the 1915 edition), pp. 19–20, 23, 25–27, 34, 48–49, 55, 82.

25. In September, Mussolini had reviewed and approved the program of "national syndicalism" in "'Tu quoque,' Jouhoux?" *Oo*, 11, pp. 356–358; and in November, Mussolini reviewed and approved, once again, the elements of "national syndicalism" as a proper socialism for a postwar Europe. See Mussolini, "Il sindacalismo nazionale: Per rinascere!" *Oo*, 12, pp. 12–14.

26. Mussolini, "Conquiste e programmi," *Oo*, 12, pp. 242–245. Mussolini applauded similar theses articulated at a workers' conference in Berne, Switzerland. See his report, "Nel mondo sindacale Italiano," and "Precisiamo," *Oo*, 12, pp. 20–21, 249–250.

27. During this period, Mussolini regularly spoke of the imperative of production and development. "'Produce!' remains the first and capital commandment of the hour." Mussolini, "Un ordine del giorno," *Oo*, 12, p. 260.

28. See the discussion in Mussolini, "Nel mondo sindacale italiano: Rettifiche di tiro," *Oo*, 12, pp. 249–252.

29. Mussolini, "Conquiste e programmi," *Oo*, 12, pp. 244, 245.

30. See Mussolini's comments to De Begnac in *Palazzo Venezia*, p. 116.

31. The following is drawn from Mussolini, "Apologia o condanna? Il 'documento' Sadoul," *Oo*, 12, pp. 301–305.

32. Mussolini regularly cited the criticisms of Leninism by Karl Kautsky to support his arguments; see, for example, Mussolini, "Fra due conferenze: Il congresso-processo di Berna," "La politica nazionale: Primo squillo," "Un ordine del giorno," "Un'altra requisitoria," *Oo*, 12, pp. 204–206, 223, 261, 275.

33. "The masters . . . of the school of socialism . . . taught us that socialism can materialize only in objective and determinate circumstances" that include "the fact that capitalism had achieved the final stage of its development, a national economy reduced to the control of a few monopolists of the means of production and exchange. Opposed to those plutocrats, there was to be a wretched mass of impoverished workers who would expropriate them. . . . Such a revolution would be possible only if the proletariat had matured to economic consciousness, enured to organization and managerial responsibilities." See Mussolini, "Divagazione," *Oo*, 11, pp. 341–342.

34. The following follows the account of Mussolini, "Babau," *Oo*, 12, pp. 184–185.

35. See the discussion in Karl Kautsky, *Die materialistische Geschichtsauffassung* (Berlin: J. H. W. Dietz Verlag, 1929), 2, part 3.

36. Karl Marx, Preface, *The Critique of Political Economy* (Chicago: Charles H. Kerr and Company, 1918), p. 12.

37. Engels had predicted just such an eventuality in circumstances where a "revolutionary leader" made revolution in primitive economic conditions. Engels, *The Peasant War in Germany* in Karl Marx and Frederick Engels, *Collected Works* (New York: International Publishers, 1978), 10, pp. 469–470.

38. See, for example, Mussolini, "Gli orrori del 'banditismo' Leninista denunciati da un socialista Russo nella rivista di Filippo Turati," *Oo*, 11, pp. 394–395.

39. Mussolini argued that Lenin had reconstructed the traditional "bourgeois" political system, resting the state on the trinity of "bureaucracy, the military, and the police." The military, Mussolini added, was used not only to protect national

borders, but also for territorial expansion. Mussolini, "Crepuscoli: I templi le gli idoli," *Oo*, 14, p. 337.

40. See Mussolini's comments in "La politica nazionale: Primo squilo," *Oo*, 12, pp. 222–223, and "Posizione," together with "Triplice condanna," *Oo*, 13, pp. 29, 77–79.

41. Mussolini, "Divagazione: Contro la bestia ritornante . . ." *Oo*, 12, pp. 231–232.

42. Mussolini, "Un altro passo," *Oo*, 12, pp. 229–230.

43. All these themes had been bruited by syndicalists and their sympathizers before and early in the course of the Great War. See the discussion in Roberto Michels, *L'imperialismo italiano* (Milan: Societa Editrice Libraria, 1914), and Corridoni, *Sindacalismo e repubblica*.

44. Mussolini, "Nel mondo sindacale Italiano: Rettifiche di tiro," *Oo*, 12, pp. 250–251.

45. The following provides a summary of Mussolini's presentation in the hall of the Industrial and Commercial Alliance at the meeting at 9 Piazza San Sepolcro, Milan, in the morning of 23 March 1919. Mussolini, "Atto di nascita del fascismo," *Oo*, 12, pp. 321–327.

46. See, for example, Mussolini, "Ideali e affari," *Oo*, 13, p. 72. There was a regular repetition of the twin themes, the *nation* and *production*, in Mussolini writings and discourses. See Mussolini, "Il fascismo e le agitazioni operaei," and "Sindacalismo francese: Una dichiarazione-programma," *Oo*, 14, pp. 245, 286.

47. Mussolini spelled out the relationship in a number of places. In one place he cataloged the elements: "There can be no greatness for the nation . . . without the development of production . . . and [that cannot be forthcoming] without the nation securing its place in the world." Mussolini, "Le minoranze sindacali in Italia: Dall'episodio alla situazione generale," *Oo*, 14, p. 329.

48. Mussolini spoke of Italians suffering a "precapitalist mentality" in a world of intense economic and political competition. He spoke of the nation's economy as a vassal to that of foreigners. He insisted that the Italy of tour guides and mandolin players was a thing of the past, and that "production" was to be the imperative guiding Italy's "marvelous rebirth." "Production, production, production" was the immediate necessity. "Producers" were to be the normative models for the new Italy. Mussolini, "Orientamenti e problemi," *Oo*, 11, pp. 282–284.

49. As has been indicated, Mussolini had long so understood the dynamics of mass movements. For a typical treatment, see Mussolini, "La data," *Oo*, 11, p. 370.

50. The explicit argument with which Mussolini, as a revolutionary socialist and syndicalist, was familiar, was that of Roberto Michels, *Zur Soziologie des Parteiwesens* of 1911, which appeared in an Italian edition as *Sociologia del partito politico nella democrazia moderna* in 1912. The central argument, common to all the antiparliamentaristic sentiments of the radicals, was that all organizations have "oligarchic tendencies," and the suggestion that parliamentary democracy might be an exception was seen as a fiction. Parliamentary democracy was the "charter myth" of bourgeois oligarchic rule. Mussolini was familiar with Michels's works as early as 1909. See Roberto Michels, *Political Parties* (New York: Dover, 1959). Before the Great War, Mussolini spoke of "parliamentary cretinism," as conducive to "fraud" and deception, created to corrupt and be corrupted—governed by those possessed of

wealth and titles. See Mussolini, "La fattucciera," "Il primo congresso dei 'destri,'" *Oo*, 5, pp. 8–9, 25.

51.   The "maximization of production" was a constant theme during the first months of organization for the *fasci*. See, for example, Mussolini, "Orientamenti e problemi," *Oo*, 11, pp. 282–28, "Nel mondo sindacale Italiano: Rettifiche di tiro," *Oo*, 12, pp. 249–251. The indifference to specific tactics for those that actually worked was a recurrent theme. Mussolini, "Le minoranze sindacali in Italia: Dall'episodio alla situazione generale," *Oo*, 14, p. 329.

52.   Marxism, in general, held government in "bourgeois" circumstances to be little other than a committee that served the interests of property. Engels clearly dismissed the representative democracy of the United States of the period as offering nothing other than opportunities for "politicians" to form "a separate and powerful section of the nation" to control the proletariat. See Engels, Introduction to "The Civil War in France," in Marx and Engels, *Selected Works* (Moscow: Foreign Languages Publishing House, 1955), 1, p. 483. See Lenin's comments on Engels's view of the "modern representative state" as an "instrument of exploitation of wage-labor by capital." Lenin, "The Proletarian Revolution and the Renegade Kautsky," *Collected Works* (Moscow: Progress Publishers, 1965), 28, p. 243. Lenin insisted that elections could only serve as indicators of public sentiment and that only the "authority of the armed people," rather than the exercise of suffrage, could determine society's future. *Ibid.*, p. 255.

53.   Mussolini, "Dopo quattro anni," *Oo*, 11, pp. 54–55. See "La vittoria fatale," *Oo*, 11, pp. 86–87.

54.   Mussolini spoke candidly of what "socialism" might be understood to be. He insisted that so much of what had been socialism had been transformed by events, that it was impossible to pretend that "socialism" had a single significance. Whatever socialism was to be after the conclusion of the Great War, it would have to address contemporary problems rather than pretend that it might simply remain "loyal" to dogmas half-a-hundred years old. See Mussolini "Divagazione," *Oo*, 11, pp. 270–272.

55.   See the discussion in Mussolini, "Dopo il congresso sindacale: Orientamenti," *Oo*, 11, p. 118.

56.   See the entire discussion in Sergio Panunzio, *Sindacalismo e medioevo (Politica contemporanea)* (Naples: Partenopea, 1911), where the objections are raised against the suppression of workers' "autonomy" under the "leaden weight of the political state." See *ibid.*, pp. 7–11, 18, 34–37, 41–43. At that time, Panunzio held that "syndicalism prepares, with the sovereignty of syndicates, for the destruction of the *unity* of the state and the advent of *particularistic and autonomous* economic, political and social regime comparable to the communes of medieval times." *Ibid.*, p. 57.

57.   Panfilo Gentile, "Stato e sindacato," *Utopia*, 2, nos. 9–10 (July 1914), pp. 273–277.

58.   These are issues raised early by Panunzio in his discussion concerning the role of law in any future syndicalist state. In 1912, about the same time that Gentile wrote his piece for *Utopia*, Panunzio published his *Il diritto e l'autorità: Contributo alla concezione filosofica del diritto* (Turin: U.T.E.T., 1912), in which he argued for the possibilty of the persistence of law and authority without the existence of a state.

59. Mussolini, "Studi socialisti: Tentativi di revisionismo," *Oo*, 5, pp. 203–207.

60. *Ibid.*, p. 206. The general index of persons named in the *Opera omnia*, volume 36 (see p. 85), does not cite Giovanni Gentile's name on the indicated page, but that is clearly an oversight. Mussolini is unmistakably referring to Giovanni Gentile as the "other Gentile" that served as a "guide" to Panfilo Gentile.

61. Years later, in his discussion with Yvon De Begnac, Mussolini said that by 1908 he had already opposed himself to the representative system of democracy—under the influence of Giovanni Gentile, among others. Yvon De Begnac, *Palazzo Venezia: Storia di un regime* (Rome: La Rocca, 1950), p. 133.

62. See Giovanni Gentile, "Una critica del materialismo storico," in *La filosofia di Marx: Studi critici*, appendix to *I fondamenti della filosofia del diritto* (Florence: G. C. Sansoni, 1955), pp. 143–196.

63. An English version of the 1899 edition of Benedetto Croce, *Historical Materialism and the Economics of Karl Marx* (New York: Macmillan, 1914) is available.

64. In his discussion, Mussolini refers to the criticisms of both Croce and Sorel. Both had argued against the strict determinist interpretation of Marxism—and both sought to provide a defensible ethical rationale for socialism. See in that regard, Georges Sorel, "La necessità e il fatalismo nel marxismo," *Saggi di critica del marxismo* (Milan: Remo Sandron, 1903), pp. 59–94.

65. Giovanni Gentile, *L'atto del pensare come atto puro* (Florence: G. C. Sansoni, 1937; reprint of the 1912 edition).

66. See Gentile's discussion of his "method of immanence" in Giovanni Gentile, *La riforma della dialettica hegeliana* (Florence: G. C. Sansoni, 1954; a third, modified edition of that published in 1913), chap. 8.

67. An excellent exposition of Gentile's social and political thought available in English is H. S. Harris, *The Social Philosophy of Giovanni Gentile* (Urbana: University of Illinois Press, 1960). An English exposition of his technical philosophy can be found in Roger W. Holmes, *The Idealism of Giovanni Gentile* (New York: The Macmillan Company, 1937). I have provided a brief, summary account of Gentile's actualism in Gregor, *The Ideology of Fascism*, chap. 5 and *Giovanni Gentile: Philosopher of Fascism* (New Brunswick: Transaction Publishers, 2004), chap. 3.

68. So seriously, as has been indicated, that V. I. Lenin recommended Gentile's work on Marx to his audiences.

69. See Gentile's discussion in "La filosofia della prassi," in *I fondamenti della filosofia del diritto*, particularly pp. 226–230.

70. The "immanence" of society in the individual is at the core of actualism's epistemology and politics. The argument appears early in his writings and runs throughout his works, in his pedagogical, religious, and technical writings. For an insight into how his method of immanence operates in the political domain, summary treatment is found in his last work, *Genesis and Structure of Society* (Urbana: University of Illinois Press, 1960), conveniently available in English translation. An early expression of the impact of his doctrine of immanence on his political thought can be found in English translation in Gentile, "The Reform of Education," in *Origins and Doctrine of Fascism* (New Brunswick: Transaction Press, 2002).

71. Mario Missiroli, an actualist of sorts, argued in the pages of Mussolini's *Utopia* that "the state and the citizen are one thing. . . . The error of democracy arises in

maintaining that liberty consists in the slackening of the ties between the state and the individual; actually these ties should be eliminated by having each citizen feel himself the state, *entirely the state*." Mario Missiroli, "L'Italia e la Triplice," *Utopia*, 2, 11–12 (15 August–1 September 1914), p. 348.

72. That was the "anti-intellectualism" that characterized actualism. It was the epistemological objection to the disposition of intellectuals to conceive human experience as composed of thinking individuals being confronted with an unthinking and opaque "external" reality. Subsequent discussants interpreted Gentilean anti-intellectualism to mean an opposition to reason and reasoning—a totally objectionable interpretation. See the more elaborate discussion in Gregor, *The Ideology of Fascism*, pp. 120–127, 205–238; and *Mussolini's Intellectuals: Fascist Social and Political Thought* (Princeton: Princeton University Press, 2005), pp. 92–98.

73. Gentile provided a didactic treatment of his notions of immanence and the ultimate reality of multiplicities in unity in his *Introduzione alla filosofia* (Rome: Treves-Treccani-Tumminelli, 1931), chaps. 1 and 2. Recognizing that his account was written in 1931, the discussion on the nature of the state and its relationship to subject individuals is instructive. See particularly p. 16. The notion of the "ethical state," the precondition for the moral "new man" of Fascism is found in its essential entirety in Gentile, *Discorsi di religione* (Florence: G. C. Sansoni, 1955; third edition of the edition of 1920), pp. 20–23.

74. As early as 1920, Gentile included labor, as a creative expression of human kind, in the very making of humanity. See Gentile, *Discorsi di religione*, p. 26. The theme persisted throughout Gentile's intellectual life and appears in his last work as "the humanism of labor." See Gentile, *Genesis and Structure of Society*, pp. 171–172.

75. See, for example, Giovanni Gentile, "La riforma della scuola media," *Rivista d'Italia* (January) 1906, pp. 1–31.

76. As has been indicated, these ideas were known to, and favored by, Giuseppe Prezzolini and the *Vociani*, thinkers and thought that had documented influence on the political convictions of Mussolini. By the end of the Great War, Sergio Panunzio was employing Gentilean ideas in his exposition of revolutionary thought. See the discussion on Panunzio in Gregor, *Mussolini's Intellectuals*.

77. They included G. Lombardo-Radice and Mario Missiroli with whose writings Mussolini was very familiar. Both were Gentileans.

78. See the entire discussion in Gentile, "Le due democrazie," *Dopo la vittoria: Nuovi frammenti politici* (Rome: La voce, 1920), pp. 107–113. See the discussion concerning the relationship of syndicates to the state in "Stati e categorie," *ibid.*, pp. 95–100. At the time, Gentile spoke of the state as being not *inter homines*, but *in interiore homine*, as a reality which "abstract individuals" intrinsically share. See "L'idea monarchica," *ibid.*, p. 154. Years later, in the "Fundamental Ideas" of the official *Dottrina del fascismo*, these thoughts are given expression in the following fashion: "Fascism reaffirms the state as the true reality of the individual. . . . [Fascism] is the most explicit form of democracy if the people are conceived, as they should be, qualitatively rather than quantitatively." Mussolini, *Dottrina del fascismo, Oo*, 34, p. 120.

79. Such notions are found throughout Gentile's early writings and they are explicit in his writings at the time of the Great War. See the discussion in *Dopo la vittoria*, where he states that political leaders have "historic significance" insofar as

they speak for an entire people. Such a leader has a "personality" that represents the will of a people, and acts effectively only insofar as he acts as they would have him act. "The will of he who governs is the same will as that of the people." See Gentile, "Il significato della vittoria," *Dopo la vittoria*, pp. 5–6, 8.

80. When the *Dottrina del fascismo* appeared, that was expressed in the following fashion: "The human being is not an individual separated from all the others to stand alone. The human being of Fascism is an individual who is nation and fatherland, a moral law that unites individuals and generations in a tradition and in a mission, that transcends the instinct of a closed and transient life of pleasure to awake a commitment to a superior life free of the limitations of space and time." Mussolini, *Dottrina del fascismo, Oo*, 34, p. 117.

81. Mussolini, "Per rinacere e progredire: Italia marinara, avanti," *Oo*, 14, pp. 203–206.

82. Mussolini spoke of Italy's lack of industrial minerals, of its lack of iron, coal, and oil—all of which contributed to the nation's lack of competitiveness on the world scene. Mussolini, "Il nostro dovere e quello di liberarci dal giogo della plutocrazia internazionale," *Oo*, 14, pp. 222–224.

83. Mussolini, "Ideale e affari," "L'Adriatico e il Mediterraneo," "Che possiede, paghi!" "Cifre da meditare," *Oo*, 13, pp. 72, 142–143, 224, 284.

84. Strikes cost the national economy 18.9 million man days of labor in 1919 and 16.4 million man days in 1920. See Gianni Toniolo, *L'economia dell'Italia fascista* (Rome: Laterza, 1980), pp. 33–34.

85. Mussolini, "Discorso di Dalmine," *Oo*, 12, 314–316.

86. See Mussolini, "Corso al disastro," "In tema ferroviario: La nostra tesi," "Lo sciopero e un enorme delitto contro la nazione!" *Oo*, 14, pp. 169–170, 242–243, 260, and particularly, "Ripresa scioperista," *Oo*, 18, pp. 195–197.

87. At about the same time, Roberto Michels, who had written on Italy's inability to support its own population as one of the motives of its struggle against the Turkish caliphate, continued to write extensively on the processes involved in the economic and industrial development of less developed nations. See Roberto Michels, *Lavoro e razza* (Milan: Vallardi, 1924). Mussolini, as has been indicated, was familiar with the work of Michels as early as 1909.

88. Corridoni, *Sindacalismo e repubblica*, pp. 55–101.

89. See the discussion in Massimo Rocca, "Un neoliberalismo?" *Risorgimento* (September 1921), reprinted in *Il primo fascismo* (Rome: Volpe, 1964), pp. 45–54. In a protracted debate within the Fascist Party itself, Rocca made the case that many syndicalists, including Filippo Corridoni, Paolo Orano, A. O. Olivetti, and Sergio Panunzio, had contributed substantially to Fascist thought. See Rocca, "Le fonti spirituali del fascismo," *L'Epoca* (10 May 1924), in *Il primo fascismo*, pp. 136–137.

90. See the entire discussion in A. O. Olivetti, "Da Gian Giacomo Rousseau alla Carta del Carnaro," *Pagine libere*, 2 November 1922, reprinted in *Battaglie sindacaliste: Dal sindacalismo al fascismo*, a manuscript copy of a collection of essays by Olivetti, made available by his daughter. To be made available to the University Library of the University of California, Berkeley.

91. Among some of the major syndicalists, like Panunzio, the state finally was recognized as the ultimate arbiter of law.

92. "Programma del PNF (1921)," in Renzo De Felice, *Mussolini il fascista: La conquista del potere 1921–1925* (Turin: Einaudi, 1966), p. 756.

93. *Ibid.*, pp. 756–760.

94. The following account follows that of Mussolini, "L'Azione e la dottrina fascista alle necessità storiche della nazione," *Oo*, 18, pp. 411–421.

95. *Ibid.*, pp. 412–413, 419.

96. See Alberto De' Stefani, *La restaurazione finanziaria: I risultati 'impossibili' della parsimonia* (Rome: Volpe, 1978) and *Una riforma al rogo* (Rome: Volpe, 1963).

97. In June 1922, months before the March on Rome, Mussolini outlined the characteristics of "Fascist syndicalism." It would be a syndicalism that was compatible with the most fundamental interests of the nation: the maintenance and expansion of production. See Mussolini, "Fascismo e sindacalismo," *Oo*, 18, pp. 225–227.

98. Sergio Panunzio, "Lo stato nazionale," in *Che cos'è il fascismo* (Milan: Alpes, 1924), pp. 14–15, and *Stato nazionale e sindacati* (Milan: "Imperia," 1924), particularly pp. 7–11, 31–42, 72–75, 94. Already in March 1922, Panunzio spoke of a "strong, powerful, and disciplined state." *Ibid.*, p. 108. In May 1923, he advocated the construction of a state that was nothing less than "a most powerful Leviathan, a state with powerful judicial capabilities enhanced by an 'economic magistrature' . . . together with a strong military." *Ibid.*, p. 107. Because of the increasing commitment to the dominance of the state, the anarchist intellectuals that had collected around Fascism, removed themselves. Anarchists of the intellectual quality of Ettore Bartolozzi, Virgilio Galbiati and Edoardo Malusardi, withdrew from the Partito nazionale fascista.

99. Mussolini, "Discorso di 3 gennaio," *Oo*, 21, pp. 235–241.

100. Mussolini, "Sulla situazione interna," "58a Riunione del Gran Consiglio del Fascismo," *Oo*, 21, pp. 248, 250–251. In April, he spoke of the imperative need to develop the industrial economy of Italy in order that its armed forces be prepared for war. See the ample discussion in Mussolini, "Per la riforma dell'esercito," *ibid.*, pp. 270–279.

101. Mussolini, "Il trattato di commercio con la Russia," *Oo*, 21, p. 340.

102. Mussolini, "Nulla deve essere al disopra dello stato," *Oo*, 21, pp. 324–336.

103. Mussolini, "Intransigenza assoluta," *Oo*, 21, pp. 357–364.

12. CONCLUSIONS

1. There were many theoreticians, during the 1930s and 1940s, who recognized the shared properties of these systems. Among the more interesting were Mihail Manoilescu, *Die einzige Partei als politische Institution der neuen Regime* (Berlin: Otto Stollberg, 1941); Renzo Bertoni, *Il trionfo del fascismo nell'U.R.S.S.* (Roma: Signorelli, 1933); Bruno Rizzi, *Dove và l'U.R.S.S.?* (Milan: La Prora, 1938); Tomasso Napolitano, "Il 'fascismo' di Stalin ovvero l'U.R.S.S. e noi," *Critica fascista*, 15, 23 (1 October 1937); B. Ricci, "Il 'fascismo' di Stalin," *Critica fascista*, 15, 18 (15 July 1937); A. Nasti, "L'Italia, il bolscevismo, la Russia," *Critica fascista*, 15, 10 (15 March 1937). Leon Trotsky spoke of the "fateful similarities" shared by the political systems of Fascist Italy and Stalin's Russia. See Leon Trotsky, *The Revolution Betrayed* (New York: Doubleday, 1937), p. 278.

2. See the discussion in Roberto Michels, "Der ethische Faktor in der Parteipolitik Italien," *Zeitschrift für Politik*, 3, no. 1 (1909), pp. 56–91.

3. Mussolini's interest in the pragmatists also was sparked by the *Vociani*. Between 1904 and 1913, Giovanni Papini published a number of essays on the pragmatists to ultimately appear as *Pragmatismo* (Florence: Vallecchi, 1943; originally published in 1913). Mussolini was familiar with Papini's work as early as 1909. See Mussolini, *Opera omnia* (Florence: La fenice, 1951; hereafter *Oo*) 1, p. 197; and the more ample discussion in A. James Gregor, *The Ideology of Fascism: The Rationale of Totalitarianism* (New York: Free Press, 1969), pp. 121–126.

4. "You socialists can testify that I was never a positivist—not even when I was a member of your party. For us, we do not acknowledge a dualism of matter and spirit; we have annulled that antithesis in the synthesis of the spirit. Spirit alone exists—nothing else, not you, not this hall, nor things or objects that appear in the fantastic cinematography of the universe. All that exists insofar as I think and only in my thought, and otherwise has no independence. It is the spirit that has returned." Mussolini in a speech delivered in December 1921, "Per la vera pacificazione," *Oo*, 17, p. 298. "Reality is not possible without the thinking . . . actual in consciousness. In order to conceive of a reality one must first conceive of a mind in which that reality represents itself. An [independent] material reality reveals itself as an absurdity." Giovanni Gentile, *Teoria generale dello Spirito come atto puro* (Bari: Laterza, 1924; first edition 1916), p. 1. In a chapter entitled "Reality as Thought," Gentile maintained, "In the first place, in conceiving reality as nature, [that nature] becomes immanent in thought. As a consequence, it becomes impossible to separate it from thought in the effort to render it independent." Gentile, *I fondamenti della filosofia del diritto* (Florence: Sansoni, 1955; first published in 1916), p. 47.

5. Mussolini, as has been indicated, suggested that he was familiar with Gentile's work as early as 1908. See Mussolini's comments to Yvon De Begnac, *Palazzo Venezia: Storia di un Regime* (Rome: La Rocca, 1950), p. 133. By that time Gentile had published his critique of Marx. Marxists were so familiar with that work that, as we have seen, Lenin recommended it. It seems eminently plausible that Mussolini was familiar with the work.

6. Panfilo Gentile, "Stato e sindacato," *Utopia*, 2, nos. 9–10 (15–31 July 1914), pp. 273–277. Sergio Panunzio, a critical intellectual in the articulation of Fascist conceptions of law, morality, and the state, cited that article in his "Il socialismo, la filosofia del diritto e lo stato," *Rivista giuridica del socialism*, 1, nos. 2–3 (June–July 1914), pp. 65–84. By that time it was clear that Mussolini was prepared to consider "critical idealism" as part of the rationale of his convictions.

7. Years later, Ugo Spirito, one of Gentile's foremost pupils, wrote, "[Gentilean] idealism was one of the fundamental theoretical presuppositions of the Fascist revolution." Spirito, *Il fallimento della scuola italiana* (Rome: Armando, 1971), p. 153. Among those works published by Gentile before the Fascist March on Rome most relevant to the development of the Fascist doctrine of the state and law, are Gentile, *La riforma dell'educazione: Discorsi ai maestri di Trieste* (Florence: Sansoni, 1955; originally published in 1919), *Discorsi di religione* (Florence: Sansoni, 1955; originally published in 1920), *I fondamenti della filosofia del diritto* (Florence: Sansoni, 1955; originally published in 1916), *Preliminari allo studio del fanciullo* (Florence: Sansoni,

1958; originally published in 1920–1921), *Sommario di pedagogia come scienza filosofica* (Florence: Sansoni, 1954; originally published in 1914).

8. "The Hegelian ethical state . . . identified with Giovanni Gentile . . . [was] a direct prefiguration of the state of which Mussolini spoke . . . and, in general, of the Fascist state, omnicomprehensive and possessed of every human value." Stelio Zeppi, *Il pensiero politico dell'idealismo italiano e il nazionalfascismo* (Florence: La Nuova Italia, 1973), p. 163.

9. Gentile's treatment of the thought of Karl Marx in *La filosofia di Marx: Studi critici* (Florence: Sansoni, 1955; originally published in 1899), was published before the turn of the twentieth century, and was recommended to Marxists by V. I. Lenin himself. By the time Gentile wrote his critique, he had already read some of Sorel's assessments, and identified Marx's conception of history with the antiliberal conviction that the essence of humankind is *social*. The human being is a *social creature*. Marxists had proceeded to lapse into a form of primitive materialism and identified humankind with the product of Darwinian evolution—to reduce humanity to the level of beasts of the field—to the neglect of consciousness, will, and ethical concerns—without which humans would have no motives to act. See *ibid.*, pp. 163–164, 167–168, 183–185, 226–230. For the critique of Marx's materialism, using a number of the objections of Sorel, see *ibid.*, pp. 210–219, 240–241, 245–255.

10. For a brief discussion of the relationship between the epistemological postures of Marxism and Gentilean idealism see A. James Gregor, *Giovanni Gentile: Philosopher of Fascism* (New Brunswick, N.J.: Transaction Press, 2004), chap. 5.

11. Gentile, *La filosofia di Marx*, p. 298; see the entire discusssion in *ibid.*, chap. 9, "The Philosophy of Praxis."

12. Sergio Panunzio, *Lo stato di diritto* (Ferrara: Taddei, 1921).

13. For a more ample discussion, see A. James Gregor, *Mussolini's Intellectuals: Fascist Social and Political Thought* (Princeton: Princeton University Press, 2005), chap. 4.

14. See particularly *ibid.*, chap. 6.

15. For a more complete account of the intellectual development of Sergio Panunzio, see *ibid.*, chaps. 4 and 7.

16. The paths taken by the two thinkers were very different. Panunzio's reforms of Marxism seem to have had their origin in his wide study of social theory. As distinct from the orthodox interpretation of historical materialism, Panunzio recognized, by way of illustration, that while "group conflict" may have supplied much of the substance of history, the "groups" involved need not always have been "classes." More than that, Panunzio, as a legal theorist, did not find the notion that law was simply the will of the ruling class convincing. Gentile, for his part, had epistemological difficulties with what the orthodox saw as the "materialism" of Marxism.

17. See Gentile's comments in "Una critica del materialismo storici," in *La filosofia di Marx*, pp. 151–155.

18. There are many expositions of Gentile's "actualism." Perhaps the best in English is Roger W. Holmes, *The Idealism of Giovanni Gentile* (New York: Macmillan, 1937) and Patrick Romanell, *The Philosophy of Giovanni Gentile* (New York: Vanni, 1938). The best devoted to his social and political thought is H. S. Harris, *The Social Philosophy of Giovanni Gentile* (Urbana: University of Illinois Press, 1960).

19. In 1914, this was expressed in the following fashion: "What must one do, with others or alone, to create a life worthy of living? . . . One can say: be a human being [*esser uomo!*]—which means to create oneself as such." Gentile, *Sommario di pedagogia come scienza filosofica*, 2, p. 45. At the end of his life, Gentile wrote: "In providing the content of the moral law. . . . I expressed it in the admonition: be a human being [*sii uomo*]." Gentile, *Genesi e struttura della società* (Florence: Sansoni, 1946), p. 44.

20. In the early twenties, Gentile expressed that conviction in the following fashion: "the moral life is the entire spiritual life of man—an ongoing act that continues without end, neither in some fancied ideal nor any probability. . . . A human being is human in so much as he continues to make himself. . . . A human being is entirely a spiritual process; forever in the making." Gentile, *Preliminari allo studio del fanciullo: Appunti* (Florence: Sansoni, 1922), p. 1; see pp. 27–28, 42–43, 52–53. "Human life is spiritual. Its development, by virtue of which it realizes its humanity, is its progressive spiritualization. . . . [One] has the infinite responsibility . . . of affirming [one's own] life." Gentile, *Discorsi di religione* (Florence: Sansoni, 1955; first published in 1920), pp. 33–55. The purpose of institutions is "that lofty mission . . . to arouse those powerful moral energies without which human beings cannot truly live as human beings." Gentile, *La riforma dell'educazione: Discorsi ai maestri di Trieste* (Florence: Sansoni, 1955; originally published in 1919), p. 55.

21. Gentile spoke of the "empirical individual," the individual of which materialists and philosophical realists speak, as an "abstraction." The "concrete person," on the other hand, he understood to be the totality of being, the living consciousness of all things, to which nothing is alien or "external."

22. "Our unity of wills is not the result of suggestion, as some maintain, or of imitation, nor the consequence of some mysterious influence of prestige, nor is it the submission of a weak will to one that is stronger. . . . It is the consequence of the very laws of spiritual development: [illustrated in the fact that] two interlocutors, even though speaking different languages, must ultimately come to some comprehension." Gentile, *Sommario di pedagogia come scienza filosofica*, 2, pp. 36–37. "A state is always governed by a force, a power, whose real and positive foundation is found in the will of its subjects." Gentile, *Dopo la vittoria* (Rome: La Voce, 1920), p. 151.

23. See the discussion in Gentile, *Discorsi di religione*, pp. 20–29, and *La riforma dell'educazione*, chap. 8.

24. Gentile, *La riforma dell' educazione*, p. 8.

25. "Fascism reaffirms the state as the true reality of the individual." *Dottrina del fascismo*, *Oo*, 34, p. 119, para. 7.

26. In the early thirties, Gentile, writing the "Fundamental Ideas" for the official *Doctrine of Fascism*, held that individuals, to achieve the fullness of self, should be prepared to sacrifice unto death for their nation. *Dottrina del fascismo*, *Oo*, 34, pp. 117–118, para. 2.

27. See Panunzio's testimony, in *Lo stato fascista* (Bologna: Cappelli, 1925), pp. 36–37.

28. At the close of the Fascist period, authors still rehearsed the essentials of the doctrine of law and the state—citing the "modern idealism" of Gentile as among their philosophic foundations. See, for example, Gerardo Pannese, *L'Etica nel fas-*

cismo e la filosofia del diritto e della storia (Rome: La voce della stampa, 1942). The same features are to be found in publications of the time when the Regime was in full flower. See Corrado Petrone, *Principi di diritto fascista* (Rome: Edizioni "Conquiste d'Impero," 1937), particularly pp. 49–55.

29. Sergio Panunzio, *Che cos'è il fascismo* (Milan: Alpes, 1924), pp. 24–25, 28–29, 40, 48, 53.

30. Panunzio, *Stato nazionale e sindacale*, pp. 117–118, 122, 167. Gentile opined that Italy "no longer wished to be the easy prey of foreigners, a negligible quantity in the world of great, imposing powers . . . locked in debilitating individualism, in abstract thought, allowing power, life, and reality to escape." Gentile, *Dopo la vittoria* (Roma: La Voce, 1920), p. 85.

31. See the discussion in Bernardo Pirro, "L'individualità scientifica del diritto fascista," *Il diritto fascista*, 3, nos. 7–9 (28 September 1935), pp. 242–243; and Oscar di Giamberardino, *L'Individuo nell'etica fascista* (Florence: Vallecchi, 1940), *passim*.

32. *Ibid.*, pp. 198–199. Panunzio, *Stato nazionale e sindacati* (Milan: Imperia, 1924), pp. 107–108, 117–118.

33. "In Fascist ethics the ends of society and the state are identical with those of the individual." Pannese, *L'Etica nel fascismo*, p. 158.

34. See the entire discussion in *ibid.*, pp. 13–45, particularly pp. 37–38.

35. "The totalitarian state . . . absorbs, in order to transform and empower, all the energies, all the interests, and all the hopes of a people." Bernardo Pirro, "Introduzione e istituzioni di diritto fascista," *Il diritto fascista*, 3, nos. 4–6 (28 April 1935), p. 134.

36. "The Fascist state is the direct and immediate source of law." Bernardo Pirro, "Il diritto fascista," *Il diritto fascista*, 1, no. 1 (28 October 1932), p. 14, and Pirro, "Il capo del governo organo costituzionale del sistema di governo fascista," *Il diritto fascista*, 1, no. 6 (7 June 1933), pp. 309–322.

37. "Carta del lavoro," in *Atti fondamentale del fascismo* (Rome: Nuova editrice lara, 1969), pp. 7, 8.

38. See Gregor, *Mussolini's Intellectuals*, chap. 8.

39. Pannese, *L'Etica nel fascismo*, p. 7.

40. Sergio Panunzio, *Teoria generale dello stato fascista* (Padua: CEDAM, 1939).

41. The account that follows draws on that of Panunzio, found in *ibid.*, pp. 507–520.

42. Roberto Michels, by that time an acknowledged Fascist theoretician, provided the account of "charisma" as it was employed by Panunzio. See Michels, "Charismatic Leadership," in *First Lectures in Political Sociology* (New York: Harper and Row, 1949), chap. 6.

43. See the discussion in A. James Gregor, *A Survey of Marxism: Problems in Philosophy and the Theory of History* (New York: Random House, 1965), chap. 3.

44. See the discussion in Alfonso U. Thiesen, *Lenins politische Ethik nach den Prinzipien seiner politischen Doktrin: Eine Quellenstudie* (Munich: Verlag Anton Pustet, 1965), pp. 322–325. Trotsky, in his time, admitted that Lenin never wrote anything extensive on ethics or morality. See Leon Trotsky, *Their Morals and Ours* (New York: Merit Publishers, 1966), p. 51.

45. Lenin, "The Tasks of the Youth Leagues," *Collected Works* (Moscow: Foreign Languages Publishing House, 1963; hereafter *LCW*), 31, pp. 291, 293.

46. As we have seen, Dietzgen sought to provide a theoretical basis for Marxist ethics by appealing to Darwinism. Kautsky spoke without hesitation of the fact that "there was no place in historical materialism for a morality that did not find its origins in prevailing economic factors." See the discussion in Karl Kautsky, *Le marxisme et son critique Bernstein* (Paris: Stock, 1900), p. 41, as cited in Georges Sorel, *Saggi di critica del marxismo* (Milan: Remo Sandron, 1903), pp. 284–285.

47. Woltmann addressed some of these issues in his discussion of Engels's treatment of "morality and law" in *Anti-Dühring* (chaps. 9–11), where Engels argued that the standards of truth varied in each domain of discourse. Engels clearly understood the varying differences in certainty between analytic and empirical truths. Woltmann made a point of the fact that Engels's allusion to a "truly human morality" rested on neither analytic nor empirical grounds. If there is a truly human morality that "stands above class antagonisms and above any recollection of them," we are left with the question of origins. "Truly human morality" does not rest on analytic truths; it does not "reflect" class struggles. It would seem that such a morality could only "reflect" prevailing social relations. That morality would be warranted by empirical facts. Why would anyone feel that any behaviors that simply "reflect" empirical fact should be morally binding? See Engels, *Anti-Dühring*, pp. 118–132; and Ludwig Woltmann, *Der historische Materialismus: Darstellung und Kritik* (Düsseldorf: Michels' Verlag, 1900), pp. 228–230.

48. Stalin was prepared to recognize that the majority of Communist Party members did not enjoy a "very high theoretical level" in their understanding of Marxism and its implications—not to speak of the total lack of theoretical sophistication of the general population. See Stalin, "Report to the Seventeenth Party Congress on the Work of the Central Committee of the C.P.S.U.(B)," *Works* (Moscow: Foreign Languages Publishing House, 1955), 13, pp. 356–357.

49. After the death of Stalin, Soviet ethicists could still argue that "the founders of Marxism demonstrated, through their study of the laws of development of capitalism, that the abolition of private property and the exploitation of man by man . . . would allow the most complete development of human personality." A. F. Schischkin, *Grundlagen der marxistischen Ethik* (Berlin: Dietz, 1964), pp. 41–42.

50. During the earliest period in the "transition" from capitalism to socialism, Lenin advocated a form of "revolutionary legality" that was calculated to foster and sustain conformity on the part of workers and peasants through the use of punishments and terror. See the account in Richard Pipes, *Russia Under the Bolshevik Regime* (New York: Random House, 1994), pp. 398–409.

51. Evgeny B. Pushukanis, *The General Theory of Law and Marxism* is available in two English editions, the more recent by Transaction Publishers in 2002, with a new introduction by Dragan Milovanovic, and an earlier edition by Ink Links Ltd., published in 1978, with an introduction by Chris Arthur and the title: *Law and Marxism: A General Theory*.

52. As cited, Dragan Milovanovic, "Introduction," to Pashukanis, *The General Theory of Law and Marxism*, p. xv.

53. In his long discourse to Soviet jurists on the role of the state and its laws in the evolving Soviet Union after the Second World War, Vyshinsky took the time to personally attack Pashukanis as a "fascist" and a national traitor. See Andrei

Vyshinsky, "Die Hauptaufgaben der Wissenshaft vom socialistischen Sowjetrecht," and U. Kudaibergenow, "Die sozialistische Rechtsbewusstsein," *Sowjetische Beiträge zur Staats- und Rechtstheorie* (Berlin: Verlag Kultur und Fortschritt, 1953), pp. 50–53, 351.

54. "Once established, the superstructure of [socialist] society [which includes the state and its laws] becomes a formidable power. It contributes to the construction and the enhancement of the [economic] base, and assists the new society to defeat the old economic system." D. I. Tschesnokov, "Die Stellung des Staates im System des Überbaus," *Sowjetische Beiträge zur Staats- und Rechtstheorie*, p. 130.

55. Evgeny B. Pashukanis, "The Marxist Theory of State and Law," in *Selected Writings on Marxism and Law* (New York: Academic Press, 1980), p. 297.

56. J. V. Stalin, "Report to the Seventeenth Party Congress," *Works*, 13, p. 374.

57. Stalin, "Report to the Eighteenth Congress of the Communist Party," *Problems of Leninism* (Moscow: Foreign Languages Publishing House, 1953), p. 792.

58. Stalin, "Political Report of the Central Committee to the Sixteenth Congress," *Works*, 12, p. 381.

59. Stalin repeated precisely the same judgment. He told his followers that the revolution "cannot abstain from breaking up the old state machine and substituting a new one for it." Stalin, "On the Problems of Leninism," *Problems of Leninism*, p. 156.

60. Lenin, *The State and Revolution*, LCW, 25, p. 470.

61. Lenin's entire conception of the state was to conceive it an apparatus of control and oppression, fabricating laws to ensure its purposes, and employing "armed organizations" to impose its will. That he expected the continued existence of the "bourgeois state" without the bourgeoisie is instructive. See *ibid.*, pp. 386–389.

62. Pipes, *Russia Under the Bolshevik Regime*, pp. 400–401. Under Stalin we were told that "Soviet law and communist morality fosters the greatest possible productivity for socialist society. It protects collective property and mobilizes Soviet workers to the fulfillment of Stalinist plans for the economic and spiritual transformation of society on the way to communism." Part of the obligation discharged by Soviet law is to "discipline" those who pursue "undisciplined life styles." I. Rjabko, "Die Wechselwirkung zwischen Recht und Moral in der sozialistischen Sowjetgesellschaft," in *Sowjetische Beiträge zur Staats- und Rechtstheorie*, pp. 383–384.

63. Thus, we are told that "the Communist Party provides the leadership and the correct direction in the formation and development of . . . all forms of the social consciousness of socialism." The purpose is to "establish the Communist order . . . by having the masses directed by the leading wisdom of the Party. . . . The leading role in all of this is exercised by the Party. . . . which, by its leading role in the process, fosters and secures the legal ideology of the Soviet society . . . which finds expression in the issuance of law by the Soviet state. . . . The politics of the Communist Party of the Soviet Union is the soul of Soviet law, and law is the embodiment of the politics of the Party." U. Kudaibergenow, "Das sozialistische Rechtsbewusstsein," *Sowjetische Beiträge zur Staats- und Rechttheorie*, pp. 351–353.

64. See Schischkin, *Grundlagen der marxistische Ethik*, pp. 11–20.

65. See A. Vyshinsky, "Die Hauptaufgaben der Wissenschaft vom sozialistischen Sowjetrecht," *Sowjetische Beiträge zur Staats- und Rechtstheorie*, p. 68. Later, in the

history of the Soviet Union, some theoreticians offered a somewhat more subtle treatment of morality: identifying it as the sum total of socially sanctioned behaviors—that had manifested itself in primitive forms before the appearance of "class society." Schischkin, *Grundlagen der marxistischen Ethik*, pp. 11–12.

66. See the discussion in I. Rjabko, "Die Wechselwirkung zwischen Recht und Moral in der Sozialistischen Sowjetgesellschaft," *Sowjetische Beiträge zur Staats- und Rechtstheorie*, pp. 383–385.

67. Vyshinsky was fond of quoting the "brilliant Comrade Stalin": "Marxism is the scientific expression of the life interests of the working class." A. Vyshinsky, "Die Hauptaufgaben der Wissenschaft vom socialistischen Sowjetrecht," *ibid.*, p. 52.

68. Stephen F. Cohen, "Bolshevism and Stalinism," in Ernest A. Menze (ed.), *Totalitarianism Reconsidered* (London: Kennikat, 1981), p. 67.

69. "One must acknowledge that at the core of the theory of the Soviet state, as well as the Soviet theory of the law, is the teaching of the dictatorship of the proletariat." A. Vyshinsky, "Über einige Fragen der Theorie des Staates und des Rechte," *Sowjetische Beiträge zur Staats-und Rechtstheorie*, p. 117.

70. *Ibid.*, pp. 109, 110.

71. "Under the dictatorship of the proletariat, law serves as a determinate means of control. . . . Law is the will of the ruling class. . . . [It] is the totality of the rules governing human behavior that the ruling class would have sanctioned by the power of the state. . . . Lenin and Stalin, further developing the teachings of Marx and Engels, taught us how we must use the law in the interests of the socialist revolution . . . stabilizing and strengthening the state in order to maintain discipline . . . instructing everyone not only of their rights, but their duties as well." Vyshinsky, "Fragen des Rechts und des Staates bei Marx," *ibid.*, pp. 15, 17, 21, 38–39, 40, 41, 46; see "Die Hauptaufgaben der Wissenschaft vom sozialistischen Sowjetrecht," *ibid.*, p. 72. "The Marxist party and state discharge a monumental responsibility in providing the workers of our land a communist education." Schischkin, *Grundlagen der marxistischen Ethik*, p. 51.

72. See Stalin, "Report to the Seventeenth Party Congress on the Work of the Central Committee of the C.P.S.U. (B)," *Works*, 13, pp. 353–355.

73. "Mussolini, having organized the people, in the unitary party, resolved all the puzzlements left behind by thinkers like Hegel and Marx. . . . The party state of Mussolini is the guarantee, in perpetuity, of the continual promotion of the social and moral unity of a people. . . . [It is] the spiritual creation of our great Leader." Panunzio, *Teoria generale*, pp. 577, 580–581.

74. For a systematic discussion of the relationship of the Kuomintang and paradigmatic Fascism, see Maria Hsia Chang, *The Chinese Blue Shirt Society: Fascism and Developmental Nationalism* (Berkeley: University of California Press, 1985); and A. James Gregor, *A Place in the Sun: Marxism and Fascism in China's Long Revolution* (Boulder, Colo.: Westview Press, 2000), chaps. 2–6.

75. See Sergio Panunzio, *Spagna nazionalsindacalista* (Milan: Editrice Bietti, 1942).

76. As a Fascist hierarch, Dino Grandi wrote: "Modern wars, the wars of tomorrow, will inevitably involve poor nations against those that are rich, between those nations that labor and produce and those nations that already possess capital

and riches. . . . It will be a class struggle between nations." Dino Grandi, "Interventismo 1915 e interventismo 1940," *Gerarchia* 19, no. 11 (1940), p. 571.

77. Grandi repeated the same sentiments in Dino Grandi, "La guerra non risolverà nulla," written in 1914, reprinted in *Giovani* (Bologna: Zanicelli, 1941), p. 39.

78. However unconvincing, Fascist theoreticians argued that Hitler's National Socialist movement, taking power in an industrially well developed nation, was still a "developmental undertaking." After the Great War, Germany was shorn of its economic advantages and reduced to a developing economic system. National Socialists were obliged to undertake a program of rapid and comprehensive development. See, for example, Guido Bortolotto, *Die Revolution der jungen Völker: Faschismus und Nationalsocialismus* (Berlin: R. Kittlers Verlag, 1935).

79. Fascism was clearly one of the first, if not the first, exemplar of those systems now identified as "political religions." Panunzio spoke of Fascism as animated by the "exaltation, . . . almost the religion of the state . . . infused by heroic and religious values . . . a moral doctrine of the heroic life of the spirit and of sacrifice . . . an *ecclesiastical* state, as opposed to an indifferent and agnostic state." Panunzio, *Teoria generale*, pp. 5, 7, 10, 19.

80. See n. 42 above.

81. The more detached Fascist theoreticians took a certain pride in the knowledge that Fascism provided the state system necessary to the circumstances of the time. Renzo Bertoni fully expected the Soviet Union to devolve in some form of Fascism. Bertoni, *Il trionfo del fascismo nell'U.R.S.S.*

82. One finds one or more of the major elements of totalitarianism, at one or another stage, in the development of the political regimes of Chiang Kaishek, Mao Zedong, Fidel Castro, Pol Pot, Jamal Abdel Nasser, Saddam Hussein, Hafiz al-Asad, Muammar Qaddafi, Kwame Nkrumah, Kim Il Sung and Kim Jong Il, among others.

83. See the discussion in A. James Gregor, *The Search for Neofascism: The Use and Abuse of Social Science* (New York: Cambridge University Press, 2006).

Index